European Cross-Border Banking and Banking Supervision

European Cross-Border Banking and Banking Supervision

DALVINDER SINGH

OXFORD
UNIVERSITY PRESS

OXFORD
UNIVERSITY PRESS

Great Clarendon Street, Oxford, OX2 6DP,
United Kingdom

Oxford University Press is a department of the University of Oxford.
It furthers the University's objective of excellence in research, scholarship,
and education by publishing worldwide. Oxford is a registered trade mark of
Oxford University Press in the UK and in certain other countries

First Edition published in 2020
Impression: 1

Published in the United States of America by Oxford University Press
198 Madison Avenue, New York, NY 10016, United States of America

British Library Cataloguing in Publication Data
Data available

Library of Congress Control Number: 2019953159

ISBN 978–0–19–884475–4

Printed and bound by
CPI Group (UK) Ltd, Croydon, CR0 4YY

Preface

The principle of home country control and the home and host relationship posed a significant asymmetry of information challenges during the European financial crises and led to ad hoc cross-nationalistic decisions aimed at safeguarding national financial stability to possibly the detriment of the integrity of the European Union. The notable EU weaknesses of minimum harmonization or no harmonization transpired, leading to different levels and capacities of oversight and intervention in the form of supervision and a lack of attention to crisis management amongst the Member States. This work provides the first holistic and, in parts, empirical analysis of the European reforms in the principal areas of bank supervision, resolution and crisis management and their attempts to address asymmetry of information problems and agency problems within the European Union. The interlinkages between the starting points of supervision through to crisis management are critical to ensure a robust analysis of the appropriateness of the reforms and indeed proposed reforms in the form of a single European deposit guarantee scheme.

The European reforms associated with the Single Rulebook and the individual pillars of the Banking Union attempt to minimize or try to eliminate the asymmetry of information problems of adverse selection and moral hazard. In many respects the reforms, as a whole, attempt to address the problems of moral hazard to protect the integrity and stability of the European banking integration project. By engaging with the legal instruments and the level of administrative discretion that resides within those instruments, the work argues a significant number of weaknesses remain that undermine the legitimacy and aspirations of the reforms leading to an expectations gap between the political and legal position. At a practical level, reference to legal form—branches and subsidiaries—in supervision, resolution and insolvency, and crisis management is made, with their impact on home-host decision-making. The third country dimension in the individual instruments and the use of international soft law instruments to bridge the gaps is also considered.

Chapter 1 explores 'push and pull' factors of cross-border banking between EU Member States in terms of, inter alia, total international loans and deposits flows between 2006 and 2016. It provides new insights into the levels of interconnection between Member States and calls into question some of the traditional assumptions that tend to exist between the large and small Member States of the European Union and accession countries. It primarily engages with the economic and political economy literature in the field to explore the implications of the different levels of exposure and concentration risks between different sets of Member States and accession countries. The level of interconnection is also analysed by using data on the level of assets held by domestic and foreign bank branches and subsidiaries; and how legal form influences behaviour between home and host authorities. The systemic risk implications of those interconnections are then used as context to gauge the adequacy of supervisory and crisis management policy responses. In Chapter 2, the centralized decision-making is explored and how centralization potentially leads to the minimization of asymmetry of information between home and host supervisory and resolution authorities. It specifically looks at the relationship between the European Central Bank (ECB) and Single Resolution Board (SRB) with participating and non-participating Member States. It specifically engages with the issue of close cooperation and what close cooperation means in practice for those Member States that decide to join the Single Supervisory Mechanism (SSM). It also embarks on exploring the different mechanisms of decision making and accountability within the SSM and wider, most notably the European Banking Authority (EBA), and how they deal with home and host supervisory and resolution decisions. The case of Bulgaria (as a non-participating Member State entering in to close cooperation) is specifically analysed and the practical benefits of close cooperation. This is an important move in view of the dominance played by Eurozone banks in countries such as Bulgaria. The chapter argues the ECB's relationship with the Member States in close cooperation is akin to an EU agency relationship like that exercised by the SRB within the Single Resolution Mechanism (SRM) and the relevant national resolution authorities, since the decision is taken at the ECB and SRB but executed by the relevant competent and resolution authority. The move to close cooperation could potentially lead to significant reduction of the asymmetry of information between home and host national authorities and in some instances may well lead to the idea of even eliminating home and host national authorities for 'pure' Eurozone banks. In Chapter 3, the practical aspects of bank supervision are considered and how they deal with the potential asymmetry of information problems between home and host authorities. It embarks on this by primarily exploring the different forms of 'classifying' banks and how those classifications could potentially contradict one another as they are made either at the centralized or decentralized level between micro- and macro-prudential decision-making authorities. The chapter then analyses the principal instruments that attempt to minimize the asymmetry of information between respective national competent authorities when supervising cross-border banks and the level of reciprocity in terms of information sharing. In this respect, techniques, such as consolidated supervision, recovery planning, supervisory colleges and stress testing, are scrutinized. It questions in a variety of ways how the individual mechanisms in practice address the home and host dilemma in view of the significant amount of administrative discretion that exists within those instruments. Chapter 4 explores the issue of non-performing loans (NPLs) and loan loss provisioning from a supervisory perspective. It first of all analyses the data to show the significance of bank and sovereign crises on NPL growth across the European Union. The lack of harmonization in the way NPLs are dealt with leads to a potential underestimation of the problem and inconsistent treatment from a supervisory perspective. In view of the findings in Chapter 1, such a dominant bank-led model of business means the NPL problem is even more serious and needs to be tackled before another spell of economic decline takes hold and exacerbates the problems of failing banks. While International Financial Reporting Standards (IFRS) 9 provides a basis to improve the accuracy of the level of NPLs, potential inconsistency arises from the capacity of banks to actually operationalize IFRS 9 compliance to determine the level of NPLs and the extent to which the bank need to provision for such loans from a forward-looking perspective. The experience so far suggests national authorities are left in a situation where the problems of NPLs appear to be significantly understated and culminating in to a position of underestimating the size of the losses in pre-insolvency or resolution decision stages leading to a lack of market confidence for any potential capital raising or restructuring initiatives. In Chapter 5, the reforms associated with resolution are explored and how they attempt to address asymmetry of information problems when banks are likely to fail. It undertakes the task by looking at the dominant role of the home country in the home and host relationship. In the first part of the chapter the mechanisms to improve resolvability are examined such as loss absorbing capacity and potential resolution schemes as well as early intervention powers. It then delves into the use of resolution tools and the home and host implications they give rise to. It analyses all the Member State decisions notified to the EBA and the techniques utilized. Finally, the chapter explores the third country perspective and the Memorandum of Understanding (MoU) the SRB has entered into with various countries to improve decision making at the preventative stage. Chapter 6 analyses the challenges that arise from the lack of a harmonized bank insolvency-liquidation regime across the EU and how national discretion plays out. It specifically argues the premise of EU resolution contradicts the premise of the Deposit Guarantee Scheme Directive. It analyses the current policy measures that attempt to address the home and host relationship when it comes to depositor protection across borders. It suggests the latter remains in perilous state if insolvency-liquidation is the primary tool to deal with a bank that is failing or likely to fail, due to the fact that it can lead to creditors and shareholders of a bank group in different Member States being treated differently. Furthermore, national authorities may not be adequately funded to deal with a spate of banks not considered to be undertaking critical functions. In view of this, it is inevitable that onus may well fall on the state due to lack of funds in the deposit guarantee scheme. The chapter explores recent cases decided by the SRB and all the national decisions that have been notified to the EBA. The third country perspective is also examined and what measures EU national authorities will need take to ensure depositors are protected. The final Chapter 7 explores the principal issue of public funding in its various forms. The lack of coherence between the different instruments and state aid rules highlights significant gaps for national discretion to wield its head. The move towards mutual support does go a significant way to minimize the asymmetry of information problems that can arise in such circumstances at the market level with pricing of assets and providing assistance to troubled institutions. In many respects, the banking structure and cross-border operations of EU banks explored in Chapter 1 question the position of large Member States opposed to further mutualization in view of the dominant role that large Member States' banks play in the smaller Member States.

The opportunity during the early days of the project to discuss some of the themes explored in the book with staff at the ECB and ESRB and also at the SRB is gratefully acknowledged. I am grateful to Professor Dr Chiara Zilioli for opening the door to talk to staff at the ECB. I would like to thank Andreas Witte, Principal Legal Counsel at the ECB, for organizing and attending the meetings with a host of team members from the Joint Supervisory Teams, crisis management, recovery planning, MoUs, and the legal division over several days. For the discussions with the ESRB staff, I would like to thank Alessandro Scopelliti, formerly of the ESRB. I also would like to thank Stefano Cappiello, formerly at the SRB. At IADI, I would like to thank Kumudini Hajra, Senior Policy Advisor, and David Hoelscher, formerly of the FDIC and IMF, for the opportunity to participate in the Technical Committee to draft the 'Deposit Insurers' Role in Contingency

Planning and System-wide Crisis Preparedness and Management', Guidance Paper, May 2019. During this time I learnt so much from both of them and indeed from the other members of the technical committee.[1]

I would like to thank a number of people who have assisted with this work. The original project was explored with Professor David Mayes who sadly passed away in November 2017. I will always be grateful for his time and support. I am also grateful to Maria Nieto for discussions and her unwavering support and encouragement. The time I spent at the European University Institute (EUI) as Fernand Braudel Fellow in 2016 really helped kick- start the project. I am grateful to Professor Grundmann, Professor Giorgio Monti, and Professor Hans Micklitz for the opportunity. I would also like to thank the lively PhD student community at the EUI, in particular, Agnieszka Smolenska and Christy Ann Petit for their perspectives. I would also like thank Jens Henrich-Binder, Ross Leckow, Charles Enoch, Giuliano Castellano, Ioannis Kokkoris, Rodrigo Olivares-Caminal, Marco Bodellini, Andrea Miglionico, Christian Guzman Mecklenburg, Biljana Biljanovska, Costanza Russo, Saveethika Leesurakarn, and Stephen Connelly for discussions on various aspects of the work. I also gratefully acknowledge the financial support provided by the Legal Research Institute, Warwick Law School, and the ESRC IAA fund.

I would particularly like to thank the many former students that have helped me during the project, Iulia Nicolescu and Theodora Papadopolou, and, more recently, Elina Rage and Chris Tassis. I would like to particularly thank Rebecca Kirk for all her help with the charts and tables.

A real big thank you goes to Rachel Mullaly and Iona Jacobs at Oxford University Press for their support and encouragement of the project and help with the publication. It's a great pleasure working with you.

Finally, I would like to thank my family, in particular my wife Sarbjit, despite all the challenges, you can still be a beacon of great strength and humour. And indeed to our children, Amaryn and Arvind. To them I dedicate this work.

[1] All errors are the author's responsibility.

Table of Contents

Table of Cases xiii
Table of Legislation xv
List of Abbreviations xxiii

1. European Cross-Border Banking
   - Introduction 1.1
   - EU Member State Cross-Border Banking Exposure 1.4
     - EU Member States—exposure to international loans and deposits and securities 1.8
     - Top three EU Member State exposures per EU Member State 1.9
   - EU Member State Local Positions of Total International Claims 1.20
     - Sub-section: EU Member State local resident cross-border claims to foreign bank counterparties 1.25
   - The Proportion of Foreign and Domestic Banks in EU Member States 1.31
     - The legal form foreign banks take in the EU Member States 1.33
     - Total assets of domestic and foreign banks 1.41
     - The intragroup position between banks and their affiliates: branches and subsidiaries 1.43
     - The third country perspective 1.44
   - Reflections on the Principal Issues 1.48

2. The ECB's Supervision and SRB Resolution—Participating and Non-Participating Member States
   - Introduction 2.1
   - Ramifications of Opting In or Out of the Banking Union 2.4
   - The SSM and Entering Close-Cooperation 2.7
   - The ECB and Decision-Making Process and Accountability 2.22
   - Single Resolution Mechanism—A Close Cooperation Perspective 2.32
   - The Role of the EBA: Supervision and Resolution Conciliation and Mediation 2.39
   - EBA Mediation: Single Resolution Board and Banca Națională a României 2.46
   - Bulgaria and the Application to Enter Close Cooperation 2.47
   - Reflections on the Principal Issues 2.52

3. The EU Home and Home-Host Dilemma: The Prudential Supervisory Perspective
   - Introduction 3.1
   - The Legal Form of Cross-Border Banking and Banking Supervision 3.3
   - Single Supervisory Mechanism—Classification of Significant Banks 3.10
   - Significant Banks—Listed and Non-Listed Significant Banks 3.15
   - The Macroprudential Classification of Banks 3.20
   - Consolidated Supervision 3.31
   - Information Sharing between Home and Host States 3.37
   - The Supervisory Colleges 3.41
   - The Role of Recovery Planning 3.51
   - Stress-Testing—The Home and Host Challenges 3.59

Reconfiguring Home Bias for Significant Subsidiaries—The Supervisory Perspective 3.65
Consolidated Supervision: A Third Country Perspective 3.69
International Soft Law Instruments Focus on Home and Host Supervisory Issues 3.77
Reflections on the Principal Issues 3.81

4. EU Non-Performing Loans and Loan Loss Provisioning
Introduction 4.1
The Size of the European NPL Problem 4.7
The Definitional Challenges of NPLs 4.17
Loan Loss Provisions—Co-mingling the Accounting and Prudential Supervision 4.26
Public and Private Mechanisms to Reduce NPLs: A Portfolio-based Approach 4.40
Reflections on the Principal Issues 4.49

5. The EU Home and Home-Host Dilemma: The Resolution Perspective
Introduction 5.1
Resolution Framework and Legal Form—Branches and Subsidiaries 5.5
Resolvability and the Minimum Required Eligible Liabilities 5.9
Single Point of Entry and Multiple Point of Entry Resolution 5.21
The Resolution Colleges 5.28
Early Intervention: Aligning Supervision and Resolution 5.39
Resolution Objectives, Conditions, and Principles 5.52
The Sale of Business Tool 5.54
The Bridge Institution Tool 5.57
Goldman Sachs International v Novo Banco SA 5.59
Bayerische Landesbank v Hypo Alpe Adria Bank International AG (now HETA Asset Resolution AG) ('Heta') 5.63
Asset Separation Tool 5.65
The Bail-in Tool 5.66
EU Member State Resolution Decisions 5.78
Cross-border Group Resolution 5.84
Relations with Third Countries 5.88
International Cooperation Arrangements 5.100
Reconfiguring Home Bias for Significant Subsidiaries—The Resolution Perspective 5.104
International Soft Law Instruments Focus on Home and Host Resolution Issues 5.108
Reflections on the Principal Issues 5.110

6. European Bank Insolvency and Liquidation Proceedings
Introduction 6.1
Bank Insolvency—Branches and Subsidiaries 6.10
The BRRD and SRMR and the 'Normal Insolvency Procedure' in Context 6.19
Normal Insolvency Proceedings 6.21
Bank Liquidation and Moratoria 6.24
The *ABLV* Case and the Cross-border Dimension 6.31
Veneto Banca and Banca Populare di Vicenza 6.40

Creditors Interests in Insolvency—Depositor Preference 6.45
The Role of the Deposit Guarantee Scheme 6.52
DGS Funding and Target Coverage Level 6.55
Liquidation Cases with DGS Payouts and Other DGS Interventions 6.59
The Role of the DGS and Cross-border Challenges 6.69
Insolvency, Liquidation, and DGS Third Country Perspective 6.77
International Soft Law Instruments Focus on Home and Host Deposit Protection Issues 6.79
Reflections on the Principal Issues 6.82

7. EU Financial Crisis Management and Containment
Introduction 7.1
Central Bank, Emergency Liquidity Assistance, and Extraordinary Financial Support 7.3
Precautionary Recapitalization 7.5
Emergency Liquidity Assistance 7.13
The Financial Support Measures and the State Aid Perspective 7.22
Liquidation Aid 7.28
ECB and Centralizing Liquidity Assistance 7.33
Single Resolution Fund 7.38
The Move Towards the Third Pillar: The Proposed European Deposit Insurance Scheme 7.51
The European Stability Mechanism 7.59
International Soft Law Guidance on Temporary Public Funding 7.70
Reflections on the Principal Issues 7.75

Appendix 1 237
Appendix 2 241
Appendix 3 247
Appendix 4 253
Appendix 5 255
Appendix 6 259
Appendix 7 265
Appendix 8 269
Appendix 9 273
Index 279

Table of Cases

INTERNATIONAL CASES

European Commission

State Aid NN 49/2008—Belgium NN 50/2008—France NN 45/2008—Luxembourg Emergency aid to Dexia in the form of a guarantee for bonds and liquidity assistance, Brussels, 19 November 2008 C(2008)7388 final 7.27
State Aid SA.42215 (2015/N)—Greece Prolongation of the Greek financial support measures (Art. 2 law 3723/2008) Brussels, 29.06.2015 C(2015) 4452 final 7.24
State Aid SA. 45664 (2017/IN)—Italy—Orderly liquidation of Banca Popolare di Vicenza and Veneto Banca—Liquidation aid (Brussels, 25 June 2017) (C(2017) 4501 final) 6.40
State Aid SA.47677 (2017/N)—Italy New aid and amended restructuring plan of Banca Monte dei Paschi di Siena, 4/7/2017 . . . . 7.23
C 14/2008—Northern Rock, Commission decision of 18 October 2009 . . . . 7.23
C 15/2009—Hypo Real Estate, Commission decision of 13 November 2009 . . . . 7.23

European Court of Justice

C-64/05 P Sweden v Commission [2007] ECR I-11389 . . . . 2.25
C-85/12 Société Landsbanki Islands HF v Kepler Capital Markets SA and Frédéric Giraux (30 May 2013) 6.11
C 370/12 Thomas Pringle v Government of Ireland and Others [2012] ECR 756 . . . . 7.60
C 526/14 Kotnik and Others (18 February 2016) 6.13, 6.14, 7.22, 7.29
C-41/15 Gerard Dowling Padraig McManus Piotr Skoczylas Scotchstone Capital Fund Limited v Minister for Finance 6.13
C-195/15 SCI Senior Home, in administration, v Gemeinde Wedemark Hannoversche Volksbank eG [2017] OJ C6/14 . . . . 6.63
C-212/15 ENEFI Energiahatekonysagi Nyrt v Direcţia Generală Regională a Finanţelor Publice Braşov (DGRFP) (9 November 2016) 6.29
C-219/17 Silvio Berlusconi, Finanziaria d'investimento Fininvest SpA (Fininvest) v Banca d'Italia, Istituto per la Vigilanza Sulle Assicurazioni (IVASS) 19 December 2018 . . . . 2.25

General Court/Court of First Instance

T-712/15 Crédit Mutuel Arkéa v ECB 2.30
T-133/16 to T-136/16 Caisse Régionale De Crédit Agricole Mutuel Alpes Provence and Others v ECB 2.29
T-323/16 Banco Cooperativo Español v SRB (2016/C 296/39) [2016] OJ C296/30 . . . . 7.48
T-661/16 Credito Fondiario v CRU (2016/C 402/71) [2016] OJ C402/59 . . . . 7.48

DOMESTIC CASES

Austria

Bayerische Landesbank v Hypo Alpe Adria Bank International AG (now HETA Asset Resolution AG) (Az 32 0 26502/ 12) (8 May 2015) 5.63, 5.64

Ireland

Dellway Investments & Ors v NAMA & Ors [2011] IESC 4 . . . . 4.45

United Kingdom

Harbinger Capital Partner v Caldwell and Another [2013] EWCA 492 . . . . .5.49
Goldman Sachs International v Novo Banco SA [2015] EWHC 2371 (Comm). 5.59–5.61
Guardians of New Zealand Superannuation Fund & Ors v Novo Banco, SA [2016] EWCA Civ 1092 . . . . .5.62
Goldman Sachs International v Novo Banco SA [2018] UKSC 34. . . . . .5.62

Table of Legislation

OTHER LEGISLATION

Hungary

Hungarian Resolution Act
Art 42(2) 5.79

Irish

Credit Institutions (Stabilisation) Act 2010
s 50 . . . . 6.10

Italy

Decree-Law 99 of 25 June 2017: Disposizioni urgenti per la liquidazione coatta amministrativa di Banca Popolare di Vicenza S.p.A. e di Veneto Banca S.p.A. 6.42

Portugal

Decree-Law No. 199/2006 of 25 October 2006
Art. 21 . . . . 6.13

United States

Patriot Act 2001
s 311 . . . . 6.31

EUROPEAN LEGISLATION

Decisions

Decision of the European Central Bank of 31 January 2014 on the close cooperation with the national competent authorities of the participating Member States whose currency is not the euro (ECB/2014/5) 2.11
Decision of the European Central Bank, 17 September 2014 on the implementation of separation between the monetary policy and supervisory functions of the European Central Bank, ECB/2014/39 (2014/723/EU) [2014] OJ L300/57 . . . . 2.22
Decision (EU) 2019/322 of the European Central Bank of 31 January 2019 on delegation of the power to adopt decisions regarding supervisory powers granted under national law (ECB/2019/4) 3.10

Directives

Directive 94/19/EC of the European Parliament and of the Council of 30 May 1994 on Deposit- Guarantee Schemes [1994] OJ L135/5 . . . . 6.49
Art 1(3)(i) 6.60
Art 1(3)(ii) 6.60
Directive 1346/2000 on Insolvency Proceedings 6.29
Directive 2001/24/EC of the European Parliament and of the Council of 4 April 2001 on the reorganization and winding up of credit institutions [2001] OJ L125/15 (RWD) 6.14, 6.28
Title II 6.13
Art 2 . . . . 6.22
Art 6 . . . . 6.10
Art 9 . . . . 6.13, 6.35
Art 13 . . . . 6.13
Art 23 . . . . 6.18
Art 25 . . . . 6.18
Directive 2002/47/EC of The European Parliament and of The Council of 6 June 2002 on financial collateral arrangements 6.28
Directive 2013/36/EU of the European Parliament and of the Council of 26 June 2013 on access to the activity of credit institutions and the prudential supervision of credit institutions and investment firms, amending Directive 2002/87/EC and repealing Directive 2006/48/EC and 2006/49/EC (Capital Requirements Directive, CRD IV) 3.3, 3.31, 3.66
Recital 25 . . . . 3.33
Recital 26 . . . . 3.33
Recital 34 . . . . 3.33
Art 2(5) 5.64
Art 15 . . . . 3.31
Art 35 . . . . 3.6
Art 36 . . . . 3.6
Art 35(2)–(5) 3.6

Art 39 .... 3.6
Arts 40–46 .... 3.41
Art 48 .... 3.69
Art 48(3) 3.69
Art 49 .... 3.31, 3.41
Art 50 .... 3.31, 3.41
Art 50(1) 3.33
Art 50(3) 3.33
Art 50(4) 3.33
Art 50(6) 3.37
Art 51 .... 3.8, 3.41
Arts 51–52 .... 3.31
Art 51(1) 3.8
Arts 53–55 .... 3.33, 3.70
Art 57 .... 3.33
Art 86(11) 3.33
Art 88(1)(e) 2.29
Art 99(2)(a) 3.33
Art 111 .... 2.43
Arts 111–115 .... 3.32
Art 113 .... 3.36
Art 114 .... 3.31
Art 117(1) 3.33
Art 127 .... 3.69
Art 133(11) 3.21
Art 136(7) 3.21
Art 138 .... 3.70
Art 139 .... 3.70
Art 158 .... 2.43

Directive 2014/49/EU of the European Parliament and of the Council of 16 April 2014 on deposit guarantee schemes (recast) [2014] OJ L173/149 (DGS) 2.39, 6.1, 6.49, 6.54, 6.70
Recital 21 .... 6.77
Recital 28 .... 6.57
Art 2 (11) 6.57
Art 9 .... 6.49
Art 10(2) 6.57
Art 10(6)(b) 6.57
Art 12 .... 6.75
Art 14 .... 6.75

Directive 2014/59/EU establishing a framework for the recovery and resolution of credit institutions and investment firms and amending Council Directive 82/891/EEC, and Directives 2001/24/EC, 2002/47/EC, 2004/25/EC, 2005/56/EC, 2007/36/EC, 2011/35/EU, 2012/30/EU and 2013/36/EU, and Regulations (EU) No. 1093/2010 and (EU) No. 648/2012, of the European Parliament and of the Council [2014] OJ L173/190 (Bank Recovery and Resolution Directive, BRRD) 2.32, 2.39, 7.4
Recital 6.1
Recital 1 .... 6.19
Recital 4 .... 6.19
Recital 15 .... 5.29
Recital 17 .... 5.29
Recital 24 .... 3.53
Recital 33 .... 5.29
Recital 38 .... 3.55
Recital 41 .... 7.9, 7.22
Recital 96 .... 3.54, 5.29
Recital 97 .... 5.29
Recital 99 .... 5.32
Recital 101 .... 5.30
Recital 102 .... 5.5
Recital 111 .... 6.49
Recital 132 .... 5.5
Art 2 .... 5.64
Art 2(1) 7.14
Art 2(1)(29) 7.14
Art 2(1)(35) 3.51
Art 2(1)(36) 3.51
Art 2(47) 6.21
Art 4(1) 3.51, 3.52
Art 5(1) 3.52
Art 5(3) 3.52
Art 5(9) 3.53
Art 6(2)(a) 3.53
Art 6(5) 3.53
Art 7 .... 3.54
Art 7(1)–(3) 3.54
Art 7(2)–(4) 3.54
Art 7(5) 3.55
Art 8 .... 2.44
Art 9 .... 3.54
Art 13 .... 5.29
Art 13(1) 5.6
Art 15 .... 5.9
Art 15(1) 5.6
Art 15(1)(a)–(c) 5.9
Art 16(a)–(c) 5.9
Art 16(2) 5.9
Art 17 .... 5.9
Art 17(1) 5.6
Art 17(5)(i) 5.10
Art 17(5)(j) 5.10
Art 18 .... 5.9
Art 18(1) 3.54
Arts 31–34 .... 5.52
Art 32(c) 5.44
Art 32(1)(a)–(c) 5.44
Art 32(1)(b) 5.44
Art 32(4)(a)–(d) 5.45
Art 34(2) 5.87

Art 36 .... 5.48
Art 36(4)(a)–(g) 5.48
Art 36(8) 5.48
Art 38(1) 5.54
Art 38(2) 5.55
Art 38(3) 5.55
Art 38(7) 5.55
Art 38(9)(a)–(f) 5.55
Art 38(12)(a)–(b) 5.55
Art 39 .... 5.55
Art 40 .... 5.57, 5.82
Art 40(1) 5.57
Art 40(1)(a) 5.57
Art 40(1)(b) 5.57
Art 40(2)(a) 5.57
Art 40(2)(b) 5.57
Art 40(3) 5.57
Art 40(7) 5.59
Art 40(12) 5.58
Art 40(13) 5.58
Art 41(3)(a)–(e) 5.58
Art 41(5) 5.58
Art 41(6) 5.58
Art 42 .... 5.65
Art 42(2)(a)–(b) 5.65
Art 42(3) 5.65
Art 42(4)(a)–(d) 5.65
Art 42(13) 5.65
Art 43 .... 5.82
Art 46 .... 5.82
Art 64(1)(a)–(f) 5.6
Art 66 .... 5.64
Art 66(3) 5.6, 5.60
Art 69 .... 6.27
Art 74(1)–(4) 5.74
Art 75 .... 5.74
Art 85(4)(b) 5.46
Art 86 .... 5.60
Art 87 .... 5.5
Art 87(a)–(l) 5.86
Art 87(h) 5.87
Art 88 .... 2.44, 3.54
Art 88(1)(a)–(i) 5.29
Art 88(2)(a)–(h) 5.29
Art 89 .... 5.30
Art 90 .... 5.31
Art 90(2) 5.31
Art 90(3) 5.31
Art 91 .... 5.32
Art 91(4) 5.32
Art 91(7) 5.32
Art 91(8) 5.32
Art 91(12) 5.32
Art 92 .... 5.32
Art 93 .... 5.89
Art 93(1)(a)–(c) 5.90
Art 94 .... 5.91
Art 94(4)(a)–(d) 5.91
Art 95 .... 5.95
Art 95(a)–(e) 5.93
Art 96 .... 5.95
Art 107(2)–(5) 7.42
Art 108 .... 6.49
Annex
Section A 3.53
Section C 5.9

Regulations

Proposal for a Regulation of the European Parliament and of the Council amending Regulation (EU) 806/2014 in order to establish a European Deposit Insurance Scheme (COM(2015) 586 final, 2015/0270 (COD) 7.51
Regulation (EU) No 1093/2010 of The European Parliament and of The Council of 24 November 2010 establishing a European Supervisory Authority (European Banking Authority), amending Decision No. 716/2009/EC and repealing Commission Decision 2009/78/EC (OJ L 331, 15.12.2010, p. 12) 2.39
Art 31 .... 2.45
Regulation (EU) No. 1215/2012 of the European Parliament and of the Council on jurisdiction and the recognition and enforcement of judgments in civil and commercial matters (recast) ('Recast Brussels Regulation') 5.60
Art 1(1) 5.61
Art 25 .... 5.61
Regulation (EU) No. 575/2013 of the European Parliament and of the Council of 26 June 2013 on prudential requirements of credit institutions and investment firms and amending Regulation EU No. 648/2012 (CRR) 2.39, 3.3, 3.31
Art 4(1) 3.33, 5.64
Art 4(1)(1) 3.5
Art 4(38) 3.34
Art 4(40) 3.5
Art 4(41) 3.5, 3.32
Art 4(43) 3.5, 3.33
Art 4(44) 3.33
Art 4(47) 3.5
Art 11(1) 3.35
Art 13 .... 3.66
Art 18 .... 3.70

Art 19(1)(a) 3.34
Art 19(1)(b) 3.34
Art 19(2)(a)–(c). 3.35
Art 20 . . . . 2.43
Art 20(1)(a) 3.36
Art 20(1)(b) 3.36
Art 21 . . . . 2.43, 3.36
Art 99(4). 4.19
Art 178(1)(a) 4.21
Art 437 . . . . 3.66
Art 438 . . . . 3.66
Art 440 . . . . 3.66
Art 442 . . . . 3.66
Art 450 . . . . 3.66
Art 451 . . . . 3.66
Art 453 . . . . 3.66
Regulation (EU) No. 1024/2013 of 15 October 2013 conferring specific tasks on the European Central Bank concerning policies relating to the prudential supervision of credit institutions [2013] OJ L287/63 (the SSM Regulation) 2.7
Art 3(6). 2.9
Art 4 . . . . 2.9, 2.13, 3.12
Art 4(1). 2.14
Art 4(2). 2.14
Art 5 . . . . 2.9, 2.13, 2.14
Art 5(2)–(5) 3.20
Art 5(2). 3.20
Art 6 . . . . 2.9
Art 6(5)(b) 3.10
Art 7 . . . . 2.2, 2.47
Art 7(1). 2.13
Art 7(2). 2.12, 2.13
Art 7(2)(b) 2.13
Art 9 . . . . 2.14
Art 16 . . . . 3.10
Art 24 . . . . 2.28
Art 26(8). 2.23
Regulation (EU) No. 468/2014 of the European Central Bank of 16 April 2014 establishing the framework for cooperation within the Single Supervisory Mechanism between the European Central Bank and national competent authorities and with national designated authorities [2014] OJ L141/1 (SSM Framework Regulation). 2.8
Art 3 . . . . 2.15
Art 4 . . . . 2.11, 2.15
Art 5 . . . . 2.11
Art 8 . . . . 2.17
Art 9 . . . . 2.13, 2.17, 2.18
Art 10 . . . . 2.13, 2.17
Art 11 . . . . 2.13
Art 12 . . . . 2.13
Art 107(2). 2.13
Art 108 . . . . 2.14
Art 108(2)(a) 2.14
Art 108(2)(b) 2.14
Art 113(1)–(3) 2.14
Art 114(1)–(4) 2.14
Art 115(3). 2.15
Art 115(5). 2.18
Art 118 . . . . 2.24
Art 118(4). 2.24
Art 119 . . . . 2.24
Art 119(4). 2.24
Art 142 . . . . 2.14
Art 143 . . . . 2.14
Regulation (EU) No. 524/2014 of 12 March 2014 supplementing Directive 2013/36/EU of the European Parliament and of the Council with regard to regulatory technical standards specifying the information that competent authorities of home and host Member States supply to one another 3.37
Chapter II 3.39
Art 14 . . . . 3.40
Regulation (EU) No. 620/2014 of June 2014 laying down implementing technical standards with regard to information exchange between competent authorities of home and host Member States, according to Directive 2013/36/EU of the European Parliament and of the Council 3.37
Art 4 . . . . 3.39
Regulation (EU) No. 650/2014 of 4 June 2014 laying down implementing technical standards with regard to the format, structure, contents list, and annual publication date of the information to be disclosed by competent authorities in accordance with Directive 2013/36/EU of the European Parliament and of the Council. 3.66
Regulation No. 806/2014 establishing uniform rules and a uniform procedure for the resolution of credit institutions and certain investment firms in the framework of a Single Resolution Mechanism and a Single Resolution Fund and amending Regulation (EU) No. 1093/2010 [2014] OJ L225/1 (the SRM Regulation). 2.32, 7.38

Recital 15 . . . . 2.34
Recital 19 . . . . 7.38
Recital 84 . . . . 5.10
Recital 91 . . . . 5.28
Recital 112 . . . . 2.34
Art 1 . . . . 2.34
Art 4(2) 2.34
Art 4(3) 2.34
Art 8(2) 5.85
Art 13 . . . . 5.43
Art 13(1) 5.43
Art 13(2) 5.43
Art 14 . . . . 5.52
Art 15 . . . . 5.52
Art 18(1) 2.38
Art 18(1)(a)–(c) 5.44
Art 18(1)(c) 6.42
Art 18(4)(a)–(d) 5.45
Art 18(4)(c) 5.45
Art 24 . . . . 5.54
Art 25 . . . . 5.57
Art 26 . . . . 5.65
Art 29 . . . . 7.20
Art 31 . . . . 5.28, 5.84
Art 32 . . . . 5.28, 5.85, 5.100
Art 33 . . . . 5.103
Art 33(2)(b) 5.28
Art 45 . . . . 2.35
Art 67 . . . . 7.41
Art 67(2) 7.40
Art 68 . . . . 7.41
Art 69 . . . . 7.41
Art 70 . . . . 7.43
Art 75 . . . . 7.41
Art 76 . . . . 7.42
Art 78 . . . . 7.42
Regulation (EU) No. 673/2014 of The European Central Bank of 2 June 2014 concerning the establishment of a Mediation Panel and its Rules of Procedure (ECB/2014/26) 2.26
Regulation (EU) No. 2015/63 of 21 October 2014 supplementing Directive 2014/59/EU of the European Parliament and of the Council with regard to ex ante contributions to resolution financing arrangements [2015] OJ L11/44 . . . . 7.44
Art 6(1) 7.45
Art 7(1) 7.46
Art 10(1)–(6) 7.46
Regulation (EU) No. 2016/98 supplementing Directive 2013/36/EU of the European Parliament and the Council with regard to regulatory technical standards for specifying the general condition for the functioning of colleges of supervisors 3.42
Recital 7 . . . . 3.45
Art 3 . . . . 3.43
Art 3(3) 3.43
Art 5 . . . . 3.43
Art 17 . . . . 3.45
Regulation (EU) No. 2016/99 of 16 October 2015 laying down implementing technical standards with regard to determining the operational functioning of the colleges of supervisors according to Directive 2013/36/EU of the European Parliament and of the Council 3.42
Art 3 . . . . 3.43
Art 3(1)(b) 3.43
Regulation (EU) No. 2016/1075 of 23 March 2016 supplementing Directive 2014/59/EU of the European Parliament and of the Council with regard to regulatory technical standards specifying the content of recovery plans, resolution plans and group resolution plans, the minimum criteria that the competent authority is to assess as regards recovery plans and group recovery plans, the conditions for group financial support, the requirements for independent valuers, the contractual recognition of write- down and conversion powers, the procedures and contents of notification requirements and of notice of suspension and the operational functioning of the resolution colleges 5.28
Recital 66 . . . . 5.36
Art 20 . . . . 3.58
Art 20(1)(a) 3.58
Art 50 . . . . 5.34
Art 54(2) 5.36
Art 61 . . . . 5.36
Art 94 . . . . 5.36, 5.37
Art 108 . . . . 5.37
Regulation (EU) No. 2016/1450 of 23 May 2016 supplementing Directive 2014/59/EU of the European Parliament and of the Council with regard to regulatory technical standards specifying the criteria relating to the methodology for

setting the minimum requirement for own funds and eligible liabilities [2016] OJ L237/1
Recital 8 . . . . . 5.14
Art 1 . . . . . 5.12
Regulation (EU) No. 2017/747 of 17 December 2015 supplementing Regulation (EU) No. 806/2014 of the European Parliament and the Council with regard to the criteria relating to the calculation of *ex ante* contributions, and on the circumstances and conditions under which the payment of extraordinary *ex post* contributions may be partially or entirely deferred [2017] OJ L113/2 . . . . . 7.39
Regulation (EU) No. 2017/1443 of 29 June 2017 amending Commission Implementing Regulation (EU) No. 680/2014 laying down implementing technical standards with regard to supervisory reporting of institutions according to Regulation (EU) No. 575/2013 of the European Parliament and of the Council [2017] OJ L213/1 . . . . . 4.20

INTERGOVERNMENTAL AGREEMENT

Agreement on the transfer and mutualization of contributions to the Single Resolution Fund, 14 May (2014) 7.40

INTERINSTITUTIONAL AGREEMENT

Agreement between the European Parliament and the Single Resolution Board on the practical modalities of the exercise of democratic accountability and oversight over the exercise of the tasks conferred on the Single Resolution Board within the framework of the Single Resolution Mechanism [2015] OJ L339/58 . . . . . 2.35

INTERNATIONAL COOPERATION ARRANGEMENTS

Cooperation Arrangement between the Banco Central Do Brasil and The Single Resolution Board (2018) 5.100
Cooperation Arrangement between the Bank of Albania and The Single Resolution Board (2018) 5.100
Cooperation Arrangement between the Institute for the Protection of Bank Savings and The Single Resolution Board (2018) 5.100
Cooperation Arrangement between the National Bank of Serbia and the Single Resolution Board (2018) 5.100
Cooperation Arrangement Concerning the Resolution of Financial Institutions with Cross- Border Operations in Canada and The European Banking Union (2017) 5.100
Cooperation Arrangement Concerning the Resolution of Insured Depository Institutions and Certain Other Financial Companies with Cross- Border Operations in the United States and The European Banking Union (2017) 5.100

INTERNATIONAL INSTRUMENTS

Consolidated version of the Treaty on the Functioning of the European Union Protocol (No. 4), on the Statute of the European System of Central Banks and of the European Central Bank [2016] OJ C202/230
Art 3 . . . . . 2.7
Arts 3.1–3.3 . . . . . 2.7
Art 9 . . . . . 2.7
Art 9(2) 2.7
Art 12.1 . . . . . 2.7
Art 14 . . . . . 2.7
Art 14.4 . . . . . 7.15
Art 25.2 . . . . . 2.7
European Stability Mechanism By-Laws (2014)
Recital 8 . . . . . 7.63
Recital 12 . . . . . 7.63
Art 4(4) 7.61
Art 4(5) 7.61
Art 13 . . . . . 7.63
Art 13(7) 7.63
Arts 14–18 . . . . . 7.64
Art 41(2) 7.61
Annex II 7.61
Protocol on the Statute of the European System of Central Banks and of the European Central Bank 7.15
Treaty Establishing the European Stability Mechanism Between the Kingdom of Belgium, the Federal

Republic of Germany, the Republic of Estonia, Ireland, the Hellenic Republic, the Kingdom of Spain, the French Republic, the Italian Republic, the Republic of Cyprus, the Republic of Latvia, the Republic of Lithuania, the Grand Duchy of Luxembourg, Malta, the Kingdom of The Netherlands, the Republic of Austria, the Portuguese Republic, the Republic of Slovenia, the Slovak Republic, and the Republic of Finland, T/ESM 2012- LT/en 1 ....7.61
Treaty on the Functioning of the European Union (The Lisbon Treaty, TFEU) [2012] OJ C326/47
Art 48(6)............................7.60
Art 105(2)............................2.7
Art 105(3)............................2.7
Art 105(5)............................2.7
Art 107 ....7.24
Art 107(1)–(3) 7.22
Art 111 ....2.7
Art 127(6)............................2.7
Art 131 ....2.7
Art 132 ....2.7
Art 136 ....7.60
Art 136(3)...........................7.60
Art 139 ....2.8
Art 141 ....2.8
Art 282(3)............................2.7

EUROPEAN BANKING AUTHORITY

Decisions

Decision of the European Banking Authority adopting the Rules of Procedure for the non- binding mediation between competent authorities, 18/06/2014..............2.45
Decision of the European Banking Authority adopting the Rules of Procedure for the settlement of disagreements between competent authorities, 20/02/14................2.45
Decision of the European Banking Authority on notifications to thc EBA relating to Directive 2014/49/EU on deposit guarantee schemes (EBA/DC/2018/243, 23 July 2018) 6.54
Decision on the Settlement of a Disagreement, Addressed to: Single Resolution Board and Banca Națională a României 2017 joint decision on group resolution plans and resolvability for [. . .], 27 April 2018 .... 2.46

Guidelines

Consultation, Guidelines on disclosure requirements under Part Eight of Regulation (EU) 575/2013, EBA/CP/2016/07, 29 June 2016 ....3.66
Final Report Guidelines on disclosure requirements under Part Eight of Regulation (EU) No. 575/2013, EBA/GL/2016/11, version 2*, 14 December 2016..................3.66
Final Report on guidelines on supervision of significant branches, EBA/GL/2017/14 (2017)..............3.9
Guidelines on disclosure of encumbered and unencumbered assets (27 June 2014).............................7.16
Guidelines on the criteria to determine the conditions of application of Art. 131(3) of Directive 2013/36/EU (CRD) in relation to the assessment of other systemically important institutions (O-SIIs), December 2014....3.21
p. 6.................................3.22
p. 10................................3.22
p. 24................................3.22
Guidelines on the interpretation of the different circumstances when an institution shall be considered as failing or likely to fail under Art. 32(6) of Directive 2014/59/EU, EBA/GL/2015/07, 26 May 2015.......5.40
Guidelines on the minimum list of qualitative and quantitative recovery plan indicators, EBA-GL-2015- 02, July 2015 .... 3.53, 3.54

Opinion

Opinion of the European Banking Authority on the Equivalence of supervisory and regulatory requirements in relation to Argentina 22/05/19
Annex 3.77, 5.108

INSTRUMENTS OF INTERNATIONAL ORGANISATIONS

Basel Committee on Banking Supervision

Basel Committee on Banking Supervision, Core Principles for Effective Banking Supervision, 2012. . . 3.78

Financial Stability Board

FSB, Key Attributes of Effective Resolution Regimes for Financial Institutions Annex 2 . . . . 5.108
FSB, Guiding principles on the temporary funding needed to support the orderly resolution of a global systemically important bank ('G- SIB') (August 2016)
Principle 1. . . . . 7.72
Principle 2. . . . . 7.72
Principle 3. . . . . 7.72
Principle 4. . . . . 7.72
Principle 5. . . . . 7.72
Principle 6. . . . . 7.73

International Association of Deposit Insurers

IADI Core Principles 2014 . . . . 6.47
Principle 5. . . . . 6.80
Principle 6. . . . . 6.80, 6.81
Principle 8. . . . . 6.80
Principle 9. . . . . 6.80

List of Abbreviations

BIS	Bank for International Settlements
BRRD	Bank Recovery and Resolution Directive
CAL	compulsory administrative liquidation
CRD IV	Capital Requirements Directive IV
CRR	Capital Requirements Regulation
DGS	deposits guarantees scheme
DIF	Deposit Insurance Fund
EBA	European Banking Authority
ECB	European Central Bank
EDIS	European Deposit Insurance Scheme
EFDI	European Forum of Deposit Insurers
EFSF	European Financial Stability Facility
ELA	emergency liquidity assistance
ESCB	European System of Central Banks
ESM	European Stability Mechanism
ESRB	European Systemic Risk Board
FDIC	Federal Deposit Insurance Corporation
FOLTF	failing, or likely to fail
FSB	Financial Stability Board
FSAP	Financial Sector Assessment Program
FSCS	Financial Services Compensation Scheme
GDP	gross domestic product
GFC	global financial crisis
G-SII	Global Systemically Important Institution
IADI	International Association of Deposit Insurers
IFRS	International Financial Reporting Standards
IMF	International Monetary Fund
JST	joint supervisory teams
LAC	loss-absorbing capacity
LOLR	lender of last resort
MPE	Multiple Point of Entry
MPS	Monte Paschi di Siena
MREL	Minimum Requirement for own funds and Eligible Liabilities
NCA	National Competent Authority
NDA	National Designated Authority
NPE	non-performing exposure
NPL	non-performing loan
NRA	National Resolution Authorities
NTMA	National Treasury Management Agency
O-SII	Other Systemically Important Institution
RF	Rresolution Ffund
RWD	Reorganisation and Winding Up Directive
SCV	Single Customer View

SME	small- and medium-sized enterprises
SPE	Single Point of Entry
SRB	Single Resolution Board
SRF	Single Resolution Fund
SRM	single resolution mechanism
SRMR	Single Resolution Mechanism Regulation
SSM	single supervisory mechanism
TFEU	Treaty on the Functioning of the European Union
TLAC	total loss-absorbing capacity

1
European Cross-Border Banking

Introduction

The move towards greater integration of banking over the last several decades has been the subject of an important debate in the European Union. The bank-based model has taken a dominant role in the reforms in view of banks' unique vulnerabilities to risks. In many ways, the existing dominant role that banking business takes in European finance, leads to a position observed by Langfield and Pagano[1] of Europe's bias towards a bank-based model of finance as a result of a variety of socio-economic factors.[2] Langfield and Pagano reflect on this model and explain how it equally gives rise to a greater risk of systemic crises and slow economic growth as a result of credit risk exposures turning sour. The global financial crisis (GFC) acutely brought this to the fore, with significant capital inflows to Member States up to 2008 and subsequently significant levels of entrenchment up to 2012, showing the fragility of European banking integration.[3] **1.1**

The internationalization of banking within the EU has occurred for a variety of reasons, significantly supported by a reduction of regulatory and supervisory barriers between Member States to create a single financial services market. As a result of those opportunities from wider access to financial markets due to distinct common entry requirements, the 'push and pull factors' of cross-border banking are prevalent: in the former case, high costs of business or static levels of return on capital and indeed surplus liquidity incentivize moves to foreign markets, and in the latter case, positive economic fundamentals such as growth rates, but also untapped domestic demand and a shortage of local liquidity. Banks have otherwise highlighted other opportunities to improve costs of business and growth by accessing new sources of finance to reduce costs based on economies of scale and diversification. This interconnection forms a mechanism for 'exporting' and 'importing' good and bad lending practices, so that the refinancing of operations in foreign markets could simply be a way to camouflage underlying business practices that may be exacerbating the domestic problems. For instance, a credit boom in the foreign local property and commercial loans markets is one such example resulting from an oversupply of liquidity from the home market where the parent entity resides. **1.2**

[1] S Langfield and M Pagano, 'Bank bias in Europe: Effects on systemic risk and growth' (2016) 31(85) Economic Policy 51–106.

[2] Ibid, 86–91.

[3] M Schmitz and M Tirpak, 'Cross-border banking in the euro area since the crisis: what is driving the great retrenchment?' (2017—Special features), Financial Stability Review 145–57; S Claessens and N Horen, 'Foreign banks: Trends and Impact' (2014) 46(s1) Journal of Money, Credit & Banking 295–326; G Maria, M Ferretti, and C Tille, 'The Great Retrenchment: International Capital Flows During the Global Financial Crisis' (IHEID Working Papers 18-2010, Economics Section, The Graduate Institute of International Studies, revised 15 Sep 2010); M K Brunnermeier, 'Deciphering the liquidity and credit crunch 2007–2008' (2009) 23(1) Journal of Economic Perspectives 77–100.

European Cross-Border Banking and Banking Supervision. Dalvinder Singh, Oxford University Press (2020). © Oxford University Press.
DOI: 10.1093/oso/9780198844754.001.0001

1.3 This chapter will show that banking integration across the EU is not homogenous. The composition of the foreign bank presence in each Member State is distinct, with specific reference to its legal form, namely the proportion of branches and subsidiaries. The level of foreign bank presence is divided into EU bank presence and non-EU bank presence. This will provide an understanding of the interconnection and the potential risk for the transmission of shocks between home and host banking markets both within and outside the EU. Notably, the size of branch presence rather than subsidiary presence in a respective Member State offers an indication of the extent it is exposed to credit risks from the home country. It illustrates from a forward-looking perspective the challenges likely to be experienced by the home and host authorities. It offers insights into the composition of international banking between EU Member States and accession countries. The chapter then provides an analysis of the contagion risk that may exist between different Member States and the accession countries.

EU Member State Cross-Border Banking Exposure

1.4 The analysis of cross-border banking between EU Member States is a useful starting point to understand the interconnection between EU Member States and ultimately the need for better coordination between the home and host authorities to minimize the asymmetries of information and improve financial stability. The greater the level of diversity in the banking market, the more likely it is able to withstand local and international shocks. Contrary, an economy is prone to experience shocks as a result of a halt in international flows of finance when there is less diversity and greater dependency on a small range of sources of finance due to a lack of competition and as a result lead to concentration risks.

1.5 The larger the presence of international banking in a domestic market, the greater the chance of cross-border shocks occurring.[4] Where the domestic banking market plays a dominant role, there is likely to be less of a chance of spillovers or transmission of risk to others due to the lack of interconnectedness. The study by de Haas and Lelyveld highlights that during a domestic banking crisis domestic banks are more likely to curtail finance in comparison to their foreign counterparts so the latter can become a critical source of liquidity in such periods.[5] The presence of foreign banks in financial markets certainly varies in terms of market share size, how this differs between large and small Member States and accession countries needs to be explored further.

1.6 In this study the Member States are divided into groups according to their contribution to EU GDP in 2018, leading to seven groups.[6] It also includes a separate group for accession countries to show the level of foreign bank business activity in those countries.[7]

[4] N Cetorelli and L S Goldberg, 'Global Banks and International Shock Transmission: Evidence from The Crisis (NBER Working Paper No. 15974, Issued in May 2010) http://www.nber.org/papers/w15974.pdf [accessed 25 February 2019].

[5] R de Haas and I van Lelyveld, 'Internal capital markets and lending by multinational bank subsidiaries' (2010) 19 Journal of Financial Intermediation 18.

[6] The monograph uses this categorization throughout the study so that comparisons can be made consistently between large Member States and also look at the interconnections between Member States both large and small. Please note there was no data on the BIS Statistics section for Kosovo.

[7] Communication from The Commission to The European Parliament, The Council, The European Economic and Social Committee and The Committee of The Regions 2016 Communication on EU Enlargement Policy, Brussels 9/11/2016, Com (2016) 715 final, see separate reports at <https://ec.europa.

These are candidate countries in formal negotiations to join the EU. Each country is at a different stage of progress with different agreements in place and moving close to formally entering the EU.

The charts provide a ten-year timeline from 2006 to 2016 which includes the banking crisis and sovereign debt crisis, to show banks' behaviour before, during, and after the crises. This is important to show how the two episodes affected bank behaviour. Rather than seeing a reduction of risks by banks during the banking crisis, they were found to be shifting risk to supposedly safer assets, namely sovereign bonds within the region. The extent to which this was a move to safer assets per se or rather camouflage to shift risk to sovereigns in an attempt to improve capital requirement levels has been explained in detail by Archarya and Steffen.[8] From the home and host perspective in Italy and Spain, Archarya and Steffen find that domestic banks increased their exposure to their respective home-sovereign, whereas foreign banks reduced their exposures to host-sovereign.[9] This can be explained by arguing that foreign banks recognize the risk of not being supported in the way domestic national champions are likely to be supported, despite their exposure. Hence, the potential need for the parent entity to refinance foreign entities to maintain credit levels, despite the fact that local banks have retracted.[10] Epstein explains this phenomena using the Eastern European experience that the importance of the Eastern European parts of the business to the foreign bank group meant there was no intention of retrenching from them. The retrenchment experienced in these markets was relatively small—in the region of 3%.[11] Nevertheless, the overall implications of these episodes have been significant economic declines in growth within the Eurozone.[12] Moreover, asymmetry of information between home and host also gives rise to the possibility of risk shifting to minimize domestic concerns about financial stability either by entrenchment or by accessing local sovereign liquidity support in addition to home country support. Moreover, where there are deep localized funding sources, the interconnection **1.7**

eu/neighbourhood-enlargement/countries/package_en> [accessed 1 March 2019]; Albania 2016: <https://ec.europa.eu/neighbourhood-enlargement/sites/near/files/pdf/key_documents/2016/20161109_report_albania.pdf>[accessed 1 March 2019]; Montenegro 2016: <https://ec.europa.eu/neighbourhood-enlargement/sites/near/files/pdf/key_documents/2016/20161109_report_montenegro.pdf> [accessed 1 March 2019]; Bosnia and Herzegovina 2016: <https://ec.europa.eu/neighbourhood-enlargement/sites/near/files/pdf/key_documents/2016/20161109_report_bosnia_and_herzegovina.pdf> [accessed 1 March 2019]; Serbia 2016: <https://ec.europa.eu/neighbourhood-enlargement/sites/near/files/pdf/key_documents/2016/20161109_report_serbia.pdf> [accessed 1 March 2019]; Former Yugoslav Republic of Macedonia 2016: <https://ec.europa.eu/neighbourhood-enlargement/sites/near/files/pdf/key_documents/2016/20161109_report_the_former_yugoslav_republic_of_macedonia.pdf> [accessed 1 March 2019]; and Kosovo 2016: <https://ec.europa.eu/neighbourhood-enlargement/sites/near/files/pdf/key_documents/2016/20161109_report_kosovo.pdf≥ [accessed 1 March 2019].

8 V V Archarya and S Steffen, 'The Greatest Carry Trade Ever? Understanding Eurozone Bank Risks' (NBER Working Paper No. 19039, Issued in May 2013) <http://www.nber.org/papers/w19039> [accessed 25 February 2019]. See also N Battistini, M Pagano, and S Simonelli, 'Systemic risk, sovereign yields and bank exposures in the euro crisis' (2014) Economic Policy 203–51, arguing for the potential wider application to core countries at 209–10.

9 Ibid, Archarya and Steffen, at 3. See Dexia and Bank of Cyprus experience and their demise as a result of this risk shifting.

10 R A Esptein, 'When do foreign banks "cut and run"? Evidence from west European bailouts and east European markets' (2014) 21 Review of International Political Economy 847–77, at 851.

11 Ibid.

12 Report by the high-level expert group on reforming the structure of the EU banking sector (2012) <https://ec.europa.eu/info/system/files/liikanen-report-02102012_en.pdf> [accessed 25 February 2019], at p. 24 and especially p. 30.

between countries in the wholesale markets poses limited risk of contagion. If the domestic financial markets set the right regulatory incentives they will shield against external spillovers undermining confidence, as was the case in Canada, with its high levels of exposure to the United States.[13]

EU Member States—exposure to international loans and deposits and securities

1.8 The Charts in Appendix 1[14] show total international bank loans and deposits and securities in the period 2006–2016 for each Member State. The charts highlight the significant bank-orientated business dominating international finance in all Member States. The charts also show evidence of the relatively small level of debt instruments offered in the respective Member States. While debt securities have remained relatively stable in the period 2006–2016, international loans and deposits show a significant amount of volatility, highlighting them as the principal channel for the transmission of international shocks between Member States. The movement in international loans and deposits identifies the peak in exposures in 2008. The decline in international loans and deposits amongst the EU Member States steadied at around the level of 2006 in most Member States. However, a number have seen significant declines further below the 2006 position: these are the Member States that have experienced sovereign debt problems and required assistance, such as, Ireland, Greece, Spain, and Portugal. However, in Group 6 (made up of Eastern European countries) it is also evident that Croatia and Slovenia have seen significant declines in international loans and deposits below the 2006 positions. These charts highlight the potential high relative exposure of the banking channel through which cross-border risks are likely to be transmitted between Member States in the Groups. The higher level of reliance on banking suggests a relatively high level of concentration risk which diversification of financial sources would otherwise mitigate. McGuire and Peter explain that the use of host deposits was partly to offset the contraction in the wholesale funding experienced in the larger home markets.[15] This can also be expressed from the perspective of the legal form banks take in the host where branches reliant on interbank funding are more susceptible to retrenchment than subsidiaries in the same host.[16]

[13] L Ratnovski and R Huang, 'Why Are Canadian Banks More Resilient?' (IMF Working Paper WP/09/152).

[14] The source of this data is the BIS Statistics Explorer on International Banking which is compiled from data provided by various national authorities. The data has been analysed and amended by the Author.

[15] P McGuire and G Von Peter, 'The resilience of banks' international operations' (March 2016) BIS Quarterly Review, 65–78, at 66: 'A robust finding is that affiliate groups more attached to their host jurisdictions at the onset of the crisis—with local claims funded by local liabilities—experienced smaller balance sheet contractions in its aftermath. The local content in these affiliates' balance sheets, which often represents retail banking activity, provided resilience to their balance sheets when global wholesale funding markets seized up in the crisis. By contrast, affiliates that relied more on non-core liabilities, such as interbank, cross-border and cross-currency funding, experienced larger balance sheet contractions.'

[16] C M Buch, K Neugebauer, and C Schroder, 'Changing Forces of Gravity: How the Crisis Affected International Banking' (2013) Centre for European Economic Research, Discussion Paper No. 14-006, <http://ftp.zew.de/pub/zew-docs/dp/dp14006.pdf> [accessed 1 March 2019], p. 23.

Top three EU Member State exposures per EU Member State

The cross-border exposures show an interesting picture of EU banking integration if one refers to the top three Member State banking exposures in the respective Member State and the changes experienced by individual Member States during the designated period. Isolating the three largest exposures at the country level gives us insights into the likely size of credit risk between individual Member States and how the credit risks are allocated between the home and host. The level of integration across the EU and the accession countries shows which groups of banks (at the aggregated level) from the respective Member States are the most integrated, expressed by the frequency with which Member State's (banks) are listed in the top three. Notably, the level of interconnection shows a top-down movement of integration with little or no bottom-up movement of integration, leading to a depiction by Allen et al of Western Europe as both home and host, and Eastern Europe as essentially host.[17] This research would suggest the Nordic countries are essentially hosts as well. It is rather unsurprising to observe that the banks from the largest economies (Group 1) are the most exposed within the EU and the accession countries. While Germany is clearly the most integrated in the EU, France, on the other hand, appears to be the most integrated when the accession countries are included. It is noticeable that the depth and breadth of integration drops significantly from Group 1 to Group 2. In respect of Group 2, banks from the Netherlands appear to be more exposed to Group 1, Group 2, and then Group 7 Member State markets, as opposed to the rest of the EU put together, and have little exposure in the accession countries. In the case of the Netherlands, there is less of a sub-regional area of dominance than is seen by banks from other Member States. While Dutch banks have a sizeable presence in the EU, there is more of a footprint in third countries, most notably in the US and Asia.[18] It can also be observed that integration takes specific geographic lines based on traditional economic and cultural ties, which have led to regional concentrations in the smaller Member States in Groups 5, 6, and 7 and the accession countries. Austrian banks are listed in the top three in Groups 5, 6, and 7 of the EU and the accession countries. In this respect, the Austrian banks have significant exposures to Eastern Europe in its widest terms, closely followed by France, Germany, and Italy. This exposure gives rise to the potential risk of contagion between large and small Member States.[19] 1.9

The charts in Appendix 2[20] show the cross-border consolidated foreign creditor banks on an ultimate risk basis allocated to the country where the final risk resides. These figures are adjusted in view of the size of net transfers of a bank's credit risk from the credit counterparty in the host country to the parent counterparty in the home country by way of guarantees, collateral, credit default swaps, and positions from a branch and subsidiaries of a foreign bank. The total international claims may be considered relatively high and show a 1.10

[17] F Allen, T Beck, E Carletti, P R Lane, D Schoenmaker, and W Wagner, *Cross-border Banking in Europe: Implications for Financial Stability and Macroeconomic Policies* (London: Centre for Economic Policy Research, 2011), p. 3.

[18] Jon Frost, Jakob de Haan, and Neeltje van Horen, 'International Banking and Cross-border Effects of Regulation: Lessons from the Netherlands' (2017) 13(S1) International Journal of Central Banking 293–313, at 295.

[19] Dirk Schoenmaker and Wolf Wagner, 'Cross-border banking in Europe and financial stability' (2013) 16(1), International Finance 1–22.

[20] The source of this data is the BIS Statistics Explorer on International Banking which is compiled from data provided by various national authorities. The data has been analysed and amended by the Author.

significant reliance on international credit but the risks posed to a counterparty country are reduced in view of the credit risk being transferred out of the counterparty country. From the perspective of the bank supervisor, it would be important to ensure such inward and outward risk transfers are managed well to ensure risks do not undermine financial stability. This is important as it reflects the kind of data consolidated supervisors would use (in different formats) to gauge the overall safety and soundness of the banking group. Likewise, the different levels of exposure could actually influence how the relationship between the home and host works in practice from the perspective of supervision, resolution, and crisis management. Moreover, the composition of the exposure is equally important since loans and deposits at the wholesale level and at the retail level give rise to different risks when loss of confidence is experienced and a downturn in the economy materializes. In the former, a speedy withdrawal from the market is almost immediately experienced to minimize losses, whereas in the latter withdrawals occur relatively slower. If the safety net arrangements are fit for purpose, then the loss of confidence can be contained, but if they are not, then an immediate bank run is likely, as experienced with Northern Rock.[21]

1.11 A number of common features indicating a decline of claims by foreign banks within the EU Member States are certainly evident between 2008 and 2016.[22] However, the general decline conceals a number of significant changes between banks highlighted by the retrenchment of international capital flows during this period.[23] This provides more observations about the importance of the need for cooperation and coordination from a home and host perspective. Cross-border banking flows peaked between 2006 and 2008, showing evidence of a clear economic boom across the countries. The charts also illustrate a significant drop in cross-border exposures after the GFC. The charts go on to illustrate how confidence stabilized and remained at a relatively constant level after 2011–2012 amongst those top three EU States.[24] Overall, the charts highlight the interrelationship between Member States large and small. This relationship appears to be much more prevalent across the EU than one simply associated with Nordic and Eastern European Member States.

1.12 The country exposure data shows a clear increase in bank exposures in the EU from 2006 to 2008. For example, German banks increased their exposure in Italy by 150% and Italian banks increased their exposure in Germany by considerable 1400% between 2006 and 2008. According to Mihaljek, the Central Eastern European (CEE) region experienced a similar increase in inflows of bank loans and deposits of approximately 79% between 2002 and 2007.[25] This suggests the start of the banking crisis in 2007 was not envisaged to be as

21 Rocco Huang and Lev Ratnovski, 'The Dark Side of Bank Wholesale Funding' (IMF Working Paper WP/10/170, 2010), p. 4.

22 Martin Schmitz and Marcel Tirpak, 'Cross-border banking in the euro area since the crisis: what is driving the great retrenchment?' (November 2017) Financial Stability Review 145, at p. 147.

23 Gian-Maria Milesi-Ferretti and Cédric Tille, 'The Great Retrenchment: International Capital Flows During the Global Financial Crisis' (IHEID Working Papers 18-2010, Economics Section, The Graduate Institute of International Studies, revised 15 September 2010).

24 The entrenchment from foreign markets to improve the home country position is explained in the report by the high-level expert group on reforming the structure of the EU banking sector (2012) <https://ec.europa.eu/info/system/files/liikanen-report-02102012_en.pdf> [accessed 25 February 2019], at p. 11.

25 D Mihaljek, 'The Spread of the Financial Crisis to Central and Eastern Europe: evidence from the BIS Data' in R Matousek (ed.) *Money, Banking and Financial Markets in Central and Eastern Europe* (Basingstoke: Palgrave Macmillan, 2010) p. 6.

serious as it materialized after 2008 with the bankruptcy of Lehman Brothers. The 2007–2008 peak in exposures is superseded by the decline in exposures across parts of the EU and the accession countries.

The following sections provide a more detailed breakdown of the top three EU exposures in the respective Member States to show how they have changed over time and how the levels of interconnection give rise to interesting home and host dilemmas. 1.13

The country exposures in Groups 1–7 (Appendix 2) overall show that the differences between the three largest countries did not change position during the period 2006–2016, albeit there is a decline. A few notable exceptions are present: In Group 1, the UK clearly shows its preeminent position as an international financial centre in view of the sheer size of international claims. In Group 1, the UK saw the most significant declines in exposures by French and German banks. In Group 2 the exposure of Belgium banks in the Netherlands experienced a very significant, almost vertical drop between 2008 and 2010 of 90%. In the same group, Spain experienced a significant reduction in exposure by German banks between 2007–2016 of 88%, which was mirrored by the UK with a reduction of 92%. In the latter case, the additional drop after 2012 could be attributed to the decline in confidence in Spain in view of its need for official assistance to avoid a default. This is mirrored in Group 3 in the case of Ireland, which also experienced the most significant increase in exposures by UK and German banks by approximately 60% and 100% between 2006 and 2008 respectively; and subsequently reduced their exposures between 2008 and 2016 by 60% and 85% respectively. The additional point of decline from 2010 to 2016 coincides with the need for official assistance to avert a sovereign default in 2010. In Group 4, following its need for official assistance, French banks appear to reduce their exposure to Greece between 2009 and 2013 by 98%. It is also important to highlight that the French banks increased their exposure to Greece by a massive 244% between 2006 and 2008. One could argue that the increase during this period may have been unlikely if the underlying problems existing in Greece were foreseeable before the banking crisis. 1.14

The level of concentration risk at the consolidated level is acutely visible between Member States, which raise concerns about potential shocks from loss of confidence in the home market threatening the financial stability of the host market in view of the size of the credit exposures. This is particularly acute in the smaller EU economies in Groups 4–7. In Group 3, Denmark shows a significant exposure to banks in Sweden. In Group 4, Finland's exposure to banks from Sweden is 695% greater than to the other Member State banks. This trend is significantly noticeable in a number of Eastern European Member States. For example, Lithuania in respect to banks from Sweden. However, in Group 6, Croatia, Latvia, and Estonia show a similar level of exposure to other Member States, most notably banks from Austria and Italy. As will be shown, the proportion of foreign banks is significantly greater than domestic banks in a number of Member States and in particular in the accession countries. The level of interconnectedness creates high concentration risks from EU foreign banks in the local economy. 1.15

The almost vertical increase was not experienced in all Member States. Indeed, the charts do suggest that a number of Member States across the different groupings did not experience the same negative boom and bust of the banking crisis. This includes Poland, Sweden, Denmark, Finland, Hungary, Romania, Slovakia, Slovenia, Latvia, Estonia, Lithuania, and 1.16

Malta. However, many of these Member States experienced very significant short-term liquidity problems because of the retrenchment of global liquidity to safeguard critical home and materially significant overseas interests. As a result of the contraction of global liquidity, the ability to raise finance in the international markets by countries such as Hungary led to the necessity for IMF assistance.[26]

1.17 The country exposure data in the charts in Appendix 3[27] expressed as percentages in the same period 2006–2016 provides a different dimension to the relationship between the top three Member States. This new dimension provides an idea of what proportion of total exposures they represent and therefore gives an idea of the level of concentration risk to foreign counterparts they represent. In terms of Group 1 Member States, it is evident that the top three amount to about 20% of total exposures in the countries, with the exception of Italy, where the exposure of banks from France presents almost 50% of total exposures, thus showing a significant concentration risk. Overall, in Group 1 there is a wider diversification of exposures. In Group 2, all four Member States have shown similar levels of exposure and represent approximately 20% of total exposures. In Group 3, on the other hand, the potential concern of concentration risk is present between Member States. Within these Member States the level of exposure to particular Member State banks is significantly higher. For example, the exposure of UK banks to Ireland is approximately 30% with it declining recently to around 25%. However, other Member States in Group 3 show a different position where concentration risk could be a concern. For example, Denmark, as mentioned above, shows a significant level of interconnection to banks from Sweden as a proportion of its total exposures since they represent almost 70% of total exposures in the Member State. A similar position is present in Belgium as well, but with banks from France. Belgium has experienced an increase from 20% in 2006 of total exposures to over 40% of total exposures in 2010–2016. The relatively high proportions of total exposure are present in Group 4 Member States as well as, most notably, in Finland where banks from Sweden represent 60% of total exposures. The position in Greece is important to note since it shows the speed with which exposures can fall, as is the case with banks from Germany where their exposures fell by approximately 41% between 2011 and 2012, and appearing to be stabilizing at between 6% and 5% in 2013–2016. The relatively high levels of concentration risk to the three largest counterparties are also present in Groups 5–7. The CEE countries show high levels amounting to approximately 40% to 50% of total exposures. Notable examples are Lithuania where it is heavily exposed to banks in Sweden at up to 72%. A similar position is also present in Latvia and Estonia where banks from Sweden represent 90% of total claims in the respective countries.

1.18 The data described above does not necessarily show reciprocal relationships between Member States. For example, the high exposure of Spanish banks in Portugal is not reciprocated by Portuguese banks in Spain nor it is the case of France and Italy, Austria and Italy, or Sweden and Eastern European Countries. In view of this position one could argue there is less reciprocal interconnection as a whole at the regional level. The proportion of total exposures made up of the top three foreign counterparties shows

[26] Page 14.

[27] The source of this data is the BIS Statistics Explorer on International Banking which is compiled from data provided by various national authorities. The data has been analysed and amended by the Author.

another dimension of the EU integration, namely the extent to which there is sustainable diversification of finance in the respective Member States. In view of this, the Groups 1 and 2 Member States show fewer concerns about concentration risk. However, as the economies get smaller, in Groups 3–7, the levels of exposure to a particular counterparty are between 40% and 90%. The levels appear to show systemic importance at the local level.

The significant peaks and troughs in the charts could partly be based on a redistribution of liquidity by banks within the EU dealing with local liquidity shortfalls by contracting from other parts of the EU and safeguarding levels of liquidity in more important markets. The pressing need for liquidity post-Lehman and post-Dexia and Fortis could be linked French banks increasing liquidity in Belgium. In view of this, the home and host relationship shows a particular vulnerability outside of the 'bilateral relationship' to obverse indirect interconnections that may exist because of factors arising elsewhere requiring careful consideration at the microprudential and macroprudential level. For instance, high levels of exposure may lead to a movement of liquidity from banks in one country to safeguard confidence in another where there are material exposures present that require support. Moreover, the concerns about exposure to sovereign risk of European banks to their home country specifically gave rise to moves to minimize exposure in the US in the Money Market Mutual Funds (MMMF), a principal source of short-term funding for EU banks' US dollar funding requirements.[28] 1.19

EU Member State Local Positions of Total International Claims

The next set of charts in Appendix 4[29] titled 'Local Positions Data' break down BIS locational data for total international claims and local foreign claims (held by subsidiaries) for each EU Member State and accession countries.[30] The local positions in the charts are expressed as a percentage of total international claims. The trend towards financing business operations via local sources, either retail or corporate deposits, as opposed to sources of finance from the home country markets, has been an area of interest in the field of international banking.[31] By comparing the local country positions, it is possible to show that between 2006 and 2016 local positions have remained relatively stable amongst the seven groups in comparison to international cross-border claims. This suggests that local positions in comparison to international claims are less prone to sudden withdrawal. In Group 1 the difference between 2006 and 2016 is approximately 10% to 15% change, with local positions declining by approximately 20% to 30% in some places. In these cases, such as the UK, the greatest decline is experienced in 2006–2009. This is in contrast to the positions explained above where country positions increased during those periods, meaning that the increase is from international foreign inflows rather than originated locally. A separate feature that is observable is the 1.20

[28] IMF, 'Global Financial Stability Report, October 2010: Sovereigns, Funding and Systemic Liquidity' (World Economic and Financial Surveys, October 2010), p. 64.

[29] The source of this data is the BIS Statistics Explorer on International Banking which is compiled from data provided by various national authorities. The data has been analysed and amended by the Author.

[30] Robert N McCauley, Judith S Ruud, and Philip D Wooldridge, 'Globalising international banking' (March 2002) BIS Quarterly Review. The data has been analysed and amended by the Author.

[31] Ibid.

proportion of foreign claims originating from local sources. In this respect, a lesser concern could possibly be raised by the position in Denmark and in Finland, given Finland's significant exposure to banks (taking the legal form of a subsidiary) from Sweden, where more than 50% to 60% are originated locally. The following countries and their interconnections between other Member States follow a similar path: in Estonia & Sweden, Croatia & Italy & Austria, and Hungary & Austria, the exposure originates from local sources, therefore conferring, as the host, possibly more control on the movement of those positions than they otherwise could exercise if they arose cross-border. However, Member States such as Sweden, with significant international and local claims in other Member States, experience a ratio similar to most others.

1.21 The local positions across the EU have remained stable from 2008–2009, therefore showing less vulnerability than cross-border claims. The decline in the level of international claims also shows how Member States that were once reliant on cross-border inflows of banking activities have seen an increase in them being locally financed rather than financed from the home country of the respective foreign banks. The data also shows that the high proportion of foreign local claims are not simply an Eastern European phenomenon but significantly wider across a number of small EU Member States with specific regional and cultural ties. In the vast majority of cases the proportion between international and local claims is approximately 60% and 40% respectively. The Member States in Group 6 provide an interesting case study of Eastern European experiences: Bulgaria has seen a decline in international claims from 70% to just below 60%. This trend is similar to Croatia where local positions represent 60% of total international claims, which has remained steady over the period. On the other hand, Lithuania and Slovenia show the opposite trend: 40% local claims and 60% international claims. This could mean that the latter two countries may experience more significant reductions of cross-border claims than the former two. A similar set of local positions are present in the accession countries as well. However, the accession countries appear to have experienced more volatility in 2006–2016 at the level of local position than their EU counterparts.

1.22 This data shows the level of cooperation and coordination needed to ensure prudent oversight of domestic banks' foreign exposures from a home country perspective and the level of local control that needs to be exercised by the host authority over those positions to ensure financial stability.[32] The charts provide evidence that local positions held by subsidiaries are significantly more resilient to external shocks than cross-border flows. An examination by McCauley, McGuire, and Peter of cross-border claims and location claims between 1999 and 2009 corroborates the position observed in this study.[33] Their paper highlights a trend towards a banking model akin to a multinational approach rather than an international model-oriented towards cross-border claims using home country funds. However, Allen et al partly support this position regarding local position. Notably, they observe that such countries, while avoiding the sudden shocks experienced by countries with large international claims, did experience aftershocks when intragroup liquidity was restricted to

[32] B N Jeon, M P Olivero, and J Wu, 'Multinational banking and the international transmission of financial shocks: Evidence from foreign bank subsidiaries' (2013) 37 Journal of Banking and Finance 952–72.

[33] R N McCauley, P McGuire, and Goetz von Peter, 'The Architecture of Global Banking: From International to Multinational?' (March 2010) BIS Quarterly Review 35, available at SSRN <https://ssrn.com/abstract=1561576≥ [accessed 28 February 2019].

support local operations.[34] Moreover, Caprio and Klingebiel note that while capital flight can lie behind bank failures, it is the aftershocks of an economic recession and poor economic growth that are the more significant factors.[35]

Host authorities are likely to be able to exercise more control of local positions in currencies originating from the domestic economy than they are on cross-border claims. This has a stabilizing effect either by capital and liquidity requirements for subsidiaries or simply liquidity requirements for branches located in their banking market, unless local circumstances change and risks such as political or economic risks increase, leading to a sudden withdrawal from the market. However, this is unlikely in the EU financial markets where wider legal protections are in place. At the same time, the potential of such occurrence varies depending on whether those positions are held by branches or subsidiaries, since the financial stability of the two is different depending on the parent entity. For branches, the risk resides with the home country rather than the host. For subsidiaries incorporated locally, the host-home does have more control but is still reliant on the home country from the consolidated supervision perspective. Decisions at the group level could significantly impact on external flows to the foreign subsidiary. In this regard, the materiality of the interest is likely to determine the level of commitment needed from the national authorities of the Member State to continue surveillance of those exposures at the macroprudential level as well as supervision at the microprudential—institutional—level. In this respect, direct cross-border credit inflows are likely to be more exposed to reductions than internal credit inflows to foreign established subsidiaries. A study by de Haas and Lelyveld shows how multinational banks form their own internal market for capital where domestic markets for capital are weak in exploiting the local needs for finance.[36] The study found foreign subsidiaries continue lending with parental support even during times of distress and so the parent acts as a source of strength. The study also found the importance of the subsidiary does not necessarily lead to a trade-off between material and immaterial subsidiaries to the group as a whole, so suggesting importance does not necessarily matter when the crisis is in the host. In particular, this is highlighted by the difference between what are referred to as 'greenfield' subsidiaries and 'takeover' subsidiaries with an existing footprint in the market. However, there is likely to be a trade-off between material and immaterial subsidiaries. In those cases where the crisis is in the home country of the banking group, the foreign subsidiary can be a source of liquidity for the parent entity. The view that bank liquidity flows to address sudden liquidity shortfalls is explored by Reinhardt and Riddiough in their study on interbank (between unrelated banks) and intragroup flow of funds in cross-border banking. Notably, the authors find that intragroup funds (between parent and its foreign affiliates) a significant source of funds for cross-border operations.[37] 1.23

[34] F Allen, T Beck, E Carletti, P R Lane, D Schoenmaker, and W Wagner, *Cross-border Banking in Europe: Implications for Financial Stability and Macroeconomic Policies* (London, Centre for Economic Policy Research, 2011), p. 3.

[35] G Caprio and D Klingebiel, 'Bank Insolvency: Bad Luck, Bad Policy, or Bad Banking?', Paper presented to the Annual Bank Conference on Development Economics. Washington, World Bank, 25–26 April, p. 13.

[36] R de Haas and I van Lelyveld, 'Internal capital markets and lending by multinational bank subsidiaries' (2010) 19(1) Journal of Financial Intermediation 1–25.

[37] D Reinhardt and S J Riddiough, 'The Two Faces of Cross-Border Banking Flows' (19 July 2015), available at SSRN <https://ssrn.com/abstract=2427644> [accessed 28 February 2019] or <http://dx.doi.org/10.2139/ssrn.2427644> [accessed 28 February 2019], p. 10; https://www.bis.org/events/cgfs_ibfsws/reinhardt_pres.pdf> [accessed 28 February 2019].

1.24 The positions of the top three EU Member State exposures in the respective Member States and accession countries show that while there were certainly significant movements in terms of their peaks and troughs of international claims, there is less evidence of a complete exit from the local foreign market. This is possibly due to the fact that a significant proportion of those international claims were actually local positions which therefore originated from the host market. In view of the fact that the positions of the top three between 2006 and 2016 stabilized around 2011–2012 to their former 2006 positions, or even increased.[38] This highlights how the home and host attempt to cope with the short-term movements that need to be considered carefully. It is also necessary to ensure that there is sufficient liquidity in the financial system to smooth out the levels of demand and supply in the local markets in periods of short-term instability. The data presented also highlights that exiting a market is more difficult than is generally perceived since there is significant investment that has occurred in the foreign market that cannot simply be replicated elsewhere.

Sub-section: EU Member State local resident cross-border claims to foreign bank counterparties

1.25 The BIS Data on Liabilities set out in Appendix 5[39] provides another dimension to understanding the cross-border relationship between Member States. It shows local resident exposures to foreign bank counterparties located outside of the respective country; the liabilities in terms of total loans and deposits; and debt securities held with banks, both in their own name and for third parties as trustees. The charts in Appendix 4 cover the period 2006–2016 in order to demonstrate the movement of loans and deposits and debt securities prior to, during and after the GFC. It is evident that, just as international claims are dominated by loans and deposits as the principal form of cross-border finance, so international liabilities are dominated by loans and deposits as opposed to debt securities.

1.26 In Group 1 the UK position as the preeminent financial centre and Luxembourg in Group 5 in Europe is illustrated by the level of liabilities held with foreign banks. In relation to the other Member States, the levels are significantly smaller. It is important to note that the liabilities charts however show less volatility than international claims. The flow of international liabilities in 2006–2016 is similar to international claims, with evidence of a slight peak in 2008, but, in comparison, it is not as prominent. The importance of the liabilities charts is to review the extent to which there is evidence of capital flight to other countries considered more stable financially. In this respect, there is less evidence of such movements during 2008–2009, albeit there is evidence that there is a drop in levels of outward exposures. This is noticeable in Germany, the Netherlands, and Belgium, and to a lesser extent, in Spain, which could be explained by the possibility that they were individually safer domestically than if liabilities were placed with banks in other countries. While there is significant inward volatility of international claims, there is relatively less outward flow of liabilities

[38] M Giannetti and L Laeven 'Flight home, flight abroad, and international credit cycles' (2012) 102(3) American Economic Review 219–24.

[39] The source of this data is the BIS Statistics Explorer on International Banking which is compiled from data provided by various national authorities. The data has been analysed and amended by the Author.

from the respective countries, with a few notable exceptions in view of the sovereign debt problems experienced by Cyprus and Greece. In terms of Greece, in Group 4, it appears to have experienced a 56% increase in terms of liabilities from 2006 to 2010, suggesting a possible loss in local confidence in the market as a result of the debt crisis. This was staved off in 2011 by the European Union agreeing a bailout for Greece, with a positive impact on confidence resulting in a gradual decline in liabilities with an equivalent reduction by 56% by 2013, and subsequently stabilization to its 2006 position by 2016. Consequently, the decision to impose capital controls was lifted in 2018. The Cyprus experience is similar in many ways, such as the gradual increase of up to 50% of international liabilities from 2006 to 2009. The impact of the sovereign debt crisis in 2012 manifests in the form of a significant drop in liabilities possibly because of the specific over-exposure of Cypriot residents to Greek banks—so not really a haven of safety at the time. Cyprus was the first to impose capital controls in 2013–2015, which possibly led to the level of international liabilities stabilizing and showing an increase from 2015 to 2016. The Eastern European Member States (in Groups 4 and 5) demonstrate relatively stable levels of international liabilities for both loans and deposits and debt securities, albeit at minimal levels in comparison to other EU Member States. This could be because they are a recipient of inward finance but not necessarily a provider of outward finance to banks.

The level of cross-border activity varies considerably from one Member State to another **1.27**
showing evidence of diversity or concentration of finance requirements in a given financial market. In view of this, Pagano et al[40] note how the credit markets of the EU have integrated at a slower rate in comparison to other financial instruments such as bond markets. This is due to the underlying idiosyncratic characteristics of the corporate and retail markets of respective Member States, which give rise to implicit barriers to full integration. It is possible to break down international claims to ascertain the proportion raised from the local market. This finding would mitigate concerns that could arise if a Member State was viewed as reliant on cross-border finance to support local economic activity, distinctly where over 70% to 90% comes from one particular foreign banking market. Therefore, it specifically reduces the concern or raises the concern about the interconnection between banking markets of Member States, since it leads to an assessment of whether the Member State is vulnerable to financial spillovers and the risk of contagion.[41] On the other hand, it also shows the level of self-reliance on the local economy needed to support its financial needs, although it is provided by foreign banks. The local positions (claims booked in the country of residence) would be based on activities of the respective foreign EU branches and subsidiaries and non-EU branches and subsidiaries.[42] The local positions charts in Appendix 4 are calculated using the BIS locational banking statistics. Importantly, finding the difference between total claims and international claims for the individual Member States in the Groups would show how the level of foreign bank activity has changed from 2006 to 2016 at

[40] T Jappelli and M Pagano, 'Financial Integration in Europe', in G Caprio, T Beck, S Claessens, and S L Schmukler, *The Evidence and Impact of Financial Globalization* (Boston: Elsevier, 2012) at p. 374.

[41] J P Bonin and D Louie, 'Did foreign banks stay committed to emerging Europe during recent financial crises?' (2017) 45 Journal of Comparative Economics 793–808 at 800.

[42] Cross-border: 'Positions where the counterparty resides in a country that is different from that where the banking office that books the claim is located' and Local: 'Positions where the counterparty resides in the same country as that where the banking office that books the claim is located', BIS locational banking statistics: notes to explain the data structure definitions, December 2017, p. 21.

a cross-border and local level regardless of the amount of total claims. The period provides an understanding of how local positions have changed before and after the GFC.

1.28 The overall picture provided by the individual charts in the respective groups does show the level of finance booked in the local market has been relatively stable with percentage movement of approximately 10%, 15%, and 20% in the period 2006–2016. Those movements are across Groups 1–7, not simply related to Member State size nor proportion of local positions. This does not come as a surprise since local positions are reliant on the business generated by foreign bank subsidiaries in the Member State. It does support the argument put forward by many that foreign banks continued or maintained liquidity in Member States during the GFC, and so are providing a stable source of funding in the local market regardless of what proportion actually is provided locally rather than cross-border. This is the case of foreign banks across the EU and not just the position in Eastern Europe, albeit they have a large preponderance of foreign banks in their markets and they have been viewed as being vulnerable to cross-border financial spillovers due to the retrenchment of large banks to support parent entity capital and liquidity.

1.29 The Member States in Groups 1–7 and the Accession Countries show the proportion of local position 2006–2016 of 30% to 40% and 40% to 50% respectively. This suggests that when it comes to local positions as a proportion of total claims, there is not necessarily a greater preponderance of international claims in smaller Member States in comparison to larger Member States. The split of approximately 30% local positions and 70% international claims has been experienced by almost half of the EU Member States in Groups 1–7.

1.30 In view of the local positions as a proportion of total claims, it is necessary to analyse the institutional form and the ratio of domestic and foreign banks in the individual Member States to gauge whether or not there is a significant need to review the level of foreign bank interconnection and foreign bank concentration risk in EU Member States. Since it is useful to deconstruct further the risk associated with consolidated positions by examining the impact of the institutional form taken by banks' foreign entities. This can show us how legal form allocates more or less credit risk in the home and host; if the legal form the foreign entity takes is a subsidiary business model, credit risk resides within the home-host,[43] whereas if the legal form takes a branch business model, credit risk is transferred out to the home country where the parent resides. It will also be important to deconstruct the consolidated positions by reflecting on their composition by analysing the level of intragroup support and their reliance on local deposits to source their business activities. This is done by analysing BIS consolidated data on a total claims basis and separating out international claims to find the level of local positions in local currencies and locational data. This is important on two levels: first, it will show how reliant the Member State is on the international flow of inward funds, and secondly the potential impact of this can be gauged by considering the legal form the foreign banks take. This is done to try and break down where that supervisory risk resides if it takes the form of branches or subsidiaries.

[43] It is technically the home authority but from a consolidated supervision perspective it is a host normally referred to as the home-host.

The Proportion of Foreign and Domestic Banks in EU Member States

The organizational form foreign banks take in the EU is an important consideration when analysing the interconnection between Member States and their relationship with third countries. It is important to ascertain the number of foreign banks as a proportion of the total number of banks in Member States when reviewing cross-border banking. The higher the proportion of foreign banks to domestic banks, the greater the need for cooperation and coordination to minimize the risks of contagion from cross-border banking. According to the ECB, a foreign bank is defined as 'controlled by either an EU or a non-EU parent that is "foreign" from the reporting country's point of view'.[44] There are different drivers to the size of the number of foreign banks in a Member State such as the size of capital markets as a source of liquidity, historic liberalization of financial markets to foreign competition, and finally, the opportunity foreign banks have taken to play a dominant role in view of the limited level of domestic banks in the Member State. Table 6.1 (Appendix 6)[45] highlights that a number of EU Member States have a very high proportion of foreign banks—between 70% and 90%. These Member States are not all relatively small either. It could be argued that the expansion of foreign banks is based on two factors: first, the harmonization of bank entry requirements through introduction of the single passporting regime leading to branch expansion, and second, the opportunities foreign banks observe to be available in other markets through the setting up of subsidiaries and acquiring domestic banks. **1.31**

In Group 1, the UK is a clear outlier with the proportion at 65% of total number of banks are foreign, but this is again due to its position as the international financial centre in Europe, followed by France at 41%. On the other hand, in the case of Germany and Italy the position appears to be the complete opposite with foreign banks representing a mere 9% and 17% of the total number of credit institutions. In relations to the other Member States in Groups 2–7 the picture is equally mixed, with countries such as Portugal, Ireland, Austria, Lithuania, and Latvia having little foreign bank presence—between 7% and 15% of the market. However, a clear dominant presence of foreign banks exists in Member States such as Belgium, the Czech Republic, Luxembourg, Slovakia, Bulgaria, and Cyprus, making-up between 69% and 96% of the market. Table 6.1 does show a significant preponderance of foreign banks in Eastern European Member States which is well recognized, but it also shows other cases such as the Nordic countries, where the foreign bank presence is between 12% and 26%. There are a few notable exceptions such as Belgium and Luxembourg which are very high at 83% and 96% respectively. They appear to be exceptions to the general position of between 30% and 60% in cases like Spain and the Netherlands. In respect of smaller Member States, the proportion of foreign banks poses challenges if a foreign bank **1.32**

[44] Definition of foreign banks: 'Foreign banks are defined as subsidiaries and branches that are controlled by either an EU or a non-EU parent that is "foreign" from the reporting country's point of view. The data for these institutions are excluded from the data on the domestic banking sector and are aggregated under the heading "foreign banks". The fact that foreign banks account for a significant proportion of the domestic banking sector in some EU countries justifies their separate analysis.' <https://www.ecb.europa.eu/stats/supervisory_prudential_statistics/consolidated_banking_data/html/index.en.html<https://www.ecb.europa.eu/stats/supervisory_prudential_statistics/consolidated_banking_data/html/index.en.html> [accessed 28 February 2019].

[45] Source: ©ECB, Statistical Data Warehouse, except material added by the Author. This information may be obtained free of charge from <https://www.ecb.europa.eu/home/html/index.en.html>.

is in distress since it could mean domestic banks are ill-equipped operationally to absorb the market share of a foreign bank when the authorities in the Member State activate a resolution scheme to minimize disruption to services for depositors and markets.[46] It is likely that another foreign bank is needed if an institution is failing or likely to fail to absorb the critical function and minimize disruption to the market and/or the economy to the services that have been transferred. This could however change with the growth of state banks in the region which have recently been found to be expanding in the market.[47] Nevertheless, the size and exposure of foreign banks still remain significant, leading to perhaps greater chances of foreign consolidation.

The legal form foreign banks take in the EU Member States

1.33 Table 6.1 shows the legal form the entities take, namely either as a subsidiary or branch. The proportion of EU branches and non-EU branches in the reporting countries show the former as a more significant presence in comparison to their subsidiary counterpart.[48] The countries in Group 1 show a significant presence of both EU and non-EU branches, highlighting the international nature of their financial markets. While the numbers appear large on face value in comparison to the number of credit institutions in the respective countries, the numbers are not high, especially when taking into account Germany which has a considerable number of credit institutions in its banking market. The UK has traditionally had a liberal approach to the setting up of branches and so has a significant number in comparison to the total number of credit institutions. However, countries in Groups 2–7 show a strong preponderance of EU branches and very few non-EU branches in their respective financial markets. The reason for this is partly due to the differential approach to branch access from non-EU countries, leading to costs equivalent to setting up a subsidiary. Moreover, the countries in Groups 2–7 also show a more EU-centric banking business model in comparison to those countries in Group 1 in all Member States, including the Eastern European and Nordic Member States. There are notable exceptions such as Belgium and Luxembourg. In the case of Luxembourg, it has a significant market presence in a number of financial services such as investment funds, attracting a large proportion of both EU and non-EU branches and subsidiaries.

1.34 The proportion of EU and non-EU subsidiaries highlights some interesting observations about EU Member States' financial markets as being either essentially Eurocentric or international in their outlook. Despite the move towards branchification (especially by Nordea), the EU Member States have a number of bank subsidiaries as well. In the latter case, subsidiaries would need to be separately incorporated and comply with local licensing requirements which may be more or less onerous than those in the home country. Moreover, local levels of capital and liquidity will need to be commensurate with the risks taken by

[46] See Chapters 5 and 6.

[47] CEE Banking Sector Report (June 2017, annually), p. 7, available at <http://www.rbinternational.com/eBusiness/services/resources/media/829189266947841370-829189181316930732_829602947997338151_829603177241218127-1250327788031332015-1-2-EN.pdf>[accessed 28 February 2019].

[48] Jonathan Fiechter, İnci Ötker-Robe, Anna Ilyina, Michael Hsu, André Santos, and Jay Surti, 'Subsidiaries or Branches: Does One Size Fit All?' (March 2011) IMF Staff Discussion Note, available at <https://www.imf.org/external/pubs/ft/sdn/2011/sdn1104.pdf> [accessed 28 February 2019].

the subsidiary in the local market. Another reason for the setting up of subsidiaries is the need to isolate, to a greater or lesser extent, the risk its business activities pose to the parent and the group as a whole. From the perspective of the home-host, the national authorities have direct responsibility and supervision of the subsidiary. However, from the perspective of the home country authority, the subsidiary and its capital and risk will form part of the overall risk and capital of the group as a whole for the purposes of consolidated supervision. The risk for the home country is the potential for the host to decide to ring-fence assets or restrict transfer of dividends to the parent, which was a quite common experience for subsidiaries in Eastern European countries including EU Member States.[49]

The Groups as a whole show there is a significant number of EU and non-EU subsidiaries in the EU Member States. It is again unsurprising that those countries in Group 1 and, most notably, Luxembourg in Group 5, have the most subsidiaries from both sets of countries—EU and non-EU. The level of internationalization of the UK and Luxembourg markets explains why they have the largest number of non-EU subsidiaries, with the UK standing at seventy-six and Luxembourg at forty. In comparison, Germany, France, and Belgium have approximately twenty each, the largest section being EU subsidiaries by a significant proportion. The Eastern European Member States show a significant presence of EU subsidiaries operating in their markets. The presence of those subsidiaries is partly answered by the historical takeovers of failing institutions in the market and the opportunity those markets present to the EU banks from Italy, France, Austria, and Germany to a lesser extent. The lack of non-EU subsidiaries in those markets is partly because of the dominant role played by EU subsidiaries and the limited role even domestic banks play in view of the economies of scale exercised by the former EU entities. The relatively high number of EU subsidiaries in Romania, Slovakia, Bulgaria, and Croatia, in comparison to branches from the respective EU and non-EU countries, may highlight the historic vulnerabilities these markets posed and the acquisitions made post-transition. On the other hand, the Nordic countries, notably Denmark, Finland, and Sweden, highlight how, as a region, they have moved towards branchification in a formal business model, leaving the number of subsidiaries in comparison to branches as a tiny proportion and indeed very few or no non-EU subsidiaries. **1.35**

The EU financial services model is premised on the single passporting regime for branches across the EU financial market. In view of this, the preponderance of EU branches in Member States is not surprising, considering the barriers to entry are eliminated. This is not the case for foreign banks that seek to establish as a branch since they would not benefit from the opportunity of the single passport regime. A third country branch would be exposed to bespoke national requirements which may require separate capital and liquidity. Foreign banks would need to set up a subsidiary to benefit from the single passporting regime The legal form is important because it has implications for bank supervision, resolution, and crisis management. As will be shown in subsequent chapters, a significant amount of reform has been undertaken to improve clarity of decision-making and legal commitments between national authorities as well as the establishment of the Banking Union and with it, the centralization of decision-making. **1.36**

[49] E Cerutti, A Ilyina, Y Makarova, and C Schmieder, 'Bankers Without Borders? Implications of Ring-Fencing for European Cross-Border Banks', IMF Working Paper, WP/10/247 (2010).

1.37 A large proportion of the legal entities are subsidiaries as opposed to branches, which is surprising since there are no obstacles preventing them from forming branches under the EU passporting regime. This could be for historical reasons, considering the number of foreign banks in the CEE markets that were operating before the passporting rules came into existence and were traditionally takeovers of former banks, either private or state-owned, in distress in the respective Member State.The argument put forward by Cerutti et al does resonate with the traditional concerns posed by operating in these markets, namely that the unstable macro-economic and political environment has led banks to limit exposure and liability by setting up subsidiaries.[50] What is significant about the Cerutti et al's article is the demonstration of the importance of penetration of foreign banks into the host market and the link with the legal form chosen which supports the need to look at the banking environment. Cerrutti's empirical study found that where foreign banks have the opportunity to acquire or have significant market share, they are likely to operate as subsidiaries. However, they are likely to form branches when there is less opportunity to penetrate deep in the domestic market. In view of these findings, however, the EU branch may be considered an exception to the general finding since the start-up costs are minimal. The responsibility of the parent entity to branches and to a lesser extent to subsidiaries (in view of its own capital and liquidity) means that the home country is more likely to be exposed to more macroeconomic shocks from the host under a branch model in comparison to a subsidiary model. This applies equally to the host country since it will be exposed to macroeconomic shocks from the home country where the parent entity is located.

1.38 The proportion of foreign banks in a banking market is also an important consideration when contemplating the potential risk of spillover effects from foreign markets to the respective domestic market. Moreover, the size of the foreign bank presence should also lead to a commensurate level of outward-looking supervision with a significantly greater attention to cooperation and coordination with their respective foreign supervisory counterparts. In view of this, a greater proportion of foreign banks to domestic banks generally would raise this concern. The EU Member States provide interesting findings in this respect. The dominance of foreign banks, EU and non-EU, as a proportion of total banks in a domestic market is evident in a range of Member States.

1.39 In a number of Member States the number of foreign banks is at significant levels: 60% to 90% in Belgium, Bulgaria, the Czech Republic, Romania, Cyprus, Slovenia, and Luxembourg. The list contains an interesting mix of countries beyond the traditional suspects of Eastern European Member States where it is traditionally observed that foreign banks outnumber domestic banks (at the top of the rankings) in their respective banking markets. Surprisingly, the list includes more developed Member States as well such as Luxembourg where foreign bank dominance is at 90%. While Luxembourg is a major financial centre for asset managers, it is particularly vulnerable to the risk of cross-border contagion as a result of risks materializing overseas simply in view of the size of the foreign bank presence, both directly through the number of foreign branches and through foreign subsidiaries. In Member States such as Spain and France, the position is approximately half foreign and half domestic, possibly offering a balance in terms of the size of the domestic banking market

[50] E Cerutti, G Dell'Ariccia, M Soledad, and Martínez Pería, 'How banks go abroad: Branches or subsidiaries?' (2007) 31 Journal of Banking and Finance 1669 at 1686.

as a proportion of the whole banking market. However, in other Member States such as in Italy, Germany, and Poland, the foreign bank presence is minuscule in comparison, with the lowest level of foreign bank presence at approximately 6.8%. As a region, the Nordic Member States show a relatively small level of foreign bank presence in their banking markets, but this may camouflage potential risks from foreign idiosyncratic failures if one considers the level of assets owned by such a small number of foreign banks. Finally, in view of the size of foreign bank presence in a respective Member State, risk to the foreign banks is a concern also as a result of a domestic downturn, as are potential sovereign debt risks as a result of the performance of the local economy. This is likely to have been the case with Member States such as Cyprus, leading to a position where foreign banks start to withdraw from such markets.[51]

Caprio and Honohan[52] suggest that domestic banks should consider their own cross-border branching and subsidiary policies to diversify risk and reliance on the home country akin to the foreign bank presence in their own domestic banking systems. This is not so simple considering that bank branching into foreign markets has a number of challenges and succeeds where the bank has an identifiable strength it can exploit in the foreign bank market to build a sustainable business, most notably following corporate customers or a gap in financial products in the market. According to Caprio and Honohan, 'Banks constrained to lend locally in such small markets will routinely fail, because they are too intimately tied to the local economy'.[53] In this respect, the cause of the Greek financial crisis was not necessarily the banking crisis, but rather the loss of confidence in the domestic economy and government, leading to a sovereign debt crisis. Nevertheless, the opportunity to diversify should lead to a lower risk of localized idiosyncratic problems threatening the viability of a bank since it is less reliant on local business. The same rationale is adopted by large EU banks in the direction of their domestic banking markets. This is less of a challenge in the EU since it operates a single passporting regime with reciprocal recognition of standards of regulation and supervision, so regulation is not necessarily a barrier to entry. There are regional players, such as the Hungarian OTP bank, with a presence in other Eastern European Member States and third countries. Despite a few notable exceptions, the level of cross-border banking operations from small Member States into large Member States is limited as shown above. 1.40

Total assets of domestic and foreign banks

The total assets of banks in the Eurozone Member States between 2008 and 2016 have also seen significant declines, as shown in Table 6.2[54] (Appendix 6) with the Euro Area overall seeing a decline of 16% in total assets. The Member States suffering sovereign debt problems have experienced the most significant declines, most notably Ireland which shows a 73% decline in total assets, with Greece and Cyprus experiencing declines of almost 50%. However, 1.41

51 See earlier in this chapter.
52 G Caprio and P Honohan, 'Restoring bank stability: beyond supervised capital requirements' (1999) 13 Journal of Economic Perspectives 43–64 at 59–60.
53 Ibid, 60.
54 ©ECB, Statistical Data Warehouse, except material added by the Author. This information may be obtained free of charge from <https://www.ecb.europa.eu/home/html/index.en.html>.

this is not observed across the EU: Slovakia and Finland, for instance, have experienced an increase in total assets of 18% and 39% respectively. The assets held by domestic Eurozone banks show a similar trend in the period between 2008 and 2016. The Member States which required official assistance, such as Ireland, Greece, and Cyprus, experienced the biggest decline in assets held by domestic banks. This trend has also been experienced by Lithuania and Slovenia.

1.42 The biggest falls are shown in assets held by foreign subsidiaries and branches in the respective Member State. The largest declines are again experienced by Ireland, Greece, and Cyprus, with 80%, 94%, and 64% declines respectively. More notable is the experience of Spain, where it saw a 59% decline but did not experience a similar change in its domestic bank assets, which increased by 5%. The position in Slovakia and Finland showed positive movements of assets held by foreign banks, which was also experienced by Slovenia although it showed a decline in domestic bank assets by 42%. The decline in assets held by domestic and foreign banks needs to be put into some context given the period investigated, since it is acutely apparent that 2006–2008 was the peak of an economic boom period and so the decline shown elsewhere shows positions have settled around the points prior to the boom.[55] The difference in the experience between domestic and foreign asset decline is indicated by Schnabel and Seckinger as a result of the ECB long-term refinancing operation offering liquidity support in Eurozone countries to increase lending levels.[56]

The intragroup position between banks and their affiliates: branches and subsidiaries

1.43 The domestic financial markets are significantly exposed to the financial market movements in the respective Member States of the parent banks.[57] A key aspect of this interconnectedness is the source of finance for group activities raised from the home financial markets and the limited ability to raise finance in the local host market.[58] The analysis of the composition of the banking system and the ratio of domestic and foreign banks is equally important when considering how they seek liquidity in the marketplace, or intragroup financing.[59]

[55] 'Report by the high-level expert group on reforming the structure of the EU banking sector' (2012) < https://ec.europa.eu/info/system/files/liikanen-report-02102012_en.pdf>, p. 31 [accessed 1 March 2019].

[56] Isabel Schnabel and Christian Seckinger, 'Financial Fragmentation and Economic Growth in Europe' (20 March 2015) GSME Discussion Paper Series, available at SSRN <https://ssrn.com/abstract=2599063> or <http://dx.doi.org/10.2139/ssrn.2599063>, p. 7 [accessed 1 March 2019].

[57] L Gattini and A Zagorisiou, 'Cross-border banking: Pull-push effects of parent banks on subsidiaries' credit extensions' (EIB Working Papers, No. 2016/07, 2016).

[58] Valentina Metz, Konrad Richter, Philipp Weiss, Bernard Rottensteiner, Daniel Unterkofler, Johannes Langthaler, and Patrick Pechmann, 'Minimum Requirements for Own Funds and Eligible Liabilities (MREL)—Initial Assessment for Austrian Banks and Selected Subsidiaries in the EU', Oesterreichische National Bank, Financial Stability Report (June 2016), 82–95; A Popov and GF Udell, 'Cross-border banking, credit access, and the financial crisis' (2012) 87 Journal of International Economics 147–61. See also Stephen G Cecchetti, R N McCauley, and P M McGuire, 'Interpreting TARGET2 Balances' (BIS Working Papers No. 393, December 2012), p. 10: 'In September 2012, BNP Paribas announced its intention to have its Italian subsidiary, Banca Nazionale del Lavoro, fund itself more completely in Italy and thus make it less reliant on cross-border inter-office funding', available at <http://www.bis.org/publ/work393.pdf> [accessed 1 March 2019].

[59] E Cerutti and S Claessens, 'The Great Cross-Border Bank Deleveraging: Supply Constraints and Intra-Group Frictions' (IMF Working Paper, WP/14/180), available at <https://www.imf.org/external/pubs/ft/wp/2014/wp14180.pdf> [accessed 1 March 2019].

It is accepted that branches are more likely to be supported by intragroup funding in contrast to subsidiaries for whom support comes from their own capital and liquidity generated by their local operations or raising finance through interbank activity. However, the reliance on intragroup funding has been a rather controversial area since it was assumed that it is equally vulnerable to sudden withdrawal like international cross-border financing. Research by Hoggarth et al concludes that cross-border intragroup lending during the GFC was relatively stable in comparison to interbank lending.[60] Nevertheless, Allen et al find that subsidiaries that are reliant on interbank finance, as opposed to local deposits via the parent entity, are affected by the liquidity of the parent.[61] There is no one-size-fits-all rule at the country level, as noted by Allen et al in their analysis of individual bank behaviour in Eastern Europe.[62] Despite this, it remains useful to separate intragroup claims and total claims to identify the reliance on intragroup financing in a given Member State and delineate how much reliance is placed on intergroup financing at the country level. This information also shows how much foreign bank finance is from the home country partly as a result of the great dominance of branch banking in the EU, but it also offers some idea of the lack of host domestic capital markets to raise finance locally. This is separate from raising loans and deposits domestically. While subsidiaries are separately capitalized, the home capital markets can be an indirect source of finance for them since countries such as those in Eastern Europe are assumed to offer limited opportunities for raising capital in the local market separate from corporate and retail deposits. The principal source of finance is likely to be local deposits from retail and corporate clients. From the home perspective, the concern could be asset quality and non-performing loans as opposed to the size of the local liabilities.[63] High leverage at group level is likely to be a concern for the host.[64]

The third country perspective

The accession countries identified above illustrate that the form foreign bank operations in terms of assets held is that of subsidiaries rather than branches.[65] This could be evidence of EU Member State banks being expected to set up (under local rules or the rules of the group regulator) as subsidiaries to ring-fence, so to speak, operations in such countries. The share of foreign bank assets is similar to those countries that are EU Member States. Moreover, **1.44**

[60] G Hoggarth, L Mahadeva, and J Martin, 'Understanding international bank capital flows during the recent financial crisis' (Financial Stability Paper No. 8—September 2010), p. 4.

[61] F Allen, A Hryckiewicz, A Kowalewski, and G Tümer-Alkan, 'Transmission of financial shocks in loan and deposit markets: role of interbank borrowing and market monitoring' (2014) 15 Journal of Financial Stability, 112–26.

[62] F Allen, K Jackowicz, O Kowalewski, and Ł Kozłowski, 'Bank lending, crises, and changing ownership structure in Central and Eastern European countries' (2017) 42 Journal of Corporate Finance 494–515.

[63] See Chapter 4, Regulation and Supervision of Non-Performing Loans and Loan Loss Provisioning.

[64] L Gattini and A Zagorisiou, 'Cross-border banking: Pull-push effects of parent banks on subsidiaries' credit extensions' (EIB Working Papers, No. 2016/07, 2016), pp. 3–4: 'Parent bank's asset quality is one of the most important and consistent predictors of subsidiaries credit growth. Also past profitability at consolidated level is an important determinant of subsidiary's credit growth.'

[65] Ismael Ahmad Fontán, Thorsten Beck, Katia D'Hulster, Pamela Lintner, and D Filiz Unsal, 'Banking Supervision and Resolution in the EU—Effects on Small Host Countries in Central, Eastern and South Eastern Europe (2019), http://pubdocs.worldbank.org/en/589991557325278014/FinSAC-BR-Effects-on-Small-Host-Countries-Europe.pdf [accessed 1 May 2019] Bank of Albania, Annual Supervision Report (2016),<https://www.bankofalbania.org/Publications/Periodic/Supervision_Annual_Report/Supervision_Annual_Report_2016.html> [accessed 1 March 2019], p. 68.

the presence of the groups identified in this study show that they have a significant presence in such third countries. In this context the percentage range between 60% and 30% in those respective third countries is quite material.[66] In a separate initiative, the Eastern Partnership with Armenia, Azerbaijan, Belarus, Georgia, Moldova, and Ukraine aims to improve cooperation and political association and is a multilateral initiative to improve, inter alia, economic integration and growth.[67] Moreover, the share of foreign ownership or minority share may not entirely originate from the EU. For instance, in Albania a sizeable proportion of the banks' minority owners are from the Middle East—Kuwait and Saudi Arabia. The challenges remain, with the countries identified still developing the capacity to undertake supervision, resolution, and crisis management.[68]

1.45 Table 6.3[69] (Appendix 6) indicates the number of European banks that undertake business in those Member States as well as the accession countries.[70] The banks that are located in the respective countries, namely Raffeisen, Unicredit, Société Générale SA, Intesa Sanpaolo SpA, KBC, Commererzbank, NBG, Alpha Bank, and Erste Group Bank AG, are classified as significant banks in the home Member State and so are supervised under the umbrella of the Single Supervisory Mechanism (SSM) by the European Central Bank (ECB).[71] The grounds for deciding their significance varies but most are considered significant because of their asset size. This includes: KBC, Commererzbank, NBG, Alpha Bank, Société Générale SA, Intesa Sanpaolo SpA, UniCredit SpA, and Erste Group Bank AG. Table 6.3 highlights the spread of European banks present in the respective Member States and accession countries. This table shows a potential for significant exposure to risk to those small countries. The EU banks listed in Table 6.3 have all been recipients of at least one state aid decision between 2007 and 2014, which also highlights the cross-border risks they potentially pose to small Member States and third countries.

1.46 The presence of EU banks in the accession countries is clearly evident. However, not all of them are listed in the top five of banks in the Accession countries in terms of assets held, as shown in Table 6.3a[72] (Appendix 6). The presence of national domestic banks is clearly shown to be relatively small or non-existent in comparison to the number of foreign owned banks. In countries such Bosnia and Herzegovina all of the top five listed banks are foreign and in others four out of five are foreign with the exception of Albania, which has a larger proportion of domestic banks in comparison to foreign EU banks. This partly could be because of the larger size of the country in comparison to the other accession countries.

[66] It is important to then assess the extent to which the prudential requirements associated with supervision, resolution, and crisis management ameliorate the challenges between the home and host Member State as well as from the perspective of the third country small host. Whether the information associated with them proposing to safeguard the interests of small hosts is shared remains a crucial question for the purposes of financial stability.

[67] <https://ec.europa.eu/neighbourhood-enlargement/neighbourhood/eastern-partnership_en> [accessed 1 March 2019].

[68] Bank of Alania Annual Report (2016) at p. 11.

[69] Source, Orbis Bank Focus, Bureau van Dijk.

[70] List of supervised entities: <https://www.bankingsupervision.europa.eu/ecb/pub/pdf/list_of_supervised_entities_201611.en.pdf?a9caa144fa232a75fb36cf1213edd990> [accessed 1 March 2019].

[71] See also Appendix 1, where, from the perspective of asset ownership, the majority of the banks indicated in 2011 ranked in the top three: G Impavido, H Rudolph, L Ruggerone, 'Bank Funding in Central, Eastern and South Eastern Europe Post Lehman: a "New Normal"?' (IMF Working Paper WP/13/148, 2013), p. 17.

[72] Source: Orbis Bank Focus, Bureau van Dijk.

The sub-regional blocks of countries are exposed to the risk of cross-border contagion.[73] The emergence of the Vienna Initiative is explained by the fragility of the respective CEE and Southeast Europe (SEE) countries when large Member States get in trouble. The GFC showed the reluctance to cooperate and coordinate unless incentivized to do so with small hosts.[74] The actions taken through the Vienna Initiative did provide finance to the local economy and stability to the banking system within the region. The collapse of local currencies led to depreciation of the property market in a number of countries, such as Estonia, Latvia, and Lithuania, leading to foreign banks experiencing liquidity problems. Spendzharova highlights the fact that the Swedish banks held between 50% to 80% of total bank assets in the respective countries and experienced losses in the region of 60% to 75%, requiring the parent entity to refinance the local entities.[75] The participating banks entered into a 'commitment letter' of support to 'maintain their exposures and to recapitalize subsidiaries'.[76] The soft law arrangements resulted in varying degrees of support to the respective countries, leading to inconsistent practices amongst states and banks. In some instances, banks would be willing to offer support under the commitment letter. Considering this experience, significant political support was needed to iron out some of the inconsistent practices. Epstein argues that the banks present in the region did not intend to 'cut and run' as foreign banks have done in previous financial crises but establish long-term commitments in the region. Nonetheless, the support provided via the Vienna Initiative did have positive spillover effects for the region as a whole. The acute problems faced by the region highlight a wider set of problems between home and host states, and of states, unsurprisingly, acting in their own self-interest. This is perhaps also partly due to the lack of complexity and opacity of the underlying business between the group and the respective subsidiary in this region. Notwithstanding the interim measures to address these asymmetry of information problems, the recent study by Gattini and Zagorisiou[77] highlights the acute vulnerability 1.47

[73] B Torbjörn, D Daianu, Z Darvas, V Gligorov, M Landesmann, P Petrovic, J Pisani-Ferry, D Rosati, A Sapir, and B Weder Di Mauro, 'Whither Growth in Central and Eastern Europe? Policy Lessons for an Integrated Europe' (2010) (Bruegel Blueprint Series, Vol XI), <https://wiiw.ac.at/whither-growth-in-central-and-eastern-europe--dlp-2268.pdf> [accessed 1 March 2019]; B Martin and P Lane, 'Debt Overhang in Emerging Europe?' (The World Bank, Policy Research Paper, No. 5784) (Washington, 2011) <http://documents.worldbank.org/curated/en/185281468256189110/pdf/WPS5784.pdf> [accessed 1 March 2019]; N Klein, 'Non-performing loans in CESEE: Determinants and impact on macroeconomic performance' (IMF Working Paper, 2013).

[74] Vienna Initiative 1.0, <http://vienna-initiative.com/vienna-initiative-part-1/> [accessed 1 March 2019]; <http://vienna-initiative.com/wp-content/uploads/2012/08/Final_Report_on_Joint_IFI_Action_Plan_Feb_20111.pdf> [accessed 1 March 2019]. This regional vulnerability where international claims were at 37% to 60% of GDP within parts of the region culminated in the establishment of the Vienna Initiative in 2009.
The Vienna initiative had four primary goals to contain the risk of contagion by coordinating commitments at the public and private sector levels to:

- 'Prevent a large-scale and uncoordinated withdrawal of cross-border bank groups from the region, which could have triggered systemic bank crises not only in individual countries but in the region as a whole.
- Ensure that parent bank groups maintain their exposures and recapitalize their subsidiaries in emerging Europe.
- Ensure that national support packages of cross-border bank groups benefited their subsidiaries in emerging Europe and thus avoided a 'home bias'.
- Agree on, and implement, basic crisis management principles in the region.'

[75] A B Spendzharova, 'Banking union through the back door? How European banking union affects Sweden and the Baltic States' (2016) 39(3) West European Politics 565–84 at 569.

[76] Ibid.

[77] Luca Gattini and Angeliki Zagorisiou, 'Cross-border banking: Pull-push effects of parent banks on subsidiaries' credit extensions' (EIB Working Papers, No. 2016/07, 2016), available at <https://www.econstor.eu/bitstream/10419/148572/1/875235824.pdf> [accessed 1 March 2019]; BN Jeon, MP Olivero, and J Wu 'Multinational banking and the international transmission of financial shocks: Evidence from foreign bank subsidiaries' (2013) 37 Journal of Banking and Finance 952–72.

of the European bank subsidiaries in the host to credit expansion and credit contraction in the large European Member States where the parent banks reside. This recent study shows the interdependency of large and small home and host states to credit expansion and credit contraction because of how loan impairment charges at the group level is managed, for instance.[78] Such movements led to moral hazard problems due to either systemic or idiosyncratic crises.

Reflections on the Principal Issues

1.48 A range of 'push and pull' factors exist leading to the growth and challenges that arise with international banking within the EU and a principal one being regulatory reforms. It is evident from the data compiled from the BIS that a significant proportion of international banking between Member States is in the form of loans and deposits. Therefore, showing the significant bias to a bank-based model of finance, as explained by Langfield and Pagano. The BIS data shows the significant exposure between Member States and how that exposure to bank business changed between 2006 and 2016, illustrating a before and after picture of the GFC. However, it was also shown that a large proportion of international banking business is locally sourced in the host Member State. This dynamic is not limited geographically within the EU Member States. In view of this, the 'push and pull' factors give rise to different potential threats to financial stability. In some Member States it was shown the high level of concentration of EU foreign banks gives rise to distinct threats from concentration risks to EU foreign group wide risks which need careful monitoring from a supervisory perspective. The BIS data also shows between 2006 and 2016 the level of local resident cross-border claims to foreign banks remained relatively stable therefore suggesting a movement of funds when confidence swayed during the crisis between banks within the local market as opposed to movement of funds to other Member States. This potentially means the host Member State is reliant on the foreign banks to act in their interest, which cannot always be assured during a crisis. Nonetheless, it is quite evident after the GFC that the level of retrenchment of foreign banks that have traditional ties with the host was an important factor.

1.49 The regulatory reforms make the legal form of banking an important consideration in the exposure of risk between Member States. The EU and the Eurozone Member States are clearly not a homogenous form when it comes to the composition (proportion of domestic and foreign) banks in their markets. There is clear evidence to show that some Member States are more internationally orientated than others. The level of assets therefore held by banks in each Member State according to legal forms and whether they are foreign held or domestically held provides a basis for considering the potential risk of contagion between Member States. The legal form of branch and subsidiary give rise to different levels of cross-border exposure to risk of contagion as well and different degrees of exposure to home country risks. The risk of retrenchment to the home market has been discussed and the reasons for it vary. A primary one being to consolidate the core business of the group within the home Member State. Finally, Eurozone-significant banks have exposures to accession countries. These exposures reside in subsidiaries rather than branches for the top five banks

[78] See also Chapter 4, Regulation and Supervision of Non-Performing Loans and Loan Loss Provisioning.

in each country. In part this is historical but from a supervisory perspective gives rise in part to a containment of risk within the countries. Overall the exposure of credit risk between Member States is prevalent and it resides in two principal legal forms branches and subsidiaries. In many respects these forms influence in part the potential exposure to the home and host. It is important to then consider how those exposures are supervised from a home country and cross-border perspective.

2

The ECB's Supervision and SRB Resolution—Participating and Non-Participating Member States

Introduction

The centralization of decision-making is a significant step towards minimizing the asymmetry of information challenges faced by Member States within the Banking Union. The move attempts to denationalize decision-making and replace it with a decision-making process in the interests of either the Eurozone or the Union as a whole. It attempts to replace decisions that were otherwise likely to be taken across national lines with decisions that attempt to provide a consensus-based approach to decisions that are likely to affect Member States unequally. In view of this, it is also part of the narrative to incentivize non-participating Member States to enter close cooperation, since decisions at the centralized level are likely to impact the decisions of non-participating Member States in view of the interconnections between participating and non-participating Member States. In view of the co-mingling of centralized supervision and resolution and decentralized decisions, the outcomes for banks in distress and precautionary recapitalization or emergency liquidity assistance and macro-prudential decisions associated with capital buffers highlight how fractures can arise and interests may fall across national lines. 2.1

The Single Supervisory Mechanism opens the door to non-Eurozone Member States to participate and have credit institutions supervised by the ECB that fulfil the criteria of significance within the Member State and have cross-border activities.[1] The ECB is required to work closely with both participating and non-participating Member States, since a significant proportion of credit institutions will invariably have business activities in both participating and non-participating Member States.[2] The participating and non-participating Member States will be expected to allow the ECB to take the lead and/or cooperate with the ECB as the competent 'home' supervisor to ensure appropriate cooperation and coordination of supervision and information sharing to inform supervisory decisions. The interaction will also be within the supervisory colleges set up for the respective cross-border credit institutions. The aim of the ECB in this respect is to safeguard financial stability and facilitate sustainable market integration. The literature appears to assume, 2.2

[1] Council Regulation (EU) No. 1024/2013 of 15 October 2013 conferring specific tasks on the European Central Bank concerning policies relating to the prudential supervision of credit institutions [2013] OJ L287/63, Art. 7, <http://eur-lex.europa.eu/legal-content/EN/TXT/PDF/?uri=CELEX:32013R1024&from=EN> (the SSM Regulation) [accessed 19 March 2019].

[2] Pia Hüttl and Dirk Schoenmaker, 'Should the "'Outs"' join the European Banking Union?' (February 2016) Breugel Policy Contribution, Issue 2016/03, p. 5, <http://bruegel.org/wp-content/uploads/2016/02/pc_2016_03.pdf> [accessed 19 March 2019].

European Cross-Border Banking and Banking Supervision. Dalvinder Singh, Oxford University Press (2020). © Oxford University Press.
DOI: 10.1093/oso/9780198844754.001.0001

notwithstanding the more significant political hurdles, close cooperation is 'equivalent' rather than 'comparable' in terms of its outcomes.[3] In view of this, it is suggested that the ECB does not have the right to direct banks as it does with banks in the Eurozone. The ECB's relationship with non-participating Member States in close cooperation is akin to that of the Single Resolution Mechanism (SRM), which is one of EU agency and participating Member States. While the ECB exercises centralized decisions, it is reliant on the National Competent Authority to execute its decisions because the ECB does not have direct jurisdiction as it does in Eurozone Member States. Nonetheless, participating Member States in close cooperation will have an equivalent presence on the Single Resolution Board (SRB), which they do not have on the ECB Governing Council.

2.3 This chapter focuses on the procedures set out to explain how a non-Eurozone Member State enters a close cooperation agreement with the ECB to come under the umbrella of the Single Supervisory Mechanism (SSM). In this respect, it asks whether the close cooperation agreement emulates the current SSM arrangements between the ECB, national competent authority (NCA), and national designated authority (NDA) for the purposes of micro-prudential and macro-prudential coordination. It is important to understand what the arrangements are likely to be for supervision and accountability of decision-making to inform the decision to opt in or not.

Ramifications of Opting In or Out of the Banking Union

2.4 The Member States opting out of the Banking Union are varied, and the benefits of opting in to the Banking Union need to be assessed on a case-by-case basis since the move to close—cooperation may not in practical terms create a level playing field between the Eurozone and those that eventually decide to enter into close cooperation. Ultimately, the linchpin is that those non-participating Member States move to adopt the euro in place of national currencies once they meet the convergence criteria. It would be for the Council to decide whether those non-participating Member States have met the convergence criteria. This decision is ultimately superseded by the political will of the Member State to adopt the euro. In this respect the EU consists of a number of sub-categories of Member States, albeit there is sovereign equality in its legal foundations. The research undertaken by Bruegel, cited by Huttl and Schoenmaker,[4] would indicate that many of the banks listed as having presence in the CEE region are essentially European-centred institutions, with the vast majority of their business—60%–70%—located in the Banking Union and a significant proportion of

[3] A Belke, A Dobrzanaska, D Gros, and P Smaga, '(When) should a non-euro country join the banking union?' (2016) 14 Vol. 14, The Journal of Economic Asymmetries 4–19; Z Kudrna, 'Governing the ins and outs of the EU's Banking Union'(2016) 17(1–2) Journal of Banking Regulation 119–32; M Katalin and D Piroska, 'Banking Union and banking nationalism—Explaining opt-out choices of Hungary, Poland and the Czech Republic' (2016) 35 Journal Policy and Society 215–26; K Mitręga-Niestrój and B Puszer, 'The Threats of the Banking Union for the Polish Banking Sector', European Financial Systems 2015, Proceedings of the 12th International Scientific Conference, 18–19 June 2015, Brno, Czech Republic, pp. 400–7; U Vollmer, 'The Asymmetric Implementation of the European Banking Union (EBU): Consequences for Financial Stability' (2016) International Journal of Management and Economics No. 50, 7–26.

[4] P Hüttl and D Schoenmaker, 'Should the "Outs" join the European Banking Union?' (February 2016) Bruegel Policy Contribution, Issue 2016/03, at p. 5, <http://bruegel.org/wp-content/uploads/2016/02/pc_2016_03.pdf> [accessed 20 March 2019].

the remaining parts of their business still within Europe. This would imply that the move towards close cooperation of the respective Member States where significant parts their banking activities are located should improve the economies of scale of centralization since it could lead to a position where 80%–90% and above moves under the umbrella of the SSM and SRM.

The challenge for the ECB as the single supervisor is then how it can balance the ambitions of the Eurozone and those of the wider economic union in its decision-making processes of safeguarding the integrity of the Eurozone, and consider the interests of those opting in. The official safeguards at the sovereign level, with the introduction of the European Stability Mechanism (ESM), are for the exclusive benefit of its Eurozone members. One particular matter that could sway the significance of the decision to opt in is whether it will change or elevate the importance of significant subsidiaries in those Member States entering close cooperation and lead to better recognition in consolidated supervision, and recovery and resolution planning. Member States entering into close cooperation is a signal that in a relatively short period of time the ECB has been able to build the reputation of being a credible supervisory authority. The counterfactual is also evident: the reluctance of Member States to enter into close cooperation signals lack of confidence in the credibility of the ECB as a Single Supervisory Authority. If one were to be elitist about the type of Member State entering close cooperation, the larger the non-participating Member State, the better for the reputation of the ECB as a supervisor. **2.5**

The relatively unique home and host relationship in the Banking Union with the ECB acting as the home and the host supervisor, is likely to be a very important factor in considering close cooperation. The Member State needs to reflect on the level of discretion it is likely to lose with the transfer of supervisory decision-making to the ECB. In close cooperation with the ECB at the helm of supervising significant banks of the Eurozone requesting information from a number of Member States national competent authorities becomes less of a concern. While it is assumed that competent authorities cooperate with one another and share information on a reciprocal basis, in practice it is not always forthcoming in a timely manner. On the surface, competent supervisory authorities can appear to be lacking an understanding but it is occasionally based on the lack of cooperation from their counterparts in sharing information and data on a reciprocal basis. **2.6**

The SSM and Entering Close-Cooperation

The ECB's relationship with Eurozone Member States is different to that between non-participating Member States. The Statute of the European System of Central Banks and of the European Central Bank (ESCB Statute)[5] sets out the authority of the ECB and its responsibilities. In view of ESCB Statute, Article 25.2, 'the ECB may perform specific tasks concerning policies relating to the prudential supervision of credit institutions and other financial institutions except for insurance undertakings'.[6] In view of Article 131, national **2.7**

[5] Consolidated version of the Treaty on the Functioning of the European Union Protocol (No. 4), on the Statute of the European System of Central Banks and of the European Central Bank [2016] OJ C202/230.

[6] Treaty on the Functioning of the European Union (The Lisbon Treaty) [2012] OJ C326/47, Art. 127(6): 'The Council, acting by means of regulations in accordance with a special legislative procedure, may unanimously, and

legislation is expected to be compatible with the Treaties of the ESCB and of the ECB. To execute the tasks conferred on the ESCB, the ECB can make regulations, recommendations, and opinions and impose fines and penalties on undertakings for failure to comply with obligations under its regulations and decisions (Art. 132). Article 9 of the Protocol (No. 4) sets out the scope of the authority of the ECB explaining:

> The ECB which, in accordance with Article 282(3) of the Treaty on the Functioning of the European Union, shall have legal personality, shall enjoy in each of the Member States the most extensive legal capacity accorded to legal persons under its law; it may, in particular, acquire or dispose of movable and immovable property and may be a party to legal proceedings.

The tasks conferred on the ESCB[7] are to be undertaken by the decision-making bodies of the ECB[8] relating to prudential supervision which are further articulated in the Single Supervisory Mechanism (SSM) Regulation 1024/2013.[9] In many respects, the SSM replicates the Treaty aspirations of the central banks of the ESCB and the ECB working together, rather than the ECB taking complete control of direct supervision of the credit institutions within the respective Eurozone Member States.

2.8 The respective Member States that are the focus of this study are classed as Member States with a derogation.[10] It excludes them from the rights and obligations within the ESCB and their respective voting rights of the Council are suspended when it comes to recommendations made to Eurozone Member States concerning surveillance, stability programmes, and warnings, and measures relating to fiscal policy, namely excessive deficits (TFEU, Art. 139). In respect of these Member States, the ECB (TFEU, Art. 141) is expected to strengthen cooperation between central banks, coordination of monetary policies, and

after consulting the European Parliament and the European Central Bank, confer specific tasks upon the European Central Bank concerning policies relating to the prudential supervision of credit institutions and other financial institutions with the exception of insurance undertakings.'

[7] Protocol (No. 4), ESCB Tasks.

Article 3

3.1. In accordance with Article 105(2) of this Treaty, the basic tasks to be carried out through the ESCB shall be:
- to define and implement the monetary policy of the Community;
- to conduct foreign-exchange operations consistent with the provisions of Article 111 of this Treaty;
- to hold and manage the official foreign reserves of the Member States;
- to promote the smooth operation of payment systems.

3.2. In accordance with Article 105(3) of this Treaty, the third indent of Article 3.1 shall be without prejudice to the holding and management by the governments of Member States of foreign-exchange working balances.

3.3. In accordance with Article 105(5) of this Treaty, the ESCB shall contribute to the smooth conduct of policies pursued by the competent authorities relating to the prudential supervision of credit institutions and the stability of the financial system.'

[8] Protocol (No. 4), Art. 9(2): 'The ECB shall ensure that the tasks conferred upon the ESCB under Article 105(2), (3), and (5) of this Treaty are implemented either by its own activities pursuant to this Statute or through the national central banks pursuant to Articles 12.1 and 14.'

[9] The SSM Regulation.

[10] Institutional Paper 26, European Commission, Convergence Report 2016 (7 June 2016) (last update on: 7 June 2016), Institutional Paper 26, <https://ec.europa.eu/info/publications/economy-finance/convergence-report-2016_en> [accessed 19 March 2019] (examining convergence progress in Bulgaria, The Czech Republic, Croatia, Hungary, Poland, Romania, and Sweden).

more specifically, hold consultations with the respective central banks for the purposes of financial stability institutions and markets. The strengthening of the cooperation is formalized, with the option of the non-participating Member States to enter close cooperation with the ECB in the SSM in accordance with the SSM Regulation which is further articulated in Regulation 468/2014[11] in terms of cooperation with the SSM and national competent authorities.

The SSM framework for cooperation between the ECB and national competent authorities and national designated authorities is set out in a further regulation, both with participating, and those seeking to became participating Member States once they enter close cooperation.[12] The SSM Framework Regulation adds practical details to Articles 4, 5, and 6 of the SSM Regulation on the respective competent authorities and designated authorities. This more formalized arrangement needs to be distinguished from the Memorandum of Understanding that non-participating Member States should enter into with the ECB to work out how they will cooperate and assess decisions with one another in terms of supervision and crisis management.[13] **2.9**

The SSM requires significant reliance on the cooperation of the ECB and the national competent authorities to achieve the aims and objectives of a single supervisory approach.[14] The complexity of the mechanism means the different cogs in it need to be synchronized in a way to achieve what is broadly a single supervisory decision-making mechanism. Considering the macro-prudential and micro-prudential requirements, it needs detailed cooperation and coordination at a variety of levels to maintain financial stability and integrity of the market. One only needs to count the number of additional decisions and regulations wrapped around the core regulations and directives to see the sheer scale of the number of legal instruments required to ensure consistency of cooperation and coordination. It is useful then to describe the cooperation and coordination measures and assess the extent to which they minimize the asymmetry of information problems. **2.10**

The Member State is required to make a request to the ECB to enter close cooperation.[15] This requires the requesting Member State to set out how it expects to adhere to ECB instructions, guidelines, and requests for information about all the supervised entities established in its jurisdiction. This will be expected to be undertaken across the areas of responsibility that come within the umbrella of the ECB's tasks within the SSM.[16] This will be to determine the significance of those supervised entities in the Member State to classify them as significant and less significant banks. But, more importantly, it will **2.11**

[11] Regulation (EU) 468/2014 of the European Central Bank of 16 April 2014 establishing the framework for cooperation within the Single Supervisory Mechanism between the European Central Bank and national competent authorities and with national designated authorities (SSM Framework Regulation) [2014] OJ L141/1, <http://eur-lex.europa.eu/legal-content/EN/TXT/PDF/?uri=CELEX:32014R0468&from=EN> [accessed 19 March 2019]. See Eilís Ferran & Valia S G Babis (2013) The European Single Supervisory Mechanism, Journal of Corporate Law Studies, 13:2, 255–85; Danny Busch and Guido Ferrarini, *European Banking Union* (Oxford: Oxford University Press 2015).

[12] Ibid.

[13] SSM Regulation, Art. 3(6).

[14] C V Gortsos, 'Competence Sharing between the ECB and the National Competent Authorities within the Single Supervisory Mechanism (SSM)', *European Business Organisation Law Review*, Vol. 16 (2015) 401–20.

[15] Decision of the European Central Bank of 31 January 2014 on the close cooperation with the national competent authorities of the participating Member States whose currency is not the euro (ECB/2014/5).

[16] SSM Framework Regulation Arts 4 and 5.

establish how viable they are as a going concern to avoid them causing a burden prematurely on the resources of the ECB and the wider resources in case of a failure. The Member State also must submit the draft legislation as part of its request so that the ECB can satisfy itself that the Member State has all the legal means in place to ensure the competent authority can comply with ECB decisions. More importantly, a significant part of this process is to ascertain the quality of the supervision and the crisis management arrangements in place to ensure the requesting Member State can fulfil the standards of supervision expected so as not to have a detrimental impact on the SSM achieving its objectives and principles. In this respect, the principle of *mutatis mutandis* applies when it comes to the respective ECB responsibilities: the assessment of significance of credit institutions; macro-prudential tools; administrative penalties; and investigatory powers. The ECB needs to be satisfied that the directions it gives in the above matters can be executed by the NCA in accordance with its standards.

2.12 The ECB makes its decision concerning the entry into close cooperation based on a comprehensive assessment of the Member State and its banking system in the widest sense. As part of the process (which is expected as a minimum to take approximately three months) the ECB can request further documentation to assist it in making the decision. The process towards close cooperation is not a simple entry but rather a continuous process of working towards close cooperation and then continuously complying with the ECB decisions and instructions associated with supervision. Once the ECB has formed a view on the close cooperation, it will then adopt a decision based on Article 7(2) of Regulation 1024/2013 addressed to the Member State. The lack of compliance in close cooperation can lead to a situation where the agreement can be suspended or terminated by the ECB. The supervisory relationship will, to all intents and purposes, be wider than simply micro-prudential decisions and instructions since it will also be applicable on the macro-prudential level, so invariably encroaching, by necessity, on the wider issues associated with the financial system and the economy in light of the interdependence of the two strands of policy.

2.13 The SSM Framework Regulation explains the role of the ECB and Member States in the SSM and how they are expected to cooperate in close cooperation. It explains the criteria and the role of the ECB decision to determine significant and less significant credit institutions and how the ECB directly supervises significant banks and, in some cases, less significant banks. A request to a national competent authority from a significant bank to branch or provide services in another Member State is expected to be communicated to the ECB immediately.[17] It also further explains how the ECB is to take on the role of Chair and Member of the supervisory college in the capacity as of consolidated supervisor of the significant bank in a participating Member State and how the national competent authority is to revert to a position of observer for the same significant bank.[18] Regulation 468/2014 does not expressly refer to the ECB as the new competent authority, albeit it undertakes the role in a quasi-competent authority role akin to as a 'shadow' competent authority role by instructing national competent authority in the way significant banks are supervised.[19]

[17] Ibid, SSM Framework Regulation Arts 11–12.
[18] Ibid, SSM Framework Regulation Arts 9–10.
[19] SSM Regulation Art. 7(1).

In view of this, the Member State has to initiate legislative reforms to ensure the national competent authority can 'abide by any guidelines or requests by the ECB'.[20] The ECB on close cooperation simply refers the 'tasks' associated with Arts 4 and 5. To understand what form close cooperation of those tasks will take it is important to refer to the SSM Framework Regulation, Article 107(2):

> If a close cooperation has been established pursuant to Article 7(2) of the SSM Regulation the ECB and the NCA in close cooperation shall, in respect of significant supervised entities and groups and less significant supervised entities and groups established in the participating Member State in close cooperation, be in a position comparable to significant supervised entities and groups and less significant supervised entities and groups established in euro area Member States, taking into account that the ECB does not have directly applicable powers over significant supervised entities and groups and less significant supervised entities and groups established in the participating Member State in close cooperation.

The SSM Framework Regulation sets out in clear terms that the ECB does not have equivalent responsibility as the competent or designated authority (as it does in Art. 9 of the SSM Regulation 1024/2013). The ECB in close cooperation will rely on the NCA of the Member State more than it does with a Eurozone Member State. In this respect, the close cooperation arrangements could give rise to a different agency relationship associated with the regional interests and national interests not being aligned in a formal sense; since it provides 'comparable' but not 'equivalent' supervision of significant entities. Therefore, it is important to analyse where it is equivalent and where it is comparable to ascertain the benefits of opting in or out. The ECB in the context of SSM Regulation Article 4(1) and 4(2), the ECB in participating Member States is given exclusive competence to exercise the tasks set out therein. In accordance with Article 108 of the SSM Framework Regulation[21] the ECB has the discretion to give 'instructions', 'make requests', **2.14**

[20] SSM Regulation Art. 7(2)(b).

[21] SSM Framework Regulation Article 108:

Legal instruments related to supervision in connection with close cooperation

1. With respect to the tasks referred to in Article 4(1) and (2) and Article 5 of the SSM Regulation, the ECB may give instructions, make requests or issue guidelines.
2. If the ECB considers that a measure relating to the tasks referred to in Article 4(1) and (2) of the SSM Regulation should be adopted by the NCA in close cooperation in relation to a supervised entity or group, it shall address to that

   NCA:
   (a) in respect of a significant supervised entity or significant supervised group, a general or specific instruction, a request or a guideline requiring the issuance of a supervisory decision in relation to that significant supervised entity or significant supervised group in the participating Member State in close cooperation, or
   (b) in respect of a less significant supervised entity or less significant supervised group, a general instruction or a guideline.
3. If the ECB considers that a measure relating to the tasks referred to in Article 5 of the SSM Regulation should be adopted by the NCA or NDA in close cooperation, it may address to that NCA or NDA a general or specific instruction, a request or a guideline requiring the application of higher requirements for capital buffers or the application of more stringent measures aimed at addressing systemic or macro-prudential risks.
4. The ECB shall specify in the instruction, request or guideline a relevant time limit for the adoption of the measure by the NCA in close cooperation, which shall be no less than 48 hours, unless earlier adoption is necessary to prevent irreparable damage. When determining the time limit, the ECB shall take into account the administrative and procedural law with which the relevant NCA in close cooperation has to comply.

and 'issue guidelines' in close cooperation. The ECB is required to address measures to the NCA when it relates to significant supervised entities and in cases relating to less significant supervised entities or less significant groups.[22] In this respect, the NCAs remain the competent authority for supervision but the instructions will come from the ECB. For example, decisions normally addressed to a supervised entity or group are addressed to the NCA to implement for the purposes of the assessment of significance of credit institutions and decisions to apply administrative penalties.[23] Moreover, in terms of investigations relating to significant banks the NCA is to undertake actions following ECB instruments and then report the findings to the ECB.[24] In such investigations, the ECB staff are present in the capacity of observers.[25] In this respect, the ECB, within the Eurozone, can exclusively conduct investigations by way of requesting documentation, obtaining evidence, and conducting interviews.[26]

2.15 The Joint Supervisory Teams (JSTs) are one area that has gathered considerable attention since it attempts to break the local nexus of oversight and responsibility. SSM Framework Regulation explicitly refers to the ECB leading the work of Joint Supervisory Teams and being responsible for their establishment. The ECB invites national competent authority staff to join the JST and appoints the Joint Supervisory Coordinator and the national competent authority sub-coordinator.[27] They essentially become the point of contact for the bank. The responsibility of the JST in terms of supervision of significant banks is to undertake the supervisory review and evaluation process (SREP) and put forward a supervisory examination plan to the Supervisory Board, which will need ECB's approval. This is not to say local supervisory staff are not important: they are crucial to ensuring the supervisory team understand the domestic banking sector. Nevertheless, the independence of the JST is likely to minimize regulatory capture or forbearance. The level of reliance on local knowledge and practices by the JST is a question of balance and experience, which will be managed by the JST coordinator and the national competent authority staff member in the role of sub-coordinator. A hurdle will be language and culture and interpretation of local laws and procedures.

2.16 The JST teams can also include other staff members of the official safety net from the Member State which also offers the benefit of better oversight since it enables the JST to get a more holistic understanding of local approaches at the macro-prudential and micro-prudential level. More importantly, the different experiences of the JST could inform the official safety net authorities of practices which could improve the alignment of information and cooperation arrangements which appear not to be in place. For example, in crisis management arrangements are there clear lines of information sharing both

> 5. An NCA in close cooperation shall take all necessary measures to comply with the ECB's instructions, requests or guidelines and it shall inform the ECB without undue delay of the measures it has taken.

[22] Ibid, SSM Framework Regulation Art. 108(2)(a)–(b).
[23] Ibid, SSM Framework Regulation Art. 113(1)–(3).
[24] Ibid, SSM Framework Regulation Art. 114(1)–(4).
[25] Ibid, SSM Framework Regulation Art. 114(4).
[26] SSM Framework Regulation Arts 142–3.
[27] Ibid, SSM Framework Regulation Arts 3, 4 and Art. 115(3).

ex ante, for preparation purposes, and *ex post* during a crisis so that supervision and resolution are better aligned? Another significant benefit of Joint Supervisory Teams, which are likely to be multi-disciplinary and from different Member States, is potentially a more holistic, less localized approach, which is also less exposed to political influences. This influence could also lead to pressure to forbear. Therefore, consistency and robust standards are likely to materialize. It is important to note that the difference between the national competent authorities on the ground and the JST flying in means local surveillance and oversight is still an important element of understanding of what is going on in the markets, which is likely to arise from surveillance and tip-offs in other parts of the financial system which do not benefit from a direct centralized form of oversight. The systematic visits on a cycle of 1-2-3 years are likely to lead to points in time when the JST is not going to be present. But that is a problem for all on-site models of supervision, since they tend to be done at fixed periods of time. An important factor in such cases is that while there is a better overall approach, what level of attention the small local entities get from JST teams could differ in terms of frequency of visits. This is an area that, in comparison to local supervision, may differ in terms of intensity of supervision. But the move to centralization does not prevent the national authorities from doing more to ensure that there is continuous dialogue.

It is no surprise the ECB is to act as the consolidated supervisor for significant banks and their group entities.[28] Since the focus of the ECB is significant banks, the responsibility for less significant banks on a consolidated supervisor is left with the NCA. More importantly, the role of consolidated supervisor and college of supervisors in the Banking Union is reconfigured. In the Eurozone, the ECB is the consolidated supervisor and the chair of supervisory colleges for significant banks and the respective Member State NCA acts in the capacity of observer.[29] Member States' national competent authorities are no longer classed as members but can join as observers. So in the Banking Union and for pure Eurozone banks, supervisory colleges are less important since the ECB is both home and host and there would be limited asymmetry of information. However, if the consolidated supervisor is in a non-participating Member State, then the ECB and the NCA with respective interests are invited per the following rules set out in Article 10 of the SSM Framework Regulation as member and observer status respectively on the supervisory college.[30] **2.17**

This would also apply to those Member States that enter in to close cooperation.[31] The Member State that is the consolidated supervisor of a significant bank decides to enter into close cooperation its national competent authority will lose the position of chair which will be replaced by the ECB and the national competent authority's position would be changed to one of observer. Moreover, if the Member State in close cooperation has a significant branch or a subsidiary and is a member of a supervisory college then its position will be changed as well to one of observer. In this capacity as a consolidated **2.18**

[28] Ibid, SSM Framework Regulation Art. 8.
[29] Ibid, SSM Framework Regulation Art. 9.
[30] Ibid, SSM Framework Regulation Art. 10.
[31] Ibid, SSM Framework Regulation Art. 115(5).

supervisor, the ECB as chair and competent authority has the discretion to give instructions to the national competent authority in close cooperation. In the Eurozone context, the national competent authority has the right to participate in the supervisory college in the capacity of an observer.[32] The ECB is reliant on the national competent authority in close cooperation to act on the ECB instructions because the ECB does not have jurisdiction to act on its own initiative and directly liaise with the significant bank as it would within a Eurozone Member State.

2.19 The approach taken is somewhat different to the guidelines published by the European Banking Authority (EBA) since in the supervisory colleges the invitation of a Member State to join the college as an observer is not automatic and it is not one equivalent to a Member of a supervisory college, in terms of access to information or input in decisions.[33] However, as the ECB acts as both home and host for Eurozone banks this becomes less of an issue, to a point where it could even be considered unnecessary to continue having a supervisory college for pure Eurozone banks with the flow of information on capital, liquidity, and insolvency between home and host, since the role of the JST and Supervisory Board bridge the information gap for dialogue between national competent authorities. This could even be extended to the role of mediation by the EBA of joint decisions since again the conflict is likely to be resolved by the ECB acting as both the home and host competent authority.

2.20 There is one question which should be reflected on in the Eurozone, has the home and host state alignment of interests changed with the introduction of a single regulator for Eurozone Member State and close cooperating Member States? If it has and the home bias explored elsewhere is indeed minimized or eradicated, then what is the impact on the relationship between consolidated supervisor and host supervisor and what role does the supervisory college have in a pure Eurozone setting? A part of this is addressed with the adoption of JSTs since it also acts to break down the obstacles host Member States tend to face with regards to seeking information and data from the consolidated supervisor. With JSTs composed of competent authorities from the different parts of the banking group, national interests tend to be dissipated.

2.21 The benefits of opting in to close cooperation would certainly address the concerns about information sharing and enabling the Member State in close cooperation to better prepare at the macro-prudential, micro-prudential and resolution levels for future crises. A recent review by the European Court of Auditors of the SSM has the composition of JSTs in areas that do need improving. Unsurprising, perhaps, given the relatively short time that has gone between the SSM establishment and it being operational.[34] It has found that a significant proportion of the JSTs are staffed from national competent authorities since the ECB simply does not have the number of staff to improve the ratio between ECB and national competent authority staff making up the teams.

[32] Ibid, SSM Framework Regulation Art. 9.

[33] See Chapter 3, *The EU Home–Host Dilemma: The Prudential Supervisory Perspective*, The Supervisory Colleges, paras 3.14–3.53.

[34] European Court of Auditors, 'Special Report: Single Supervisory Mechanism—Good Start but further improvement needed' (No. 29, 2016).

The ECB and Decision-Making Process and Accountability

The SSM is composed of a number of committees to ensure that it complies with good governance practices and that participating Member States comply with its decisions. The complex nature of the SSM means the governance arrangements are multifaceted, with internal arrangements for ensuring the ECB's decision-making complies with the requirements of the Regulation. This results in a lack of a clear Treaty mandate to undertake and make supervisory decisions. As part of this, the governance arrangements aim primarily to ensure the ECB is acting in an independent manner when it arrives at its decisions and avoids claims of bias when it comes to the treatment of credit institutions from different participating Member States. Moreover, it resides within two broad mandates, namely the ECB's first mandate for monetary and economic policy for the Eurozone and the ECB's second mandate for the SSM.[35] These two functions of the ECB need to be operationally separate in order to minimize the risk of bias undermining their integrity. **2.22**

The Supervisory Board of the SSM organizes the day-to-day tasks and drafts the decisions of the ECB.[36] The decisions need to be proposed to the ECB's Governing Council following the 'non-objection' procedure for the supervisory board to adopt the decision.[37] The draft decisions also need to be sent to the NCA which is addressed at the same time. The Governing Council, however, could object to a draft decision of the supervisory board. In this case, the Mediation Panel would act to resolve the differences between the Governing Council and the supervisory board and ensure the functions of the ECB as a monetary authority and supervisory authority are clearly separated and do not influence one another's decisions. The NCA could also raise an objection to either the supervisory board's or the Governing Council's position. **2.23**

The Governing Council is the principal decision-making body of the ECB for the purposes of monetary and economic policy.[38] It is made up of six members of the executive board and the governors of the nineteen Eurozone central banks. In contrast, the supervisory board is made up of participating Member States which would include Member States in close cooperation with the ECB. The Supervisory Board is composed of a chair, vice chair, four ECB representatives, and nineteen representatives of national competent authorities. In respect to the SSM, the ECB's Governing Council has an extended jurisdiction over these Member States which it would normally not have, with the national central bank having the principal responsibility for monetary policy. In light of the fact that safeguarding financial stability and integrity is very broad and can spill over into monetary and economic matters, the decisions need to be assessed a lot more closely by non-Eurozone-participating Member States. Therefore, the Regulation confers a right on those non-Eurozone-participating Member **2.24**

[35] Decision of the European Central Bank, 17 September 2014 on the implementation of separation between the monetary policy and supervisory functions of the European Central Bank, ECB/2014/39 (2014/723/EU) [2014] OJ L300/57.

[36] SSM Regulation Art. 26(8).

[37] SSM Regulation Art. 26(8); <https://www.bankingsupervision.europa.eu/organisation/decision-making/html/index.en.html>: Decision Making: 'The Supervisory Board, as an internal body of the ECB, prepares the draft decisions, which are adopted by the Governing Council under the non-objection procedure. If the Governing Council does not object within a defined period of time, the decision is deemed adopted.'

[38] The Governing Council, <https://www.ecb.europa.eu/ecb/orga/decisions/govc/html/index.en.html> [accessed 20 March 2019].

States to raise objections to an ECB draft decision to the Governing Council for a decision on the matter.[39] The Supervisory Board, on the basis of the decision of the Governing Council, could amend the decision. However, the participating Member State is given a limited range of options of either to comply with the decision or terminate the close cooperation agreement.[40]

2.25 The final decision of the ECB can only be reviewed by the Court of Justice even though it may be reliant on the opinion expressed by the NCA in the preparatory stages. In such instances, where the decision emanates from a composite administrative procedure where decisions are made between national authorities and EU institutions it can be difficult to untangle with whom responsibility for the decision lies and with whom jurisdiction exists to review the decision. The Advocate General's Campos Sánchez-Bordona Opinion regarding Silvio Berlusconi and Fininvest (a company he controlled) and the subsequent ownership of Banco Mediolanum explored this issue.[41] The Bank of Italy objected to this and asked Fininvest to apply for authorization of its qualifying shareholding holding in Banco Mediolanum. The Bank of Italy put this decision to the ECB, since the ECB has exclusive competence to assess and decide on acquisitions of and increases in qualifying holdings in all financial institution that fall within the Single Supervisory Mechanism. The ECB Supervisory Board accepted it and subsequently approved the draft decision which was put to the Governing Council and adopted it and raised no objections to the decision. In the opinion of the Advocate General: 'I should stress that, in legal terms, the draft submitted by the NCA does not determine the subsequent decision by the ECB. Depending on its merits, it may influence that decision to a greater or lesser extent, but such a situation is also to be found in other processes (such as a non-binding opinion, for example) in any procedure.' The NCA has no specific decision-making power, beyond its responsibility for conducting the first stage of the procedure once an application for authorization has been submitted.[42] In view of this the Advocate General concluded the decision falls within the composite administrative procedure as explained in *Sweden v Commission* because the final decision falls on the shoulders of an EU institution.

2.26 The Mediation Panel is composed of representatives of both the Governing Council and the Supervisory Board.[43] The Case Committee of the Mediation Panel which is made up of members of the Mediation Panel reviews the decision. The Mediation Panel is composed of one member per participating Member State, so technically making its membership wider in terms of including Eurozone and non-Eurozone-participating Member States. The Mediation Panel is likely to play an important role in resolving disagreements between the Supervisory Board, Governing Council, and the NCA regarding a draft decision. In such matters, the Mediation Panel is expected to take a position in the interests of the Banking Union as a whole. However, the opinion of the Mediation Panel is not

[39] SSM Framework Regulation Arts 118–19.

[40] SSM Framework Regulation Arts 118(4) and 119(4).

[41] Opinion of Advocate General Campos Sánchez-Bordona, delivered on 27 June 2018 Case C-219/17 *Silvio Berlusconi, Finanziaria d'investimento Fininvest SpA (Fininvest) v Banca d'Italia, Istituto per la Vigilanza Sulle Assicurazioni (IVASS)*, third parties: Ministero dell'Economia e delle Finanze, Banca Mediolanum SpA, Holding Italiana Quarta SpA, Fin. Prog. Italia di E. Doris & C. s.a.p.a., Sirefid SpA, Ennio Doris.

[42] Ibid, 19.

[43] Regulation (EU) No 673/2014 of The European Central Bank of 2 June 2014 concerning the establishment of a Mediation Panel and its Rules of Procedure (ECB/2014/26).

binding on the Supervisory Board and the Governing Council. It should also be noted that, while mediation is open to all participating Member States, the right to mediation does differ between Eurozone and non-Eurozone participating Member States. In the former case, the participating Member State may require assurance that the decision reflects the separation of monetary policy and supervisory tasks. However, in the case of non-Eurozone participating Member States objecting to a draft decision, the ECB is not obliged to pursue mediation. Moreover, if the competent authority of the non-Eurozone Member State requests mediation over its objection to a draft decision and formally submits its disagreement, then the Governing Council will have thirty days to respond with its opinion on the disagreement. If the Member State still objects to the decision, despite the opinion of the Governing Council, then the ECB could suspend or terminate the close cooperation agreement notwithstanding the impact on the integrity of the SSM and the fiscal impact on the Member State in question. The ECB could reconsider the position provided the credit institutions in the Member State are not in a more favourable position than credit institutions in other Member States. In such circumstances, the 'request for mediation shall be deemed withdrawn'. A participating Member State could as a last resort terminate the close cooperation agreement and would not be able to re-join for three years.

The administrative decision-making process requires internal verification before a credit institution and/or an NCA needs to act upon the decision. The Governing Council would be reliant on the expertise and judgment of the Supervisory Board which has the technical competence to decide the importance of a decision. The decisions can emanate from various parts of the SSM relating to the classification of credit institutions, authorizations, and capital, to enforcement penalties and corporate governance arrangements. However, there is likely to be a significant amount of home and host dilemmas in this conversation, despite the fact that the ECB with its more centralised role of supervisor is acting as the home and host competent authority. The wider legal framework confers distinct roles on the home state supervisor as opposed to the host state which will invariably impact on the interests of cross-border credit institutions. In this respect, the Mediation Panel is likely to be called on to ensure the decisions are based on the appropriate supervisory reasons rather than economic concerns about burden sharing. Moreover, the forbearance of decisions also poses a risk, particularly if the matter relates to, in the ECB's opinion, supervisory intervention such as raising higher capital requirements. The monetary and economic arguments may have a different view of this decision in light of their technical expertise. However, more complex decisions relating to countercyclical capital buffers may gain a significantly higher level of scrutiny. These decisions are in the national discretion but require notification to the ECB and the ESRB, as the Member State decides to enter in a close cooperation. The role of the Mediation Panel will likely decrease the possibility of a Member State putting its national interests and the interests of national flagship credit institutions at the forefront, rather than the wider interests of the Banking Union and interests of other Member States where it undertakes its business activities. However, the position of a non-Eurozone Member State needs special consideration since the view of its central bank will not be reflected on the Governing Council, whereas a Eurozone participating Member State's central bank will be. The Mediation Panel will also need to seek the views of the other stakeholders of the official safety net to determine their opinion. 2.27

2.28 The role of the Administrative Board of Review (ABoR) is to review ECB final decisions to determine its in opinion whether they are in compliance with the Regulation.[44] For instance, if a credit institution or individual disapproves of the ECB final decision it can ask the ABoR to assess it. The review is wider than simply procedural due process since it encompasses the assessment of the facts and errors in law and compliance with prudential requirements. The Supervisory Board is expected to take the opinion of the ABoR into account and amend the decision and issue another draft decision to the Governing Council. The quality assurance role of the Administrative Board of Review within the ECB is constituted separately and does not replicate the governance models of the other mechanisms of decision-making in that it is not based on national supervisory competences. The Administrative Board of Review is independent and composed of five members of 'high repute' that are not current staff of a Member State's competent authority or central bank. The review is expected to be conducted impartially with interests, either direct or indirect, declared before they can decide a case in the wider public interest. The party requesting the review funds the decision of the Administrative Board of Review separately. While the opinions are confidential, the following decisions provide some insights into the opinion and the scope of its jurisdiction to be taken into account.

2.29 In one such matter where the applicant objected to an ECB final decision,[45] the court found in favour of the ECB's interpretation regarding its position on separating the chairman and executive director roles in accordance with French company law. Crédit Agricole's requested the appointment of a number of individuals of different entities within the group. The ECB approved the appointment of them as chairmen of each of the entities but opposed their appointment as effective directors of each of the applicants. In view of the ECB decision the applicants requested a review of the decisions. The ABoR opinion favoured the ECB's decision and considered it lawful. It explained while the tasks of 'effective director' were not defined it envisaged a separation of executive and non-executive roles and such dual role were prohibited in accordance with Article 88(1)(e) of Directive 2013/36 and indeed domestic company law. The decision highlights the scope of the mandate of ABoR is a lot wider when it forms its opinion than simply procedural due process as in this case the assessment of the final decision encompasses both Union law and domestic law in its assessment.

2.30 The role of ABoR is considered in the judgment in *Crédit Mutuel Arkéa v ECB* (2017)[46] where the cooperative group objected to the ECB decision to exercise consolidated supervision once it was designated a significant bank. Crédit Mutuel sought review of the ECB final decision about the need to supervise it on a consolidated basis and in part the revision to its CET Tier 1. The judgment is illustrative of the ABoR role once a request is made for an opinion. In part the position of Crédit Mutuel group the Confédération National du Crédit Mutuel ('the CNCM') was based on the argument that it was not a credit institution so it could not be subject to direct consolidated supervision by the ECB as a significant entity.

[44] SSM Regulation Art. 24; Administrative Board of Review <https://www.bankingsupervision.europa.eu/organisation/whoiswho/administrativeboardofreview/html/index.en.html> [accessed 20 March 2019]; C. Brescia Morra, R. Smits, and A. Magliari, 'The Administrative Board of Review of the European Central Bank: Experience After 2 Years' (2017) 18 European Business Organizational Law Review 568–89.

[45] *Caisse Régionale De Crédit Agricole Mutuel Alpes Provence and Others v ECB* Cases T-133/16 to T-136/16 24 April 2018.

[46] Judgment of 13 December 2017—CASE T-712/15 *Crédit Mutuel Arkéa v ECB*.

The ABoR found the ECB decision was lawful. It explained how the group was previously supervised on a consolidated basis from the French authorities and saw no reason why it could not continue by the ECB as the supervisor of significant banks. Indeed it is normal practice to exercise consolidated supervision of the group at the highest level, which in this case would be from the vantage point of CNCM, since it is standard practice for responsibility for the risks of the group entities to be captured by tasks such as consolidated accounts and supervision for the purposes of solvency and liquidity. In part of the assessment, the ABoR provided a statement of reasons which did not appear in the original final decision of the ECB which the ECB endorsed. In this assessment, the ECB guidelines explaining the level of responsibility the central body of the group has to its affiliates were equally assessed and considered to be an aspect of the legal context that forms the SSM legal regime.

Since the ECB leads the process of close cooperation as part of the SSM, the question that arises is whether the ECB should provide the green light for the Member State to also enter the SRM in a close cooperation arrangements. In view of how the ECB and SRB work to form decisions about failing institutions at the point of whether an institution is 'Failing' or 'Likely to Fail' an understanding of what relationship a Member State in close cooperation is it likely to have with the SRB is important. As will be shown below in this instance, both the ECB and SRB are partly reliant on the national competent and resolution authorities to help form the decision albeit the ECB and SRB make the final decision. What coordination framework is in place to ensure the supervisory green light also extends to reassurances that the resolution authority is also competent to undertake the task of resolution? A significant difference between the SSM and SRM is the level of reliance on the home and host competent and resolution authorities. In the former case there is clearly more centralized decision-making and direct supervisory oversight, whereas in the SRM there is centralized decision-making but the heavy work of resolution remains with the national resolution authorities. In both instances simply having in place the prudential and resolution requirements and tools set out in the Single Rulebook is not enough in practice to minimize home and host conflicts. For instance, the way banks are resolved through resolution or insolvency and liquidation. The cases highlight differences in the interpretation of the public interest criteria and determining whether a bank undertakes critical functions. Therefore, the SRB should be expected to put in place a framework for close cooperation equivalent to that found in the SSM framework. The SRM framework for cooperation would need to set out how it will incorporate Member States within close cooperation into the SRM decision-making process and strategically review the extent to which the national resolution authorities are likely to work with the SRB. This is important on several counts: **2.31**

(1) The measures to ensure resolution plans can be assessed by the SRB and, secondly, can implement the mandate for Minimum Required Eligible Liabilities (MREL), considering this is also a mandate for resolution authorities rather than competent authorities.[47]
(2) The resolvability and impediments to resolvability of designated significant banks will need to be closely assessed.

[47] See Chapter 5, *The EU Home and Host Dilemma: The Resolution Perspective*, 'Resolvability and the Minimum Required Eligible Liabilities', para 5.9.

(3) It will be important to determine which approach, Single Point of Entry (SPE) or Multiple Point of Entry (MPE), it is likely to adopt *ex ante* for of designated significant banks that operate in the market.[48]
(4) Finally, the SRB will also need to incorporate the review and decision-making regarding designated significant banks into the resolution college framework, if this has not been done already.

Single Resolution Mechanism—A Close Cooperation Perspective

2.32 The response to the European banking and sovereign debt crisis resulted in the introduction of the Bank Recovery and Resolution Directive 2015[49] (BRRD) and the Single Resolution Mechanism (SRM), to form the second Pillar of the Banking Union.[50] This was considered necessary due to the lack of a common approach towards the resolution of banks and investment firms, leading to situations where Member States primarily acted in their own public interest rather than in a coordinated way with commonly understood outcomes. As the regulator has a significant role as supervisor to play in the proceedings, a particular concern was the over-reliance on corporate insolvency procedures which were not considered fit for purpose to deal with the wider stakeholder concerns arising from a bank failure. In part, the reforms of both macro-prudential and micro-prudential oversight include a more coherent approach to improvements to resolution of banks and financial firms in distress. The key policy objective of those reforms is espoused to minimize both the possibility of taxpayer bail-outs and spillover effects of banks and financial firms and replace it with a resolution regime that places the primary burden on its shareholders and particular creditors, while also introducing new techniques to resolve problems experienced by them. Moreover, it aims to provide a structure to ensure cooperation and coordination between regulators and resolution authorities of Member States.

2.33 The responsibility of the SRB in the SRM is more akin to the relationship between the ECB and those participating Member States in close cooperation in the SSM: the national resolution authority act under the instructions of the SRB rather than the SRB undertaking the resolution in the same way as the ECB undertakes supervision for significant banks. How will Member States achieve close cooperation status within the SRM? Is it based on the principle of *mutatis mutandis*?

2.34 The SRMR in Recital 15 explains how it applies to banks that are supervised by the ECB and to those banks present in Member States in close cooperation. But unlike the SSMR

[48] See Chapter 5, *The EU Home and Host Dilemma: The Resolution Perspective*, 'Single Point of Entry (SPE) and/or Multiple Point of Entry Resolution (MPE)', para 5.22.

[49] Directive 2014/59/EU establishing a framework for the recovery and resolution of credit institutions and investment firms and amending Council Directive 82/891/EEC, and Directives 2001/24/EC, 2002/47/EC, 2004/25/EC, 2005/56/EC, 2007/36/EC, 2011/35/EU, 2012/30/EU and 2013/36/EU, and Regulations (EU) No. 1093/2010 and (EU) No. 648/2012, of the European Parliament and of the Council [2014] OJ L173/190.

[50] Regulation No. 806/2014 establishing uniform rules and a uniform procedure for the resolution of credit institutions and certain investment firms in the framework of a Single Resolution Mechanism and a Single Resolution Fund and amending Regulation (EU) No. 1093/2010 [2014] OJ L225/1 (the SRM Regulation).

it does not provide an administrative procedure for interested Member States to follow to enter close cooperation. A Member State that decides to terminate its relationship or its suspended with the ECB in close cooperation it will also put to an end or suspend its relationship within the SRM as well. The SRB will then need to work out 'a fair partition of the cumulated contributions' by the participating Member State to the SRF.[51] In view of how the fund is financially resourced it means either a recoupment of the non-mutualized part or the totality of part post-mutualization. Equally, if resolution funds are accessed by the Member State then those funds are required to be deducted from the contribution made.

The SRM is not a single cohesive entity but a set of multiple sets of bodies and agencies with discretionary responsibilities.[52] The SRB, described as a Union Agency,[53] is accountable to the European Parliament, the Council, and the Commission in various ways.[54] The national parliaments of participating Member States in the SRM are also able to call the Board to give written responses to questions they may have. This creates an avenue of communication and accountability between the national parliament and the SRB which does not replace the national arrangements of accountability for national resolution authorities. The SRM Regulation put in place the requirement that the SRB is expected to act independently and in the interests of the Banking Union as a whole, as a Union Agency, rather than solely in the interests of the Eurozone, albeit the primary purpose of the SRM is to improve the resilience of the Eurozone and complement the SSM. 2.35

The administrative framework sets out how the SRB takes responsibility for significant banks and how it expects national resolution authorities to exercise their responsibility.[55] In this respect, the SRB attempts to set the necessary tone for resolution within the Eurozone. This means that the role and functions of the SRB are not simply devoted to significant banks and their cross-border activities. The SRB in this role, as the resolution authority, has responsibility for a variety of decisions such as resolution plans, the setting of MREL and the premiums banks are expected to contribute to the Single Resolution Fund (SRF) and indeed the resolution scheme. The SRB has the discretion to include other cross-border groups as well, along similar terms as those allowing the ECB to include other groups as it considers necessary. Those institutions that do not fall into these categories remain the responsibility of the national resolution authority. In this respect, the national resolution authority is exercising responsibilities within the wider administrative framework of the SRM rather than simply under the terms of the BRRD. In view of this, the national resolution authority is expected to inform the SRB of any impending decisions, especially if the national resolution authority requires access to the resolution fund to support resolution. In this case, the SRB needs to be satisfied with the resolution scheme devised by the national resolution authority and then adopt it. 2.36

51 SRM Regulation, Recital 112 and Art. 4(2)–(3).

52 SRM Regulation, Art. 1.

53 Interinstitutional Agreements, Agreement between the European Parliament and the Single Resolution Board on the practical modalities of the exercise of democratic accountability and oversight over the exercise of the tasks conferred on the Single Resolution Board within the framework of the Single Resolution Mechanism [2015] OJ L339/58.

54 SRM Regulation Art. 45.

55 Framework for Cooperation between the SRB and NRAs: SRB, Decision of the Single Resolution Board of 17 December 2018 establishing the framework for the practical arrangements for the cooperation within the Single Resolution Mechanism between the Single Resolution Board and National Resolution Authorities (SRB/PS/2018/15), <https://srb.europa.eu/sites/srbsite/files/decision_of_the_srb_on_cofra.pdf> [accessed March 2019].

2.37 The cross-border resolution of institutions and groups requires a significant degree of timely cooperation and coordination between the home and host Member State or between Banking Union participating and non-participating Member States. The SRB is expected to cooperate closely with national resolution authorities. It is expected that the ECB and the SRB will publish a Memorandum of Understanding (MoU) with national resolution authorities in non-participating Member States. The national resolution authority will also assist with information to enable the SRB to formulate its decisions. The SRB will represent entities in participating Member States. In light of this, the SRB will represent the national resolution authority when working out how best to cooperate and coordinate with national resolution authorities of non-participating Member States. It is expected the Board will communicate its plans, decisions and/or measures to the national resolution authorities in non-participating Member States. The lack of success in ensuring binding commitments in the past where MoU's where present would lead one to conclude such an approach is unlikely to get the binding results.

2.38 The most critical element of the arrangements in resolution is the Board decides the resolution scheme in its executive session by determining the entity is failing or likely to fail, and there is no reasonable prospect of a private sector intervention and resolution action is in the public interest.[56] In respect of the first condition, the SRB would be reliant on the ECB to form the opinion. In respect of a Member State in close cooperation the ECB would be reliant on the competent authority to form the opinion whether the bank is failing or likely to fail and the ECB either agrees or disagrees to the assessment in the final decision which the competent authority would need to ultimately execute. In respect of assessing the prospects of a private sector solution the SRB is specifically reliant on the national resolution authority of the Member State, in close cooperation with the ECB, to assess its likelihood. Therefore, in both supervision and resolution the ECB and the SRB are heavily reliant on the Member State authorities in close cooperation to execute those decisions.

The Role of the EBA: Supervision and Resolution Conciliation and Mediation

2.39 The EBA plays a critical role in micro-prudential and macro-prudential matters within the SSM and the SRM by providing a more standardized approach to bank regulation and supervision across all the EU Member States regardless of whether they are participating or non-participating or in close cooperation.[57] Through the process of standardization, the outcome is a more consistent approach amongst Member States so that their approaches to supervision and resolution converge to better and consistent standards of practice. The rationale of consistency is to minimize the risk of regulatory arbitrage so banking does not

[56] SRM Regulation, Art. 18(1).

[57] Regulation (EU) No 1093/2010 of The European Parliament and of The Council of 24 November 2010 establishing a European Supervisory Authority (European Banking Authority), amending Decision No. 716/2009/EC and repealing Commission Decision 2009/78/EC (OJ L 331, 15.12.2010, p. 12). See Eilís Ferran, 'The Existential Search of the European Banking Authority' (2016), Vol. 17, Issue 3, European Business Organisation Law Review 285–317.

converge to the Member State that emulates the minima of the common denominator. The Single Rulebook is the principal outcome of this process, with the supportive role of the Q&A process to ensure Member States have a consist understanding of inter alia the Capital Requirements Directive (CRD IV), the Capital Requirements Regulation (CRR), Bank Recovery and Resolution Directive (BRRD), and Deposit Guarantee Schemes Directive (DGSD).[58] The production of technical standards, guidelines, recommendations, advice, and opinions gives rise to a wealth of support to interpret the principal legal instruments that form the Single Rulebook.

A recognizable challenge is really the outcome of consistent approaches amongst Member States through the process of conciliation and mediation to form joint decisions at critical junctures within the respective Singe Rulebook. However, equally important is the role of the EBA in the supervisory colleges and resolution colleges and in supporting the efforts of competent authorities and resolution authorities to come to a consensus on decisions. The process of forming joint decisions amongst Member States is perhaps the most contentious and the closest the EBA gets to 'simple rule formation', with supervisory intervention through the conciliation and mediation process. **2.40**

The Single Rulebook is premised on the principle of home country control within the relationship between home and host. The points of the Single Rulebook for joint decisions are potential areas of conflict between the home and host. In part the Banking Union where the ECB and SRB is both the home and the host competent authority and resolution authority respectively lead to decisions that may not go along national lines. It leads to a position where a pure Eurozone significant bank with a Single Supervisory Authority potentially has limited or no home and host conflicts. The EBA has a specific role in the not-so-perfect Eurozone banking context. It is, therefore, surprising to see the very few cases that have reached the point of binding and non-binding mediation. In light of the growing number of points within the instruments that require joint decisions, this is possibly the result of a lack of will by the competent authorities and resolution authorities to take matters formally to mediation. The opportunity to take matters to mediation could in itself be enough to lead competent authorities to agree amongst themselves, rather than face situation where the decision-making process is taken out of their control. **2.41**

The responsibility of the EBA in addressing joint decisions of the home and host competent authority perhaps puts it at the front line of supervision disputes. This area can be divided between prudential supervision and resolution joint decisions. Moreover, they do not simply reside in the principal legal instruments but in a much wider context, notably, in the EBA's secondary technical standards where joint decisions are also expected. Importantly, prior to the SSM or the SRM there was little cooperation or coordination since the national interest tended to prevail. In such cases, the supervisory college may have played a significant role in conciliation and arriving at some form of consensus. **2.42**

In the context of the CRD IV and the CRR, joint decisions between the home and host states are required at various points, most notably when deciding significant branches[59] and, at **2.43**

[58] Single Rulebook: <https://eba.europa.eu/regulation-and-policy/single-rulebook> [accessed 20 March 2019].
[59] CRD IV Art. 158.

more technical points, determining own funds, liquidity provisions and large exposures.[60] The scope of the CRD IV requirements is wider and, in many respects, the gaps in administrative discretion are bridged by the technical requirements set out in CRR. The process of the EBA Q&A assists in developing an understanding of rule application in practice. The competent authorities are recognized but the consolidated supervisor does take an important lead since it is likely to be in a better bargaining position when it comes to matters associated with capital and liquidity support where the latter is the principal source for a subsidiary in another Member State or third country. In such decisions, the consolidated supervisor and the competent authority are expected to take into consideration the EBA's views but may, nevertheless, formulate their own position. However, the EBA is mandated to assist in formulating the decision. This places the EBA in a very important position in reconciling the differences between home and host Member States. In light of the EBA's experience, it would be difficult for Member States to ignore its views since it is very likely that it will appear as the approach taken by other Member States also seeking to arrive at joint decisions. A time period of four months or even six months is set out in the respective principal legal instruments. Since joint decisions are by their very nature difficult and highly politicized, the respective consolidated supervisor and the competent authority can formulate decisions to fulfil their own respective interests. However, more importantly, the issue of consolidated supervision and the authority of the host Member State and host third country means that the EBA can have input into the levels of capital and liquidity at the sub-consolidated levels and decisions associated with waivers of decisions.[61] The decision-making processes formulate a position where both the consolidated supervisor and the host Member State can form their own decisions when a joint decision is not forthcoming. The option of aligning incentives in line with national interests is possibly likely to be more acute in more intense times of financial distress. However, the EBA appreciates the difficulty of formulating joint decisions.

2.44 The EBA also plays an important role in the joint decision-making process in the resolution proceedings set out in the BRRD. This applies at a range of points during the prevention phase of recovery and resolution planning as well as at the point of deciding resolution options. For example, joint decisions are expected when preparing group recovery plans between the consolidated supervisor and the competent authorities as well as when there is an opportunity to assess recovery plans.[62] In these instances, the conciliation period is four months and during this time the EBA could support the competent authorities to come to a consensus. In the absence of a joint decision, the consolidated supervisor is able to form its own decision. These similar powers and responsibilities also exist for the production of resolution plans where a larger number of parties are likely to be involved. On a more granular level, joint decisions are also expected to address impediments to resolvability. In this instance, the views of resolution colleges are important as well and should be utilised to form a view.[63] Whereas in the above cases the conciliation period is relatively long at four months, in more intensive periods of supervision, where decisions on intervention require relatively quick decisions, the conciliation period is

60 CRR Arts 20 and 21.
61 CRD IV Art. 111.
62 BRRD Art. 8.
63 BRRD Art. 88.

shorter (five days) when it comes to reaching joint decisions on the appointment of a temporary administrator prior to early intervention. The lack of joint decisions in other parts of the BRRD is also interesting since it highlights that, at critical points, a single decision-maker is more beneficial and leads to a speedier decision. However, this is likely to be the competent authority pulling the trigger for resolution, from a group perspective, it is the responsibility of the consolidated competent authority in terms of failing or likely to fail and the group resolution authority when it comes to deciding resolution options. It is expected that joint decisions are taken by the competent authority for the subsidiary and by the consolidated supervisor on an individual level, while ensuring that minimum requirements are in place at the entity level and group level. The authorities will also need to take joint decisions on the write-down and conversion of capital if own funds at the subsidiary level are taken into consideration at the consolidated level. In forming this decision, the Member State needs to take into consideration the viability of the group, since it is not compelled to write down and convert in the group's or parent's interests. In other more critical areas, joint decisions regarding the resolution scheme are also expected but it is not necessarily the case that the resolution authority of the subsidiary is required to agree to a joint scheme. Finally, in the case of recognition of third country proceedings, the European resolution college will need to consider whether it recognizes proceedings in the third country and to form a joint decision. If, on the other hand, a joint decision is not forthcoming, then the individual resolution authorities can decide whether to recognize the proceedings.

The EBA plays a crucial role in the mediation process and in the resolution process.[64] The mediation process consists of binding and non-binding mediation between the competent authorities. However, it is evident that the role of the EBA is also, if not, more important in assisting competent authorities and resolution authorities to develop their case for a joint decision. This suggests that the EBA plays a very important role at the boundaries of binding and non-binding mediation and, in a more informal manner, during the conciliation phase to get competent authorities to reconcile their differences prior to triggering binding and non-binding mediation. In this respect, the EBA does sit in a very powerful position in this process with almost a quasi-adversarial function. It also highlights the intricacy of rule-making and rule compliance. The separation of regulation and supervision into distinct silos creates an imperfect balance since rule interpretation involves dialogue among competent authorities and that implies a form of supervisory intervention in many ways. It could argue that the EBA is a rather underutilized resource to address regulatory forbearance and lack of cooperation and coordination. An important point for Member States and third country authorities is to utilize the EBA to improve levels of cooperation and coordination and to get access to supervisory and resolution colleges as either observers or members. It is also important to utilize the EBA to improve cooperation and coordination in the completion of recovery and resolution plans. This will enable the competent and resolution authorities to sufficiently understand and prepare for supervision and resolution. **2.45**

[64] Regulation (EU) No. 1093/2010 Art. 31. See EBA, Decision of the European Banking Authority adopting the Rules of Procedure for the non-binding mediation between competent authorities, 18/06/2014; and EBA, Decision of the European Banking Authority adopting the Rules of Procedure for the settlement of disagreements between competent authorities, 20/02/14.

EBA Mediation: Single Resolution Board and Banca Naţională a României

2.46 The first public joint decision illustrates very well the tenses explored in this work relating to home and host dilemmas.[65] The joint decision between Single Resolution Board (the SRB) and Banca Naţională a României (NBR), after its disagreement about the group resolution plan and the resolvability assessment underpinning the proposed resolution options, illustrates the potential conflicts that can arise between the Eurozone and non-participating Member States but also on another level the conflicts between the two if the policy aims of resolution do not align. In this context, emphasis is placed on resolution options and insolvency for non-core parts of the group. The potential underlying assumption that narrow banks are unlikely to be undertaking critical functions leads to a misalignment of outcomes for the different parts of the group and its entities, and ultimately impacts on the domestic market in which it can play a dominant role. Once the parties failed to reach a joint decision during the conciliation period. A Panel was set up by the EBA to assess the evidence to propose a decision to resolve the disagreement. The redacted public statement highlights the disagreement was about how different parts of the group and how entities within the group were likely to be resolved and the viability of those choices. The potential conflict has likely arisen because the SRB concludes the resolvability option for the group is liquidation and insolvency since in its view the group does not undertake critical functions that, if discontinued, would not cause financial stability concerns. The Romanian authorities are likely to have disagreed with this since, in their view, the subsidiary of the group in its financial markets is viewed as undertaking critical functions by the authorities so if it were to be considered failing or likely to fail its preferred option would be for the exercise of resolution options rather than insolvency-liquidation. In view of the circumstance, the following principle decisions were made: one, resolution plan adopted by either party needs to take into consideration the assessment of resolvability and potential impediments to achieve the preferred resolution strategy; and two, the SRB and the NBR are expected to cooperate to ensure a coordinated approach and to keep the EBA informed about the joint decision relating to the resolution plan.

Bulgaria and the Application to Enter Close Cooperation

2.47 Bulgaria made a formal request on 18 July 2018 to enter into close cooperation with the ECB pursuant to Art 7 of the SSM Regulation.[66] This included submission of draft legislation to amend their legislation on credit institutions and on resolution, to ensure it is compliant with the close cooperation mandate and that it can legally follow the ECB's specific instructions, guidelines, requests, and measures in relations to significant supervised entities and the ECB's general instructions, guidelines, requests, and measures in relation to less significant supervised entities.[67] The draft legislation provided for consultation explains how the

[65] EBA, Decision on the Settlement of a Disagreement, Addressed to: Single Resolution Board and Banca Naţională a României 2017 joint decision on group resolution plans and resolvability for [. . .], 27 April 2018.

[66] <http://www.minfin.bg/en/1291> [accessed 19 March 2019].

[67] Request to Enter into Close Cooperation pursuant to Art. 7 of Regulation (EU) No. 1024/2013 by the Republic of Bulgaria.

Bulgarian central bank will legislate to allow its exclusive jurisdiction over the banks to be under the direction of the ECB. It clearly explains, as pointed out before, that the ECB does not have direct relationship and powers with the banks designated as significant. The ECB will instruct the Bulgarian central bank both in terms of micro-prudential supervision and macro-prudential supervision. The latter is primarily within the discretion of the Bulgarian national bank but will now be open to scrutiny by the ECB who may request to increase levels of capital and liquidity. In order for the ECB to fulfil its task, the Bulgarian central bank is expected to provide data and documents, access to accounting records, and oral and written explanations.

The benefit from the Bulgarian perspective is certainly the improved oversight of foreign risk exposures in view of the large number of EU foreign banks present in its market. In view of the fact that they are Eurozone banks means that the ECB will have a far better understanding of the risk exposures from a home and host perspective. It is interesting to note that while the supervision of non-bank activities has been an area that has been considered important, it is yet not under the supervision of the ECB. The review of close co-operation does consider the quality of non-bank supervision. While it is not clear yet what it consists of, it presumably includes a review of their ability to understand and request information about the risk exposure of non-bank activities by the banks. It has also consisted of improving the Bulgarian Financial Supervision Commission's ability to undertake risk-based supervision. Finally, the review process also extends to anti-money laundering measures, insolvency, auditing, and accounting. This is particularly important in view of the focus on non-performing loans and the needs to assess rights associated with recoveries and how they are accounted for by the country. This highlights how the tentacles of supervision are reliant on areas indirectly associated with the supervisory mandate. In many respects this involves ensuring the 'preconditions' for supervision do not pose obstacles to the execution of supervision. **2.48**

However, it is important to consider the implications of the redistribution of resources between the ECB and the Bulgarian central bank. In terms of supervisory fees for significant banks and the resolution fee for significant banks, these are collected by the central bank on behalf of the ECB and SRB. In a separate piece of legislation, agreement has been entered into for the transfer and mutual use of contributions to the Single Resolution Fund.[68] While there are certainly benefits from close cooperation, the national authorities are very much reliant on existing budgetary resources to execute supervision and resolution. If these are limited, then there is going to be further strain on resources, especially when the central bank will need them to execute the tasks which the ECB decides. Notwithstanding this it has been explained earlier that supervision by the ECB is significantly reliant on national authorities. The needs of macro-prudential oversight is reliant on national authority's recourses. In view of this, when the number of banks is relatively small and foreign-owned in a constrained budgetary environment, this could result in a significant loss of budgetary resources. **2.49**

[68] Law on the ratification of the Agreement on the Transfer and Mutual Use of Contributions in the Single Fund for Restructuring, <https://www.parliament.bg/bg/laws/ID/78201> [accessed 19 March 2019].

2.50 The ECB carries out a comprehensive asset quality review as part of the close cooperation review process. This is likely to identify how well the banks have been supervised in practice, the quality of their balance sheet, and their resilience to withstand the shocks that feature in the stress tests.[69] The six banks listed consist of the four largest banks in Bulgaria and two banks from its second tier. Of the four largest banks, three are foreign European banks from Italy (UniCredit Bulbank), Hungary (DSK Bank), and Belgium (United Bulgarian Bank). The other three are Bulgarian banks, two of which are publically listed (First Investment Bank AD and Central Cooperative Bank AD). While it is sensible and obviously necessary to undertake a comprehensive asset quality review of these banks, one would have thought it would have been useful to extend it to a larger proportion of Bulgarian banks to gauge the quality of the balance on a wider scale. This is especially important when the ECB's reach includes significant and less significant institutions. The number of banks listed in other smaller Member States would lead to the conclusion that only the three largest banks are likely to fall under 'direct' supervision. In this case, as in those cases, it is likely to be the foreign bank subsidiaries. Therefore, from a home and host perspective the move is likely to mean the ECB is going to be both the home and host for the Italian and Belgian subsidiaries from a consolidated supervisory standpoint, since both subsidiaries have ultimate parent entities that are designated as significant banks in the Eurozone. In the case of DSK Bank, its parent is OTP Bank in Hungary, so it will need to continue liaising with Hungary as a non-participating Member State.

2.51 The most controversial aspect of close—cooperation is likely to be in the field of resolution decision-making. The ECB will decide for significant banks whether it is failing or likely to fail and the SRB will decide how the bank will be resolved either in resolution or insolvency-liquidation. The findings in Chapters 5 and 6 in the work clearly point out that the public interest test for resolution strategy is interpreted differently leading to a decision that the national authorities may not have taken it if they were responsible for making the decision. The national authorities may take a more cautious approach to ensure continuity of critical functions which the SRB may not consider as critical to the real economy and so decide after its assessment that national insolvency law can be used to liquidate the bank and orchestrate a payout for covered deposits.

Reflections on the Principal Issues

2.52 The SSM and SRM provide formal decision-making mechanisms to provide principal decisions about supervision and resolution for participating Member States. The scope for non-participating Member States to interclose cooperation clearly shows the relationship does differ in a formal legal perspective. This is important to understand since the legal form will ultimately impact the way decisions are made within the SSM and SRB. In view of this it has been important to also analyse the formal administrative mechanisms to take supervisory decisions and how those decisions are scrutinised. The nature of bank supervision is a complex affair where it is assumed rules exist the administrative discretion within those rules is

[69] 'ECB to conduct comprehensive assessment of six Bulgarian banks', <https://www.bankingsupervision.europa.eu/press/pr/date/2018/html/ssm.pr181112.en.html> [accessed 19 March 2019].

evident and requires additional legal scrutiny to analyse their purpose, as shown through the work of ABoR and EBA mediation. Nonetheless the move towards close cooperation relies more on the national competent and resolution authorities to discharge decisions. Therefore, it was shown that the relationship between the ECB and those Member States in close cooperation is akin to an agency relationship. Indeed, the announcement of Bulgaria entering into close cooperation is a very good illustration of the relationship between the Bulgarian authorities and the ECB and the legislative acceptance of the ECB's decisions with execution remaining with the Bulgarian authorities. The legislative reforms go beyond supervision but also extend to the mutualization of resolution funds. The data from Orbis Bank Focus shows that a significant proportion of the largest banks in Bulgaria are EU foreign bank subsidiaries and are significant banks in their respective home country. In view of this the ECB is likely to have a good position to see the operations of those banks from another home and host perspective. The Bulgarian authorities will now have the leverage of the SRB to insist on cooperation and coordination at the supervisory and resolution levels where forbearance at one point in time may have been prevalent. Therefore minimizing, in part, the asymmetry of information between home and host. However, the recent opinion published by the EBA between the SRB and Romania shows there is still a long way to minimizing the asymmetry of information between home and host when either the group interests and or policy interests are not aligned.

3

The EU Home and Home-Host Dilemma

The Prudential Supervisory Perspective

Introduction

The integration of EU banking identifies potential exposures of risks of contagion and concentration risks as a result of the relationship between Member States. Cross-border prudential supervision, in various forms, attempts to address the potential risk posed by home and host bias about cross-border banking business creeping in to their decision-making. The idea of home bias has been a material concern after the global financial crisis and, in particular, when considering the limited powers of the host Member State to intervene in the business affairs of a branch undertaking regulated activities under the single passport regime. However, it is important that the home bias is reviewed when considering the position of the subsidiary of an EU parent institution. In this context, it is assumed once the subsidiary is authorized, the supervisor can undertake the necessary supervision of its activities on an isolated level. It is argued that the subsidiary is left in a rather precarious position because it is assumed that there will be cooperation and coordination with the group consolidated supervisor of the parent institution and the subsidiaries respective supervisor. **3.1**

This chapter analyses the issues from the perspective of home country control and host responsibilities and the role of the ECB as a single supervisor to minimize the potential conflicts between home and host participating Member States. It first of all analyses the relationship of home and host supervisory authorities for branches and subsidiaries. The criteria for deciding which banks in participating Member States fall within the ECB jurisdiction of responsibilities is specifically analysed. Implicit in this narrative is the importance of financial stability. Where financial stability is more explicit in determining which banks are domestically important (O-SIIs), a contrasting (and inconsistent) position arises to the number of banks listed as significant in Member States. These show the first signs of the misalignment of the EU instruments between the centralized (ECB) and decentralized (Member State) position. Another approach is also explored namely the composition of significant banks as publicly listed and non-listed. It is argued later this factor could have implications for raising finance and managing the information channel such markets expose listed banks to. It is then necessary to explore the use of consolidated supervision of bank groups. It is the starting point for addressing the home and host issue. The controversial aspect of it is premised on the home country taking the lead and so for significant banks the ECB would be designated the consolidated supervisor. In addition to this, requirements are in place for information sharing for the purposes of crisis preparation. This analysis is linked to the role of supervisory colleges. It will consider the role of supervisory colleges **3.2**

European Cross-Border Banking and Banking Supervision. Dalvinder Singh, Oxford University Press (2020). © Oxford University Press.
DOI: 10.1093/oso/9780198844754.001.0001

and whether they could open up an expectations gap in group supervision. In terms of how membership is decided and the level of discretion it confers to its members to actually form decisions. In addition to supervisory colleges, the other principal mechanism to address potential risks to financial stability is the preparation of the recovery plans. However, it is argued recovery options open up a range of unintended consequences and they suggest a narrow group think and do not reflect properly the cross-border dimension. The use of stress-testing is also considered and the challenges faced by Member States attempting to embark on cross-border stress tests. The chapter further proposes a more coherent supervisory framework for 'significant subsidiaries' those material to the local market of the host Member State. In the context of the European Union banking groups, there is a mix of branches and subsidiaries with a preponderance of branches over subsidiaries in most Member States.[1] The chapter finally considers the third country perspective and the use of international soft law instruments to bridge some of the gaps left by the consolidated supervision of EU third country institutions.

The Legal Form of Cross-Border Banking and Banking Supervision

3.3 The composition of foreign banks in the EU Member States takes two broad forms, namely branches and subsidiaries. As shown earlier, the number of foreign branches in comparison to foreign subsidiaries is larger relatively to a few exceptions regionally. The right of establishment of branches is incentivized with the introduction of the single passporting regime. In this respect it should not come as a surprise therefore the number of foreign branches is higher than the number of subsidiaries in EU Member States since the branch is legally dependent part of an institution and so does not require separate capital for its business in the host Member State. The branch can undertake the activities of the parent entity in a host Member State as a result of the authorization of its parent to undertake those activities by the home Member State. In addition to the right to branch in a host Member State, the right to provide cross-border services on the same basis also exists. In contrast the subsidiary is authorized separately by the 'host-home' and for the purposes of consolidated supervision the 'host-home' is responsible for Capital Requirements Directive (CRD IV) and Capital Requirements Regulation (CRR) requirements. The principle of mutual recognition and minimum harmonization is integral to the right of establishment and the provision services in one another's financial markets. Since it requires recognition of a Member State's authorization and supervision practices of banks and their activities, the other underlying principles is home country control which confers on the competent authorities regulatory and supervisory powers in terms of solvency and liquidity requirements for the parent entity and the group as a whole.

3.4 The principle of home country control appears to be relatively straightforward and uncontroversial. However, its origins from a legal perspective provides a perspective which is couched in legal administrative discretion and so much so it is less set in concrete as one

[1] Cf F Allen, T Beck, E Carletti, PR Lane, D Schoenmaker, and W Wagner, *Cross Border Banking in Europe: Implications for Financial Stability and Macroeconomic Policies*, Centre for Economic Policy Research (CEPR) (2011) p. 21.

appears to first believe. This gives rise to the need to assess the approach to home country principle within the context of the legal instruments that give rise to conferring responsibilities to the home and host competent authorities. In simple terms the application of home country control provides a starting point to divide responsibilities for the purposes of cross-border bank supervision and its counterparts in the host country. The simplification of separate roles and functions of the home and host avoids, in part, the attempt to apply national laws to the different component parts of a banking group. Leading to the proposition, whether it addresses concerns associated with asymmetry of information problems between the different legal entities.

The demarcation lines of the home and host country are in the first instance determined according to the legal form banks take namely subsidiary, and branches and provision of services. According to the CRR, the home Member State[2] is defined as where the credit institution is authorized to undertake the business of accepting deposits or other repayable funds,[3] by a national competent authority.[4] The competent authority in the home state undertakes the task of supervision of that business and also undertakes the task of consolidated supervision of the parent entity or the holding company in either the form of a financial holding or mixed holding company.[5] Member States where a subsidiary is incorporated and authorized to undertake business of a credit institution is classed as a home Member State and is also conferred responsibility for consolidated supervision. Albeit the Member State where the 'ultimate' legal parent entity or holding company is incorporated will undertake consolidated supervision as if it were a 'single institution'.[6] This does not negate the ability of the 'host-home' Member State to undertake sub-consolidated supervision of the activities of the incorporated subsidiary by its competent authority. 3.5

The host Member State is simply the Member State where the credit institution has a branch or provides cross-border services. Therefore, foreign group subsidiaries incorporated to undertake the business of a credit institution in other Member States are not technically a host Member State but its home state. Therefore conferring on it the principle of home country control over the incorporated branches and services provided by the subsidiary. The presumption here is potential conflicts of interests between the home and home-host authority can be ameliorated by each competent authority undertaking their responsibilities conferred by CRD IV and CRR and by applying the technical standards devised by the EBA. In respect to branches that want to set up in a host Member State, the competent authorities have within two months to prepare for supervision.[7] In order to assist the process of decision-making, the home Member State is required to assess the credit institutions decision and its management and provide information about the credit institutions level of own funds and risk exposures.[8] More importantly, it can also indicate conditions in accordance 3.6

[2] CRR Art. 4(43).
[3] CRR Art. 4(1)(1).
[4] CRR Art. 4(40).
[5] CRR Art. 4(41).
[6] CRR Art. 4(47).
[7] CRD IV 35–36; see EBA FINAL draft implementing technical standards on passport notifications under Arts 35, 36, and 39 of Directive 2013/36/EU; EBA, Report on the Peer Review of The RTS on Passport Notifications, 10 July 2018.
[8] CRD IV Art. 35(2)–(5).

with the general good how those activities can be carried out in the host Member State.[9] The Member State in this respect can impose restrictions on the activities of the branch and these restrictions would need to be communicated to the home Member State. What are restrictions in this context? In part, the function of general good is addressed by CRD IV and CRR by the use of joint decisions and the elaboration of some discretionary elements by requiring technical standards produced by the EBA to structure the administrative discretion of the competent authorities. At the SSM level, the ECB partly relies on the national competent authorities to undertake due diligence according to their responsibilities with the ECB deciding whether the requirements are met.[10]

3.7 The interpretation and application of the general good principle is deferred to the national competent authority and is able to apply national law in these circumstances to safeguard the 'public interest'. The EBA review found, on the whole, good practices when it came to branch notification and activities amongst Member States, but did recommend better dialogue between the two and recommended the host Member State to meet management of the branch, especially in cases where the branch undertakes significant levels of business in the host Member State.[11] In respect of the general good requirement only four competent authorities expressed that they had set out restrictions in the general good which related to national law conferring on the competent authority to require branches to comply with specific treatment of financial services such as deposit taking requiring a separate licence or to undertake mortgage business.

3.8 The level of assets held by foreign branches and subsidiaries in a Member State highlights there importance since both give rise to different risk outcomes from a home and host supervisory perspective. The importance of branches and the risks they pose in a Member States was acutely apparent in the GFC especially when the risks posed by them could not be mitigated by the commitments to protect depositors at their respective branches, most notably Iceland and its obligations to depositors in the Netherlands and the UK.[12] In view of the importance of branches the EBA requires Member States to apply guidelines to identify a new set of significant branches classed as 'significant-plus branches' present in their

[9] CRD IV Art. 36.

[10] EBA, 2018 p. 8. The ongoing consolidation in the EU banking sector affects the number of branches, which has shrunk since the onset of the financial crisis. In this regard, Question 4 seeks to assess how many subsidiaries cancelled their authorization and transferred the majority of their business to a branch. See also ANNEX 4: Sharing of responsibilities between CAs and the ECB/SSM with regard to passport notifications Home CAs—Act as entry point of the application from the supervised entity—Assess the completeness of the notification—Create passporting procedures in IMAS (branch/services) —Decide in cases of branch and outgoing branch procedures of less significant credit institutions (LSIs)—Notify host CA in cases of passporting LSIs (branch/services within or outside the SSM) and passporting SI within the SSM. Host CAs—Receive notification from home CA/ECB—Inform the supervised entity about the conditions under which, under national law in the interest of general good, activities can be carried out—Create passporting procedures in IMAS (incoming branch/incoming services). ECB—Monitors the passporting procedures in IMAS—Assesses whether or not the requirements for passporting branch of SI within or outside the SSM are met—Assesses the significance of incoming branches—If requirements for passporting branch SI are met, notifies the host CA—Notifies the host CA in cases of outgoing services of an SI—If the requirements are not met, prepares proposal for a complete draft decision to oppose the establishment of the branch and notifies the applicant and home and host CAs. At p. 46.
There has been hardly any noticeable cancellation activity on authorization of branches during the reference period (Figure 4). Indeed, 20 CAs did not report any cancellation. Seven CAs reported one cancellation and only three CAs reported two cancellations, excluding the ECB/SSM. P. 16.

[11] EBA 2018, p. 26.

[12] M Elvira Méndez-Pinedo, 'Iceland and the EU: Bitter Lessons After the Bank Collapse and the Icesave Dispute, 9-42' in Ivana Barković Bojanić and Mira Lulić (eds) Contemporary Legal and Economic Issues III, Faculty of Law Osijek (Josip Juraj Strossmayer University of Osijek: Croatia, 2011).

market.[13] However, CRD IV Article 51 does not provide a complete criteria to identify such important branches. These branches are expected to be either significantly important to the group or systemically important in the market of the host Member State. The challenge partly is to ensure Member States take a consistent view of the importance of certain branches and ensure it is a joint decision to avoid the interests of either the home or host influencing the decision. The classification of significant branches in view of their importance can be duplicative as well since there is, as will be shown below, a potential for misalignment with other decisions taken by the home and host Member State when it comes to decisions about capital buffers for the purposes of macroprudential supervision, which do apply to branches. This is a risk where subsidiaries are converted in to branches through a branchification strategy which changes oversight of the legal entity but not its importance or significance either to the group as a whole or the host market. In the latter, however, formal powers of supervision are moved to the home competent authority and leaves the newly designated host reliant on the home to provide information which it could once insist directly from the subsidiary; albeit the host can inspect and seek information if it considers its financial stability is at stake. Moreover, the responsibilities of the host also extend to market conduct risks associated with money laundering requirements and terrorist financing compliance.

The EBA Report on Significant Branch Guidelines 2017[14] explain the identification of significant-plus branches does not change the existing responsibilities of the home and host supervision of such significant branches. The EBA Guidelines suggest a new framework to structure the relationship for these specifically importance branches by providing a point of reference to improve information sharing and recovery planning for the purposes of supervisory colleges. For purposes of classifying a branch as significant-plus, the competent authorities of either the home or host or both jointly need to meet a higher threshold and require a separate supervisory approach in view of the branches importance. A separate intensification test is provided to formulate their decision. From the home perspective whether or not the branch provides critical functions and is important to the group. From the host perspective, the branches importance for the purposes of financial stability but more specifically its position in terms of market share and whether or not its deposit base exceeds 4% of total domestic deposits or it holds total assets that are greater than 4% of GDP or is as domestically important as other branches that are classed as systemically important.[15] The findings of on-site inspections that could be carried out by both home and host or separately are expected to be shared with one another and with the management of the branch. However, this requirement falls short of complete sharing of information which illustrates the point about how coordination and cooperation may transpire in practice. Since the guidelines qualify the sharing of information by 'at least, in a proportionate 3.9

[13] CRD IV Art. 51(1) Significant Branches: 'That request shall provide reasons for considering the branch to be significant with particular regard to the following: (a) whether the market share of the branch in terms of deposits exceeds 2% in the host Member State; (b) the likely impact of a suspension or closure of the operations of the institution on systemic liquidity and the payment, clearing and settlement systems in the host Member State; 27.6.2013 Official Journal of the European Union L 176/367 EN; (c) the size and the importance of the branch in terms of number of clients within the context of the banking or financial system of the host Member State.' EBA, Final Report on guidelines on supervision of significant branches (2017).

[14] EBA, Final Report on guidelines on supervision of significant branches, EBA/GL/2017/14 (2017).

[15] Ibid. p. 17.

and appropriate manner, adequate information',[16] there is a risk of inconsistency of practice between home and host authorities which may play out in line with their own self-interest. An important element of this process however is the possibility of aligning the decision and monitoring of a branch as a significant-plus entity with decisions about capital buffers for the purposes of macroprudential supervision, since those decisions give rise to reciprocal rights of action. The information from the ground would be useful for these decisions. Finally, the information garnered would also assist with the decision of how the branch fits within the recovery plan considering it is assessed as providing critical functions and would be included in the dialogue of the supervisory college.

Single Supervisory Mechanism—Classification of Significant Banks

3.10 The ECB and its relationship with national authorities resides in an interesting position within European Banking Union with what may be referred to as general tasks and specific tasks of bank supervision. The ECB's general tasks of bank supervision apply to all credit institutions in participating Member States and equate to assessing applications, requests, and ensuring compliance and supervisory reviews. These general tasks are wide and include responsibility for all applications of authorization and withdrawal of authorization, to exercise the task conferred on the home competent authority and host competent authority with requests to establish a branch or provide services in a non-participating Member State, and assess requests for acquisitions and disposal of qualifying holdings of credit institutions in the participating Member States.[17] More specific general tasks include ensuring compliance with Union law matters relating to own funds requirements, securitization, large exposure limits, liquidity, leverage and disclosure requirements, and requirements associated with credit institution governance arrangements such as fit and proper requirements. In addition to these tasks the ECB in coordination with the EBA carries out supervisory reviews such as stress tests. As a result of those stress-test findings impose additional own funds and or liquidity requirements. It is only tasks relating to authorization and acquisitions for all credit institution that reside with the ECB. The ECB is reliant on national competent authorities to undertake the rest of the general tasks on their own initiative and keep the ECB informed of the measures taken. These tasks are then specifically divided between significant and less significant credit institutions. The SSM Regulation, therefore conferring on the ECB either direct or indirect powers that involve interaction with credit institutions either directly or via the national competent authorities with significant banks. Notwithstanding the division of responsibility based on significance, the ECB does have significant supervisory powers of intervention regarding all credit institutions conferred by Article 6(5)(b) and Article 16 to address prudential and governance matters at credit institutions within participating Member States to ensure consistency of practices.

3.11 The ECB is the competent authority and undertakes direct prudential supervision of banks and their groups designated as significant, in an attempt to contribute to improving market

[16] Ibid. p. 25.

[17] Decision (EU) 2019/322 of the European Central Bank of 31 January 2019 on delegation of the power to adopt decisions regarding supervisory powers granted under national law (ECB/2019/4).

integration and overall financial stability and economic growth. The ECB is conferred the task of overseeing the banking system in terms of safeguarding the entry into the banking system. However, what can constitute prudential supervision is very broad but is qualified to focus on capital requirements, liquidity requirements, internal governance controls, fit and proper management, ownership, and indeed early intervention powers to support resolution. Mindful of different approaches to the design of regulation and supervision, the SSM Regulation also confers a range of explicit idiosyncratic responsibilities on the ECB which are generally implicit to the tasks of supervision. However, notwithstanding the explicit reference to those tasks, the ECB as the competent authority will be responsible for exercising specific supervisory tasks which NCAs would be required to comply with under Union law and administer them in accordance with their responsibilities in day-to-day bank supervision. The challenges of ensuring compliance with Union law in a consistent manner are due to the level of discretion that exists within parts of it and the different interpretations amongst Member States.

The banks classed as significant according to their consolidated position in the participating Member State by the ECB and so falling within the remit of the SSM is based on a wide encompassing criteria.[18] Implicit in this decision of classifying an institution significant and less significant is the idea that large credit institutions are likely to threaten financial stability in contrast to small credit institutions. The threshold of most significant banks is based on: **3.12**

(1) size;
(2) importance for the economy of the Union or participating Member State; and
(3) significance of cross-border activities.

The significance of the bank is qualified further by reference to its asset size: **3.13**

- more than €30 billion; or
- ratio of total assets and GDP is more than 20%; or
- one of the three largest banks; or
- directly assisted by the European Stability Mechanism (ESM); or
- based on cross-border activities, the credit institution has total assets exceeding €5 billion and its cross-border activities in a participating Member State exceed 20% of its total assets, or
- its liabilities in a participating Member State exceed 20% of total liabilities.

The ECB can also consider a bank significant if it has subsidiaries in two or more participating Member States; or if the bank is supported by the European Financial Stability Facility (EFSF) or ESM; or finally, if the ECB, in agreement with the local competent authority, decides that the institution should come under the umbrella of the SSM rather than remain under the helm of the local competent authority.

The classification of significant banks in each Eurozone Member State according to the different categories. The most significant banks according to the highest asset size €1000bn and 500–1000nb reside in Member States in Group 1 and Group 2 with banks from France, Germany, and Italy, and the Netherlands and Spain represented, and with France having the **3.14**

[18] Art. 4 SSM Regulation 2013. List of supervised entities: <https://www.bankingsupervision.europa.eu/ecb/pub/pdf/list_of_supervised_entities_201611.en.pdf?a9caa144fa232a75fb36cf1213edd990>.

highest proportion of banks in this EU G-SIB category. The majority of significant banks is unsurprisingly in the smallest category of assets between €30–50bn and the number reduces significantly in the subsequent categories. The significant banks in Member States in Group 5–6 which are Member States including Eastern Europe do not have significant banks based on asset size. These banks come within the category of total assets above 20% of GDP and or among the three largest banks in the Member State. This points to the idea that the banks which are primarily foreign EU and non-EU banks are not essentially significant parts of the banking group but are significant within the respective Member State. Finally, while the respective Member States have relatively few significant banks in comparison to other Member States, the position when it comes to banks considered domestically important is different. This contributes to the argument that a separate coherent policy narrative for significant branches and subsidiaries is required to ensure a more balance approach to their respective position within the group and indeed the decision making of the home country national competent authority.

Significant Banks—Listed and Non-Listed Significant Banks

3.15 The significance of banks for the purposes of financial stability as explained has been used to determine their system importance. As a result of this, some banks are also required to hold additional capital buffers. Another signal of significance is whether the bank is publicly listed or not. This information would serve as an indicator of how an institution can raise capital either from a closed set of investors or an open set of investors. The risk of the bank in the former is likely to be held by a small set of investors and the latter is likely to be held by a more diversified set of investors in the market. The level of liquidity that a bank could access is equally dependent on whether it is publicly listed or private. The information about the bank in the latter is again in a small set of hands, so only they can truly assess whether the institution is investor worthy. The opportunity for a publicly listed bank arises to raise finance or indeed not, as often is the case based on market appetite. The monitoring capacity of private and public investors causes its own controversy, with the former possibly providing more scrutiny in comparison to the latter, which can be captured by investor apathy.[19]

3.16 Information about the importance of a bank if it is publicly listed is more readily available and the market can gauge relatively quickly the importance of the institution in terms of market capitalization as well as other publicly disclosed information. However, for privately owned banks the information is not as transparent and reside in private hands, so the market may be slow to respond. The implications of this are important from a policy perspective since banks that may be interconnected with the private institution may underestimate the systemic importance of the institution and could be found to be ill-prepared if problems come to light. The market may be unprepared for the spillover effects of such a bank failing in comparison to those that are publicly quoted and obligated to disclose market sensitive information to the market. On the other hand, the problems of a bank not

[19] Avanidhar Subrahmanyam and Sheridan Titman, 'The Going-Public Decision and the Development of Financial Markets' (1999) Journal of Finance 1045–1082 p. 1046.

listed could be concealed from the market allowing itself to work out its problems behind closed doors. Equally important is the ability of a publicly listed corporation to issue debt instruments to potential new investors. The creditworthiness of a publicly listed corporation is easier to assess and so the pricing of corporate bonds is likely to be more accurate. This form of finance is an acute problem in the European banking industry as is explored further below.

Table 7.1 (Appendix 7) shows the proportion of ECB significant banks that are publicly listed and private in each jurisdiction.[20] **3.17**

The 2018 list of significant banks per Member State are set out in Table 7.1 (Appendix 7). The Eurozone average of non-listed is high at 65%, with only 35% as listed institutions. The table shows that the division between small and large Member States is not so clear cut, with the latter having comparable level of unlisted significant banks. While it is clear those with only unlisted significant banks are indeed smaller Member States, it also includes Luxembourg, which has a very large banking market relative to the economy. With smaller Member States put to one side, the rest of the picture is one of the Eurozone average of a 60–40 split between unlisted and listed banks. The exception in this overall group is Germany, with a 80–20 split between unlisted and list banks. A significant proportion of EU foreign banks are subsidiaries in other participating Member States and large enough to reach the significance threshold in their own right. Yet, they may decide that they do not need to be listed as they are able to depend on local corporate and retail financing to support business operations and support from the parent entity in the home Member State. This is particularly distinct in the Eastern European jurisdictions. Notwithstanding this, the similar balance sheet of those institutions gives rise to certain challenges as well. In many respects, the markets are reliant on proper supervision of both listed and non-listed and possibly more so in the latter case because shareholder monitoring is not as transparent. The introduction of recovery plans needs to undertake robust due diligence of bank's chances of raising capital. **3.18**

The important point about this data is the implications of being unlisted. The first thing the banks would find it more challenging to raise capital in the marketplace like their listed counterparts. In many respects, the banks are self-financing through their business operations. Therefore, the majority of these banks will find it difficult to issue external Minimum Requirement for Own Funds and Eligible Liabilities (MREL), which is explored further in Chapter 5. This point is highlighted by Restoy, who explains that for significant banks a considerable challenge exists to raise MREL. He echoes, 'it is estimated that the European banking industry will need to make up a large shortfall of eligible liabilities. According to data provided by the SRB, corresponding to banks representing 80% of total assets of SRB banks as of 31 December 2016, that shortfall could exceed €117 billion.'[21] How that shortfall would be covered is a considerable challenge when the banks do not have the kind of access to financial markets as one would assume. This is exasperated by the fact noted by Restoy as well, and echoed in Chapter 1, that the EU market is heavily reliant on loans and deposits as a form of finance and issues very little subordinated instruments. In view of this, and the **3.19**

[20] Source: Orbis Bank Focus, Bureau van Dijk.

[21] Fernando Restoy, 'Bail-in in the new bank resolution framework: is there an issue with the middle class?' At the IADI-ERC International Conference: 'Resolution and deposit guarantee schemes in Europe: incomplete processes and uncertain outcomes', Naples, Italy, 23 March 2018, <https://www.bis.org/speeches/sp180323.pdf>.

data presented in Table 7.1 (Appendix 7), it is possible to conclude that in some Member States it will be unlikely to raise external debt finance as is anticipated in those Member States where the significant banks are not listed. In smaller Member States where banks are listed it could be a challenge because of a lack of market for such instruments. Indeed recent experience with Metro Bank in the UK clearly indicates the challenges banks can experience when trying to issue MREL. Confidence in the institution is critical at such points in time and where it in doubt investors may not be inclined to purchase the new instruments.[22] Another option in such circumstances would be to arrange a private issuance rather than a public issuance to manage expectations. While these are private decisions supervisors will need to be flexible in terms of the timing of such decisions to issue new instruments.

The Macroprudential Classification of Banks

3.20 The responsibility of macroprudential supervision is primarily a national competency, however the ECB within the context of participating Member States does have a significant influence on national decisions. The ECB is conferred the responsibility of ensuring consistency to the extent it can 'apply higher capital buffer requirements and more stringent measures than those adopted by the national authorities to address systemic or macroprudential risks at the level of credit institutions'.[23] The supranational position it has places it in an important position to deal with potential asymmetry of information challenges when macroprudential measures have an impact on other Member States.[24]

3.21 The soft arrangements associated with macroprudential matters through the introduction of formal Systemic Risk Buffers with Article 133(11) of CRD IV and the Counter Cyclical Buffer with Article 136(7) leaves room for national discretion when going about setting these two buffers in accordance with EBA Guidelines.[25] The EBA Guidelines enable the national authorities to, first of all, identify the O-SII buffer, and, secondly, set the two other buffers according to their assessment of the systemic risk associated with the individual subsidiary or sub-consolidated division and/or the economic cycle the economy is moving in. Despite this broad discretion, the national authorities would need to be mindful of their decisions being comparable to levels set by other Member States and the cross-border effect of setting the levels. With buffer rate simply requiring notification to the ESRB, it is argued that, while prudential capital requirements may reside in the decision-making authority of the ECB as the single supervisor, the movement of these at the group level could have implications for the host authorities. Where the ECB seeks to change these at the consolidated level, it could place pressure on the local subsidiaries to enable them to comply. However, it could be the view of the central bank that the systemic importance of the subsidiary and/or the concerns of economic cycle , mean they need to be maintained or increased.

3.22 The Member States use the EBA's guidelines to determine whether banks, branches or subsidiaries, should be classed as O-SIIs and may require to hold between 0–1.5% and 2%

[22] *Financial Times*, 'Metro Bank shares tumble 30% after bond sale pulled', 24 September 2019.

[23] SSM Regulation Art. 5(2).

[24] SSM Regulation Art. 5(2)–(5).

[25] EBA, Guidelines: On the criteria to determine the conditions of application of Article 131(3) of Directive 2013/36/EU (CRD) in relation to the assessment of other systemically important institutions (O-SIIs), December 2014.

additional capital.[26] Some Member States do not differentiate between EEA and non-EEA branches.[27] The rational to assess both forms of entities highlights how they can both be a channel for the transmission of systemic risk in to a host Member State. However, in the case of branches no buffer (unless it is a third country branch) is applied but need to be assessed nevertheless in view of the potential threat posed by branches to financial stability. The move towards branchification by some banks highlights the need for such monitoring as well since the systemic importance of the entity remains the same but with the added obstacle on relying on the home competent authority to undertake prudential supervision. The dominance of the branch model for expansion across borders explained earlier also highlights the importance of considering them for such matters. Despite this, not all Member States have identified branches as O-SIIs, especially whether foreign branches were included in the assessment. Instances where branches are not assigned a score the EBA recommends the designated authority to provide a score to a cluster of branch entities to identify their threat to financial stability.[28] The Banking Stakeholder Group also emphasizes the importance of considering branches in the group structure.[29]

The criteria consist of qualitative and quantitative measures of size, importance to the economy, complexity, and interconnectedness.[30] More specifically, O-SIIs are likely to be exercising critical functions in the wider financial system, in terms of volume of payment transaction, private sector deposits and loans, cross-border complexity, sizeable OTC derivatives positions, cross-border liabilities and claims, intra-financial system liabilities and/or assets and debt securities. A significant proportion of these banks are EU banks. The level of administrative discretion conferred on national authorities and the lack of need to enter in to joint decisions on matters relating to capital buffers means the home and host are not necessarily obliged to coordinate and cooperate with one another in such decisions. In addition to these indicators the EBA Review (2017),[31] found some national authorities considered other indicators to be important as well to better reflect the systemic importance in their banking systems such as (1) financing to the real economy based on loans to non-financial and financial sector; (2) contribution to financial intermediation based on level of deposits held by households and corporations; (3) level of exposure to the respective interbank markets; (4) payment services; (5) vulnerability to contagion through parent bank-subsidiary relationship; (6) contagion through a conglomerate relationship; (7) vulnerability through shareholding; (8) reputational contagion; and (9) connectivity with foreign banking systems. Implications for higher capital buffers is nevertheless an important consideration for the cost of business especially in markets with very high levels of bank concentration and acute levels of foreign bank presence. 3.23

The wider set of bespoke indicators provide a wide level of administrative discretion to national designated authorities determine the importance of an institution and whether capital buffers should be applicable. It is understandable why small Member States have 3.24

[26] EBA, Final Peer Review Report, On the peer review of the Guidelines on the criteria to determine the conditions of application of Article 131(3) of Directive 2013/36/EU (CRD) in relation to the assessment of other systemically important institutions (O-SIIs), November 2017.

[27] EBA, Guidelines 2014, p. 10.

[28] EBA Review 2017, p. 29.

[29] EBA Guidelines 2014, p. 24.

[30] EBA Guidelines 2014, p. 6.

[31] EBA Review 2017, at p. 32.

designated more banks as a percentage as O-SIIs than in comparison to larger Member States with their more diversified banking systems. The dominant role played by foreign banks in such Member States means the additional criteria associated with contagion risk become critical indicators to determine whether capital buffers should be applied. Indeed as was shown in Chapter 1, smaller Member States tended to have as a proportion of total banks a large number of subsidiaries in comparison to branches as well. This is also particularly more acute if there is reliance on intragroup support and indeed there is a higher proportion of international claims through interbank financing rather than locally sourced financing.

3.25 The policy of classifying banks as significant subsidiaries and, more specifically, O-SIIs, in order to apply capital buffers, should then lead to a consistent application of other requirements set out in the CRR and the CRD IV, namely in terms of information sharing and contingency planning on a cross-border level. The listing of an O-SII should also be linked to a significant subsidiary in order to give it more specificity since it lacks a granular criterion to improve its visibility in the legal framework. It is arguable that the recognition should go further by requiring that the supervisory authority of the parent bank of an O-SII designated by the host authority leads to mandatory membership of the supervisory college and resolution college, rather than it being left to the discretion of the home authority. It should be able to then *ex ante* prepare for resolution or insolvency with a significant degree of confidence. In the Eurozone context, the issue is less important perhaps with centralized supervision leading to the importance of the home and host dilemma being reduced. However, one is still assuming the centralization of supervision is more inclusive when it comes to matters relating to supervisory colleges and resolution colleges. This may not be the case when the entity in question is part of a larger foreign bank that is reluctant to have smaller Member States included in the core part of the college. More importantly, the assumption that these banks are narrow and at the periphery, so they can be simply placed into insolvency due to their relative size in comparison to other parts of the group is misleading and gives rise to a number of misalignment of incentives and agency problems for the host Member State.

3.26 Table 7.2 (Appendix 7)[32] shows the proportion of total banks that are significant banks and the proportion that are classed as systemically important in the country for the purposes of capital buffers. It is clear that the proportion of banks classed as significant is relatively small in comparison to the total number of banks. The largest Member States appear to have the smallest proportion. However, small Member States with relatively small banking systems appear to have the largest proportion above; 10%–17% in the case of Slovenia. Whereas those banks classed by the national authorities as O-SIIs is significantly higher for small Member States or at least in line with the number classed as significant banks. In this respect small Member States consider at least 10% of their banks as systemically important in their market with a few notable exceptions such as Slovenia considering approximately 40% of its banks systemically important while it has only classed 18% as significant banks according to the ECB criteria. This is in contrast to the position in Germany, France, and Italy, where the proportion of total banks classed as significant is less than 5% and the proportion

[32] <https://eba.europa.eu/risk-analysis-and-data/other-systemically-important-institutions-o-siis-/2018>.

classed as O-SIIs is less than 2% which is rather unsurprising since all three Member States have the largest proportion of significant banks based on asset size. The reason for this position is because of the level of diversity within the banking system giving rise to less concentration and shows a more competitive banking market. Table 7.3[33] (Appendix 7), on the other hand, shows a similar picture for all EU Member States. In this table it shows those outside the Eurozone a similar position with Bulgaria, Croatia, and Romania classifying 29%–42% of their banks as systemically important, with notable exception of Poland with less than 2% represented as O-SIIs. The position in the Nordic countries is stark contrast to the position in Eastern Europe as a whole showing 1%–7% classed as O-SIIs to the total number of banks.

A sizeable proportion of the banks classed as O-SIIs are also foreign banks (EU or non-EU), which indicates how important foreign banks are in the domestic market and representing an important level of exposure to the respective home market. The EBA review (2017) found home and hosts did not place a priority on communication between the respective home and host authorities.[34] Both opting to apply the capital buffers according to their own findings according to their interpretation of the scoring system. However, the EBA does consider it important that some form of communication is made between the home and host and other respective national authorities for the purposes of supervisory information sharing either bilaterally or through the supervisory colleges. This is surprising when local subsidiaries or branches are designated as O-SIIs and so determining how best to manage their systemic importance as a result of the risk of contagion is all the more critical from the host country perspective. They are unlikely to command the same commitment by the host authorities as would local domestic banks, since they are not the Member State's 'national champions'.[35] The experience from the global financial crisis is one of Member States and their central banks standing behind their respective national champions, meaning that in the Eastern European markets and Nordic markets such political commitments may not be forthcoming albeit they have a significant market share. This appear to be an acute problem in small countries per se as highlighted by Dermine showing how the largest five banks have significant market share and those with a very diversified banking industry with a large mix of financial services provide the concentration ratios are relatively low.[36] **3.27**

The recent assessment by the EBA on the approach taken by Member States to determine O-SIIs strongly indicates the difference in interpretations of the criteria to form such decisions leading to the potential of designating too few or too many institutions as O-SIIs in comparison to their EU neighbours. The differences in practice show that some Member States take a significantly stricter approach to classifying institutions as O-SIIs. This could be partly minimized in the Eurozone, since banks considered systemically important at the domestic level at the Eurozone level as O-SIIs by the national designated authority could be reviewed on a case-by-case basis to assess whether they should come under the umbrella of **3.28**

33 <https://eba.europa.eu/risk-analysis-and-data/other-systemically-important-institutions-o-siis-/2018>.

34 EBA Review 2017, at pp. 24–6.

35 Nicolas Véron, Banking Nationalism and the European Crisis, 'The Transformation of Europe's Financial Landscape' at the 30th Anniversary Symposium of the European Private Equity and Venture Capital Association (EVCA) in Istanbul, Turkey, on 27 June 2013, <https://piie.com/publications/papers/veron20130627.pdf>.

36 J Dermine, 'Bank Mergers in Europe: The Public Policy Issues' (2000) Vol. 38, Journal of Common Market Studies 409–25 at pp. 419–20.

the SSM. The relatively large proportion of foreign banks in a number of Eurozone banking markets suggests that they are systemically important in the country but may not be systemically important to the group as a whole.

3.29 The national designated authorities appear to view banks differently from the competent authority. The emphasis on systemic risk in macroprudential supervision is not necessarily leading to an over-accommodation of banks. The move by the smaller Member States may well be in line with findings by Altunbas et al that find emerging market economies in comparison to advanced economies are more likely to be more sensitive to external factors associated with the economy and financial system.[37] Altunbas et al advocate the need to pool information as a result of different experiences to improve decision-making between advanced and emerging markets authorities in the field of macroprudential supervision to curb bank risks associated with credit growth or risk taking in times of low interest rate policies. Cerutti et al explain from their research the attempts by macroprudential supervisory authorities using such tools to minimize systemic risks emanating from the relationship between 'dominant banks and interconnections among banks'.[38] Therefore highlighting the importance of how macroprudential supervision tools assist to improve the resilience of banks.

3.30 In view of this it is important to show how the home and host consolidated supervision cooperate and coordinate to oversee the different elements of a bank group and the extent the two reciprocate with one another when it comes to sharing information.

Consolidated Supervision

3.31 The quality of supervision at the home and host state level is crucial to the success of consolidated supervision and indeed the stability and integrity of both the home and host states financial markets. A considerable level of trust is also needed to ensure home and host Member States cooperate with one another at critical times.[39] To achieve this, trust requires a significant degree of reciprocity in terms of information sharing.[40] In my view, supervisory cooperation and coordination between parent-home and home-host, where the subsidiary is located, is almost taken for granted and could lead to a number of unintended consequences.[41] Supervisory cooperation is almost assumed for subsidiaries whereas for branches it is explicitly referred to at junctures of supervisory cooperation and coordination. This is particularly due to the problems associated with branches during the global financial crisis. More importantly, it highlights a gap in the current arrangements which show the importance of formulating a framework for significant subsidiaries from a wider supervisory perspective.

[37] Y Altunbas, M Binici, and L Gambacorta, Macroprudential Policy and Bank Risk, 81, Journal of International Money and Finance (2018) 203–20; see also E Cerutti, S Claessens, and L Laeven, 'The use and effectiveness of macroprudential policies: New evidence', 28, Journal of Financial Stability (2017) 203–24.

[38] Ibid., Cerutti et al, p. 204.

[39] Directive 2013/36/EU of the European Parliament and of the Council of 26 June 2013 on access to the activity of credit institutions and the prudential supervision of credit institutions and investment firms, amending Directive 2002/87/EC and repealing Directives 2006/48/EC and 2006/49/EC; Regulation (EU) No. 575/2013 of the European Parliament and of the Council of 26 June 2013 on prudential requirements for credit institutions and investment firms and amending Regulation (EU) No. 648/2012; CRD IV Art. 15 and Art. 49.

[40] CRD IV Art. 50; see also Art. 114

[41] CRD IV Arts 51–52.

The approach to undertake supervision of groups and their domestic and cross-border activities is undertaken by the home state through consolidated supervision.[42] The requirements for consolidated supervision are set out in the CRD IV.[43] The purpose of consolidated supervision is to ensure activities undertaken by way of subsidiaries and branches do not undermine the stability of the parent entity or the group as a whole.[44] In view of this, a banking group's desire to expand its activities into new markets geographically or new lines of business could be considered sufficient threats to warrant refusal of authorization and could even be seen as a move to changing the consolidated supervisor in view of the distribution of its business. A particular challenge for supervisors has been to understand bank and non-bank risks that can materialize. Mindful of this, a significant attention in consolidated supervision has been devoted to solvency associated with adequate levels of capital and liquidity for the purposes of the group as a whole. In this respect, the CRR provides a number of specific requirements associated with intragroup exposures, capital, and liquidity that need to be calculated on a consolidated level. The purpose of these requirements and information sharing between home and host is to try and ensure the risks from the host can be captured and mitigated before they become material risks to the group and group entities. The counter balance to this is the authority of the host to be able to intervene if risks at the group parent level are a concern and to avoid putting at risk entities for which it is responsible. The 2017 EBA Report on the functioning of supervisory colleges found improvements on joint decisions about capital requirements but found the number of final decisions about liquidity falling short of the EBA expectations in terms of specificity when it came to the needs of subsidiaries.[45] **3.32**

In the EU framework the definition of home Member State and host Member State is defined in accordance with an authorized entity of the home state with a branch that provides services in the host state.[46] This definition of home and host Member State is very specific and the reforms introduced to address home bias address the problem associated with the risks of a branch and its solvency and the ability of the host state to take precautionary measures to minimise risks to its financial stability.[47] The CRD IV expects home and host states to cooperate with one another for the purposes of determining financial soundness and solvency of a credit institution and at the group consolidated level.[48] In addition to this, home and host states are expected to cooperate to exchange information and data for the purpose of producing recovery plans and resolution plans.[49] **3.33**

In the context of a parent having control of a subsidiary and exercising a dominant influence the close links requirement provides some basis to expect cooperation and coordination.[50] **3.34**

42 CRR Art. 4(41).

43 CRD IV Arts 111–115.

44 CRD IV para. 47.

45 EBA Report 2017 p.31; see also p. 32: 'Host authorities and the EBA raised their objections to this approach to the consolidating supervisor in various colleges in order to ensure reciprocity on the timing of sharing proposed quantitative and qualitative measures between college members. All colleges that followed this approach have been assigned an 'improvement needed' score for the process aspect of the joint decision process, as can be seen in Figure 11.'

46 CRR Art. 4(1), (43), and (44) respectively.

47 CRD IV Arts 53, 54, 55, and 57 regarding information sharing between the constituents of the official safety net.

48 CRD IV Recital 25, 26, 34, Art. 50(1), Art. 99(2)(a), Art. 117(1).

49 CRD IV Art. 50(3)–(4); Art. 86(11).

50 CRR Art. 4(38).

The decision to include subsidiaries in consolidated supervision is prima facie applied to all financial, investment and/or credit institutions in the form of subsidiaries.[51] The competent authority could apply full or partial consolidated supervision on a case-by-case basis depending on the proportion the holding or the parent entity has in a subsidiary. The competent authority could also exclude a subsidiary from consolidated supervision if its assets and off-balance sheet items amount to €10 million, or 1% of the total amount of assets and off-balance sheet items of the parent.[52] In practice, this is highly unlikely.

3.35 The competent authority of the parent entity is required to put in place organizational structure to identify subsidiaries that are covered by the CRR. This is for the transfer of data for the purposes of consolidation and, therefore, the competent authority of the parent entity is expected to receive the data to comply with consolidation requirements.[53] In practice, countries have complied with the requests for data but, in return, receive information in a more generalized format so offering limited assistance to oversee the risks to a subsidiary. In other cases, the competent authority can decide to exclude a subsidiary from consolidated supervision if it is incorporated in a third country where impediments for information sharing exist or where the subsidiary is of negligible interest to actually monitor its activities from a consolidated basis.[54]

3.36 The CRR expects competent authorities to arrive at joint decisions on prudential requirements.[55] This illustrates the importance placed on the consolidated supervisor in forming decisions associated with prudential requirements, such as intragroup treatment and the distribution of operational risk capital across the group entities, Advance Measurement Approach, or Internal Risk Based Approach, and with liquidity requirements that could apply either on a consolidated, sub-consolidated, or individual basis. The joint decisions are expected to be reached within six months and, if they fail to reach a joint decision, then the consolidated supervisor can decide and provide the other competent authorities its reasons for the decision. The competent authority could decide itself and is then expected to notify the consolidated supervisor of its decision. The competent authorities or the consolidated supervisor can refer the matter to the EBA for mediation within a month.[56] In the case of joint decisions, for example relating to liquidity requirements, the CRR specifically refers to the EBA being able to undertake non-binding mediation if a decision has not been reached within six months.[57] If after mediation a joint decision is not reach on liquidity requirements, then the competent authorities are expected to take a proportionate decision with the interests of the parent entity taken into consideration. The consolidated supervisor's role in taking the lead on these matters and initiating the joint decision. Notwithstanding this position, the individual competent authority could take its own decision or reach a compromise. However, the important point here is the fact that the competent authority is essentially reaching its own decision which could be at odds with the consolidated supervisor.

[51] CRD IV para 47.
[52] CRR Art. 19(1)(a and (b).
[53] CRR Art.11(1).
[54] CRR Art. 19 (2)(a)–(c).
[55] CRR Art. 20 (1)(a)–(b).
[56] CRD IV Art. 113.
[57] CRR Art. 21.

Information Sharing between Home and Host States

The importance of information sharing to improve supervisory decisions is crucial to ensure cross-border financial stability and market integrity. Information sharing needs to be at two levels; firstly, during the supervisory process, governing the banks as going concerns, and secondly, during periods of distress.[58] These Regulations supplement the requirements set out in the CRD IV.[59] The mandate of the CRD IV is wide with measures to improve corporate governance, remuneration practices, enforcement sanctions, and supervisory practices between home and host Member States. On the whole, they form one of three parts of the EBA Single Rulebook.[60] This section will review the requirements set out in the supplementary Regulations to ascertain whether they provide the appropriate level of incentives and reciprocity to fulfil the home and host Member States' interests, and those of third countries. It was evident during the financial crisis that, in many instances, host states were in the dark about the state of banks that operated within their jurisdiction, particularly in the form of a branch. **3.37**

The requirements, as set out in CRD IV and CRR, expect the exchange of a wide range of information between Member States. This includes information relating to capital, liquidity, solvency, large exposures, accounting procedures, internal controls, evidence of non-compliance and sanctions, leverage, and crisis preparedness. A particular challenge in many of the provisions is whether the home and host states interpret material 'risks', 'deficiencies', or 'complexity' in a similar way to ensure different interpretations do not lead to excessive over- or under-accommodation of problems and so misalign the incentives of Member States cooperating and coordinating their decisions in a timely fashion. **3.38**

The EU Regulation 524/2014 sets out the requirements both home and host states are expected to share with one another so that both can take timely precautionary measures on a consolidated or institutional or branch level.[61] The EU Regulation 620/2014 provides further requirements on sharing information between the home and host state when it comes to branches. It expects the home and host Member States to share information relating to stress scenarios and supervisory information from supervisory inspections carried out at the branch in a timely manner and within set formats.[62] The Regulation 524/2014 refers to the importance of information as a two-way process. It highlights how the home state dominance of the EU approach to allocate responsibilities between home and host cannot and should not give rise to a priority of information going disproportionately in one way, **3.39**

[58] Commission Delegated Regulation (EU) No. 524/2014 of 12 March 2014 supplementing Directive 2013/36/EU of the European Parliament and of the Council with regard to regulatory technical standards specifying the information that competent authorities of home and host Member States supply to one another; Commission Implementing Regulation (EU) No. 620/2014 of June 2014 laying down implementing technical standards with regard to information exchange between competent authorities of home and host Member States, according to Directive 2013/36/EU of the European Parliament and of the Council.

[59] Directive 2013/36/EU of the European Parliament and of the Council of 26 June 2013 on access to the activity of credit institutions and the prudential supervision of credit institutions and investment firms, amending Directive 2002/87/EC and repealing Directive 2006/48/EC and 2006/49/EC, and in particular Article 50(6) thereof.

[60] Interactive Single Rulebook: <https://www.eba.europa.eu/regulation-and-policy/single-rulebook/interactive-single-rulebook>.

[61] Delegated Regulation No. 524/2014, Chapter II.

[62] Regulation No. 620/2014, Art. 4.

namely to the home supervisor, considering the equal risks faced by the host regulator if a cross-border failure were to occur. The information exchanged and/or requested also needs to be appropriate in light of the size and complexity of the different risks. The onus is, however, on the home state in many places to ensure they share information with the host state to improve their decision-making.

3.40 The risk of the home and host state forbearing on the sharing of information will ultimately mean that, during periods of crisis or loss of confidence, they are likely in resolution to act in their own interests rather than the collective interests of the group as a whole. But not just then, since the requirements do not necessarily indicate the timeliness of sharing of information to inform decisions. It is without a doubt, however, that the home state, as the consolidated supervisor, and the group resolution authority need to be sharing information. It is important to emphasize that the requirements apply equally to all Member States as home and host states and do not depend on whether the Member State is a participating or non-participating Member State within the SSM. However, the requirements set out in the Regulations do not really go far enough and, therefore, a significant amount of responsibility is conferred on the colleges to decide when and what type of information should be shared as well as the form it takes. Moreover, the level of cooperation and coordination is primarily led by the consolidated supervisor for supervisory colleges and the group level resolution authority for the resolution colleges. For instance, the need for the home state to inform the host state about the likely systemic risk posed by a G-SII and an O-SII, and the need for the home and host state to share information about crisis preparedness—preparations for emergency situations such as contact details and communication plans.[63] The areas of crisis preparedness and management are much wider and complex than simply the exchange of contact details.

The Supervisory Colleges

3.41 A central plank to improve cooperation and supervision of cross-border banks is the introduction of supervisory colleges. The primary aim of the reforms is to improve supervisory coordination and cooperation between home and host states within the European Union by reducing home bias when it comes to credit institutions' branches. The attempts to do this have been aimed at improving some of the powers of host states, such as information requests, to take supervisory decisions in circumstances where the branch is significant.[64] The host state can request the home state to undertake supervisory decisions if the host state is of the view the branch is not complying. The host state can take precautionary measures as well. In circumstances where the host state is of the view the branch is not complying or indeed the home state is not taking matters seriously, then it can report the matter to the EBA to mediate between the home and host state. It should be noted that implicit in these new host state powers is the right of the home state to review whether the decisions are proportionate and the right to utilize EBA mediation if decisions are not resolved.

[63] Delegated Regulation No. 524 / 2014 Art. 14.
[64] CRD IV Arts 40–46. To determine significance see Art. 51, and for prudential matters see Arts 49–50.

The CRD IV requirements to set up supervisory colleges are further fleshed out in Regulation 2016/98[65] and Regulation 2016/99.[66] These two Regulations set out the frameworks for the exchange of supervisory information and measures for dealing with a cross-border crisis, contingency planning, and emergency scenarios. The first, Regulation 2016/98, provides for a broad set of requirements and expectations of the consolidated supervisor and the other members of the colleges from both Member States and third countries. The first part of the Regulation requires the consolidated supervisor to take the lead in providing information about the group in a mapping exercise of the group entities, in terms of authorized institutions and branches in Member States and third countries and the financial sector they undertake business in. A key component of this exercise is to appreciate the importance of the institution from the perspective of the Member State and from the perspective of the group. This is based on the total assets of the institution in question, within the Member State, being in excess of 1% of the group's total assets on a consolidated basis. While the size of the total assets and liabilities may not exceed 1% of the consolidated balance sheet, the size of foreign owned assets in the respective jurisdictions ranges from approximately 30–95% in the majority of these countries. These assets are held by a large proportion of foreign subsidiaries and, therefore, give rise to the need for coherent cross-border coordination and cooperation. 3.42

The decision of who can join the supervisory college is the responsibility of the consolidated supervisor.[67] The membership of supervisory colleges is divided into members and observers.[68] The former group plays a more significant role within the supervisory colleges than the observers. The members of the college are required to include the competent authorities that supervise institutions and significant branches in host Member States. The consolidated supervisor will need to invite other parts of the official safety net at the regional level, the EBA, and Member States' central banks if they do not have supervisory responsibilities. It is within the discretion of the consolidated supervisor whether or not competent authorities where non-significant branches are located also join as observers.[69] The consolidated supervisor with the members of the supervisory college may also invite supervisory authorities of third countries to join the supervisory college as observers.[70] Moreover, the consolidated supervisor has the discretion to determine the terms and conditions of observers so, in some supervisory colleges, observers may be conferred more access to information and involvement in decision-making than observers in other supervisory colleges. 3.43

The tasks of the supervisory college to formulate the plans to set out the arrangements for cooperation and coordination within the college, at the going concern and crisis levels, highlight how important it is to be a part of the college whether as a member or observer.[71] The arrangements will include the timeliness and frequency of exchange of information, 3.44

[65] Commission Delegated Regulation (EU) 2016/98 supplementing Directive 2013/36/EU of the European Parliament and the Council with regard to regulatory technical standards for specifying the general condition for the functioning of colleges of supervisors.

[66] Commission Implementing Regulation (EU) 2016/99 of 16 October 2015 laying down implementing technical standards with regard to determining the operational functioning of the colleges of supervisors according to Directive 2013/36/EU of the European Parliament and of the Council.

[67] Regulation 2016/98, Art. 3 and Regulation 2016/99 Art. 3.

[68] Ibid. See also Regulation 2016/99 Art. 3(1)(b).

[69] Regulation 2016/99 Art. 3(1)(b).

[70] Regulation 2016/98, Art. 3(3).

[71] Regulation 2016/98 Art. 5.

planning cross-border examinations and supervision, contingency planning, early warning signs, and other potential risks and vulnerabilities. The type of information expected to be included in the arrangements is absolutely crucial for competent authorities to manage and respond effectively to supervision and crisis management at the institutional and market level. However, who has access to this information and decision-making means the detailed framework still risks significant misalignment of incentives for cross-border supervision and crisis management. The consolidated supervisor primarily decides the agenda for the meetings as well as who can attend those meetings and what information is shared and with whom, including competent authorities of Member States where there are institutions or significant branches. It is not mandatory for the consolidated supervisor to share information with all members of the supervisory college all of the time. On one level, this may be considered impractical due to the number of members. However, the risk of not sharing with all members means the consolidated supervisor acts as the judge over who then should receive it, since it will have to determine whether the members for instance 'are affected or likely to be affected', in which case, it is likely to exchange information both on a going concern level and in times of emergency situations.

3.45 The arrangements provide for clear incentives for members of the college to work closely together,[72] but this is not necessarily the case when it comes to those categorized as observers. In the case of the latter group, they are more than likely only going to receive general pieces of information whereas the members of the colleges will receive more granular information to inform their decision-making. For example, the consolidated supervisor and the members of the supervisory college are required to formulate joint decisions about the risks within a group both at financial and non-financial prudential levels gathered through information sharing, stress-testing, and on-site inspections. In addition to this, they are required to produce a 'college framework for emergency situations',[73] setting out procedures about the exchange of information to enable members to support the crisis management efforts. The observers are expected, in practice, to provide information for these specific purposes, but they are then not given access to the reports or made privy to the decisions reached on the basis of the information. In practice, the intensity of supervision and scrutiny of the viability of the group and its respective institutions, is likely to be heightened to a point where the consolidated supervisor at the group level will decide on whether to act on its early intervention powers, if it is found an institution or the group is failing or likely to fail.

3.46 However, this crucial information and data are not expected to be shared with observers of the supervisory college. Moreover, there will be a group of Member States and third countries that simply do not have access to the kind of information necessary to assist their supervisory decision-making either. Within both categories, observers and those excluded from the supervisory college, a relatively large pool of states appear likely to act in their self-interest rather than the collective interests articulated in the reforms. Indeed, there appears to be relatively little incentives for this category of states to cooperate when they are not going to receive quality supervisory information to inform their decision from the competent authorities that are overseeing large parts of the group deemed significant for the

[72] Regulation 2016/98 Rec. 7.
[73] Regulation 2016/98 Art. 17.

respective reasons. However, they are expected to provide supervisory data to improve the consolidated supervisor's understanding of the strengths and risks within the group.

In cases where such states are participating in the supervisory college, the level of interaction is rather mixed, as the EBA has found in its 2015 Action Plan.[74] Those that have joined supervisory colleges as observers have not been given specific terms of reference or conditions. More concerning is that the respective states are denied information that would assist their supervisory decision-making and crisis preparedness and contingency planning. The very matters the supervisory colleges have been set up for were to fulfil the purposes of the CRD IV. In relation to those matters, while the states are cooperating by sharing sensitive information, both of a quantitative and qualitative level, it is not reciprocated. The states are in the dark in terms of specific decisions taken on the basis of the information provided, since only general information will be exchanged. This type of information is not going to be useful for proper planning purposes. For example, the required level of cooperation and coordination at the recovery and resolution planning level was essentially non-existent, which is, however, crucial to assist a whole range of decisions, as noted above. The frequency of meetings and invites to the meetings can also vary but, in the case of states with observer status, the frequency is more likely to be once a year. A starting point is likely to be the initiation of the supervisory assessments but this is essentially one of requesting information and data rather than a dialogue of sharing. **3.47**

The EBA 2017 report highlights significant improvement has been made in terms of supervisory colleges and the level of engagement between members with them meeting at least once and some of the colleges meeting twice or three times within the year. The report highlights an increase in willingness of information sharing between home and host members which feeds in to the level of engagement and interaction within the college. However, in view of the home consolidated supervisor preparing the agenda it was evident that host members needed more time to prepare to improve their contribution to the discussion.[75] The view of there being an inner core college and a periphery college is evident with information said to be flowing better between the two albeit what that information is and how useful it is to inform decisions is open to question; but suffice to say the two parts are linking up which should improve decision-making. Nevertheless, there is evidence to suggest the form of information differed between members of the colleges.[76] The level of information shared to complete better recovery plans has not been consistent in them of sharing information to inform members about recovery options: **3.48**

> While in 2014, only half of the closely monitored colleges were assigned a 'good' score, this percentage in 2015 was 74% and in 2016 was 90%. This trend clearly shows the significant accomplishment of colleges and that the EBA's practice of setting minimum expectations

[74] EBA, Report On The Functioning of Supervisory Colleges In 2015 2016 EBA Colleges Action Plan 1 March 2016, <http://www.eba.europa.eu/documents/10180/1390624/Report+on+the+functioning+of+supervisory+colleges+in+2015.pdf/eafde612-f85d-4ec4-baaf-14db0b03fccd>.
Accomplishment of the EBA Colleges Action Plan for 2014 and establishment of the EBA Colleges Action Plan for 2015: Assessment of the Colleges Action Plan for 2014 Promoting and monitoring colleges in 2014 EBA Colleges Action Plan for 2015, <http://www.eba.europa.eu/documents/10180/1042260/Accomplishment+of+2014+EBA+Colleges+Action+Plan+and+2015+EBA+Colleges+Action+Plan.pdf>.

[75] p. 17.

[76] p. 17.

encouraged more intensive cooperation among banking supervisors and contributed to better functioning supervisory colleges throughout the EU.

3.49 The 2017 Report[77] highlights the work of supervisory colleges on the Written Cooperation and Coordination Arrangement (WCCA) protocol that facilitates the assessment of how the consolidated supervisor and the members and observers of the college work together.[78] Some of the key findings emphasize the importance of home and host cooperating to better understanding 'use of waivers for prudential and liquidity requirements, the designation of the entities as other systematically important institutions and criteria to assess importance for the group or for the local market.'[79] The EBA Report 2017, also highlights how within the EEA more focus is being placed on sharing information between home and host but this does not extend to non-EEA entities when it came to the same categories of information. The willingness to complete the WCCA is not forthcoming as it has been in the past by the consolidated supervisor and the members.[80] The emphasis on the WCCA is suggested needs to be extended to resolution and how supervision feeds in to resolution decision-making.

3.50 The supervisory frameworks after the European financial crisis have, in terms of form, come a considerable way. A larger proportion of Member States are likely to be in a position to cooperate and coordinate better with the respective home and host states.[81] The agency problem remains for those outside of the traditional group of systemic Member States in terms of how much information is shared with them. The misalignment of these incentives will likely lead to a possible breakdown of the supervisory college very quickly if the interests of resolving the group do not align with the interests of members presiding over important subsidiaries and, thus, still facing a position of not acting in the collective interests but in the national interests. The supervisory assessment process does not address or try to mitigate the misalignment of incentives of the home and host state. This is important as it prevents, firstly, the host states from addressing supervisory risks as a going concern and, secondly, the consolidated supervisor from recognizing the fact that, in practice, some Member States are likely to act in their own interests. In many ways, factoring this reality into the recovery and resolution stage is important because it provides a more pragmatic approach to resolution and enables the host states to work out for themselves how best to resolve the subsidiary in their jurisdiction. Currently, the uncertainty arising from the misalignment of the reciprocal powers prevents them to undertake this task in a timely manner. It opens up the opportunity for possible mediation to form joint decisions between the competent authority acting as the consolidated supervisor and, therefore, it is necessary for home-host states to put their case forward as to why it is important.

[77] EBA Report: On the functioning of supervisory colleges in 2016, 22 March 2017, <https://www.eba.europa.eu/documents/10180/1720738/EBA+Report+on+the+functioning+of+supervisory+colleges+in+2016.pdf/283f550a-1a1d-4b7a-abce-66e8c9b445fb>.

[78] p. 8: Template on written cooperation and coordination arrangements College, CP/2014/12 Annex II, 3 July 2014, <http://www.eba.europa.eu/documents/10180/746034/EBA-CP-2014-12+Annex+II+%28Template+on+written+coordination+and+cooperation+arrangements%29.pdf>.

[79] p. 14.

[80] p. 44.

[81] EBA Report: On the functioning of supervisory colleges in 2016, 22 March 2017, <https://www.eba.europa.eu/documents/10180/1720738/EBA+Report+on+the+functioning+of+supervisory+colleges+in+2016.pdf/283f550a-1a1d-4b7a-abce-66e8c9b445fb>.

The Role of Recovery Planning

The BRRD first of all provides the basis for the competent authority to understand better the size and complexity of the institutions and groups it is responsible for overseeing on a solo or consolidated supervisory level.[82] The Recovery plan forms an important part of the process to minimize the asymmetry of information between the supervisor and the bank.[83] This forms the basis of the requirements to request certain institutions or groups to prepare recovery and resolution plans to enable the competent and resolution authorities to work out *ex ante* the areas of risk in terms of their critical functions[84] and core business lines[85] and possible resolution tools likely to be used to deal with banks in distress. The directive does not elaborate on what a critical function or business line is, but leaves it to the discretion of the competent authority, and possibly the resolution authority, to work this out with the institution and group. The directive is assisted by the technical advice offered by the EBA in this respect to improve the consistency between Member States in their application of the requirements set out in the Single Rulebook.[86] The directive refers to 'critical functions' in the context of a whole manner of areas and is interlinked with the recovery and resolution planning process and assessment of the utility of resolution tools. The term critical functions is given a wide interpretation covering business activities, internal and external services, and operations in the form of back office or front office support either to the firm itself or to a third party, business units, and legal entities. The impact of not providing a critical function needs to be assessed as part of the recovery and resolution, which needs to include the possible impact of the disruption or loss of the critical function to itself and third parties. Moreover, the institution or group will need to assess the substitutability of the critical function in the impact assessment. **3.51**

The competent authority and the resolution authority have the discretion to decide whether an institution or group is required to prepare a recovery and resolution plan.[87] Those institutions considered to have a relatively complex business model and risk profile that incorporates a significant level of interconnection with the wider financial system will be required to produce a recovery plan which would form the basis of the resolution plan. Notwithstanding the discretion of the competent authorities to request such plans, it is not a barrier to taking the necessary action to prevent resolution tools being exercised to safeguard an institution's critical financial functions. The requirement to produce a recovery plan applies to both individual institutions and groups. The primary aim of the recovery **3.52**

[82] Art. 4(1).

[83] E Avgouleas, C Goodhart, and D Schoenmaker, 'Bank Resolution Plans as a Catalyst for Global Financial Reform', Vol. 9 Issue 2, Journal of Financial Stability (2013) pp. 210–18, at p. 211. See also D Singh, 'Recovery and Resolution Planning: Reconfiguring Financial Regulation and Supervision' in Jens-Hinrich Binder and Dalvinder Singh (eds), *Bank Resolution: The European Regime* (2016) (Oxford: Oxford University Press) pp. 1–24.

[84] Art. 2(1) (35): '"[C]ritical functions" means activities, services or operations the discontinuance of which is likely in one or more Member States, to lead to the disruption of services that are essential to the real economy or to disrupt financial stability due to the size, market share, external and internal interconnectedness, complexity or cross-border activities of an institution or group, with particular regard to the substitutability of those activities, services or operations.'

[85] Art. 2(1) (36): '"[C]ore business lines" means business lines and associated services which represent material sources of revenue, profit or franchise value for an institution or for a group of which an institution forms part.'

[86] Technical advice on the delegated acts on critical functions and core business lines, EBA/ Op/2015/ 05, March 2015.

[87] BRRD, Art. 4(1).

plan is for the institution to explain how it will 'restore its financial position following a significant deterioration of its financial situation'.[88] The plan cannot assume in the risk assessment of the business activities and financing arrangements that the authorities will provide extraordinary public financial support.[89] However, what is considered extraordinary during stable times may form part of ordinary financial support offered by a ministry of finance or central bank. This is captured by the need to explain how the institution would access central bank facilities in circumstances where it can provide the appropriate assets as collateral in the normal course of its daily business.

3.53 The key features of recovery planning operate at a high level of the firm, with responsibility for completing and approving it resting at the board level.[90] The management body will need to set out in a systemic manner the steps and actions the institution will take within the timeframe it sets itself to fulfil its options. The plans require the institution to explain how in various scenarios it will attempt to remedy problems it faces either at the international, national, sector, or institutional level. The information that needs to be included in the recovery plan is set out in the Annex to the BRRD, Section A. The list is quite large and significantly it includes, inter alia: the capital and liquidity actions it would need to take; impediments to being able to implement the planned actions; identifying critical functions; the marketability of core business areas; identifying areas of risk and leverage within the business; and arrangements to restructure liabilities and business lines. The responsibility of reviewing the recovery plan falls on the competent authority in accordance with the aims of the directive and technical standards and guidance provided by the EBA.[91] The competent authority is required to assess the plan according to whether it is 'reasonably likely to maintain or restore the viability and financial position of the institution or of the group, taking into account the preparatory measures that the institution has taken or has planned to take',[92] in accordance with the requirements set out in the Annex to the BRRD. The competent authority can require the institution to resubmit the plan if it is of the view that there is a 'material deficiency' or 'material impediment' that would prevent the institution from implementing the options that it sets out to be utilized in a given scenario.[93]

3.54 The requirement for recovery plans is more likely to apply to those institutions part of a group.[94] In this respect, the group-parent undertaking is required to produce a plan for the whole group capturing the issues identified above, and also intra-group support arrangements. The management body of the group entity is required to assume responsibility for drawing the plan. The group recovery plan will need to include subsidiaries and significant branches in Member States.[95] In some cases the group entity will likely include subsidiaries that are required to produce a recovery plan in their own right if the home state so decides.[96] In circumstances where Member States cannot agree on the group plan and

88 Art. 5(1).
89 Art. 5(3).
90 Art. 5(9).
91 EBA Guidelines on the minimum list of qualitative and quantitative recovery plan indicators, EBA- GL- 2015- 02, July 2015, <http:// www.eba.europa.eu/ documents/ 10180/ 1147256/ EBA- GL- 2015-02_ EN+Guidelines+on+recovery+plan+indicators.pdf/ 485181d4- f8f1- 4604- 9a78- 17a12164e793>.
92 BRRD, Art. 6(2)(a).
93 BRRD, Art. 6(5) see also Recital 24 and the wide implications of the discretion of the competent authority.
94 BRRD, Art. 7.
95 BRRD, Art. 7(1)–(3).
96 BRRD, Art. 7(2).

its more important constituent parts then the EBA is required to intervene and decide or, alternatively, the decision of the consolidated supervisor will be given precedence.[97] The group entity will need to coordinate in those circumstances so that there are minimal impediments. Moreover, the group entity would also, on a practical level, ensure that its group recovery plan has appropriate synergies with other recovery and resolution plans in other third countries. As with the individual recovery plans, the group recovery plans are also assessed to ensure that obstacles to resolution are minimized.[98] In many respects the likely cross-border nature of group activities will mean that more effort is needed to co-ordinate with other competent and resolution authorities. In this respect the supervisory college and resolution college will take an important role to assist the process.[99] The EBA Guidelines 2015 elaborate on the recovery plan indicators; explaining how it is important that the recovery plans assess areas such as capital, liquidity, asset quality, market- based in-formation, macroeconomic information, and profit levels. It is evident that the EBA expects institutions and groups to comply with these minimum indicators but it important to note that competent authorities can request additional indicators and further detail to be provided relative to the complexity of the business and risks associated with the institution or group.[100] A particular challenge is likely to be coordinating the different indicators across the group and its sub groups in other third countries.

In addition to drawing up the group-wide recovery plan, as mentioned above, the group-parent undertaking is also responsible for intra-group financial support arrangements where applicable.[101] The agreement may provide for financial support to one or more subsidiaries in any combination of entities within the group, such as from the parent to subsidiaries or vice versa, or between subsidiaries. The support may include, inter alia, loans, guarantees, or assets to be used as collateral, in different transactions including as between the beneficiary and a third party. For any transaction made in pursuance to it, the group financial support agreement will need to specify the calculation principles of the relevant consideration. The purpose of intra-group financial support is to ensure the financial stability of the group as a whole, mindful also of the solvency and liquidity of the group undertaking providing the support.[102] This is intended to be voluntary and subject to appropriate safeguards, for instance, cross-guarantees protecting the participating institutions.[103] In addition, Member States are required to remove impediments to the application of the agreement in national laws. Several conditions must be met in order to provide group financial support. Notably, there needs to be 'reasonable prospect' that the support will significantly redress the financial difficulties of the group entity; the support must have the objective of 'preserving or restoring the financial stability of the group as a whole or any of **3.55**

97 BRRD, Art. 7(3)–(4).

98 BRRD, Art. 9.

99 BRRD, Art. 18(1); recital 96: 'Resolution colleges should be established around the core of the existing supervisory colleges through the inclusion of resolution authorities and the involvement of competent ministries, central banks, EBA and, where appropriate, authorities responsible for the deposit guarantee schemes. In the event of a crisis, the resolution college should provide a forum for the exchange of information and the coordination of resolution actions.' For further details about the role of Resolution Colleges see, Art. 88.

100 EBA, on the minimum list of qualitative and quantitative recovery plan indicators, EBA- GL- 2015- 02, July 2015.

101 BRRD, Art. 7(5).

102 BRRD Recital 38.

103 BRRD Recital 38.

the entities of the group' and be 'in the interests of the group entity providing the support'; there must also be reasonable prospect that the consideration for the support will be paid and that, for instance, the loan will be reimbursed (if a loan was made). Further, the support must not jeopardize the liquidity or solvency of the group entity providing it or its resolvability, and it must not create a threat to financial stability, particularly in the group entity's Member State. The EBA has developed technical standards in relation to some of the conditions, submitted to the European Commission in July 2015.

3.56 The recent review by the EBA of recovery plans provides interesting insights about bank behaviour in order to initiate recovery options at the group level in times of firm or market distress.[104] In respects the most popular recovery options for the 123 banking group's recovery plans reviewed for the report may not be beneficial to the small host. It is rather unsurprising that the report highlights the amount of work still needed for recovery plans to provide some kind of credible assurance the firms of identified options in distress that are feasible in the relative time and circumstances of a potential idiosyncratic or systemwide crisis. With a considerable level of assumption of past options will be equally credible in future crises.

3.57 The home and host national competent authority of the parent and subsidiary respectively are particularly vulnerable to the decisions made at the group level and so calling in to question whether they should be approved. The home-host dilemma can only be addressed if both are able to properly prepare for an adverse event at the sole institution or market level. Since the four most popular recovery options put forward: (a) disposal of subsidiaries; (b) sale of assets/loan portfolios; and (c) liquidity improvement measures; and (d) capital raising expose the small host to vulnerabilities outside of its control that may not be possible to safeguard via ringfencing.[105] In respect of capital or liquidity: in small Member States, the subsidiary is likely to be dependent on the home capital markets of its parent for the purposes of capital raising due to a lack of capital markets to raise finance. Moreover, the assumption of ease with which capital can be raised is entirely predicated on investor confidence at the time which may not be high and evidence of the past would suggest investors in the future maybe more hesitant since the potential losses from initial due diligence and reassurances may not be reliable.[106] The option of sale of subsidiary is a very likely recovery option for a business line in a small host since it is not material to the parent in terms of size of profits but compact enough for ease of sale to a competitor. This could give rise to further concentration risks that a small host is unlikely to be pleased about. The option of local interest in the subsidiary may not be forthcoming since the comparable competitor is another EU financial or banking institution. A competitor could view this as a good opportunity to consolidate further in the small host market. The materiality of the sale of loans or assets in a small host Member State may not necessarily raise the appropriate amounts to stabilize the parent entity so the material host subsidiary may avoid such directions from the parent. Nevertheless, if it were requested to do so it could have destabilizing effects in the market in view of the concentration of assets in foreign ownership, as explained above.

[104] EBA, Recovery Planning Comparative Report On Recovery Options, 1 March 2017, <http://www.eba.europa.eu/documents/10180/1720738/EBA+Comparative+report+on+recovery+options+-+March+2017.pdf>.

[105] EBA Comparative Report, 2017 at p. 11.

[106] The experience of banks is explored in Chapter 7.

The EBA also found group recovery plans are produced from the 'parent perspective' and a significant level of confidence is expressed that capital and liquidity from the parent would be forthcoming for a subsidiary.[107] The outcome is not surprising in view of how supervision is essentially led from the consolidated group perspective. . The emphasis is evident, for example, 'the extent to which the plan can stabilize the group as a whole and any institution of the group';[108] 'the availability of recovery options at the group level to restore where necessary the financial position of a subsidiary, without disturbing the group's financial soundness.'[109] This could lead to a position where the individual subsidiary entities are minimally capitalized or hold only sufficient liquidity but not in a position to be overly capitalized or hold higher liquid funds as they are likely to be up streamed to ensure the parent-group retains the higher levels of capital and liquidity. Moreover, the 2017 Report on Supervisory colleges highlights a lack of joint decisions about individual entity level recovery plans.[110] From supervisory college perspective the finding about recovery plans also indicate an emphasis on the home and a lack of emphasis on some subsidiaries which lends to the need to complete individual plans. The EBA concludes: 'While the lack of such information in and of itself should be seen more as a deficiency of the group plan than as a justification to request individual plans, there have been instances where competent authorities have requested individual subsidiary plans owing to a lack of information or adequate coverage in the group plan.'[111] 3.58

Stress-Testing—The Home and Host Challenges

The use of stress-testing of individual institutions minimizes the asymmetry of information between institution and supervisors. Stress-testing on the one hand improves bank supervisors' understanding of the banks business model and the associated risks, but also, since the findings are disclosed to the market, it enables the market to better price its risk in terms of cost of finance. Transparency of such findings also improves the markets sensitivity to what may be traditionally considered adverse news that could undermine confidence in the institution within the market. In part disclosure of stress-testing findings chips away at the notion of banks being special and so need to be supervised in a rather conservative way that avoids disclosing their vulnerability in view of fractional reserve banking and the recognition that capital only provides a limited buffer to adverse risks materializing. The importance of liquidity and the level of liquidity was found to be equally important if not the most underappreciated aspect of supervision and so the most important lesson of the GFC. The other matter that gathered considerable attention was leverage and the level of leverage amongst many banks. Nonetheless, the credibility of stress-testing is akin to the level of confidence the official safety net secured from the market about the capital position of banks during the GFC which was little and so expected the official safety net to go further in their efforts to support their banks. In many ways, the market will always expect more but stress-testing minimizes the ability of the 3.59

107 EBA Report 2017 Supervisory Colleges, p. 16.
108 Regulation 2016/1075 Art. 20.
109 Regulation 2016/1075 Art. 20(1)(a).
110 EBA Report 2017 Supervisory Colleges, p. 6 and p. 18.
111 EBA Report 2017 Supervisory Colleges, p. 42.

market to game more protection of their interests than it could in the past with the focus of stress-testing being part of improving the resilience of banks to shocks from a resolution and crisis management perspective.

3.60 The use of stress-testing is a significantly important preventative tool to apply to the understanding of banks risks to the sector or indeed the system as a whole. The use of adverse scenarios therefore informs both macroprudential and microprudential policy in terms of risk to the real economy and financial system going forward. In view of this information it is hoped the tools of macroprudential supervisors such as capital buffers and counter cyclical tools can be put in place to minimize such risks materializing albeit the scenarios maybe to assess the resilience of firms to extreme scenarios. But the limits of these tool cannot be forgotten especially when legacy issues are so systemically important which forward looking capital buffers cannot capture. Equally, the tools of microprudential supervision to require and or exercise formal enforcement measures to improve capital and or liquidity or even better bank governance to understand risk exposures. If risk and knowable uncertainty is illustrated as a continuum between low risks and extreme adverse knowable uncertainty, information about firms on that spectrum provides a better understanding of the firms' position between risk and knowable uncertainties. Enabling the official 'safety-net' players to prepare and understand the limits of their own resources and understanding and capacity to initiate changes. In this respect the BIS explain scenarios need to be 'severe yet plausible'.[112] Indeed Gambetta et al note 'the 2008 market collapse was driven by systemic events so complex and difficult to predict that such scenario could have been dismissed ex-ante as implausible'.[113]

3.61 Stress-testing is not a one-size-fits-all exercise, nor should it focus on one kind of risk such as credit risk or market risk, but a multitude of risks. Since the 'cocktail of risks' together is likely to give rise to different adverse outcomes. As explained by Borio et al, an important purpose of stress-testing is its ability to question underlying assumptions of stakeholders and their associated position and thinking of the financial system in different ways so providing a more holistic perspective.[114] The information gained through stress-testing is required to be shared between national authorities through the supervisory colleges. As shown earlier, the interconnection between Member States clearly highlights the possibility of shocks being transmitted between some Member States than others, especially those that are perhaps more reliant on cross-border financing. The local entity can also be a conduit of such shocks, especially if the entity requires refinancing to improve its capital position in light of a write-down of assets as a result of non-performing loans. A recent report by the BIS highlighted the importance of cross-border stress-testing. In more integrated regional banking systems there is more need of it, since the EU model places significant reliance on the home competent authority to coordinate supervisory information sharing. Information garnered from stress-testing needs to be shared more widely. But sensitivity of the findings

[112] M Quagliarello, *Stress Testing the Banking System: Methodologies and Applications* (2009) Cambridge, Cambridge University Press 3–15, p. 9.

[113] N Gambetta, M A Garcia-Benau, and A Zorio-Grima, Stress test impact and bank risk profile: Evidence from Macro Stress testing in Europe, *International Review of Economics and Finance* (2017) 1–8.

[114] C Borio, M Drehmann, and K Tsatsaronis, 'Stress-Testing macro stress testing: Does it live up to expectations? 12 *Journal of Financial Stability*, (2014).

may lead some authorities to forbear disclosure or down play findings in concern of the home or host response.[115]

The framework for the parent entity and its branches and subsidiaries in foreign markets requires national interests to be set aside for such exercises. This exercise of cross-border stress-testing would also go some way to appease those that fear burden sharing and mutualization of funding to deal with cross-border failures, since it would lead to the ability to identify vulnerable points within the group and the extent to which national designated authorities for subsidiaries and branches are able to see how shocks across certain asset classes would be managed and the extent to which individual entities would need refinancing. The host Member States with a significant bank presence need to push such coordinated efforts, since they are perhaps more vulnerable. Equally, the political position of large Member States exposed to the risks of smaller Member States could be tested to ascertain whether this is in fact a material point in the policy debate. It may well be the case that the risk relationship is in fact going in the opposite direction. It is likely, however, that the home Member State for the ultimate parent entity is likely to coordinate with those home-host and host Member States that are material to the ultimate parent entity; gauging the potential impact via the information channels of the equity and bond markets. This in itself is perfectly reasonable and, in need as well, but it could also include smaller Member States. However, this is not just important from the perspective of home to host risk transmission the opposite is equally important, since the GFC included episodes of the need for foreign entities requiring refinancing as a result of collapse of asset prices. The interlinkages between macro-event at the home and host level and the impact on the parent entity and branches and subsidiaries would be an important scenario to use to determine whether recovery options and resolution options are appropriate to deal with cross-border decision-making in crisis management.[116] The limits of stress-testing as explained by Arnold et al highlight and emphasize the importance for crisis management and resolution as opposed to an early warning system.[117] 3.62

The stumbling blocks for a cross-border stress test is similar to the weaknesses of consolidated supervision, namely a lack of reciprocity in the approach to sharing information between the home and host Member States with different information standards at the competent authorities exposing an asymmetry of information. The data provided earlier shows the level of interconnection between Member States while there is a significant amount of finance through the interbank market for the large Member States a significant proportion 3.63

[115] Basel Committee on Banking Supervision, December 2017, 'Supervisory and bank stress-testing: range of practices "Greater coordination could have a number of potential benefits. Within an interconnected global financial system, nationally focused stress tests may only give a partial view of banking sector risks. Jurisdictions that host foreign banks are, on their own, unable to gain a complete picture of the resilience of those banks and their likely behaviour under stress, and may have less visibility into group structure or management actions by parent companies that could affect the resilience of subsidiaries. These arguments are particularly true for smaller supervisors or those with higher resource constraints. Jurisdictions that are home to banks that have significant foreign operations could also benefit from coordination with the host authorities of the foreign subsidiaries/branches. For example, the host authorities may be better placed to provide information on local risks that could impact the subsidiaries and branches and ultimately impact the parent of the group, or the group as a whole.' (p. 37).

[116] C Borio, 'Towards a Macroprudential Framework for Financial Supervision and Regulation?' (2003) CESifo Economic Studies, pp. 181–215 at 190.

[117] B Arnold et al, 'Systemic risk, macroprudential policy frameworks, monitoring financial systems and the evolution of capital adequacy', *Journal of Banking & Finance* (2012) 3125–32 at p. 3127.

of foreign claims are locally sourced. The challenges of undertaking cross-country stress-testing has been explored by Castren et al suggest the identification of a common risk within the network of interconnections which requires the parent entity and the foreign banks in other markets to response to such as requirement to refinance their business. A similar scenario may be linked to the Swedish banks and their foreign establishments in the Baltics. Where the network of links expose different adverse risks.

3.64 The work of the EBA with the ESRB is particularly important in this respect since it provides a platform for cross-country comparison and disclosure. The study undertaken by Ellahie in 2012[118] points towards the reduction of the asymmetry of information between the industry and the markets with the disclosure of the findings. The work of the EBA improves consistency by requiring competent authorities to apply a common approach to overcome national approaches to supervision and information sharing. In the 2018 exercise the number of banks included in the stress test equated to 70% of the EU banking sector at the ultimate parent entity level of consolidation. The common methodology provides the basis for banks to apply an adverse scenario and provide information about the outcomes. The move towards the Single Supervisory Mechanism does move towards minimizing national interests for SSM banks where the ECB is both home and host competent authority. The scope of the exercise included reference to credit risk, market risk, fee- and interest-earning income, and conduct risk losses. But there is still a risk of national approaches differing to the interpretation of the adverse scenario. The other concern is the use of historical data and so the impact of the adverse shocks is limited since the outcome of such shocks would be to respond by sale of assets but to retain the assets and identify the losses rather than factor in the sale of those assets or restructuring through mergers, for instance.[119] Moreover, the UK use of a dynamic model rather than the static model means liquidity constraints are not considered. The coordination of results and supervisory actions has been raised as a limitation of the EBA in comparison to the US approach which is considered far more rigorous since the US require more disclosure of regulatory action needed to be taken by the individual banks.

Reconfiguring Home Bias for Significant Subsidiaries—The Supervisory Perspective

3.65 The idea of home bias in the European framework of cross-border supervision has been a specific issue associated with the relationship between home and host states and branches. However, as evident from the analysis above, home bias in respect to branches has been addressed to a certain extent. The host state can intervene in certain instances and there are explicit requirements for the sharing of information associated with management and, more specifically, liquidity, insolvency and supervisory finding as a result of on-site inspections and evidence of non-compliance. The home state is required to share information on those matters and decisions. This extends to macro-prudential decisions taken by

[118] A Ellahie, Capital Market Consequences of EU Bank Stress Tests (2012), <https://www.newyorkfed.org/medialibrary/media/research/conference/2012/FinancialServices2012/Ellahie.pdf>.

[119] A Resti, How demanding and consistent is the 2018 stress test design in comparison to previous exercises?, Directorate-General for Internal Policies of the Union PE 614.511, (2018).

other parts of the official safety net in the home state relating to capital conversation buffers. Those reforms are an attempt to enable the host state, where branches are located, to have a better understanding of the group or parent. Based on this information, the asymmetry of information between home and host is, to an extent, reduced. In cases where the host designates a branch as significant, there is the possibility of its competent authority joining supervisory colleges. However, since the branch is primarily a part of the institution within the home state, it is suggested the improvements in sharing of information and the powers of intervention serve home states just as much as host states since the host state's intervention is open to home state scrutiny.

The principle of a 'significant subsidiary' is recognized under the CRR but only for the purposes of disclosure requirements.[120] In this decision, either the EU parent entity or the EU parent holding company or the host Member State can designate a subsidiary as significant to the group or is of material significance in the local market.[121] The disclosures relate to a range of important matters either on an individual or sub-consolidated basis: own funds;[122] capital requirements;[123] capital buffers;[124] credit risk adjustments;[125] remuneration policy;[126] leverage;[127] and credit risk mitigation techniques.[128] The Regulation allows the competent authority of the parent entity or the financial holding company to either take an integrated or individual approach to the calculation of prudential requirements.[129] The consultation on disclosure emphasized the way significance could be determine which is primarily based on the ECB criteria for establishing significant banks.[130] The consultation chapter highlights the discrepancy between the ECB list of significant banks list and those banks listed as O-SIIs with a number of institutions categorized in the latter not falling within the remit of the ECB designated list. The final requirements enable Member States to exercise their discretion to identify institutions that need to comply with the designated disclosure requirements. 3.66

The decision to classify subsidiaries as significant needs to be expanded to ensure reciprocal arrangements between the home and home-host competent authority for the purposes of information and data sharing about supervision, resolution and crisis management. Therefore, it is argued that criteria should be devised to set out how a subsidiary is classed 3.67

[120] Directive 2013/36/EU of the European Parliament And of the Council, of 26 June 2013, on access to the activity of credit institutions and the prudential supervision of credit institutions and investment firms, amending Directive 2002/87/EC and repealing Directives 2006/48/EC and 2006/49/EC.

[121] Art. 13; Commission Implementing Regulation (EU) No. 650/2014 of 4 June 2014 laying down implementing technical standards with regard to the format, structure, contents list, and annual publication date of the information to be disclosed by competent authorities in accordance with Directive 2013/36/EU of the European Parliament and of the Council.

[122] CRR Art. 437.

[123] CRR Art. 438.

[124] CRR Art. 440.

[125] CRR Art. 442.

[126] CRR Art. 450.

[127] CRR Art. 451.

[128] CRR Art. 453.

[129] EBA, Consultation, Guidelines on disclosure requirements under Part Eight of Regulation (EU) 575/2013: 'Although drafted with the example of an institution, it applies *mutatis mutandis* for a significant subsidiary or a subsidiary of material significance for its local market.' EBA/CP/2016/07, 29 June 2016 pp. 19–20. EBA, Final Report Guidelines on disclosure requirements under Part Eight of Regulation (EU) No. 575/2013, EBA/GL/2016/11, version 2*, 14 December 2016.

[130] p. 21.

as significant under the different purposes to ensure better policy coordination. It would require the consolidated supervisor and the competent authorities to also share information with one another so that they can improve oversight of the group and individual institutions on a reciprocal basis, rather than now with a significant bias to the interests of the group on a consolidated basis. The resolution policy framework needs to be better aligned, for significant subsidiaries from both the perspective of the group as a whole and the perspective of Member States. It is argued that a more coherent policy framework is likely to lead to a more orderly resolution from a group perspective and a single subsidiary perspective. Therefore, better aligning the interests of home (as group consolidated supervisor) and host-home Member States and third countries where a significant subsidiary is located.

3.68 The threat of ringfencing by the host-home state is not likely to have a material impact on the decisions of the consolidated supervisor, since it has already carved out the impact of the subsidiary *ex ante*. The implications of this decision needs to be *ex ante* rather than *ex post* and should provide the host-home the opportunity to build the sufficient levels of capital and liquidity to ensure a solo resolution. The threat of measures to address non-viability at the early intervention stage of supervision and resolution could also assist the competent authority to introduce powers that can be exercised *ex post* to ensure viability, such as retain earnings and prohibit the payment of dividends to the parent.

Consolidated Supervision: A Third Country Perspective

3.69 The CRD IV and CRR requirements set out separate requirements for third country compliance for supervisory cooperation and coordination.[131] This is, broadly speaking, based on the principle of reciprocity determined by assessing whether the third country has equivalent standards to those adopted in the European Union.[132] The NCA is expected to work with the Commission and the EBA in this process of assessing equivalence. In this respect, the assessment of equivalence is not reciprocal but one of meeting the EU standards.[133] A significant proportion of the focus is on market access to the Union but other parts of the CRD IV requirements focus on equivalence of standards and approaches to determine whether quantitative and qualitative information and data is calculated on similar levels to the EU so that the Member State competent authority can confidentially consider it for the purposes of consolidated supervision.

3.70 The Member State competent authority will need to assess the likely impediments that exist for the exchange of information from the competent authority of the third country to the consolidated supervisor.[134] On the basis of the assessment by the EBA, a third country can be included in EU supervisory colleges, as has been the case with Albania.[135] Professional

[131] CRD IV Art. 48; CRR Art. 18.

[132] CRD IV Art. 48(3).

[133] CRD IV Art. 127.

[134] CRR Art. 18; CRD Equivalence Methodology for the assessment of the equivalence of Third Country Professional Secrecy Standards with the Capital Requirements Directive for the purposes of colleges of supervisors, <http://www.eba.europa.eu/documents/10180/557531/Methodology+assessment+of+confidentiality+regimes.pdf>.

[135] EBA includes Bank of Albania in EU supervisory colleges, 11 September 2015, <http://www.eba.europa.eu/-/eba-includes-bank-of-albania-in-eu-supervisory-colleges>.

secrecy laws need to be assessed to determine whether the information and data received by the competent authority can be shared in trust and can also be shared with other parts of the EU official safety net such as the EBA.[136] In this respect, the Commission can take on the responsibility of negotiating bilateral and multilateral agreements with the authority of the third country to ensure the exchange of information and data and minimize impediments thereto. The areas of particular focus are capital adequacy assessments and liquidity recovery plans to ensure shortfalls in liquidity and for the purposes of minimizing large exposures. Disclosure is also expected on a country-by-country basis to ensure there is a clear understanding of the names and activities, geographical location, number of employees, profit and loss before tax, and whether or not the institution is supported by public subsidies on an institution-by-institution level. More evidently, the decisions associated with buffer levels requires the ESRB to determine whether the third country is in line with EU expectations of where those buffers should be set.[137] For example, if the ESRB considers that the third country is benefiting from setting low buffers, then it can require the Union institutions to hold higher buffers to counter any risk posed by the exposures in the third country.[138] However, in this case, and in the other cases, the point of equivalence is to ensure the safety and soundness of the EU parts of a group or entity from the risks posed from a third country and there is little in the way of equivalence in their interests in the other direction.

The requirements in the CRR build on this and attempt to incentivize the competent authority of the third country to comply with EU requirements. For example, in a number of instances, the CRR requirements put in place penalty risk weightings if the third country's prudential requirements are not in line, therefore, increasing the cost of EU groups with subsidiaries doing business in third countries. Hence, the approach to equivalency is not reciprocal and is primarily designed to improve oversight of the parent and the group since the CRD IV requirements are directed to minimize impediments to information sharing from the perspective of the consolidated supervisor rather than from the perspective of the third country's host supervisor or home supervisor. **3.71**

The lack of reference to third countries and the need for information-sharing initiatives with EU Member States and non-EU countries is surprising since a large number of EU banks undertake business in third countries in the form of subsidiaries and branches. This is particularly acute for those third countries classed as EU candidates and EU potential countries. In these respective countries, European banks, as we have explained above, have a significant presence. Although the information sharing initiatives at the home and host state level do not formally include third countries, it will mean the home and host state are more than likely going to develop their own information sharing arrangements. The different approaches will result in inconsistency amongst Member States, which is not likely to improve the understanding of group activities in third countries. Moreover, it will also result in some third countries getting preferential treatment and, therefore, be in a better **3.72**

[136] CRD IV Art. 55 relating to CRD IV Art. 53 and Art. 54: Final Report: On recommendations on the equivalence of confidentiality regimes, EBA/REC/2015/02, 11 September 2015, <http://www.eba.europa.eu/documents/10180/1187373/EBA-Rec-2015-02+Recommendation+amending+EBA-Rec-2015-01+on+the+equivalence+of+confidentiality+regimes.pdf>.

[137] CRD IV Art. 138.

[138] CRD IV Art. 139.

position to prepare for supervision and resolution than other third countries that are excluded. In many respects, this reinforces the self-interests of some Member States over others and results in poor levels of cooperation and coordination.

3.73 It would be important for the SSM to develop a framework to ensure Member States are consistent in their approach, in terms of information sharing with third countries, to prevent incentives to align with third countries that simply preserve their own self-interest. At the same time, there is no doubt some third countries would cooperate and seek to coordinate more proactively than others, perhaps due to concerns of systemic risk being more likely to be transmitted between some third countries and the European Union. Due consideration needs to be given to those third countries where the individual subsidiary is systemically important, albeit from the group's perspective or indeed the consolidated supervisor's perspective it is not. Finally, the level of reciprocity needs to be on an equal footing, rather than it simply being a case of information going from the third country to the respective EU Member States or to the EBA. Otherwise, in times of crisis, it is likely to result in entrenchment to serve self-interests rather than collective interests.

3.74 The Memorandum of Cooperation between the EBA and six of the South-Eastern European Countries is a step in the right direction since it shows evidence of willingness to cooperate regarding information exchange.[139] The MoU certainly recognizes the importance of information sharing and vulnerability of the signatory countries to the risks posed to them by EU banks located in their respective jurisdictions. In particular, it sets out the right incentives for cooperation in the form of establishing the right principles and the need to have in place similar arrangements for cooperation—namely trust in the form of confidentiality of information. However, it is important to assess the extent to which the MoU offers reciprocal arrangements or, rather, aligns the incentives of cooperation in the interests of the European Union and its efforts to safeguard market integrity and financial stability. As with all MoUs, the framework is couched in broad terms and lacks the detail in terms of what information should be shared. Moreover, the lack of enforcement will ultimately mean it is reliant on the good will of the signatories. From the perspective of the EBA, it assists in building up its understanding of the various risks, as poor attention to rule design and supervisory practice need to be ironed out. The MoU highlights that 'the EBA express their willingness to cooperate in areas related to the EBA's tasks, as specified in Article 8 of the EBA Regulation, which involves the development of the Single Rulebook, promoting the convergence of supervisory practices and the consistent and coherent functioning of supervisory colleges, and monitoring risks and vulnerabilities in the EU banking system'.[140] The design of the MoU does raise concerns about whether it is actually based on mutual trust and understanding. In many ways, it is designed to ensure information is given to the

[139] EBA signs memorandum of cooperation with South Eastern European supervisors, 23 October 2015, <http://www.eba.europa.eu/-/eba-signs-memorandum-of-cooperation-with-south-eastern-european-supervisors>; Memorandum of Cooperation between the European Banking Authority (The 'EBA') and the Banking Agency of the Federation of Bosnia and Herzegovina, The Banking Agency of The Republic of Srpska, The National Bank of The Republic of Macedonia, The Central Bank of Montenegro, The National Bank of Serbia, and The Bank of Albania (The 'Signatory Supervisory Authorities'), <http://www.eba.europa.eu/documents/10180/1244268/Memorandum+of+Cooperation.pdf/950f264e-8b3b-48b1-b6c6-e01634188bcb>; EBA welcomes Central Bank of Kosovo to the Memorandum of Cooperation with South Eastern European banking supervisors, March 2017, <http://www.eba.europa.eu/-/eba-welcomes-central-bank-of-kosovo-to-the-memorandum-of-cooperation-with-south-eastern-european-banking-supervisors>.

[140] Ibid.

EBA which it could certainly circulate to the Members of the European System of Financial Supervision. In return, what is provided seems to be already in the public domain, such as the annual EBA colleges' action plan and colleges' newsletters. The exceptions are the lists of contact details for respective competent authorities and the assistance the EBA provides in the form of training. It highlights the aspiration to assist the signatories to participate in the supervisory colleges, but it cannot guarantee access to the respective colleges. More importantly, '[t]he Signatory Supervisory Authorities will regularly inform the EBA of the main risks and vulnerabilities affecting their national banking sectors. They will also regularly report data and indicators on their national banking sectors to the EBA as well as ad hoc requests for information, which might be needed in the context of the EBA's risk analysis work.'[141] Current practice would suggest that the requests for information and the sharing of information are not currently reciprocal. This is perhaps not surprising since the specific requests for information are on the signatories to be provided to the EBA. Therefore, requests for information are respected but the requests from the signatory countries are not likely to be honoured to the same extent on the lines of the details they are expected to provide both on a qualitative and quantitative level.

The lack of reciprocity of sharing information is a concern since the signatories are, in all intents and purposes, reliant on the goodwill of the respective Member States. As we have experienced, the lack of coherent rules-based frameworks is unlikely to lead to concrete commitments in times of crisis. It will simply lead to a situation of acting in the national interest. If requests for information are not reciprocal in the medium to long term, it means the signatory countries are unlikely to cooperate. What are the incentives to cooperate with such a misalignment of incentives? The lack of information sharing will also mean the signatory countries are unlikely to be able to prepare for supervision, let alone prepare for resolution. **3.75**

A principal barrier to cooperation between EU Member States and third countries within a supervisory college and the confidence in terms of sharing information has been whether the state in question has professional secrecy measures equivalent to those of EU Member States. The EBA has been conducting this work and its recent findings indicate the majority of EU candidates and potential candidate countries do meet the thresholds of professional secrecy.[142] On the basis of these findings, one would expect those states are more likely to be invited to join supervisory colleges. However, this is not the case, as, in many cases, it depends on the consolidated supervisor even after the fact they have passed the equivalency test. A state could find itself invited to join one supervisory college but excluded from other supervisory colleges, despite the fact that subsidiaries of equal importance in terms of systemic risk undertake business in their jurisdiction and are part of a large EU banking group. The tendency, in practice, has been that smaller competent authorities are more willing to invite states where subsidiaries are located. The more concerning issue is that those Member **3.76**

141 Ibid.

142 CRD Equivalence Methodology for the assessment of the equivalence of Third Country Professional Secrecy Standards with the Capital Requirements Directive for the purposes of colleges of supervisors, <http://www.eba.europa.eu/documents/10180/557531/Methodology+assessment+of+confidentiality+regimes.pdf>. On the basis of this methodology and the subsequent assessment EBA has published the following recommendations. EBA, Recommendations on the equivalence of confidentiality regimes, 2 April 2015, <http://www.eba.europa.eu/documents/10180/1032035/EBA-REC-2015-01+Recommendations+on+the+equivalence+of+confidentiality+regimes.pdf/e445957c-23b4-4b07-9710-7ba3a7c70fbd>.

States that are responsible for systemically important institutions are more likely to exclude such states, despite the fact that the subsidiaries from the group are systemically important in the respective states and undertake profitable business in their jurisdictions. A surprising anomaly of this is that, in these cases, the ECB would actually be the competent authority for consolidated supervision and so leads the supervisory colleges. It is not necessarily the case that post-crisis reforms have improved cross-border relations, but rather pre-existing relationships have continued to be sufficiently strong in some cases and hostile, in terms of cooperation, in other cases. Whether or not this is because consolidated supervisors have not yet realized the need to invite all competent authorities that may qualify for observer status could be one of the reasons.

International Soft Law Instruments Focus on Home and Host Supervisory Issues

3.77 The use of international soft law instruments is very important for setting the tone of what is broadly necessary in international financial regulation. Where the third country elements of instruments are of concern, such as those discussed above, it is important that attention is drawn to relevant international soft law instruments. In the case of supervision, the Basel III capital requirements are specifically reviewed alongside the introduction of capital buffers. The Argentina equivalence assessment shows that the requirements assessed thereafter are primarily equivalent to the EU prudential supervisory instruments.[143] In this section the focus is on the possible impasse between home and host countries when it comes to supervisory coordination and cooperation. The gaps that possibly exist are somewhat limited at the supervisory level. Nonetheless, the supervisory soft law expectations are necessary to reinforce the importance of cooperation and coordination starting early at the supervisory stage to inform preparations. The joint decision between the SRB and the National Bank of Romania regarding resolution plans, as noted in Chapter 2, illustrates the problem when the cooperation and coordination is not reciprocal, the legal framework can address it. In the third country context such legal administrative mechanisms do not exist and so political will is essentially counted on to reach agreements, which is not always forthcoming. The possible tensions are real and are likely to be just as significant from the third country perspective when incentives are not necessarily aligned with the legal administrative instruments. A key challenge in some cases is the political will to bring supervision and resolution regimes up to the international best standards. The gaps in administrative measures can in themselves form obstacles to cooperate even when it is in their mutual interests to do so, as it raises the question with whom can I cooperate and work with. In view of this, the work of the IMF and World Bank is imperative to ensure practical efforts are being made to achieve appropriate supervisory outcomes. The EU equivalence regime emphasizes its interests and so it will be useful to explore whether the international soft law instruments and guidance provide something that is more reciprocal in its emphasis on cooperation and coordination between home and host and so reduce a home country-centred approach. In particular, the

[143] EBA, Opinion of the European Banking Authority on the Equivalence of supervisory and regulatory requirements in relation to Argentina 22/05/19; ANNEX—Republic of Argentina, <https://eba.europa.eu/documents/10180/2740473/Annex+to+EBA+Opinion+on+third+country+equivalence+-+Argentina.pdf>.

spread of banking from the EU in the accession countries highlights the challenges posed by their presence and the importance of reciprocal information sharing since those banks play a dominant role in the jurisdiction.

The Basel Core Principles 2012[144] set the expectations about how home and host authorities should be expected to cooperate and coordinate supervision of cross-border banks. In addition to emphasizing the need for effective consolidate supervision, it explicitly refers to home and host issues as well. It sets the expectations that standards of bank conduct should not be lower than those of domestic banks. While the point of the principle is useful, if the recognition of standards by supervisors of both jurisdictions is relatively poor, then the outcomes for both jurisdictions are going to be negative externalities. An important element that is emphasized is the information to be shared for the purposes of risk management. The Principles, however, implicitly emphasize home country interests. In this case, emphasis needs to be placed on the needs of the host and whether information is reciprocally provided to assist preparations for resolution plans, for instance, when the entity is material to the host but not necessarily material to the group. In part, this is answered in the positive, with the needs of such host recognized by the Principles that emphasize the importance of them to be included in the supervisory college of the bank. In practice, however, membership is simply a starting point; it does not necessarily guarantee that the information that is actually needed will be shared or the interests of the host in such circumstances are likely to influence recovery and resolution plans. **3.78**

The FSB issued guidance in 2015 to support efforts of host authorities where Globally Systematically Important Financial Institutions (G-SIFIs) have a systemic presence but not represented on the Crisis Management Group. This is an important step forward to address the issues of membership. However, it is unlikely to be of significant impact in view of its limited scope of application. The Basel Committee Progress report 2017 highlights the finding that '[o]verall, home supervisors felt more positive about crisis preparedness in colleges than host supervisors.'[145] This response illuminates the problem of a lack of reciprocity between the two parties and is echoed in the Report 2017 in other areas of crisis preparedness. In view of the way supervisors and resolution authorities collaborate to work out recovery and resolution plans, it is equally necessary for this to occur across borders as well. The Report 2017 emphasizes the willingness of host to share information, yet the same is not reciprocated by its home counterpart. The report highlights, '[w]hile host supervisors agree that their effective contribution at forums such as supervisory colleges and CMGs, can enhance crisis preparedness discussions, expectations of host supervisors' crisis preparedness contributions do not align with assessment of their actual contributions. Most host supervisors assessed their contribution in crisis preparedness discussions at supervisory colleges as either "limited contribution" or "no contribution"'. In part, the importance of risk management information being shared between home and host is equally emphasized as well as the lack of information sharing on the part of the home with host. As a minimum, risk management reviews should be a joint initiative between the home and the host, where **3.79**

[144] Basel Committee on Banking Supervision, Core Principles for Effective Banking Supervision, 2012, <https://www.bis.org/publ/bcbs230.pdf>.

[145] Basel Committee on Banking Supervision, Progress report on the implementation of principles for effective supervisory colleges, December 2017, <https://www.bis.org/bcbs/publ/d430.pdf>.

material entities of the group and material entities to the host are part of. This is in contrast to a trickle-down approach of general information going from the home to the host where entities are only material to the host. A critical feature of the decision-making process is some form of a sign-off to ensure that effective preparation can be achieved based on the information provided.

3.80 The general view of the analysis above suggests the international soft law guidance and reported experience highlight the problem clearly. The lack of reciprocity in the guidelines is evident and the host experience echoes this. It is therefore important for hosts to lobby and insist on reciprocity in terms of information sharing to ensure they are equally well prepared as their home counterparts. This extends to material entities that are important to the group, but equally extends to entities that are material to the host. The experience of host with a dominant foreign bank presence therefore exasperates the problem since it would certainly mean it is a systemic problem rather than simply an idiosyncratic one. This is important from the perspective where the risk management of NPLs, for instance, is centralized, but the levels of exposure to NPLs are decentralized and dispersed across different jurisdictions. The implications of the centralized approach will have repercussions in the host in terms of loan loss provisioning and whether the centralized assessment takes into account the challenges of managing NPLs off the balance sheet at the local level, see Chapter 4.

Reflections on the Principal Issues

3.81 The criteria to determine the importance of banks has been shown to be inconsistent from number of fronts and this leads to problems later in the EU crisis management discourse. The inconsistency of practice could lead to potential conflicts of interest between Member States and the ECB at this juncture. From a cross-border dimension, the use of consolidated supervision is traditionally the starting point to configure the relationship between home and host and in the EU context it is clearly positioned on home country control. However, it is evident that there is a potential threat with the lack of reciprocity within the consolidated supervisory relationship. This is particularly acute for those supervising group subsidiaries where the criteria for cooperation is not as clear as it is for branches. It was argued that this can potentially lead to conflicting interests between the parent and the subsidiary since risks on either side may not be visible to each other. Supervisory colleges and recovery planning are principal mechanisms for group perspectives and host perspectives. However, the level of administrative discretion that exists within the current mechanisms can lead to home country bias. Since the ECB is in the shoes of the group consolidated supervisor it will really need to demonstrate that it truly reflects both sides. From the recovery planning perspective, it is not so clear the host perspective is considered in them. The assumption of the core recovery options likely to be exercised at the same time is overly optimistic. As is evident later when banks require precautionary recapitalization or liquidity assistance, the opportunity to raise capital in the market is shown to be far too optimistic. A key way to assess the underlying strength of banks is the formal stress-testing exercise. The need for cross-border stress-testing is necessary to understand how exposures within the group can materially impact the different parts. The home bias is particularly problematic for significant subsidiaries of groups and why there is a need for better cooperation and coordination particularly for putting in place preparations of crisis. Finally, the third country perspective is explored and the importance of confidentially requirements being a starting point for information sharing. Again, the lack of reciprocity was particularly prevalent between the EU and third countries. This needs to be addressed at the supervisory point to provide confidence in the relationships to mitigate chances of crises. The international soft law principles firstly premised on home country and essentially focused on the importance of coordination and cooperation to address the concerns about global institutions. This neglects very large parts of the banking industry that have cross-border exposures and can pose threats to financial stability in both the home and the host. This should not be based on the bargaining power of the host country.

4

EU Non-Performing Loans and Loan Loss Provisioning

Introduction

The European banking and sovereign debt crisis triggered a huge non-performing loan (NPL) problem.[1] These triggers during the global financial crisis (GFC) left banks straddling large amounts of non-performing debts and ultimately increasing their probability of failure but also hindering levels of credit in the economy and so slowing economic growth.[2] This is particularly acute in the European context. As was shown earlier, the lack of diversity of financing techniques means it is heavily reliant on commercial banking business as its primary source of finance. So when commercial banks are choked with NPLs, it reduces their profitability and hinders their ability to provide credit in the economy.[3] At the bank level, the risk attached to the assets will require the need for higher capital to be held, which at the time of an adverse economic cycle may not be readily available. In view of the primary importance of loans and credit facilities, it is critical to assess how this is addressed before distress is experienced in such facilities. This requires consideration of the matter at the supervisory level to minimize the chance of triggering resolution or insolvency proceeding. In view of the different Member State standards of practice, consistency from the point of origination of loans to liquidation of collateral and recoveries as a continuum is necessary in order to ensure a level playing field. **4.1**

The question about how best to deal with the NPLs problem is a critical one, and one that needs to be considered at both the public and private level of law and regulation. We have already seen that doubts about the quality of the assets banks hold determine whether they can raise finance in the market as and when they wish to do so. In view of this, there are both adverse selection and moral hazard problems that co-exist due to the information **4.2**

[1] European Banking Authority, 'Final Report: Guidelines on management of non-performing and forborne exposures' (EBA, 2018), pp. 4–6, <https://eba.europa.eu/documents/10180/2425705/Final+Guidelines+on+management+of+non-performing+and+forborne+exposures.pdf> [accessed 6 June 2019]; Lars Nyberg 'Resolution of NPLs in the cross-border bank' (2016), 1 <http://npl.vienna-initiative.com/wp-content/uploads/sites/2/2016/07/Nyberg-Lehmann-on-cross-border-banks.pdf>.

[2] Patrizia Baudino and Hyuncheol Yun, 'FSI Insights on policy implementation No 3 Resolution of non- performing loans – policy options' (Bank for International Settlements (BIS), 2017), <https://www.bis.org/fsi/publ/insights3.pdf> [accessed 6 June 2019]; European Central Bank, 'Guidance to banks on NPLs' (ECB, 2017), p. 5, <https://www.bankingsupervision.europa.eu/ecb/pub/pdf/guidance_on_npl.en.pdf>. [accessed 6 June 2019]; J Temesvary and A Banai, 'The drivers of foreign bank lending in Central and Eastern Europe: The roles of parent, subsidiary and host market traits' (2017) 79 Journal of International Money and Finance 157–73; Dimitrios Anastasiou 'Management and Resolution methods of NPLs: A Review of the Literature' Munich Personal RePEc Archive (MPRA), p. 5, <https://mpra.ub.unimuenchen.de/77581/1/MPRA_paper_77581.pdf> [accessed 6 June 2019].

[3] EBA Report on Statutory Prudential Backstops: Response to the Commission's Call for Advice of November 2017, p. 11, <https://eba.europa.eu/documents/10180/2087449/EBA+Report+on+Statutory+Prudential+Backstops.pdf>.

European Cross-Border Banking and Banking Supervision. Dalvinder Singh, Oxford University Press (2020). © Oxford University Press.
DOI: 10.1093/oso/9780198844754.001.0001

asymmetry and lack of transparent information.[4] Regarding adverse selection, the quality of assets is so interlinked with the duration of their non-performance that distinguishing the 'good' from 'bad' based on pricing alone is difficult. Concerning moral hazard, the extent of the problem on the balance sheet and the level of risk taking to increase profits are opaque. In view of this insufficient transparency, the ability of the bank to raise capital in the market becomes virtually impossible due to a lack of confidence in the balance sheet. As pointed out earlier in this study, a significant number of banks in the Banking Union for instance are not publicly listed, so access to investors is going be limited. Moreover, the loss of market access leads to possible assistance either from precautionary recapitalisation or emergency liquidity assistance necessary but the size of this assistance is not easy to determine with any accuracy. The issue of asymmetry of information is made more problematic when the cross-border dimension is factored into the analysis: the lack of harmonization and consistency of practice between the host and the home exasperate the underlying problems within the banking group and its different subsidiaries or branches when it comes to NPLs.[5] For instance, from a cross-border perspective, European banks operate almost in equal measure via branches and subsidiaries. In the latter case, the subsidiary may have more autonomy over how NPLs are managed according to local foreign requirements and these are then consolidated with the parent entity balance sheet at the consolidated supervisory level. However, in the case of NPLs, at branch level these are on the balance sheet of the parent entity, albeit originated in a foreign jurisdiction.[6] From a home and host perspective, the macro-prudential oversight and micro-prudential supervision need to factor this into their decision making.

4.3 The issue of NPLs is critical in the home and host dilemma because of the significant level of cross-border banking that exists at the European level.[7] The NPL problem is one of the negative consequences of the push and pull factors of cross-border banking. The move towards consistent practices in the management of NPLs is exemplified by regulatory measures concerning loan loss provisions. In particular, the interlinkages between loan loss provisioning and capital requirements and how they interact with banks and their balance sheet combine a multitude of regulatory decisions directly and indirectly at the accounting and prudential supervisory level. The dynamics of private and public forms of regulation require a systematic discussion of how best to combine and interpret the reforms at European level. It is evident that the opacity of the NPL problem hinders decision-making at both macro-prudential level and micro-prudential level.[8] In the context of the latter, it is particularly important to consider how supervision interacts with banks' strategic and operational decision making and if it potentially encroaches on the autonomy of corporate decision-making in terms of managing and making provision for losses. Provisions for greater transparency

[4] Giorgio Barba Navaretti, Giacomo Calzolari, and Alberto Pozzolo, 'NPL's European Economy-Banks, regulation, and the real sector' (Europeye srl, preliminary draft: 27 June 2017), p. 152, <https://european-economy.eu/wp-content/uploads/2017/07/EE_1.2017.pdf> [accessed 6 June 2019].

[5] Alexander Plekhanov and Marta Skrzypinska, 'Cross-border spillovers from reducing NPLs' (2018) European Bank for Reconstruction and Development 11–15; EBA, 'Consultation Paper on Draft Guidelines on disclosure of non-performing and forborne exposures' (27 April 2018, EBA/CP/2018/06).

[6] Shekhar Aiyar, 'How did the crisis in international funding markets affect bank lending? Balance sheet evidence from the United Kingdom' (Bank of England Working Paper No. 424, 2016), 10.

[7] Alexander Plekhanov and Marta Skrzypińska, 'Cross-border spillovers from reducing non-performing loans' (European Bank for Reconstruction and Development Working Paper, 2018).

[8] From General Secretariat of the Council to Delegations, Report of the FSC Subgroup on Non-Performing Loans (9854/17) (Council of the European Union, 2017), <http://data.consilium.europa.eu/doc/document/ST-9854-2017-INIT/en/pdf> [accessed 6 June 2019].

and consistency of supervisory practices amongst competent authorities within the EU have recently been introduced,[9] and so it is timely to consider them in view of the home and host dilemma that has been explored in this work. This is especially the case since the reforms associated with capital levels, such as the introduction of capital buffers, do not specifically address legacy issues related to the stock of NPLs. The move towards a forward-looking, judgment-based approach requires consideration of such legacy issues to minimize repetition of past mistakes. The home and host perspective is particularly pertinent because the different treatment of NPLs by the two authorities is likely to lead to different incentives in the way they are recognized and managed across national lines, thus resulting in an uneven playing field.

It is important to gauge the extent to which the NPL problem is addressed at the bank group strategic level between parent entity and subsidiary and branches.[10] This is especially the case in Member States that host a significant number of foreign banks, so much so that the foreign bank presence is larger than that of domestic banks, with the former being the primary provider of credit finance and holder of NPLs.[11] Therefore, the behaviour of foreign banks in such markets becomes critically important from a financial stability and economic growth perspective. From a home-host perspective the dominant role played by foreign banks in the region would suggest the strong loan growth prior to the GFC and subsequent deleveraging is indicative of a pattern of behaviour across the EU and not one of simply being regionally specific. Moreover, the presence of foreign banks may not have led necessarily to improvements in due diligence expected with foreign competitors in comparison to domestic banks which may be more attracted by local market interests. From the host Member State perspective, it could be the case that the pace of deleveraging is greater than that experienced in the home Member State (due to decisions taken in the home Member State), which would pose additional macro-prudential challenges for the host. Therefore, the asymmetry of information between foreign and local could lead to suboptimal levels of deleveraging due to a lack of both commitment and local knowledge resulting in an adverse selection problem with the unnecessary levels of deleveraging.[12] As explained by R De Haas et al, the significant risks within the sub-regions include the risk of capital flight and potential fire sale of assets. This is due to efforts to minimize exposures to the local host banking system and repatriate capital to the parent of the group to stabilize the group.[13] The study 4.4

[9] Rolf Klug, 'Next steps for the Completion of Banking Union and the reduction of non-performing loans' (ECB, 2018); ECB, 'Guidance to banks on non-performing loans' (ECB, 2017), <https://www.bankingsupervision.europa.eu/ecb/pub/pdf/guidance_on_npl.en.pdf> [accessed 6 June 2019].

[10] Alexander Plekhanov and Marta Skrzypińska, 'Cross-border spillovers from reducing NPLs' (European Bank for Reconstruction and Development Working Paper, 2018).

[11] Kimberly Beaton, Alla Myrvoda (IMF), and Shernnel Thompson, 'NPLs in the ECCU: Determinants and Macroeconomic Impact' (IMF Working Paper WP/16/229, 2016).

[12] Resolving Europe's NPL burden: challenges and benefits', keynote speech by Vítor Constâncio, Vice-President of the ECB, at an event entitled 'Tackling Europe's non-performing loans crisis: restructuring debt, reviving growth' organised by Bruegel, Brussels, 3 February 2017, available at <https://www.ecb.europa.eu/press/key/date/2017/html/sp170203.en.html> [accessed 1 March 2019].

[13] R De Haas and I Van Lelyveld, 'Multinational banks and the global financial crisis: weathering the perfect storm?' (Working Paper No 135, December 2011); F Allen, L Bartilori, and O Kowalewski, 'The Financial System of the EU 25' (Working Paper No. 05-44, Wharton Financial Institutions Center, University of Pennsylvania, 2005), pp. 5–6, available at <http://finance.wharton.upenn.edu/~allenf/download/Vita/financial%20system%20of%20the%20eu%20short%20version.pdf> [accessed 1 March 2019]; R De Haas and I Van Lelyveld, 'Foreign Banks and Credit Stability in Central and Eastern Europe: Friends or Foes?' (2006) 30(7) Journal of Banking and Finance 1927–52.

undertaken by R De Haas et al shows the exposure of the respective host states to the risk of such uncoordinated actions by foreign banks with an adverse impact on credit levels to the local economy.

4.5 The poor conduct of business practices in terms of credit underwriting in the home and host Member State may create a climate of weak assessments of counterparties and/or collateral that is secured against the loan. As such, these standards may not be sufficient to protect against the credit risk to which the bank is truly exposed, with deteriorating external economic factors having an adverse impact on the customers' ability to repay the loan. The importance of credit risk adjustment policies is equally needed to manage such exposures to maturity. The ability to redistribute risks of NPLs in a secondary market is lacking in many jurisdictions, so the capacity with which banks can offload such loans differs from one jurisdiction to another.[14] In view of this, it is important that any strategy dealing with NPLs starts at origination which implies a greater emphasis on supervision. Equally, the plumbing surrounding NPLs requires consistent legal preconditions for corporate and personal insolvency as well as restructuring to be in place to ensure an appropriate level to the playing field. At the Banking Union level the jurisdiction of the ECB is limited as it does not extend to conduct of business but rather prudential matters only. The interconnection between conduct of business and prudential matters is interlinked in the way NPLs are likely to be addressed. This would mean the conduct of business reforms to modify bank behaviour is reliant on the respective National Competent Authority (NCA).

4.6 This chapter explores the NPL issues from a supervisory perspective and explores the reforms to improve bank transparency and accountability by limiting bank forbearance of dealing with their NPL problem. It suggests the private mechanisms are more suitable to deal with the problem and are currently underutilized. The chapter first of all analyses using World Bank data the Member State level of exposure to NPLs. It undertakes this task by looking at the change in NPLs between 2006 and 2016, before, during and after the different crises points namely the banking and sovereign debt crisis. It shows the heterogeneity of the composition per Member State of the European Union and the different impacts of the two crises leading to the conclusion that the sovereign debt crisis and its spillover effects was far more detrimental and led to significant increases of NPLs. Following this the different definitions of NPLs is explored and the challenges it poses to addressing the problems, namely the transparency issue at the domestic level. In part the issue relates directly to the accounting treatment of NPLs and loan loss provisioning. The perverse consequences of IFRS 9 are explored and the challenges it leads to as a result of its complexity. Finally the chapter explores the challenges of utilizing public and private mechanisms to reduce the burden of NPLs. It suggests the move to separating out the NPL problem to a group subsidiary with improved supervisory oversight is likely to be the most appropriate solution in view of the importance of minimising the fire sale of assets and protect market best value.

[14] European Systemic Risk Board, 'Resolving NPLs in Europe' (July 2017), 16–17 <https://www.esrb.europa.eu/pub/pdf/reports/20170711_resolving_npl_report.en.pdf> [accessed 6 June 2019].

The Size of the European NPL Problem

The market context of the NPL problem is important before addressing and evaluating the regulatory and accounting response. The size of international cross-border banking within the European Union, shown in Chapter 1, demonstrates a clear trend between 2006 and 2016 where the sizeable growth of international bank activity led to significant levels of cross-border exposures between Member States in 2006–08, followed by significant declines between 2010 and 2014. It also shows the level of local positions as a significant source of finance. Finance raised in the local market from local creditors remained as a relatively stable source of funding. Although the peak was earlier 2006–07 and after 2007 a notable decline or remaining relatively stable within a range of 5%–10%. The 'push and pull' factors for smaller Member States in terms of credit finance opened a significant opportunity for foreign bank subsidiaries and branches to fill the gap for retail and commercial loans. However, the risk in a downturn is that such loans are the first casualty and so a direct cause of NPLs. 4.7

The fallout of the European banking and sovereign debt crisis shows a similar trend regarding NPLs, but in negative terms. The charts of NPLs to gross loans (loans past due over 90 days)[15] are set out in Appendix 8[16] and employ the same criteria as used in Chapter 1, i.e. the Member States are grouped according to their overall contribution to the European GDP and so showing their relative size in comparison to their peers. In view of this, the Member States are set out in seven groups according to their contributions, with Group 8 showing the accession countries. 4.8

The graphs in Appendix 8 can be explained in three significant periods 2006–17, the expansionary period, the banking crisis 2008 onwards and the sovereign debt crisis triggered at various points within the period. The ratio of non-performing loans to total loans is in line with the economic boom and bust cycle, with relatively low levels of NPLs during the boom period, followed by bust and high levels of NPLs. According to the IMF, 'NPLs in the European Union (EU) stood at about €1 trillion (or over 9% of the region's GDP) at end-2014, more than double the level in 2009.'[17] Between 2006 and 2008 the level of NPLs averaged around 0%–5%, which indicates a relatively small number of NPLs against the total number of loans. In this period the EU experienced a significant level of economic growth and so the level of NPLs is commensurately low. However, in 2008–11 the first peak of NPL surfaces in line with the fallout from the banking crisis and credit crunch. As the banking crisis takes hold over the real economy and the great recession ensues, the number of NPLs start to increase significantly, resulting in a doubling and even tripling of the percentage of NPLs between 2008 and 2011. The level of unemployment and the economic decline fed into a set of circumstances in which the economic environment was 4.9

[15] K D'Hulster, R Letelier, and V Salomao-Garcia, 'Loan Classification and Provisioning: Current Practices in 26 Countries (World Bank Group Financial Sector Advisory Centre Overview Paper August 2016): 'NPL ratios are commonly calculated as total NPLs over the gross loan portfolio. Noteworthy is that in some jurisdictions, it is not the full outstanding value of the loan that is recorded as non-performing, but the net value (after deduction of the provisions). Another practice is to include only the amount that is overdue in the measurement of the NPL' (p. 11).

[16] The authors own analysis based on data from The World Bank Data, Bank non-performing loans to total gross loans data, <https://data.worldbank.org/indicator/fb.ast.nper.zs>.

[17] Shekhar Aiyar et al, 'A Strategy for Resolving Europe's Loan Problems' (IMF Staff Discussion Note SDN 15/ 19, September 2015), p. 5.

ripe for NPLs to grow. This trend is evident for countries such as Italy in Group 1, Ireland in Group 2, Greece in Group 3, Romania and Hungary in Group 5, Bulgaria, Croatia, Lithuania, and Slovenia in Group 6, and Latvia and Cyprus in Group 7. With the exception of Italy in Group 1, the Member States suffering from the banking crisis were predominantly Central and Eastern European countries. It is evident these countries, to varying degrees, saw increases in NPLs as a result of the banking crisis, albeit they were not within the epicentre of the crisis, with the exception of Ireland. Once the international financial markets closed their doors on some countries, the growth in NPLs was almost immediate, as in the case of Hungary. The second peak occurs in 2011–13, with the great recession spreading across Italy, Ireland, Greece, Hungary, and Romania, where NPLs saw another 5%–10% increase. In exceptional cases, such as Greece and Cyprus, increases of 17%–30% were seen as the sovereign debt crisis took hold and structural adjustment policies were put in place for stabilization purposes. A further peak was experienced by Greece and Cyprus between 2013 and 2016, whereas in all the other Member States a decline in the percentage of NPLs is evident. This fourth peak in the NPL narrative is the result of the impact of the capital controls implemented in 2015 to stave off the capital flight from the country. However, the aftermath of the capital controls is the further erosion of confidence in the countries. Whereas Cyprus ultimately experienced a decline in NPLs from the heights of approximately 48% to 40% in 2016, Greece, on the other hand, saw another increase to above 45% in 2017.

4.10 The significant impact of the sovereign and banking crisis in some Member States is clear. The euro area NPLs average, albeit relatively low, was higher than that of the EU, as the euro area average grew from 2010–14, with its peak reaching approximately 7% in 2012. This is no real surprise. However, the charts equally show Member States that did experience banking crises have not necessarily encountered a significant NPL problem in comparison to those that experienced a sovereign debt problem. This is evident in Germany, France, Finland, Sweden, Netherlands, Austria, and the UK, to name a few. Here, the percentage change between 2006–17 has been relatively small at less than 5%. This trend was experienced by some Eastern European Member States as well, such as the Czech Republic and Poland. In the case of the Czech Republic, while it increased deposit coverage levels to safeguard confidence in its financial system, it avoided the need to introduce either market-based solutions or individual bank solutions.

4.11 The above data suggests that those Member States that experienced significant bank runs but not a sovereign debt crisis had less of a problem with the growth of NPLs. The idiosyncratic nature of bank failures in such jurisdictions was certainly serious and required significant state intervention, but the failures were not systemic to the point that they lost access to the international financial markets to raise funds or refinance public debt. Moreover, the state of recession was significant but not as deep as in those countries suffering a sovereign debt crisis. The Member State that is an exception to this is Italy. While Italy did not experience a significant banking crisis and avoided the need to increase deposit coverage levels simply because of its high level of deposit insurance coverage level in the first place, as was the case in France. Italy also avoided the sovereign debt crisis its counterparts experienced. In view of this, it could be concluded that the position in Italy has been purely self-inflicted through poor counterparty credit assessments. But this would be rather unfair, perhaps, since it could also be the result of the overall collapse in economic growth of the EU, leading to a deterioration in Italy's economic situation, accompanied by an exponential growth of problem loans.

A consideration highlighted linked to the advantage of the too-big-to-fail (TBTF) scenario and whether banks deemed systemically important globally or domestically abused their position to lend more freely than smaller banks. The smaller banks may be described as more cautious and less risk averse in the face of significant appetite for credit. The role of TBTF is suggested to raise the moral hazard of large banks being able to shift risks without incurring the appropriate costs to others by moving to a position where higher risk loans are taken on without the commensurate levels of capital in view of the high probability of the state to intervene to prevent it from failing. **4.12**

The ECB and EBA research indicates the opposite, that the NPL problem is more prevalent in the small- and medium-sized bank category than amongst banks with large assets.[18] The reason for this is the ability of large banks to raise capital during an economic decline to facilitate lending, something that smaller banks may not be able to do as efficiently. Notably, a large proportion of banks in the Eurozone are not listed, hence their ability to raise market finance and access a diversity of funding sources are hindered. The banks with assets sizes between €200 billion and €300 billion and above, up to €1,000 billion, reside in the largest Member States, which were least affected by the NPL problem. Moreover, the in-country picture of the NPL problem is heterogeneous, as will be shown later. The economies of scale that large banks have given them the resources and advantage to deal with the problem more efficiently than their smaller counterparts. In the latter case, smaller banks may have closer business ties with their business counterparts and may be more reluctant to write-off problem loans. **4.13**

The persistent NPL problem, rather than changes to prudential requirements, is also found to be a significant reason for the entrenchment of EU banks to their core markets and businesses. The deteriorating quality of bank assets had an adverse impact on the growth of cross-border bank activities as banks undertook a systemic process of deleveraging. The research by Emter et al[19] refers to work by Gianetti and Laeven to explain how different approaches to NPLs could be exploited to an extent that the bank group decides assets in the home market are potentially treated more favourably than assets held in foreign markets. This is further supported by ECB findings, with Emter et al concluding: **4.14**

> As domestic loans in the EU have remained above their pre-crisis level over the same period, this points to an increasing home bias (Figure 6) which supports the evidence of a 'pecking order' in banks' deleveraging in the EU as banks cut significantly their cross-border assets, while largely sheltered domestic assets (ECB, 2012).[20]

[18] M Magnus, J Deslandes, and C Dias, 'NPLs in the Banking Union Stocktaking and challenges' (European Parliament, 2018) <http://www.europarl.europa.eu/RegData/etudes/BRIE/2018/614491/IPOL_BRI(2018)614491_EN.pdf> [accessed 6 June 2019], and EBA, 'Consultation Paper: Draft Guidelines on management of non-performing and forborne exposures' (EBA/CP/2018/01, 2018), p. 85.

[19] L Emter, M Schmitz, and M Tirpák, Cross-border banking in the EU since the crisis: what is driving the great retrenchment? (ECB Working Paper, No. 2130, 2018), p. 3.

[20] Ibid, p. 5.

4.15 The above analysis highlights how the macroeconomic factors resulting from the banking and sovereign debt crisis led to an increase in NPLs. Mechanisms to address the significant NPL problems in the EU have recently been introduced; as such, it is important to assess the principle aims of these mechanisms and the extent to which they are likely to reduce the stockpile, while also considering how banks will manage them in the future. In view of the significant presence of EU foreign banks in the smaller Member States, these reforms can be reviewed from a cross-border perspective. Despite this cross-border element, it will later be questioned whether an EU level Asset Management Corporation (AMC) is the right step since the problem is acutely one of a few domestic problems that could be addressed by legal and regulatory reforms and local asset management corporations in view of the importance of local knowledge. Local knowledge would lead to approach where 'best value' is achieved at a rate that does not lead to a rate of sale leading to a collapse in market prices. The exercise of sale of non-performing loans is inherently interlink with bank knowledge about their counterparties.

4.16 Recent data provided by Raiffeisen Research indicates the level of NPLs in the Eastern European region is generally falling, with a decrease from 19% to 15% in 2015, but the variation does differ from country to country. For instance, Romania has seen its NPL levels drop from 20% to 13%, whereas in Bulgaria there has been an increase.[21] The concentration risk argument is reflected within the CEE by the high proportion of the NPLs held by foreign banks such as Intesa, Soc Gen and KBC. From a home-host perspective, the dominant role played by foreign banks in the region would suggest a strong loan growth prior to the GFC. The subsequent deleveraging is indicative of a pattern of behaviour across the EU, not one of simply being regionally specific.[22] Moreover, the presence of foreign banks may not have necessarily led to an improvement in due diligence of conduct of business and pricing of loans which assumed to be the case with foreign competitors in comparison to domestic banks. From the host Member State perspective, it could be the case that the pace of deleveraging is greater than that experienced in the home Member State (due to decisions taken in the home Member State), which would pose additional macroprudential challenges for the host. The fact that a large proportion of loans is held by foreign banks exploiting local demand may not necessarily mean a greater understanding of local markets. Therefore, the asymmetry of information between foreign and local could lead to a heterogeneity of levels of deleveraging due to the lack of both commitment and local knowledge. Moreover, the speed of deleveraging could cause an adverse selection problem in the market, preventing participants to price assets accurately in view of the fear that only the 'very bad' assets are being sold.[23]

[21] IMF Paper (above fn 15), p. 18.

[22] Robert Cull and Maria Soledad Martinez Peria, 'Foreign Bank Participation in Developing Countries: What Do We Know about the Drivers and Consequences of This Phenomenon?' (World Bank Development Research Group, Policy Research Working Paper 5398, 2010).

[23] 'Resolving Europe's NPL burden: challenges and benefits': keynote speech by Vítor Constâncio, Vice-President of the ECB, at an event entitled 'Tackling Europe's NPLs crisis: restructuring debt, reviving growth' organized by Bruegel, Brussels, 3 February 2017 <https://www.ecb.europa.eu/press/key/date/2017/html/sp170203.en.html> [accessed 6 June 2019].

The Definitional Challenges of NPLs

The definition of NPLs has been controversial in its own right, so leading to different interpretations of when a problem loan is a NPL.[24] Most interpretations of NPLs essentially focus on either failure to pay interest or principal. The modern description of determining a loan as non-performing involves the period of time the borrower has either neglected to pay the principal or interest, that is, for more than 90 days.[25] The definition of NPLs is, on the one hand, relatively straightforward in terms of the number of days the principal and/or interest is overdue. Yet, Bloem and Gorter identify a level of ambiguity that enables countries to use their interpretation which makes comparisons difficult: 4.17

> [s]ome countries use quantitative criteria (e.g., number of days overdue scheduled payments), while other countries exclusively rely on qualitative norms (such as availability of information about the client's financial status, management judgement about future payments).[26]

This highlights how the interpretation of NPLs is sensitive to the way the rules are constructed and the extent to which there is an administrative discretion to take into account quantitative and qualitative evidence when determining whether or not a loan is non-performing. If the rule is over-accommodating, it may capture loans that are problematic with sufficient evidence that payments are likely to be resumed. On the other hand, if the rule is under-accommodating, the number of loans classed as non-performing is higher, with the repercussions for the bank being a high NPL ratio that calls into question the quality of its loan book. In view of this, the definition of NPLs is likely to lead to potential conflicts of interest that both the bank and the supervisor will need to be aware of when exercising judgement about the likelihood of bank's failure. In the latter case, the supervisor may forebear to an extent that it is hoped that an economic recovery will reduce the overall number of NPLs without any formal supervisory intervention. This conflict of interest extends to the state level as well, since the number of NPLs in the economy will influence the state's credit rating. The reforms in part attempt to provide clarity of the more principles-based approach since the use of guidance and rulebooks can and should exist in such an approach.[27] The utility of a principles-based approach is its flexibility to capture behaviour that is not in line with principles but may not breach a particular rule or indeed a rule may not exist to capture such behaviour. The move towards a judgment-based approach should lead to scrutiny of the space within principles in order to enable banks to understand how NPLs are expected to be managed. This is likely to reconfigure the level of trust between banks and supervisors. 4.18

[24] European Central Bank, 'Draft guidance to banks on NPLs' (ECB, 2016); Katia D'Hulster, Raquel Letelier, and Valeria Salomao-Garcia, 'Loan classification and provisioning: Current practices in 26 countries' (World Bank Financial Sector Advisory Center (FinSAC) Overview paper, August 2014;) Roland Beck, Petr Jakubik and Anamaria Piloiu, 'NPLs What matters in addition to the economic cycle?' (ECB Working Paper Series No. 1515, 2013).

[25] Patrizia Baudino, Jacopo Orlandi, and Raihan Zamil, 'The identification and measurement of non-performing assets: a cross-country comparison' (Financial Stability Institution (FSI) Insights on Policy Implementation No, 7, 2018).

[26] Adriaan Bloem and Cornelis Gorter, 'The Treatment of Nonperforming Loans in Macroeconomic Statistics' (IMF Working Paper, WP/01/209, 2001), p. 6.

[27] See J Black, 'Forms and paradoxes of principles-based regulation' (2008) 3 CMLJ 425.

4.19 In 2014 the EBA introduced standards on supervisory reporting on forbearance and non-performing exposures. The work by the EBA has primarily been to improve supervisory consistency in the field of NPLs and NPEs. The definitions are one such attempt to improve consistency of supervisory practice in the field and build on the work of asset quality review.[28] Moving away from a situation where there are numerous country practices and indeed capacities to capture and manage data on asset quality. The capturing of accurate data improves not only supervisory but also resolution and insolvency-liquidation decision making. This is not to underestimate the preconditions for managing NPLs off the balance sheet, such as the need for efficient insolvency and bankruptcy law in order to reduce the length of time to complete such legal processes.

4.20 The adoption of a consistent definition is likely to assist both home and host supervisory authorities. A consistent definition would lead them to appreciate in a more comparable way the exposure to the NPLs at the group and individual entity level. It would enable the competent authority responsible for consolidated supervision to ask the bank to either raise capital at the group level and/or reduce NPLs in other jurisdictions. It is the case within the EU that a Member State may experience relatively low levels of NPLs in its home jurisdiction but find their banks exposed to NPLs in their foreign operations. The process will arguably improve transparency of NPLs and NPEs in the different Member States and assist supervisory authorities in deciding the kinds of measures needed to address this legacy issue. As such, theoretically, supervisory intervention is more likely to be open to assessment since it is open to comparative analysis. In an area where Member States are doing similar things but yet are so different that it leads to significant inconsistency in practices. The EBA and CRR requirements attempt to reduce the camouflage that exists by requiring banks to report at regular intervals information about NPLs and forbearance activities that are distinct from those exposures classed as impaired or in default.[29] While there is an overlap with these categorizations, the classification of impairment is at the extreme end of the spectrum. In order to manage judgements in those decisions, the bank is expected to use 'automatic triggers' to structure banks discretion and avoid a situation where differing judgements mean incomparable information within the Member State's own banking sector and at a cross-border level between Member States.

4.21 The regulation provides criteria to determine when an exposure is non-performing and how exposures can cease to be non-performing and need to be reclassified. NPLs are defined as those exposures to all classes of debt instruments that are either or both more than 90 days past-due, and the debtor is assessed as unlikely to pay its credit obligations in full without realization of collateral, regardless of the past due date. The regulation even requires banks to report separately exposures that are past due date but less than 90 days, where the bank has evidence that the debtor is unlikely to comply with their obligations. In respect of past due, it is interpreted to mean the principal or interest has not been paid

[28] EBA, 'EBA Final draft Implementing Technical Standards on Supervisory reporting on forbearance and non-performing exposures under article 99(4) of Regulation (EU) No. 575/2013' <https://eba.europa.eu/documents/10180/449824/EBA-ITS-2013-03+Final+draft+ITS+on+Forbearance+and+Non-performing+exposures.pdf/a55b9933-be43-4cae-b872-9184c90135b9> [accessed 6 June 2019].

[29] Commission Implementing Regulation (EU) No. 2017/1443 of 29 June 2017 amending Commission Implementing Regulation (EU) No. 680/2014 laying down implementing technical standards with regard to supervisory reporting of institutions according to Regulation (EU) No. 575/2013 of the European Parliament and of the Council [2017] OJ L213/1.

on the due date. The regulation requires for exposures to be assessed as non-performing either by taking a transactional approach or a debtor approach. For the latter, more than 20% of the debtor's gross exposures are classed as non-performing. The regulation also enables banks to cease the classification of loans as non-performing if the loan is no longer impaired or in default according to its criteria and, if in the bank judgement, the debtor can now pay in full or complies with modified arrangements put in place; and the debtor is no longer more than 90 days due. However, the bank does have a wide discretion in classifying exposures as non-performing when determining the debtor is 'unlikely to pay'.[30] In this case, the bank could use qualitative information about the debtor. To avoid lack of consistency in practice, the ECB advocates the use of 'automatic triggers' to move exposures between the different categories and to categorize according to changes to the debtor's creditworthiness.

The regulation also requires banks to have in place criteria to manage their non-performing exposures that are placed in forbearance measures. Non-performing exposures are placed in forbearance when the bank is of the view the exposure is unlikely to be honoured and offering some concessions will enable the debtor to continue to repay interest and/or principal. The bank needs to decide whether or not concessions are put in place and so give the debtor more time and restructure their payment obligations. Alternatively, the bank could exercise its judgement and classify the exposures as impaired or in default without opting to use these interim measures if it is convinced concessions are unlikely to work. If concessions are provided, these equally need to be reported and the impact on the classification of the non-performing exposure explained. **4.22**

The move towards structuring banks' decision-making and formalizing points for reporting is necessary to improve supervisory decision-making. However, the complexity of the decision making at the bank level means inconsistency is inevitable when classifying exposures. This requires the asset quality review process to be even deeper than before to ensure there is some consistency between Member States. For example, it could be improved by using both external and internal information to evaluate the collateral that is held against the exposures. At the Eurozone level, the significant banks, the ECB and the national competent authorities do have significant advantages to ensure consistency. In particular, the ECB guidance should assist with improving consistency amongst its Joint Supervisory Teams and on-site supervision. The centralization of decision-making is likely to assist with better understanding of cross-border exposures and ensure that discretion, albeit structured, is not applied inconsistently amongst the home and host jurisdictions. The technical capacity of supervisory authorities will need to be assessed and the sharing of information between the authorities needs to be timely and accurate. Apart from that, national competent authorities will need to enter into a dialogue with banks and provide guidance on how compliance can be ensured rather than simply rely on the prescription in the EBA Implementing Technical Standards (ITS), for example. **4.23**

From the home authority perspective, its reporting requirements will include foreign branch exposures. Therefore, at the branch level there are likely to be significant improvements of understanding cross-border exposures. Moreover, where banking groups **4.24**

[30] CRR, Art. 178(1)(a): 'The institution considers that the obligor is unlikely to pay its credit obligations to the institution, the parent undertaking or any of its subsidiaries in full, without recourse by the institution to actions such as realising security.'

have undertaken a process of branchification, it certainly highlights a significant reliance on the standards at the parent entity level to be applied across the foreign branch network. However, the real test will be when reporting subsidiaries' exposures. As shown in Chapter 1, the number of EU subsidiaries and branches does vary between Member States and in some instances, they exist in almost equal numbers. Invariably, in this case the home authority is likely to require reporting using one template for the purposes of consolidated reporting and the host-home authority could require reporting using a slightly different variant. The ECB is cognisant to this problem and requires an assessment of the reporting standards in place to determine whether they are lenient or stringent. In order to mitigate this problem, the ECB expects both to be used and reported.[31] It is hopeful then that during the process of asset quality review greater consistency could be achieved by minimizing the discrepancies between those with lenient and those with stringent reporting standards. Moreover, the level of forbearance on the part of the banks to hold out for a better bid-ask spread is likely to leave NPLs on some banks' books, thus leading to distortions in practice between home and host.

4.25 The mechanisms analysed above are an attempt to manage NPLs as they occur, with the reforms attempting to harmonize the identification of NPLs, and the opportunities to initiate forbearance measures to minimize the risks of NPLs crystallizing to a point of being written off. The primary aim of the criteria is to provide an early trigger to classify loans as non-performing and, more importantly, to then start the process of either forbearance or write-off in a more timely fashion. Indeed, if forbearance measures work, then the number of NPLs will reduce. Another mechanism to manage the risk exposures of NPLs exists in accounting and prudential requirements, namely the loan loss provision and capital adequacy. In the former, the accounting rules require banks to set aside provisions/reserves to cover the expected loss and, in the latter, adequate levels of capital to cover unexpected loss. These issues are the focus of analysis in the following section.

Loan Loss Provisions—Co-mingling the Accounting and Prudential Supervision

4.26 The management of risk of NPLs is critical for banks as they are a primary cause of bank failures.[32] To mitigate the risk of NPLs on the balance sheet, banks are required to set aside provisions to cover the expected losses Gross NPLs.[33] The analysis above has demonstrated that both external and internal factors associated with banking can change the size of NPLs to its total loans. It is likely that the number of NPLs, as was shown, will increase during an

[31] ECB, 'Draft guidance to banks on NPLs' (2016), p. 58: '[I]n the event that local standards for non-performing recognition requirements substantially diverge from the standards of Commission Implementing Regulation (EU) No 680/2014, banks will be recommended to provide reporting in both standards for internal risk management purposes.'

[32] Hennie Van Greuning and Sonja Bratanovic, 'Analyzing and managing banking risk: a framework for assessing corporate governance and financial risk management' (The World Bank, 2003); Patrizia Baudino and Hyuncheol Yun, 'FSI Insights on policy implementation No 3: Resolution of non-performing loans – policy options' (Bank for International Settlements (BIS), 2017) <https://www.bis.org/fsi/publ/insights3.pdf> [accessed 6 June 2019].

[33] David Bholat, Rosa Lastra, Sheri Markose, Andrea Miglionico, and Kallol Sen, 'NPLs: regulatory and accounting treatments of assets' (Bank of England Staff Working Paper No. 594, 2016).

economic decline. Banks with a high level of NPLs to Gross Loans would be expected to set aside higher levels of provisions to cover those expected losses if and when they materialize. Banks that are prudently managed will be able to set and build that provision up in order to cover the expected loss. The provision for expected losses will impact, nonetheless, a bank's Tier 1 capital, since the level of provision in the judgement of the banks will reduce the value of the gross loan portfolio on the asset side of the balance sheet. In view of this change, it is generally considered that the net loans value (gross loans minus loan loss provisions) on the balance sheet provides the market with information about the current value of the bank's portfolio of loans. The supervisory authority, correspondingly, will monitor the level of loan loss provision, since it is a signal of the potential riskiness of a bank balance sheet, by reviewing information from on-site and off-site inspections concerning the quality of the bank's loan portfolios and its collateral, so it can form a view about the banks resilience to withstand the impact of those loans written off. Indeed, the competent authority, as part of the credit risk adjustment powers, can request the bank to increase its provisions if, in its judgement, it is low relative to the quality of the loan portfolio and the quality of its collateral is deemed insufficient to mitigate expected losses. Notably, in the view of the competent authority, the bank could be under-estimating the size of the NPLs to avoid reducing its Tier 1 capital. Borio and Lowe explain that '[t]his pattern is a major factor driving the strongly procyclical nature of recorded bank profits'.[34] The bank may do that because the competent authority wants the bank to increase Tier 1 capital but it will be difficult to do, if it has to equally increase its loan loss provision. The market will view the increase in loan loss provision as a signal that its balance sheet is not as strong as it previously thought. Again, Borio and Lowe highlight that the credit risk is normally addressed by way of interest rates being set in accordance with the perceived riskiness of the counterparty. However, this may not be an accurate reflection of riskiness when interest rates are at historical lows and credit is readily available. Indeed, the study by Beatty and Liao[35] shows that provisioning that is too little too late exacerbates the impact of economic decline and recession.

The identification of NPLs requires robust corporate governance arrangements and internal system and controls to efficiently manage the life cycle of the loan. The management of a bank can manipulate loan loss provisioning to smooth outcome earnings in the income statement by building provisioning during profitable times and reducing those provisions over subsequent years when profits are expected to be lower. Laeven and Majnoni's[36] study explains the pro-cyclical nature of provisioning and economic performance. This, however, gives the false impression that the management of the bank are doing a good job in terms of the stewardship of the bank and acting prudentially. Similarly, Ozilia and Outab[37] highlight the ethical dilemma of smoothing or 'camouflaging' uneven earnings by the business and so providing a false impression about the strength of the business to the market. **4.27**

[34] C Borio and P Lowe, 'To provision or not to provision' (September 2001) BIS Quarterly Review, pp. 36–48, at 37.

[35] A Beatty and S Liao, 'Do delays in expected loss recognition affect banks' willingness to lend?' (2011) Journal of Accounting and Economics, Vol. 52 Issue 1, pp. 1–20.

[36] L Laeven and G Majnoni, 'Loan loss provisioning and economic slowdowns: too much, too late?' (2003), Vol. 12 No. 2, Journal of Financial Intermediation, pp. 178–97.

[37] Peterson Ozili and Erika Outab, 'Bank loan loss provisions research: a review' (2017) Vol. 17, No. 3, Borsa Istanbul Review, pp. 144–63.

4.28 Notably, the banking group could decide to smooth earnings in the home market and/or host markets to provide the impression of a stable cross-border business. Alternatively, the parent could smooth the income in the home market to avoid scrutiny by the parent supervisor, but not in host markets with weak oversight, to give the impression the fragility of the group is in foreign markets in terms of earnings, as opposed to the benign home market. A degree of mistrust of foreign bank activities may lead supervisors at the group level to expect banks to set provisions higher against their foreign bank activities. In addition to this, the lack of data to accurately provision against future NPLs in some jurisdictions, in comparison to the home, may equally lead to a situation of increasing provisioning in foreign markets, more so than in the home one. In this respect, the bank group may set the criteria for a group level provisioning strategy to capture these issues, rather than leave it to the discretion of local management and supervisors. In view of these practices, it is critical that the supervisory authorities take a consistent, judgement-based approach to ascertain the underlying rationale of the provisioning policy, which may not entirely be able to cover expected losses. However, this may not be due to home and host issues but the result of different business units performing at different rates. For example, Unicredit recently experienced a 59% reduction in trading income in the final quarter of 2018, but saw its fortunes in commercial banking improve in both its home and host Eastern European markets.[38]

4.29 The setting of loan loss provisions requires these to be in place since the approach to provisioning can be pro-cyclical or counter-cyclical.[39] The argument in the former context suggests banks are likely to increase provisions during periods of economic decline and reduce lending in view of the probability of losses and so perpetuate the current economic decline.[40] According to Borio and Lowe[41], the latter provisioning approach would increase provisioning during periods of economic growth and reduce provisions during periods of economic decline. The provisions built up during the good times can then be used to absorb the expected losses that are later charged off. The bank would then remain solvent as it has not depleted its Tier 1 capital because it was able to cover and manage the credit risk exposures. In view of these two perspectives to provisioning, competent authorities, unsurprisingly, have opted for the counter-cyclical approach since it is viewed to be more forward-looking in its approach and so should improve the resilience of the bank to future potential expected losses. It is important to note, as Ozili and Outa highlight, that this in part defeats the purpose of provisioning for loan losses, as it could distort the view of the balance sheet in the market and provisioning unnecessarily when losses are unlikely to be expected.[42]

[38] S Morris and C R Oooley, 'Italy's UniCredit posts best underlying profits in a decade', Financial Times, 7 February 2019.

[39] Luc Laeven and Giovanni Majnoni, 'Loan loss provisioning and economic slowdowns: too much too late?' (2003) 12 Journal of Financial Intermediation 178–97 <http://www.bostonfed.org/bankinfo/conevent/slowdown/laeven_majnoni.pdf> [accessed 6 June 2012].

[40] Kiridaran Kanagaretnam, Gerald Lobo, and Robert Mathieu, 'Managerial Incentives for Income Smoothing through Bank Loan Loss Provisions' (2003) 20 Review of Quantitative Finance and Accounting 63–80.

[41] C Borio and P Lowe, 'To provision or not to provision' (September 2001) BIS Quarterly Review, pp. 36–48.

[42] Peterson Ozilia and Erick Outab, 'Bank loan loss provisions research: A review' (2017) 17 Borsa Istanbul Review 133.

The GFC bought under the spotlight the accounting regime governing loan loss provisioning, with the G20 providing the mandate to rethink the accounting standards and their role in perpetuating some of the problems that surfaced during the crisis. However, it is an open debate as to whether the reforms are likely to achieve their expected benefits or rather lead to a range of unintended consequences. **4.30**

IAS 39 has been replaced by IFRS 9 which leads to a number of reforms, including loan loss provisioning. These changes signal a move away from an incurred loss model to an expected credit loss model, with the former labelled as 'backward looking' since loan losses resulting in provisions are set too late based on historical data when the impairment based on objective evidence materializes. The fragility of banks is exposed by this approach because it leads banks to provision 'too low – too late' during an adverse business-economic cycle. This is when the business-economic cycle least needs provisions to be built up by banks, as it leads to lower levels of lending and so perpetuates the cycle. In view of the lack of provisioning during periods of economic expansion for such incurred losses, profits of banks are considered to be artificially high because they do not relay the true position of the business and its earnings. Therefore, the trigger of incurred loss essentially leads to banks herding towards provisioning for losses when the market least needs the banks to do this, that is, at the point of economic decline. **4.31**

The scope of the final version of IFRS 9[43] is relatively wide, covering the business model of the bank, the classification and measurement of financial assets and liabilities, alongside how credit losses are reflected in the financial statements. The 'life of an assets' 'impairment' starts once the contract is executed. The financial asset is classified according to the bank's business model and cash flow characteristics. It is categorised as 'amortised cost', where the financial asset in a bank's business model is held for the purpose of payment of principal and interest over the life of the instrument. It is categorized as 'fair value' where financial asset in a bank's business model is held for the purpose of collecting contractual cash flows and realization of cash flows from selling financial assets. Banks are expected to apply in the following impairment of financial assets: **4.32**

- Stage 1—as soon as a financial instrument is originated or purchased, 12-month expected credit losses are recognised in profit or loss and a loss allowance is established. This serves as a proxy for the initial expectations of credit losses. For financial assets, interest revenue is calculated on the gross carrying amount (i.e. without deduction for expected credit losses).
- Stage 2—if the credit risk increases significantly and is not considered low, full lifetime expected credit losses are recognised in profit or loss. The calculation of interest revenue is the same as for Stage 1.
- Stage 3—if the credit risk of a financial asset increases to the point that it is considered credit-impaired, interest revenue is calculated based on the amortised cost (ie the gross carrying amount less the loss allowance). Financial assets in this stage will generally be assessed individually. Lifetime expected credit losses are recognized on these financial assets.[44]

[43] IFRS 9 Financial Instruments <https://www.ifrs.org/issued-standards/list-of-standards/ifrs-9-financial-instruments/> [accessed 9 June 2019].
[44] IFRS 9 Impairment.

4.33 The provisioning approach, as highlighted above, is initiated once the contract is executed and governs the life of the loan until maturity. The approach in stage 1 relies on the bank working out the expected credit loss within a 12-month period based on potential default events it identifies with the use of internal and external information. If there is a significant increase of credit risk and the probability of losses occurring is not considered low, then the loan is moved to stage 2. In stage 2, expected losses are calculated differently over the expected life of the loan and the life-time expected losses from all possible events of default that are envisaged. In stage 3, the default event has occurred and the financial instrument is classed as 'credit impaired', with the life-time expected losses recognized on the profit and loss account and the balance sheet. In view of the life time of the loan, the bank exercises forbearance measures and the loan can move back to stage 1 if the bank thinks it no longer meets criteria set in stages 2 and 3.

4.34 IFRS 9 provides a provisioning approach that is expected to be 'forward-looking', since it requires banks to forecast for potential losses significantly sooner over the maturity of the loan. It essentially means that evidence of the counterparty not likely to pay either principal or interest could trigger the need for management to start allocate provisions against the future potential losses sooner.[45] This is different from IAS 39 since banks do not have to wait for an event to account for credit losses. The expected credit loss is estimated and forecasted based on all reasonable sources of information by using both internal information about the counterparty and external information about prevailing economic conditions. This is expected to make provisioning more risk-sensitive and provide a better reflection of the market value of the loan book managed by banks. In view of this, it will be more critical for banks to improve their credit risk assessments of counterparties significantly better than in the past. The move is likely to require banks to reconsider the robustness of lending standards since they tend to decline during periods of credit expansion and increase during periods of economic contraction. As such, banks will need to have in place a more responsive approach to forecast for expected losses during periods of both economic expansion and economic contraction. This also entails the necessity for continuous evaluation of the credit quality of the loan book's portfolio.

4.35 The approach to losses by IFRS 9 and Basel III capital requirements differ, with the former relating to expected losses and the latter to unexpected ones. In many respects both are forward-looking 'life-time expected losses' and the 'through-the-cycle' and expect losses to be booked a lot sooner. However, the IFRS 9 lifetime expected loss approach is different from Basel III, with losses calculated on a 12-month basis. Both IFRS 9 and Basel III require significantly improved systems and controls to decide provisions. The degree of bank autonomy in respect of IFRS 9 and Basel III deciding provisions remains a critical area for supervisory oversight. A distinction that needs emphasizing is the banks' approach to deciding capital levels: the standardized approach or the internal risk based approach. Notably, findings by Deloitte[46] raise concerns that the impact of provisioning is not proportionate, with a more adverse impact likely materializing for the smaller banks that

[45] David Bholat et al, 'NPLs at the dawn of IFRS 9: regulatory and accounting treatment of asset quality' (2017) 19 Journal of Bank Regulation 33.

[46] Deloittes, 'A Drain on Resources? The Impact of IFRS 9 on Banking Sector Regulatory Capital' (November 2016) <https://www2.deloitte.com/content/dam/Deloitte/ch/Documents/financial-services/ch-en-fs-impact-of-ifrs-9-on-banking-sector-regulatory-capital.pdf> [accessed 7 June 2019].

apply the standardized approach, in comparison to their larger counterparts that adopt the internal ratings based approach. According to their survey, Deloitte concludes: 'On average, we expect Standardised banks to suffer twice the capital reduction of IRB peers.'[47] However, this is partly offset by the need for larger banks to hold capital buffers and manage dividend payouts.

The pro-cyclicality of provisioning has been a critical element to the debate concerning the forward-looking approach. It is open to debate as to whether IFRS 9 minimizes pro-cyclical capital levels in the short to medium term, when banks are under significant scrutiny, with stress testing scenarios requiring the building of capital, despite it being broadly difficult to raise due to the fragility of investor confidence. Domikosky[48] et al put forward the capital crunch theory to explain their support for a forward-looking provisioning approach. They argue a forward-looking provisioning approach adopted by banks that provision early should minimize capital crunch during the contraction–recession cycle. Equally, Beatty et al, using the credit crunch argument, explain how banks contract lending during periods of recession to conserve capital.[49] According to Krüger et al,[50] IFRS 9 has a negative impact on capital levels, as a counterfactual to the forward-looking approach, when banks are required to hold higher levels of capital but have high credit risk loan portfolios during an economic slowdown. In their study on IFRS 9, they find that: 4.36

> [it] would have led to a capital deduction of 1.45% during past recessions and 2.21% in the Global Financial Crisis. As banks are constrained in Tier 1 capital and required to hold even more Tier 1 capital in upcoming years, IFRS 9 and GAAP 326 are highly likely to require banks to raise additional Tier 1 capital.[51]

The decision to give all banks a five year phase-in period for IFRS 9 has increased provisions during this time without it adversely impacting on their compliance with Tier 1 capital requirements. This is perhaps a sensible decision, to offset the difficulty of increasing provisions and capital during recessionary periods.[52] The *Financial Times*, shows moves to increase provisions for expected losses from the sale of NPLs.[53] For example, Intesea Sanpaolo took the opportunity to sell bad loans worth €10.8 billion to Swedish company Intrum; UniCredit sold NPLs worth €18 billion, and Monte dei Paschi di Siena is expected to sell bad loans worth €26 billion.[54] 4.37

The introduction of IFRS 9 and the favourable supervisory treatment offered by the ECB has resulted a significant move in European banks to increase provisions by €14 billion and accelerate the management of NPLs off their balance sheets. The report in the FT explains that 'the size of provisions at some banks – particularly in Italy and Spain – has surprised 4.38

[47] Deloitte, A Drain on Resources? The Impact of IFRS 9 on Banking Sector Regulatory Capital, November (2016) p. 1.

[48] C Domikowsky, D Foos, and M Pramor, 'Loan Loss Accounting Rules and Bank Lending over the Cycle: Evidence from a Global Sample', Working Paper, Deutsche Bundesbank 2017.

[49] A Beatty and S Liao, 'Do delays in expected loss recognition affect banks' willingness to lend?' (2011), Journal of Accounting and Economics, Vol. 52 Issue 1, pp. 1–20.

[50] S Krüger, D Rösch, and H Scheule, 'The impact of loan loss provisioning on bank capital requirement' (2018) 36(C) Journal of Financial Stability 114–29.

[51] Ibid, 127.

[52] M Arnold, 'EU banks rush to "have cake and eat it" with bad loan sales', Financial Times, 23 April 2018.

[53] Ibid.

[54] Ibid.

officials at the European Central Bank, who worry they are "front-loading" losses to benefit from the favourable capital treatment'. Perhaps, the transition period sets the right incentives, particularly where a degree of flexibility is needed to address the two competing issues of increasing provisions and capital raising since both could have a negative impact on lending levels.

4.39 The discussion above has analysed the core features of the supervisory and accounting reforms. These need to be in place to address the potential adverse selection and moral hazard problems. Regarding the former, it is necessary to improve knowledge about the actual risk and price of such exposures to minimize the dangers of cherry-picking and placing only the worst kind of NPLs on the market. On the latter, the risk of shareholders and management concealing the extent of the problem by camouflaging the risk and minimize the impact on the balance sheet is a matter that the authorities need to consider in their decision making. It is crucial to emphasize the importance of the role of the supervisory authority in bringing these different strands together, seeking to improve the capacity of banks' governance, internal systems and controls to manage their NPLs' exposures. The development of consistent approaches to data and information are likely to lead to cross-country comparisons and clearer picture of this legacy issue. The move to an EU minima at 5% NPL level is likely to pose the greatest of challenges, particularly in the short and medium term, as a one-size-fits-all approach may not be suitable to such a heterogeneous position. In view of this supervisory move, it is inevitable that additional techniques are required, which are explored below.

Public and Private Mechanisms to Reduce NPLs: A Portfolio-based Approach

4.40 The techniques to deal with the removal of NPLs take a variety of forms. Primarily there are two: a 'decentralized model' of a private route to a market solution or a 'centralized model' of a public route to a market solution. A critical problem with the EU and, in particular the Eurozone, is the level of forbearance and/or lack of market for distressed debt. The forbearance arises in part with the market valuation of NPLs and the bid–ask–price at the point of sale. In view of this, states have tended to adopt their own approach to the disposal of NPLs, yet it has been inconsistent, resulting in a drag on economic growth and the provision of credit in the market. Since commercial banking is the primary form of finance in many EU Member States, it means the NPL problem needs to be addressed as efficiently as possible. As noted above, the regulatory incentives with the introduction of IFRS 9 and the reforms introduced by the ECB and EBA appear to be working, especially with the added capital requirements incentive. Despite these reforms working towards compliance with a 5% level of NPLs, it still requires additional techniques to be considered at both the private and public level. It is necessary to have a clear approach and defined roles for both the supervisory authority and the resolution authority that are sensitive to what point the bank is at in its business cycle and the extent of the NPLs at hand.

4.41 The primary goal behind the analysis of these market reforms is to address the asymmetry of information problem that NPLs create, namely, the lack of accurate pricing, giving rise to adverse selection problems and the level of forbearance leading to moral hazards stemming from risk shifting due to poor lending standards. This is acutely relevant with the advent of AMC set up by the state since the AMC will certainly influence the market's perception of its creditworthiness and its ability to sustain short-term and long-term losses and returns from the operation of the sale of assets. Indeed, the private-based solution is likely to provide some 'skin in the game', which may lead to less risk of adverse selection occurring in the newly created secondary market because of the propensity of banks to exercise 'cherry-picking' to off-load the 'very bad' loans rather than their 'less so bad' loans, which they think can be turned around in forborne measures. This, however, implicitly creates a 'good bank' and 'bad bank' scenario.

The debate about private and public means to assist with the disposal of NPLs gives rise to different competing issues for concern, such as whether private or public initiatives can achieve policy outcomes. These concerns are not new, nor are the techniques proposed, which have been adopted by various countries during a number of financial crises over the last several decades and, most notably, as a result of the GFC.[55] This has particularly been the case when countries have lacked the appropriate tools to contain a financial crisis and attempted to restructure failing or failed banks. One must wonder, to what extent is it appropriate to transfer the obligation to the state when the reforms associated with the Banking Union essentially seek to minimize the role and burden on the state? Should a sufficient amount of time be given to enable a new market for distressed debt to evolve and provide an avenue for liquidity to be created through orderly sale of NPLs? The alternative is private solutions, to transfer NPLs through the banking group itself to a designated subsidiary, which then manages the sale of said NPLs to private investment funds. Since the banks are the main culprits of the NPL problem and ultimately have better knowledge of their customers, this should be the first port of call, that is, at the self-regulatory level. It must make some sense to allow them to manage the process by reforming the supervisory, legal, and accounting environment. Indeed, another proposal is to centralize the process at the Banking Union level and set up a regional asset management vehicle. The move to centralization for the significant banks and less significant banks, in view of the fact that policy framework could evolve, would lead to consistent, proportionate treatment and a level playing field for both sets of banks. But a considerable amount of local knowledge is required for this to be executed economically which may weigh against a centralized approach. However, in order to achieve this, the regulatory, legal, and accounting environment would need to be uniform across the Member States, which is not the case at the moment. Ultimately, the moves at this juncture should be pre-resolution and pre-insolvency, classed as initiatives at the supervisory level akin to intensive supervision and part of the asset quality review process. Nevertheless, what is distinct about the EU is the introduction of significant reforms to push recapitalization and resolve problem banks. In the past, asset management corporations (AMCs) were introduced as crisis management tools to restructure banks and separate good and bad assets. In part, the asset management vehicle in EU resolution provides an enabling environment for such a technique. **4.42**

[55] Charles Enoch, Gillian Garcia, and V Sundarajan, 'Recapitalizing Banks with Public Funds: Select Issues', WP/99/139 IMF Working Paper (1999); David Woo, 'Two Approaches to Resolving Non-performing Assets During Financial Crises'(March 2000), IMF Working Paper WP/00/33; John Fell, Maciej Grodzicki, Reiner Martin, and Edward O'Brien, 'A Role for Systemic Asset Management Companies in Solving Europe's Non-Performing Loan Problems', European Economy 2017.1, pp. 71–85.

4.43 The EU context of the NPL problem raises different challenges because they are held by solvent banks that are provisioned for on the balance sheet. Moreover, a NPL is not a homogenous asset class, so one must ask which 'badly' performing loans (unlikely to pay, forborne or written off) would be transferred? How would good or bad loans be defined? Would quantitative and/or qualitative methods be applied to inform such judgements? The policy dilemma is that NPLs on the balance sheet hinder credit in the market and act as a drag on the economy. It is this issue that has given rise to the consideration of NPLs and their wholesale management off individual bank balance sheets, rather than the process of crisis containment that has traditionally spawned the set-up of AMCs as an option of last resort. In such circumstances, controversial as it sounds, portfolios of performing and non-performing assets were transferred once banks came under state control. This gives rise to competing interests between bid-ask-price and policy objectives. This section will analyse the role and function of AMCs and how they attempt to address such problems.

4.44 The European Commission Report 2018[56] explains the key features of the design and challenges concerning the establishment of an AMC. The Report is essentially the culmination of current practices and experiences of AMC's set up during the GFC. The aims and objectives of the corporation need careful consideration both in terms of aligning pre-insolvency options, resolution options and insolvency and liquidation options and maximizing returns from asset sales and recoveries. Notably, the wider the ambit of the corporation, the more complex its operational functions in terms of capitalization and funding sources. The independence of the corporation is also important in order to ensure that market rates from sales are not influenced by political factors and business relationships. In view of this, the corporation should operate at arm's length and on prevalent commercial terms in relation to corporate governance, expertise, and remuneration arrangements. The scope of the corporation is also essential to consider in terms of the volume of assets it is competent to manage and the sought of assets, retail, real estate, and/or corporate. The quality and level of data and information is a significant challenge when pricing assets and assessing the quality of collateral, which has led the Commission to introduce the concept of 'underlying long term economic value of the assets, on the basis of underlying cash flows and broader time horizons'.[57] In view of the lack of market information and price for some assets, the risk of under-pricing or over-pricing is acute. In order to address this problem, the more experienced AMCs are likely to build their own data houses based on their own (as well as what has been transferred to them) due diligence on asset quality for the purposes of valuation.

4.45 The transfer to a state AMC may provide a quick solution, but does it provide the right burden sharing incentives to banks, particularly when the moral hazard risk has crystallized once state intervention occurs? Current examples have tended to be set up for problem banks, with the primary focus to isolate the threat to financial stability, followed by the sale of problem loans—a by-product of their establishment. A concern that could be experienced by the setting up of such a public entity is itself becoming 'too big to fail' if insufficient market demand is not found by the state organ. Regardless of how the AMC is held,

[56] European Commission, Commission Staff Working Document, AMC Blueprint, Accompanying the document Communication from the Commission to the European Parliament, the European Council, The Council and the European Central Bank: Second Progress Report on the Reduction of Non-Performing Loans in Europe, Com(2018) 133 final.
[57] Ibid., p. 50.

it will remain, from both the market and public account perspective, a state corporation. That is, unless, the exposure of the state is restricted to a specific percentage and shared with other interested market participants within the distressed debt market. In view of the position of the AMC, it will need to be overseen by those in charge of the official safety net from different angles: supervisory, resolution, and crisis management vantage points. This is because the past experience with AMCs cannot be viewed in isolation—the AMC was simply one technique against a number of other crisis containment techniques administrated during the GFC. Moreover, at the time, the transfer of assets to the AMC involved both performing and NPLs, hence the high level of litigation brought by disgruntled creditors.[58] Therefore, the argument that it can be successful needs to be considered carefully in view of other techniques that improved market and economic conditions while reducing the ratio of problem loans.

The exposure to the NPLs' problems is not homogeneous across the EU, so how Member States attempt to deal with the problem at the portfolio level gives rise to different issues from a home and host perspective. Indeed, given the level of bank ownership in a number of Member States, it is important that the way it is dealt with leads to a proportionate approach that addresses the interests of the bank group as well as those of the Member State's economy. If a group-wide strategy is adopted, the home-host issues need to be considered. For example, the move to wholesale selling of portfolios to AMCs at the group level of foreign assets means the portfolio that was once owned by a regulated entity is now owned by a separate corporation that has little interest in the sale and recovery concerns of the Member State. As such, the Member State will have legitimate concerns regarding the speed with which disposal occurs and indeed the price, since it would impact on the recovery in the economy. The lack of knowledge of the local market is equally a concern, since it will be retained by the foreign bank branch or subsidiary once the portfolio of assets is sold. More pertinently, the transfer of assets will break the potential dilemma of bank forbearance associated with close business relationships, which could lead to continuous restructuring rather than writing them off. **4.46**

A coherent EU strategy would also contribute to the diversification of NPL credit risk in Member States to interested investors in other Member States that seek opportunities across borders. The development of secondary markets for NPLs would improve liquidity in the EU market and minimize the risks associated with concentration risk, which is prevalent in the EU banking market, as shown in Chapter 1. In view of this, the move to develop the secondary market, with banks taking the lead in the disposal of NPLs, is important. It has been shown how specific banks and Member States are particularly exposed to the NPL problem. This suggests that it is necessary to take both a country-specific and a bank-specific approach. **4.47**

In view of this, the one-size-fits-all approach needs to be carefully reviewed to ensure there is local capacity to undertake the task. Moreover, considering the fact that commercial bank lending in many Member States is the primary source of finance creating a new secondary market for distressed debt may take time. **4.48**

[58] *Dellway Investments & Ors v NAMA & Ors* [2011] IESC 4; Carol and John Morrissey, Plaintiffs and the National Asset Management Agency Limited, Capita Asset Services (Ireland) Limited, the Minister for Finance, Ireland, and the Attorney General [2017] IEHC 193.

Reflections on the Principal Issues

4.49 The importance of credit finance in the EU is clearly evident and with this can come the principal risk of bad debts primarily non-performing loans. It is equally evident the problem of NPLs has significantly hit some Member States more than others. Those primarily experiencing a sovereign debt crisis where specifically hit. The overall economic decline in the EU exposed others such as Italy to its own perhaps idiosyncratic NPLs problem because of its subsequent economic decline. In view of this evidence it is critical that more focus is placed on the quality of supervising institutions and ensuring internal governance mechanisms exist to minimize the growth of NPLs and now to reduce the size of the NPL problem in several Member States. The opportunity for corporate growth needs to be sustainable and the quality of the collateral and its value and forecasting for potential risks that can trigger NPLs needs to be overseen at the supervisory and corporate level. The focus at the cross-border level is consistency of practice in minimizing and managing NPL growth. In view of this the 'push and pull' factors of cross-border banking cannot be exclusively couched in the positive of exporting good practice it is evident a significant proportion of bad practice travels with equal voracity. The introduction of prudential reforms to manage at a system level bank exposure to NPLs equally requires improved conduct of business in the field of credit finance regulation and supervision.

4.50 The introduction of IFRS 9 accounting rules and its forward-looking approach complements the forward-looking approach to bank supervision that is now expected to be in place to complement risk based regulation. The move to comply with IFRS 9 is clearly a challenge for banks since in many respects there is a lack of technical expertise to fulfil the requirements of such monitoring of the loan books. In view of this bank supervision is critically important to be able to assess systems of managing loan books to assess compliance. The way IFRS 9 interacts with capital requirements and the different methods of calculating capital leads to small banks disproportionally treated by its introduction. The introduction of the five-year phase in approach is sensible and is likely to lead to more of an orderly approach to managing off NPLs rather than set off a fire sale of assets.

4.51 Finally, a principal part of the debate about NPLs is the strategy to manage the bulk of the problem should it be a public state-centred or corporate-centred approach to the managing of NPLs. In view of the supervisory perspective taken it has been argued that a combination of improved supervision and banks creating their own bad bank divisions needs to be given time. Allowing banks to manage off NPLs is not risk-free, as was shown, the potential for abuse of power needs to closely monitored by the supervisor to ensure clients are treated appropriately. It was argued that the banks have better understanding of the local knowledge but require scrutiny to ensure enough attention is placed on minimizing those risks. It is argued that the state-centred approach to deal with NPLs should be part of a wider strategy of dealing with banks in resolution and insolvency-liquidation. It is argued that more banks should be entering in this phase of the business lifecycle than is currently being experienced.

5

The EU Home and Home-Host Dilemma

The Resolution Perspective

Introduction

The challenges arising from bank failures during the global financial crisis (GFC) exposed significant asymmetry of information problems. The inability of the official safety net to differentiate between banks that could be a threat to financial stability and those that are not a threat to financial stability at the height of the crisis resulted in individual bank rescues and market-based support operations when in some cases this may not have been necessary. The EU reforms address issues of asymmetry of information by improving the preparation for resolution and introduce tools for restructuring failed banks to safeguard those banks in resolution undertaking critical functions in the financial system and within the real economy. The process of preparation *ex ante* minimizes the asymmetry of information problem by identifying banks that are important for the purposes of financial stability and so require the use of resolution options to mitigate the risks that could arise from a disorderly failure. Those banks considered not to be providing critical functions can be separated out and designated for insolvency/liquidation proceedings outside the formal resolution objectives and principles, if they were to fail. **5.1**

The efforts to execute resolution reconfigures the incentives by providing the resolution authority with the decision to decide whether a bank is failing or likely to fail and also minimizes the moral hazard problem by placing the burden on shareholders and some creditors rather than it being placed on the shoulders of states and taxpayers. The starting point is supervision and preparation for resolution to minimize hidden information problems between banks and supervisors at an early stage. The discovery of those hidden information problems at an early stage will enable the supervisory authority to assist the resolution authority. The resolution authorities require accurate information to improve their decision-making when it comes to failing banks to ensure their resources for the purposes of resolution are used only for those banks considered a threat to financial stability. More importantly this ensures the losses that accrue in the first instance are absorbed by shareholders and creditors. **5.2**

The asymmetry of information challenges faced at the domestic level are intensified when the decisions are associated with failing banks across jurisdictions. The decisions relating to cross border failures require a significant degree of coordination and cooperation to minimize adverse spillover effects both for resolution and insolvency decisions. At both the *ex-ante* preparation and *ex post* crisis management and containment level, the interplay between competing authorities and the significance of different parts of the bank group can create conflict where information between them is not complete. The focus on bank group **5.3**

European Cross-Border Banking and Banking Supervision. Dalvinder Singh, Oxford University Press (2020). © Oxford University Press.
DOI: 10.1093/oso/9780198844754.001.0001

resolution requires a serious consideration of the techniques to manage bank failures, by deconstructing the risk profile of banks and groups from the perspective of the home and host. In part the construction of the approach to resolution leads to resolution potentially falling along national lines if a strict analysis is taken in view of the level of discretion that exists within the legal instruments. The administrative powers and techniques set out in the instruments will be analysed to assess the level of administrative discretion and how that administrative discretion is likely to play out in the scenario where the home and host may or may not cooperate since their national interests may not align. The level of discretion between home and host could lead to a position where the interests of some hosts, in view of their relative exposure either at the branch or subsidiary level, may not play out in a way that properly reflects their interests or their interests are prioritized differently in view of the economic importance they represent at the group level and at the local level. In view of this a significant level of home bias can influence decisions associated with resolution both directly and indirectly. Moreover, centralized decisions exercised by the ECB and SRB can underestimate the local importance of credit finance as a critical function and so designate narrow banks in relatively smaller Member States to insolvency-liquidation.

5.4 This chapter focuses on the relationship between home and host when it comes to resolution of banks. The relationship between home and host is not a simple binary relationship where either of the interests of the two can influence outcomes. It analyses the responsibilities of each when it comes to branches and subsidiaries. This essentially leads to two potential outcomes group resolution and entity-level resolution. However, the linchpin for cooperation remains national interests which can be partly mitigated by centralization of decision-making. The role of the ECB and SRB at the centralized level can deal with coordination and timing risks in terms of announcements. This is a significant improvement and can ensure consistency of treatment. The preparation for resolution is long and complex and this is addressed in the following section on resolvability. An analysis of the underlying requirements is necessary. It is evident a significant amount of cross-border coordination and cooperation is needed to address the impediments to orderly resolution. The construction of the Minimum Requirement for Own Funds and Eligible Liabilities (MREL) and the decision about resolution strategies Single Point of Entry (SPE) or Multiple Point of Entry (MPE) are explored and it is evident who forms part of either approach gives rise to a range of questions. The resolution colleges play an important role to inform resolution decisions. However it will be shown that a significant level of discretion exists and the home resolution authority can play a role that influences the way information is shared. The ECB and SRB role in forming the decision of whether a bank is failing or likely to fail is then explored. The ability to intervene in the restructuring of banks inside resolution is specifically considered. The options for resolution are also explored in terms of their function in resolution. The chapter will show that a one-size-fits-all approach to resolution is unlikely and a multiple set of tools will be used in resolution. This is illustrated by the following section which reviews the outcomes of Member State resolution decisions notified to the EBA. It is evident the national resolution authorities have interpreted the public interest test flexibly than the SRB. The final part of the chapter will then explore the third-country perspective and the level of discretion that exists within the instruments to coordinate and cooperate. It is argued the level of discretion inevitably leads to a position where EU Member States can act in their own self-interest. Equally the SRB has entered in to various Memoranda of

Understanding (MoUs) with various third countries and indeed some accession countries. Notwithstanding these initiatives, effective preparations are still likely to fall along material risks. It is argued that reciprocal measures need to be in place so all can prepare for resolution at the group or entity level. The pre-commitment to this at least will minimize the potential conflicts that can invariably arise once a crisis ensues.

Resolution Framework and Legal Form—Branches and Subsidiaries

The legal form of banks influenceds the responsibility of the home and host competent authorities for the purposes of supervision, and resolution is no exception. In respect of the legal form of branches and subsidiaries, the Banking Recovery and Resolution Directive[1] (BRRD) determines the specific responsibilities of the home and host resolution authorities and how they are expected to cooperate and coordinate to form a coherent approach to bank-group resolution scheme and safeguard financial stability and minimize the potential risks of a systemic crisis. In view of the potential spillover effects of the financial crisis, Member States are expected to take into account the impact of their decisions at the *ex ante* and *ex post* levels on the financial stability of other Member States. More specifically, Member State authorities are expected to take into consideration the interests of other Member States, even when it is not of mutual benefit but rather in the interest of the host Member State, where it is more important than it is to the interests of the consolidated group.[2] It is important to note that in respect of subsidiaries, the host-home Member State resolution has the discretion to decide whether or not it will form an integral part of the home parent entity group resolution strategy. This will be determined by how material the parent entity group resolution authority considers the subsidiary to be. Equally important is the approach to deal with the subsidiary the home Member States has recommended for the subsidiary since the host-home may be unwilling to opt for the group strategy. But as will be shown below, the resolution authority of the subsidiary can exercise its discretion to resolve the problems at the subsidiary level in accordance with its concerns about market financial stability. This power to exercise national discretion does not exist for branches or significant branches. 5.5

To simplify and delineate clear lines of responsibility, the BRRD does set out specific functions to the home and host resolution authorities. Member States responsible for consolidated supervision are responsible for group recovery plans and recovery plans for individual incorporated institutions. Where institutions have significant branches, these would need to be incorporated into the recovery plan as well. The competent authority responsible for consolidated supervision is expected to 'transmit' what is relevant of the group recovery plan to the host competent authorities of a significant branch. This is primarily likely to be 5.6

[1] Directive 2014/59/EU of the European Parliament and of the Council of 15 May 2014 establishing a framework for the recovery and resolution of credit institutions and investment firms and amending Council Directive 82/891/EEC, and Directives 2001/24/EC, 2002/47/EC, 2004/25/EC, 2005/56/EC, 2007/36/EC, 2011/35/EU, 2012/30/EU and 2013/36/EU, and Regulations (EU) No. 1093/2010 and (EU) No. 648/2012, of the European Parliament and of the Council [2013] OJ L173/90 (BRRD), Recital 102.

[2] BRRD, Recital 132; Art. 87.

information regarding the continuity of intra-group finance or alternative forms of finance from the parent to the significant branch. In respect of subsidiaries, either a group recovery plan or an individual recovery plan may require such information about intra-group financial support. In view of the earlier finding, it is evident a significant proportion of subsidiary finance is locally sourced in foreign markets but it is nevertheless important that intra-group and interbank finance is understood to ensure the risks of a liquidity shortage can be mitigated. From the perspective of the resolution authority, the commitment to draw up resolution plans is to liaise with their counterparts responsible for subsidiaries and those responsible for significant branches. Significant branches will fall within the parent entity recovery and resolution plan, but in view of their significance in the host Member State it would be important for the host to be aware of what is likely to happen in resolution to the parent in view of its impact on the significant branch. For foreign banks with ultimate foreign parents in a third country, the sub-group in a Member State will be required to draw up a resolution plan for the European part of the group. In terms of information-sharing, the commitment is to share what is relevant to the respective entity,[3] for instance in relation to assessment of impediments to resolvability.[4] It will be important to evaluate how this discretion power is interpreted. The BRRD requires Member States to give effect to transfer orders relating to instruments of ownership, assets, rights, and liabilities from other Member States.[5] Member States are required to provide all reasonable assistance to ensure compliance with such orders. Member States 'are not entitled to prevent, challenge, or set aside the transfer under any provision of the law of the Member State where the assets are located or of the law governing the shares, other instruments of ownership, rights or liabilities'.[6]

5.7 The presence of branches and subsidiaries in a foreign Member State confers specific obligations on the host and host-home authority for the purposes of crisis management assistance. It acutely highlights the fragmented nature the group can appear to have, despite operating as a single economic entity from business and operational perspectives. This requirement means at some levels that crises within a group and sub-group structure can be isolated at the local level rather than at the ultimate risk basis at the highest level of the group as set out earlier in Chapter 1. The implications of this approach mean that at the host and home-host level a problem at the branch and subsidiary level could be contained by the local competent and central bank authorities. At the pre-insolvency period, in terms of precautionary recapitalization or emergency liquidity assistance, this falls within the national administrative discretion of the national authorities and is left to their opinion of the seriousness of the circumstances.[7] In view of this, Member State authorities need to take seriously their commitment to cooperate and coordinate their efforts to contain a crisis and minimize its spillover effects in to other interconnected markets. It also means the national authorities at the ultimate risk basis could possibly minimize their exposure or indeed show their commitment to the parent entity, therefore highlighting the importance of *ex ante* commitments to such efforts if circumstances arose.

[3] BRRD, Art. 13(1).
[4] BRRD, Art. 15(1), Art. 17(1).
[5] BRRD, Art. 64(1)(a)–(f).
[6] BRRD, Art. 66(3).
[7] See Chapter 7, 'The EU Mechanisms of Financial Crisis Management and Containment: Decentralized and Centralized Approaches'.

The material importance of the branch and subsidiary in the local market is a key determinant of such assistance being provided. It equally highlights the material importance of the branch or subsidiary to the group as well, which could step in to refinance the business. Financial support via intra-group arrangements between the parent or other subsidiaries within the group can be formally agreed *ex ante* and act as a first order line of defence if the entity is experiencing liquidity problems.[8] The requests could come either downstream, upstream or even side-stream between the different entities within the group. The relevant point here is the fact that the competent authority at the consolidated supervisory level or even at the entity level could prohibit or restrict such financing requests to ensure it does not jeopardize liquidity position of the provider. **5.8**

Resolvability and the Minimum Required Eligible Liabilities

The focus on resolvability of the institution or group, from the perspective of the BRRD, is very much tied to the process of supervision and resolution in a continuum across national lines.[9] The assessment of resolvability needs to be made based on the criteria set out in the Annex Section C of BRRD. The assumption that there is no extraordinary support, central bank emergency liquidity assistance or liquidity assistance on the basis of non-standard forms of collateral is incorporated in evaluating whether the institution or group is resolvable.[10] In the context of groups, the supervisory college and the resolution college play a crucial role in determining the best way to overcome impediments at a cross-border level.[11] The competent authorities and resolution authorities can require changes in the business organization of an institution or group to resolve impediments, such as addressing the level of large exposures or divesture of assets or business lines, new or old.[12] Moreover, the competent authority or resolution authority could require the institution or group to make changes to its own funds and/or liabilities to improve the level of eligible instruments for conversion or write-down.[13] **5.9**

The introduction of MREL into the resolvability assessment of banks has been an important addition to the process of assessing the options for resolution and the chances of recapitalization in periods of distress.[14] The EBA published in 2016 its report mandated by the BRRD on the implementation of MREL looking at the different challenges that exist with its adoption.[15] In many respects the introduction of MREL provides the tools for the resolution authority to work with institutions it is responsible for on a more continuous basis. In contrast to perhaps the more annual process of resolution planning **5.10**

8 See Chapter 3, 'The EU Home and Home-Host Dilemma: The Prudential Supervisory Perspective', para. 3.36.

9 BRRD, Art. 15.

10 BRRD, Arts 15(1)(a)–(c) and 16(a)–(c).

11 BRRD, Arts 16(2) and 17.

12 BRRD, Art. 18.

13 BRRD, Arts 17 and 18.

14 SRMR, Recital 84; BRRD.

15 EBA, Final Report on MREL: Report on the implementation and design of the MREL framework, EBA-Op-2016, 14 December 2016 (EBA MREL Report 2016). Cf Tröger and Hans, 'Why MREL Won't Help Much' (21 August 2017), Journal of Banking Regulation Vol. 20, 2019, Forthcoming; SAFE Working Paper No. 180; European Banking Institute Working Paper No. 13. Available at SSRN: <https://ssrn.com/abstract=3023185> or <http://dx.doi.org/10.2139/ssrn.3023185>.

and in addition to working with firms that have failed and are moved to resolution or insolvency. Requiring the resolution authority to work with the other parts of the crisis management official safety net players. The development of loss absorbing (MREL or total loss-absorbing capacity (TLAC)) requirements replicates in some ways the move towards introducing common capital requirements at the international level. In this respect the international and regional focus needs to be on creating a level playing field and ensuring the rules associated with loss absorbing capacity are proportionate between large 'complex' and small 'narrow' banks, but equally important for those included in the single point of entry and multiple point of entry resolution strategy. Indeed the Single Resolution Mechanism Regulation (SRMR) goes as far to highlight the importance of loss absorbing capacity to be located across the group rather than what is advocated at the international level of it being centralised in a single location.[16] The EBA report notes that the expectation would be coordinated with the resolution authority for the entity to pass on the losses that would be absorbed by the resolution entity.[17] In view of this resolution, authorities need to develop the capacity to undertake the various responsibilities conferred to them to act as a line of defence and minimize the disruption of not having a sufficient amount of loss-absorbing capacity to prevent a disorderly resolution. This also extends the responsibility of the resolution authority and would need to be complemented to include the authority to take administrative enforcement actions against individual banks for breach of loss-absorbing requirements.[18] This would offer middle ground sanctions rather than relying on the threat of triggering whether the bank is failing or likely to fail.

5.11 The MREL requirements form the basis of internal financial resources to absorb losses and, by deciding which options are likely to be utilized in a given stress scenario, to recapitalize the institution.[19] In this respect, capital requirements are outward-facing and do form the basis of the external cushion for absorbing losses, whereas the MREL are seen as internally facing and form the basis of an internal cushion for absorbing losses by utilizing funds for recapitalization. In the former case, capital requirements form the basis of a going concern scenario and, in the latter case, MREL requirements form the basis of a gone concern scenario and the likely options for recapitalization.[20] The challenge for institutions is whether they have such internal own funds and eligible liabilities to form the basis of finance to recapitalize the bank.[21] What impact will compliance with the MREL requirements have on the business model in these jurisdictions? Is there sufficient discretion with the resolution authority to enable existing externally facing capital requirements to form the basis of internal MREL? In this respect, the competent and resolution authorities need to align their efforts to ensure banks are not moving to a position of doubling on own funds and eligible liabilities and reducing the level of finance they can utilize in the market.[22] These matters are important because they also influence decisions associated with the use of the resolution fund (RF) and the deposits guarantees scheme (DGS) during

16 SRMR, Recital 84.
17 EBA MREL Report 2016, p. 9.
18 BRRD, Art. 17(5)(i) and Art. 17(5)(j); See EBA MREL Report 2016, pp. 91–9.
19 EBA MREL Report 2016.
20 EBA MREL Report 2016, p. 86.
21 EBA MREL Report 2016, at pp. 82–3.
22 EBA MREL Report 2016, at p. 111.

the resolution process, since their roles are factored into the assessment of resolvability for the purposes of setting the MREL.

The MREL requirements are premised on a broad and, in some respects, ambiguous idea of determining the amount of loss-absorbing capacity of the bank.[23] In this respect, the resolution authority is required to take into account the supervisor's decision on how it has gone about setting capital requirements for the bank.[24] It has to ensure that the bank complies with CRD IV and CRR requirements: 5.12

(1) own funds requirements:
   (a) CET 1 capital ratio of 4.5% of the total risk exposure amount;
   (b) Tier 1 capital ratio of 6% of the total risk exposure amount;
   (c) a total capital ratio of 8% of the total risk exposure amount;
(2) requirements to hold additional own funds in excess of the requirements above;
(3) combined buffer requirements;
(4) the Basel I floor; and
(5) applicable leverage ratio.

In light of these supervisory requirements, the resolution authority takes into consideration (1), (2), and (3) and in some circumstances, (4) and (5). Therefore, the MREL requirements are negotiated between the bank and the resolution authority. Moreover, the resolution authority is expected to exclude those liabilities that are not eligible for bail-in. The calculation of loss-absorbing capital is, therefore, likely to be made up of both regulatory capital and set levels of capital buffers, namely the systemic risk buffer and the counter-cyclical buffer. The level of loss absorption is likely to lead to a position where the bank is compliant with regulatory capital levels at the minimum, or even above, but that does not necessarily imply it will be recapitalized to the same level as before, maintaining, in this way, its G-SII or O-SII position. For it to retain such a position, the level of loss-absorbing capacity is likely to be extremely high which is not likely to be the aim of the resolution authority. 5.13

The complexity of setting the MREL therefore requires very close cooperation between the supervisory authority and the resolution authority to avoid a position of what the industry refers to as doubling capital requirements, since it gives rise to an overlapping mandate between the two authorities in this process. The asymmetry of information between the two authorities means they need to work closely together in setting the MREL. In light of this fact, many of the banks in these jurisdictions weathered the GFC reasonably unscathed. Recital 8 of the MREL highlights an important principle that should influence these decisions: 'Resolution authorities should set MREL consistently with those arrangements where they are integral to the institution or group's preferred resolution strategy'.[25] This principle improves the level of buy-in to the move that introduces these reforms and improves the 5.14

[23] Commission Delegated Regulation (EU) 2016/1450 of 23 May 2016 supplementing Directive 2014/59/EU of the European Parliament and of the Council with regard to regulatory technical standards specifying the criteria relating to the methodology for setting the minimum requirement for own funds and eligible liabilities [2016] OJ L237/1.

[24] Delegated Regulation 2016/1450 Art. 1.

[25] Commission Delegated Regulation (EU) 2016/1450 of 23 May 2016 supplementing Directive 2014/59/EU of the European Parliament and of the Council with regard to regulatory technical standards specifying the criteria relating to the methodology for setting the minimum requirement for own funds and eligible liabilities [2016] OJ L237/1.

outcomes by fitting existing business and funding models rather than it being transposed from above with little regard of the idiosyncratic features of the business. However, as noted in different parts of the report, it would be appropriate for the group resolution authority and the other resolution authorities to be informed of how the MREL will be set. If it is simply going to involve only those members of the resolution college with significant interests to the group, then a number of Member States are unlikely to be involved in how it is calculated.

5.15 The resolution authority is expected to decide the amount of loss absorbance expected to fulfil the resolution options decided by the bank.[26] In this decision, it could be decided that the bank is not expected to hold additional capital for the MREL, namely for recapitalization purposes, since the option in resolution is insolvency. Alternatively, the resolution authority has the discretion to argue that insolvency is not the appropriate option in the public interest and, therefore, requires an amount of capital for recapitalization purposes. This decision is likely to be made on the bank's assessment of its business operations. It depends on whether the bank undertakes business lines that are deemed critical by the supervisory authority in terms of their importance and lack of substitutability and perhaps the level of market concentration it could result in if critical functions formed part of a private sector sale to a direct competitor. The resolution authority then needs to assess the costs of implementing the resolution option and decide the level of contribution to achieve that resolution option the bank is expected to make to execute it. In setting the amount the resolution authority is expected to factor in the level of additional support, the bank would need to return it in compliance with regulatory capital requirements as well as supporting the intended resolution option to safeguard the continuity of the critical functions the bank undertakes. The resolution authority is expected to assess the feasibility of complying with the MREL from the perspective of the bank, but also the credibility of achieving the intended outcomes in order to maintain market confidence.

5.16 The decision to set the MREL by the resolution authority will differ on whether it is the group-wide resolution authority or the resolution authority of an individual subsidiary; more specifically, whether the resolution strategy is likely to be a SPE or an MPE or a combination of both a SPE and an MPE during resolution.[27] In this scenario, the group-wide decision on recapitalization is likely to lead to greater economies of scale and, therefore, lower levels of loss-absorbing funds, whereas the alternative is likely to mean higher or even no loss-absorbing funds at the local level. The important policy point here is that there is no uncertainty as to the options taken, even if it is a combination of a SPE and an MPE, as long as the local resolution authority is able to set the MREL adequate for the local operations to achieve the desired resolution option set for the bank to safeguard local critical functions. From the group resolution perspective, while resolution options may be set out for the group as a whole to safeguard critical functions, it could be the case that peripheral banks have been designated for insolvency-liquidation. At the local level this is not likely to get much support, hence, the need to have both options of SPE and MPE at their disposal with options set out to achieve both ends. This point is given more emphasis in light of the fact that Member States have exercised their discretion to classify subsidiaries in their

[26] EBA MREL Report 2016, at p. 63.
[27] See section Single Point of Entry and Multiple Point of Entry Resolution, para 5.22.

market as O-SIIs for the purposes of countercyclical and systemic risk buffers. It is therefore important that this flows to other parts of micro-prudential decision-making as well, such as setting MREL and the contribution to loss-absorbing capacity. For the purposes of group MREL, it is important that the third country can contribute to the level set and also know whether the level of loss absorbency would cover subsidiaries in its jurisdiction as well. However, the draft technical standard is silent on the third country position. The resolution authority of a Member State should exercise their discretion to formally include entities in third countries to ensure a more orderly group resolution taking into account local entities as well or at least enabling them to decide for themselves the options most appropriate for their local needs.

The setting of the MREL incorporates the role of the RF[28] and the DGS in the decision-making process.[29] This is at two levels: 5.17

(1) First, at the resolution level and the extent to which the criteria for resolution support is achieved by the conversion or write down of at least 8% of eligible own funds and liabilities. In this respect, therefore, as a minimum, the MREL do exist in the form of the obligation to have sufficient own funds and liabilities for the purposes of recapitalization to access the resolution fund.
(2) Secondly, at the insolvency level, with the factoring in of DGS support if losses to covered deposits ensued and payment from the DGS is executed.

The opportunity to stress test the banking system and the likelihood of requiring this support from both ends enables the resolution authority to gauge the level of the MREL at the market level as well as the institutional level. Taking into consideration the point that the RF and the DGF are exhausted if the Member State was to experience a multiple bank failure, in the case of the DGS, as argued in Chapter 6,[30] the level of contribution expected to be provided in real time is likely to open up an expectations gap considering its limited purpose in a systemic crisis or a crisis where there was a multiple bank failure. In such circumstances, the lack of a sufficiently funded resolution and deposit guarantee fund means government intervention is inevitable.[31] The outcome of such an exercise is useful to gauge the level of support necessary to enable an orderly resolution or insolvency. However, it is important to also consider the position that it may be unlikely as well that these funds would be needed for large complex banks that have other business lines which could be sold to cover such exposures. Therefore, the reliance on them would be very much a last resort for such institutions in the category of Global Systemically Important Institutions (G-SII) or Other Systemically Important Institution (O-SII). In such circumstances, it is unlikely they would be depleted of own funds and liabilities for the purposes of recapitalization. The discretion will be with the supervisory authority to determine whether authorization requirements continue to be fulfilled.[32] 5.18

The differing mandates of supervision and resolution may need to be worked out in advance to minimize conflicts of interests and align their mandates. In part this is challenged by 5.19

[28] EBA MREL Report 2016, at p. 130.
[29] EBA MREL Report 2016, at p. 129.
[30] Chapter 6, European Bank Insolvency and Liquidation Proceedings.
[31] EBA MREL Report 2016, at 139.
[32] EBA MREL Report 2016, at pp. 70 and 92.

the political willingness to move banks into insolvency rather than resolution. Invariably the process of structuring administrative oversight of this space will take a considerable amount of effort just as it did with capital requirements and the recent emphasis on liquidity requirements. An important element that will complement resolution authorities in this area is disclosure as another monitoring and policing mechanism. The market should be able to play a role to ensure the levels of loss absorbing at individual banks are fit for purpose, which can only be assured if banks explain their strategy to improve their loss-absorbing capacity. According to S&P Global, the greater visibility of such requirements can contribute to improving the credit rating of banks, so providing a positive incentive to improving its visibility and levels of market confidence.[33] A lack of transparency is likely to lead to asymmetry of information problems that could lead to undermining confidence in the individual bank or indeed the sector. The role of enforcement powers for non-compliance is equally important, providing the resolution authority with a set of powers if a breach of compliance is identified.

5.20 An inevitable challenge of looking at the composition of the balance sheet of a bank in a variety of ways is the problems associated with such a perspective. Moreover, the level of heterogeneity within the banking system of the EU highlights that a single approach is less likely to be effective or proportionate and so requires a significant degree of discretion at the local level. A need exists to ensure small and medium size banks do not issue bail-in-able instruments to retail customers which is common in the sector.[34] A recognition of narrow banks can equally provide critical functions such as credit finance in the market. Therefore, if the national designated authority considers institutions systemically important and requiring additional capital buffers then they also need to be considered more seriously as candidates for resolution rather than insolvency. Since the critical functions they provide in the real economy are not substitutable, for instance, then insolvency-liquidation may not be the appropriate solution. Unless techniques of insolvency consist of tools present in resolution. For instance, the Italian Compulsory Liquidation Regime, referred to in Chapter 6, used for the two banks from the Veneto region.[35]

Single Point of Entry and Multiple Point of Entry Resolution

5.21 The centralization of resolution decision-making is a significant move towards diminishing the incentives of Member States to resolve groups and/or institutions across national lines and in their own interests. This is formally achieved at the Eurozone level where participating Member States of significant banks in the capacity of home and host will have the Board to undertake resolution at the group level and so technically reduce the incentives of home bias within the SRM. The view of the Financial Stability Board (FSB) is that there is

[33] S&P Global Ratings, 'Proposals for EU Banks' Bail-in Buffer could lead to broader ALAC Rating Uplift' (August 2016).

[34] EACB Comments on EBA Public Consultation on 'Interim report on the implementation and design of the minimum requirement for own funds and eligible liabilities (MREL) 30 August 2016, p. 7.

[35] See Chapter 6, European Bank Insolvency and Liquidation Proceedings, para. 6.40.

no one-size-fits-all approach and it is perfectly feasible for both approaches to be used simultaneously and result in an orderly resolution.[36]

The SPE model assumes resolution will be initiated by the group resolution authority at the group parent level or at the holding company level. In order to execute this, a number of key requirements need to be in place or at least worked out *ex ante*. First, the parent and/or the holding company needs to have in place the appropriate amount of loss-absorbing capacity (LAC) and a pre-commitment that it will be accessible to important subsidiaries in pre-identified host states. In this model, the large proportion of the LAC is at the parent level or holding company level and if such a subsidiary experiences a loss those losses are upstreamed and absorbed by the parent or holding company, either as a whole or partially. The parent or the holding company is committed to downstream capital and liquidity for the subsidiary to enable it to continue as a going concern or enable further restructuring. Since it is likely to be part of a resolution strategy, the other parts of the resolution may well include the other tools in the resolution tool kit, namely bail-in, bridge bank, and asset separation. The challenge for an SPE approach is that the group level resolution authority needs to be well prepared to ensure full coordination and cooperation and indeed confidence and trust among the different states and minimize impediments to resolution. **5.22**

The MPE assumes resolution of a banking group will be initiated by a number of national resolution authorities. The combination may well be the group resolution authority and/or one or two other national resolution authorities. In terms of the LAC, it will need to be in place at various points within the group. It is expected that the LAC exists in sufficient amounts at the entity level. The subsidiary needs to be self-reliant on a number of levels. In particular, the national resolution authorities will need to ensure continuity of support services, such as IT services, to the entity to ensure it can continue its critical functions. These critical functions are primarily for the purposes of the domestic market and so the resolution scheme is expected to be aimed at ensuring financial stability at the local level. The challenge for the MPE approach from a coordination and cooperation perspective is greater from a cross-border perspective than that for the SPE. In view of this it is argued the MPE strategy cannot be assumed to be one of liquidation but rather a separate resolution technique such as sale of business or asset separation in addition to the SPE for the parent entity and the most material entities of the group to safeguard local critical functions. Even in circumstances where a SPE has been executed, additional measures to recapitalise the parent entity may still be purposed leading to the sale of business technique *ex post*. **5.23**

Implicit in the SRB's role as group resolution authority will be the benefit of the home Member States and those hosts that are participating Member States where important subsidiaries are located. Mindful of this, the Board is likely to want to assess, when devising resolution plans, whether or not a SPE approach or a MPE is needed to ensure orderly resolution. The Board is likely to want the quickest and most orderly outcome that will enable it to maximise **5.24**

[36] See Jeremy Jennings-Mares, Anna T Pinedo, and Oliver Ireland, 'The Single Point of Entry Approach to Bank Resolution' in Jens-Henrich Binder and Dalvinder Singh (eds), Bank Resolution: The European Regime (Oxford: Oxford University Press, 2016) para 14.11. See also Costanza A Russo, 'Resolution Plans and Resolution Strategies: Do They Make G-SIBs Resolvable and Avoid Ring Fence?' European Business Organization Law Review (2019) pp. 1–43.

coordination as the group resolution authority to the widest extent possible. This can be achieved by addressing the most significant parts of the group, but it implies that those on the 'periphery' are likely to be outside this single scheme with the assumption that insolvency is the likely option. However, the issue with this option is that it fails to consider the importance those entities on the 'periphery' have to the host Member State. An SPE approach is likely to be preferred where there is a joint decision amongst the majority of the home and host Member States. However, where a joint decision is not likely, an MPE approach is likely to be the outcome as well which will mean parts of the resolution coordination remain with some participating or non-participating Member States, since there will still be a risk that a Member State is not satisfied with the outcome of the SPE resolution set out in the resolution scheme. In light of this, it is important for the home state to put in place the right incentives for a particular approach or indeed a combination of approaches. However, this section will consider the implications for those small host states where a significant subsidiary is incorporated.

5.25 The fact that the national authorities are expected to have sufficient levels of local capital and liquidity and LAC means that the national resolution authorities will still need to work with the group level resolution authority to work out the level of capital and liquidity the former expects the bank to have. If the subsidiary is not significant for the group but it is to the host state, then there is a possibility the host state has not been given access to the group resolution plan. In many respects, this leads to further moves towards an MPE approach. The move away from centralized to decentralized capital and liquidity oversight means the cost of business can be higher for the local subsidiary since there is no advantage from the pooled financial resources as it is not able to exploit the economies of scale of a centralized treasury function. The level of host state confidence needs to be gauged where the parent entity has important subsidiary operations, as the incentives are more aligned to cooperate and coordinate for a SPE approach.

5.26 A recognition of this challenge is also highlighted by the incentives to decide whether or not the group resolution authority considers it best to adopt an SPE or MPE approach. In many ways, the former places significant importance on the group resolution authority which is also going to be the lead consolidated supervisor so ultimately the home state for the parent entity. The latter is likely to be the option where a joint decision amongst the participating Member States and non-participating Member States and those third countries is unlikely. In their case, they may consider the former is not likely to serve their interests and so opt for resolution that serves their particular circumstances, therefore, leading to multiple points of entry for the purposes of resolution. The circumstances surrounding membership of resolution colleges and the lack of reciprocal information sharing leads to a position where the MPE approach is more likely for the small host states with significant subsidiaries.

5.27 The asymmetry of information between some Member States due to their position in terms of group entities means that, for those at the periphery of the core part of the group which is less systemic for the purposes of the group and the home state parent, there is little alternative for such host states but to organise resolution in accordance with national interests which, therefore, leads to an MPE approach. However, it is important for such hosts to be able to ensure *ex ante* that with the appropriate measures in place, in terms of capital and liquidity, there is sufficient loss-absorbing capacity to provide the kind of buffer necessary for an orderly resolution of local interests. In view of this, *ex ante* MPE is similar to the *ex post* decision to ringfence to protect the local interests.

The Resolution Colleges

The SRM highlights the importance of cooperation within the SRM and with non-participating Member States and third countries.[37] However, it does not offer much in the way of clarifying how the SRB will lead resolution colleges as the group resolution authority for the banks it is responsible for. Therefore, specific reliance needs to be given to the BRRD for clarification and directions as well as to the EBA's draft guidelines for the role of the group resolution authority and resolution colleges.[38] As with the SSM and the role of the ECB, and here with the role of the SRB, it is rather surprising that little is mentioned of the respective supervisory and resolution colleges[39] since they are such a crucial vehicle for coordination and cooperation among the Member States and third countries. The focus on the group and the 'material' subsidiaries implies that a number of Member States at the 'periphery' are members of the resolution college albeit may not be privy to the information within core resolution college. **5.28**

The BRRD requires the establishment of resolution colleges for groups that operate within the EU.[40] The rationale of such colleges is necessary to ensure an appropriate platform for consultation between the respective authorities, both at the crisis prevention level and the crisis management level. The consideration of the recovery and resolution plans is the first matter to be settled. Those plans will be an important basis on which to assess the resolvability of groups and possible impediments to orderly resolution.[41] The selection of competent and resolution authorities as members of the resolution colleges is perhaps a rather contentious matter with the resolution authority for the group taking a lead role over other members selected where subsidiaries and significant branches are located. The level of cooperation and coordination required seeks to minimize the impact of such decisions on the markets and the wider financial and economic stability.[42] While the written arrangements within the EU provide the basis for an *ex ante* understanding of how the resolution of the group is likely to be executed with the objectives, conditions, and principles in mind, the matter of who is and who is not a member of the resolution college could pose challenges in terms of the timing of decision-making and those in the non-core part of the resolution college respecting the decisions of the lead resolution authority for the purposes of leading the resolution for the group.[43] Despite the fact that the membership criteria are indicated,[44] **5.29**

37 SRMR, Art. 31 and Art. 32.

38 Commission Delegated Regulation (EU) 2016/1075 of 23 March 2016 supplementing Directive 2014/59/EU of the European Parliament and of the Council with regard to regulatory technical standards specifying the content of recovery plans, resolution plans and group resolution plans, the minimum criteria that the competent authority is to assess as regards recovery plans and group recovery plans, the conditions for group financial support, the requirements for independent valuers, the contractual recognition of write-down and conversion powers, the procedures and contents of notification requirements and of notice of suspension and the operational functioning of the resolution colleges.

39 SRMR Recital 91 and Art. 33(2)(b).

40 BRRD, Recital 15; Art. 88(1)(a)–(i).

41 BRRD, Recital 17; Art. 13.

42 BRRD, Recitals 33 and 96.

43 BRRD, Recital 97.

44 BRRD, Art. 88(2)(a)–(h).

the directive leaves it to the lead resolution authority to decide which members to invite to attend a given meeting.

5.30 A special regime applies to cross-border groups with principal business activities in a third country and with a European presence in the form of a subsidiary or significant branches.[45] In this type of case, the competent authority and resolution authority for those entities will need to set up a European resolution college. The authority of the host Member State where a subsidiary or group holding company is located will take responsibility for it as group resolution authority. However, if those institutions are located by way of branches, then it is likely that the resolution authority of the significant branch will take responsibility and co-ordinate the organization of the European resolution college.

5.31 A crucial element in the cooperation between Member States themselves, as well as between third countries, is information exchange.[46] In this respect, the institution's or group's consolidated supervisor and the resolution authority are responsible for ensuring relevant information is exchanged between the respective authorities. In order to prevent the creation of panic amongst the Member States, resulting in disjointed responses, the information exchange needs to be timely. In this respect, consent is required for the onward sharing of information. In such cases, resolution authorities will be expected to provide their EU counterparts with 'all the relevant information in a timely manner';[47] and in respect to third countries, the resolution authority must seek the consent of the third country's resolution authority for the onward transmission of that information.[48] The consent is unlikely to be always forthcoming unless the information is heavily redacted.

5.32 Member States with different levels of exposure and interests located within them can pose considerable challenges for the lead resolution authority in terms of managing expectations of their counterparts. This risk could arise where a subsidiary of the group is placed in resolution by its resolution authority. In this case, the relevant resolution authority will be required to notify the group-level resolution authority and the members of the resolution college. In such a case, the group resolution authority is expected to assess the impact of the decision on the group as a whole.[49] After the assessment at group level, the resolution authority will be expected to provide a group resolution scheme and share it with the resolution members within 24 hours or a longer period, depending on what was agreed.[50] If the group-level resolution authority has not initiated a resolution scheme within that timeframe, then the resolution authority for the subsidiary can continue with its resolution actions. In such circumstances, the EBA is expected to mediate in order for national resolution authorities to come to a joint decision.[51] Irrespective of the consensus-based approach, the BRRD does envisage disagreements amongst Member States. In those cases, the dissenting resolution authority need to identify the reasons for not following the group-level resolution authority and the resolution plan, which it must then circulate amongst the other resolution authorities.[52] The resolution authorities in such circumstances are still

45 BRRD, Recital 101, Art. 89.
46 BRRD, Art. 90.
47 BRRD, Art. 90(2).
48 BRRD, Art. 90(3).
49 BRRD, Art. 91.
50 BRRD, Art. 91(4).
51 BRRD, Art. 91(7).
52 BRRD, Art. 91(8).

required to cooperate closely and inform the resolution college about the measures they are taking to coordinate their efforts at the group level.[53] A number of similar measures apply to the group-level resolution authority responsible for the parent undertaking of the group. However, the extent to which the group resolution scheme includes all parts of the group and the parent essentially depends on the extent of the problem and whether it is likely to impact other parts of the group after determining whether the parent and/or other parts of the group are failing or likely to failure.[54] The resolution authorities responsible for the different parts of the group will also need to determine whether to follow the resolution scheme and so act jointly, or whether to act separately but still inform the other resolution authorities of the actions taken.[55] The BRRD requires that a resolution authority, which decides to act independently, must notify the group-level resolution authority and other resolution authorities and provide reasons for the departure.

The issues highlighted explore a number of underlying sets of assumptions and incentives which suggest resolution coordination could remain a challenge and lead to a misalignment of incentives if they are not addressed effectively. The EBA does take a monitoring role to assess their work.[56] The lead taken by the group resolution authority to invite members and observers provides the group resolution authority with a significant amount of discretion as to which members and observers to invite. The resolution college's technical standards set out the important areas featured in a coherent resolution framework, namely coordination and cooperation at the crisis prevention and at the crisis management stage. The identification of members and observers is an area that is quite contentious since it provides the very basis of who can contribute to the dialogue and decision-making process and ultimately benefit from the reporting and decisions for oversight of their respective banking and financial system. The underlying assumption is that membership is almost automatic based on the general criteria provided, but that is not the case in practice. The group resolution authority primarily decides and other members closer to the interests of the group resolution authority can influence its decision as well. The group resolution authority will also invite observers to participate in the resolution colleges and in most cases this is likely to be those third countries with large exposures to the parent or holding company. While their ability to contribute formally is limited, that could differ from one resolution college to another since the group resolution authority has the discretion to set specific terms and conditions for observers. While resolution colleges can allow other members of an official safety net onto the resolution colleges as observers, in practice, this was not really taken up by other parts that did not either have supervisory or resolution responsibilities. For instance, in one case the central bank that lacked both a resolution and a supervisory authority was not on either college. In some cases, third countries with, in their view, a significant subsidiary were not invited to join the resolution college.[57] In fact, in some instances, since the move to adopting resolution authorities and administrative powers to orchestrate resolution are non-existent, it means some third countries are not **5.33**

[53] BRRD, Art. 91(12).
[54] BRRD, Recital 99; Art. 91(8).
[55] BRRD, Art. 92.
[56] EBA, Report on the Functioning of Resolution Colleges in 2017, July 2018.
[57] EBA Annual Report (2018) 'Resolution colleges for third-country banks. 'In 2016, the EBA was not aware of the organization of resolution colleges for subsidiaries of third-country banks. In 2017, the EBA was made aware of six such colleges, held mostly by means of conference calls.' At p. 8.

able to credibly have any expectation of joining. Nevertheless, the central bank, considering it would be the backstop for the significant subsidiary, should be able to join in such cases, if invited. There is no official right to appeal a decision regarding a Member State or a third country joining the resolution college other than lobbying the Member State of the group resolution authority.

5.34 The group resolution authority leads the management of the resolution college.[58] It arranges the meeting and decides which members and observers will be invited to the meetings either on an annual basis or ad hoc. The EBA reports found a number of annual meetings postponed which meant resolution plans were not reviewed.[59] The annual meetings are attended by the majority of members and observers whereas, at the more ad hoc meetings, only a select few are invited. The first important exercise undertaken by the resolution college is the mapping of entities and authorities responsible for their resolution.[60] The complexity of some groups with sub-groups with different business lines means a resolution college can have sub-resolution colleges of members and observers preparing for resolution for that particular part. The EBA Report found that minutes of meetings were not circulated and assessments of impediments to resolvability still a challenge that needed to be addressed.[61] This could lend itself to an option of having different resolution positions, one of an SPE and one of an MPE, being prepared at resolution college level. However, it is important to note that while members are expected to be informed about decisions and have a contribution to the decision-making process, observers, on the other hand, are not part of that process and are implicitly excluded. It could be the case, however, that a third country is given special status, albeit equivalent to a member, where the terms and conditions allow them to participate more fully.

5.35 The benefits of the resolution college are considerable since it enables members to put in place the channels to share information and data to improve the understanding of the group and the respective entities to prepare resolution, either on a group level or subgroup level. However, the EBA Report found the commitment to them by the different stakeholders as a result of expertise varied so undermined the importance of the work on resolution plans.[62] It is important to note that while resolution colleges are a conduit for information sharing, the information is not shared equally to all parties, even within the members, and the position of observers is such that no information, such as resolution plans, is expected to be shared bar only the broad conclusions of the resolution planning exercise. This is particularly the case with resolvability: the joint decision on resolvability may mean members and observers are part of the process of improving resolvability and resolution planning from the perspective of the group resolution authority but then not necessarily have the opportunity to see the full assessment. It can be the case that observers are asked for information and data to develop group resolution plans but do not have the opportunity to see them in the end. This obviously leads to a position where they do not necessarily have a clear idea of the position on group resolution. The other option is

[58] Regulation 2016/1075 Art. 50.
[59] EBA Annual Report (2018) at p. 8.
[60] Regulation 2016/1075 Art. 50.
[61] EBA Report (2018) at p. 9.
[62] EBA Report (2018) at p. 10.

that they are provided with the broad conclusions which lead to a decision of moving to an MPE position of a separate resolution plan and resolution scheme. This in itself requires considerable planning at the capital and liquidity management level for it to be exercised in an orderly manner.

There are a number of points at the planning stage that require joint decisions.[63] These are likely to be negotiated areas where Member States are likely to bargain to ensure national interests are safeguarded.[64] It is likely that ensuring the integrity and the interests of the group as a whole has benefits since it safeguards national and international franchise value. The way to achieve this is probably going to occur on business lines. However, for this to be executed, the joint decisions at the planning stage need consensus on a number of areas. First of all, there needs to be confidence in the group resolution authority to undertake resolution with the interests of host states in mind. The SRB is likely to have such credibility and large home Member States with large groups with presences in other hosts of systemic importance to the group are likely to work closely together since their incentives are aligned. However, there is a misalignment of incentives when it comes to host states that have 'significant subsidiaries', in a number of cases classified as O-SIIs. In this case, the SRB's focus is likely to take a prima facie narrow banking view of such subsidiaries. Therefore view them as suitable for liquidation and insolvency proceedings rather than resolution which secures continuity of critical functions and minimizes the destruction of value of the franchise.[65] This defeats the objective of having broad reciprocal arrangements in the interests of the EU as a whole, since the SRM's focus on material subsidiaries does imply the respective Member States are unlikely to have a significant voice in the resolution college. 5.36

The interests of other hosts are likely to be addressed along national lines taking in to account the relative impact on the group as a whole.[66] This means that incentives are not aligned to the group as a whole and, therefore, national authorities will need to address them using their own resources. This is not necessarily a bad option for the purposes of resolution since an SPE option is likely to be a compromised position. However, what is crucial is the importance of *ex ante* working towards this position rather than the resolution college working for its own interests instead of the interests of all, regardless of the resolution plans in place. Preparation is likely to take time since capital and liquidity levels have to be worked out and to ensure that they are in the right places and offer the appropriate loss-absorbing capacity needed. The challenge here is to ensure continuity of critical functions with the appropriate support and back office facilities. The question the national resolution authority needs to ask *ex ante* is, 'which resolution options are likely?' In order to address this question, it will be required to undertake its own resolution plan. The BRRD does not incentivize much else and the subsidiary is likely to need its own capital and liquidity lines on a self-reliant basis. It is possible for the group to step in on a voluntary basis 5.37

[63] Regulation 2016/1075 Recital 66, Art. 54(2) and Art. 61.

[64] Regulation 2016/1075 Art. 94: Joint decisions taken at each subsidiary level in the absence of a joint decision at consolidated level.

[65] See EBA, Decision on the Settlement of a Disagreement, Addressed to: Single Resolution Board and Banca Naţională a României 2017 joint decision on group resolution plans and resolvability for [. . .] 27 April 2018 analysed in Chapter 2, section EBA Mediation: Single Resolution Board and Banca Naţională a României, para 2.46.

[66] Regulation 2016/1075 Art. 94. See also Regulation 2016/1075 Art. 108 Disagreements and decisions taken in the absence of a joint decision.

if the problems it is facing are in other parts of the group and not necessarily with the dominant home operation.

5.38 The interesting position with the resolution college's technical standards is the fact that it has built into it the opportunity for dissent and the option to put forward an alternative option in terms of resolution schemes.

Early Intervention: Aligning Supervision and Resolution

5.39 The important synergies between supervision and resolution on a going concern and gone concern basis are set out in the context of preparation for resolution of distress institutions and groups. The intensity of the level of supervision will increase as matters escalate in terms of seriousness of the issues identified by the supervisor. The powers of early intervention in this respect are, therefore, similarly interlinked to the relationship between supervision and resolution. This is a critical phase, in that the more work undertaken at the point of supervision the more efficient the competent and resolution authorities are likely to be in avoiding formal resolution or improving its chances of achieving the resolution's objectives. At other levels though, it is important that the supervisor and the resolution authority work closely together to minimise the risks of asymmetry of information in the exercise of their roles. This is particularly acute in the setting of the Minimum Requirement for Own Funds and Eligible Liabilities (MREL) by the resolution authority and its reliance on capital requirements set by the supervisor. The decisions associated with failing banks has led to arguments that two public interest tests reside at the national level and that adopted at the centralized level co-managed by the ECB and SRB.[67] The power of early intervention is an integral part of supervision and resolution. The lack of clarity has been criticized since there is a lack of predictability for some about the ultimate outcomes.

5.40 The infringements emphasize the balance sheet; the competent authority and resolution authority will need to be mindful of the fact that such risks to balance sheet insolvency are a time lag indicator of ensuing problems, and, once they materialize, it could be too late. Certainly, the recent EBA 2015 Guidelines[68] rightly place appropriate emphasis on a broader range of significant events as well, including conduct of business failures, and prudential failures.[69] It may be argued that the introduction of infringement limits the discretion of the competent authority. Evidence of one of those infringements may result in there being little time to resolve the matter. In light of this, a range of other indicators such as management behaviour and culture could be factored into the decision-making process as precursors to the explicit infringements indicated above. When it is evident that an infringement has occurred, the competent authority can require the institution or group

[67] See Danny Busch, Governance of the Single Resolution Mechanism in Danny Busch and Guido Ferrarini (eds) European Banking Union, (Oxford: Oxford University Press) (2015) 281–335.

[68] EBA, Guidelines on the interpretation of the different circumstances when an institution shall be considered as failing or likely to fail under Art. 32(6) of Directive 2014/59/EU, EBA/GL/2015/07, 26 May 2015.

[69] See generally Chapter 5 EU Member State Resolution Decisions and Chapter 6, ABLV Case and the Cross-Border Dimension and Liquidation Cases and Other DGS interventions for the reasons why the banks are considered to be failing or likely to fail.

management body to initiate measures set out in the recovery plan or take alternative actions within the decided timeframe to resolve the infringement. The competent authority or the resolution authority could inter alia ask the management to restructure its debt or find a private sector purchaser, for instance. In circumstances where there is personal culpability of management, the competent authority should have the power to be able to remove them and appoint new management or a temporary administrator. The EBA's guidelines leave the competent authority with the discretion to determine when the trigger is expected to be pulled, as the guidelines does not explain the level of evidence it needs to pull the trigger, should it 'reasonably likely' or 'highly likely' infringe on the requirements. The evidentiary burden for the administrative decision will determine how much time the competent resolution authority will need to allow for the institution to work out its position. Moreover, the guidelines will implicitly require the competent authority for resolution and prudential purposes to cooperate and coordinate with the markets and conduct of business regulator, since some of the significant events can possibly trigger events that are market-based, linked to rogue trading or fraud. Even though this is necessary, it does not change the fact that it will mean cooperation agreements will need to be in place to ensure this type of information is shared in a timely manner.

The competent authority can appoint a temporary administrator, not with the remit **5.41**
to decide in lieu of them, but primarily for the purposes of identifying the financial position and putting in place proposals to either preserve or restore the institution's or group's financial position. In the case of groups, early intervention powers require a lot more coordination since a decision like that will have an impact on the confidence in other parts of the group. In this scenario, the consolidated supervisor is responsible for notifying the other competent authorities and resolution authorities. The competent authorities in a group scenario may face the challenge and indeed criticism of either not intervening early enough or intervening too late, and so prematurely giving rise to conflicts. Moreover, where multiple administrators are appointed by competent authorities, there is the risk that the powers and authority of temporary administrators could differ, giving rise to an inconsistent approach across the EU for single entities or groups.

The regulatory space between supervision and resolution simply provides a continuum for **5.42**
points of intervention so that the competent authority intensifies supervision to ascertain the extent of a problem that has surfaced. Indeed Enriques and Hertig refer to this space as 'shadow resolutions' outside of formal resolution which they argue undermines the credibility of formal resolution decisions.[70] Since the former can be captured by political reasons possibly protecting the integrity of a 'national champion', for instance. The classic example of this would be the decision by the Co-operative Bank in the UK to orchestrate a voluntary bail in with its creditors as part of its measures to improve its capital position.[71] In such circumstances it could well be the view capital levels need improving and the bank may well seek to sell non-core businesses to improve their capital levels. The opportunity

[70] Luca Enriques and Gerard Hertig, 'Shadow resolutions as a no-no in a sound Banking Union' in Ester Faia, Andreas Hackethal, Michael Haliassos, and Katja Langenbucher (eds) *Financial Regulation: A Transatlantic Perspective* (Cambridge: Cambridge University Press) (2015) 150–66.

[71] Barney Reynolds, 'UK Co-operative Bank: Resolution via Negotiated Bail-in Outside the BRRD' (2013) in *World Bank, Bank Resolution and 'Bail-In' in the EU: Selected Case Studies pre and post BRRD* (2016) 73–5.

to take such actions at the supervisory stage is likely to be on the surface as decisions taken by the firm rather than the supervisor. In this respect, the bank appears to be in control and its autonomy intact, leading to a position where business judgement is the order of the day in terms of decisions. But market speculation may not assist and may have a detrimental impact on the success of such decisions, especially if the option is to raise capital in the markets. The important point here would be that the matter is undertaken confidentially. This could be a challenge when a supervisory recommendation is given to several banks simultaneously, which is not likely to lead to credible outcomes, for instance, raising capital or the sale of parts of the business to improve capital requirements which may lead to negative market responses. A concern as well would be a decision to put a bank into resolution can spook the markets to think of other banks equally being vulnerable after reviewing their balance sheet and identifying similarities. While resolution is premised on it not leading to a destruction of value it invariably would and the loss of confidence is likely to be visible for those banks publicly listed in the market. The formal criteria is now analysed at the centralized and decentralized level.

5.43 The SRMR requires the ECB or the NCA to notify the SRB of its decision to exercise early intervention powers.[72] On the basis of the information the SRB is expected to notify the Commission and prepare for resolution.[73] Within this time, the ECB or the NCA is expected to provide information to the SRB and prepare, if it is obliged to, or order the NCA to produce a resolution scheme for the institution or the group.[74]

5.44 The composition of the SRMR and BRRD are broadly in line with one another when deciding whether a bank is failing or likely to fail.[75] The SRB or the NRA will have to assess the circumstances the bank finds itself and consider the possibility of a private sector solution for the failing bank.[76] In this respect the feasibility of the potential private sector interest needs to be assessed and whether it can be agreed within a relatively reasonable amount of time, albeit this is not stipulated in the provisions. The final requirement that needs to be considered is whether resolution is in the public interest.[77] This has been the most contentious of issues since it has been argued that the SRB and NRA interpretation of public interest outcomes for failing banks has differed from one another.[78] The SRB is viewed to have taken a stricter view and placing banks in to national insolvency-liquidation rather than resolution. The two Italian cases in the Venato region and in contrast the Croatian bank decisions explored in chapter 6 are illustrative of this contrasting position where concerns about sub-regional real economy surfaced and assessed differently.[79] The former were declared not in the public interest to be put in to resolution since they were not undertaking critical functions at the time of the ECB-SRB decision. The principle point in terms of public interest assessment is whether normal insolvency proceedings would lead to the

[72] SRMR, Art. 13.
[73] SRMR, Art. 13(1).
[74] SRMR, Art. 13(2).
[75] SRMR, Art. 18(1)(a)–(c) and BRRD, Art. 32(1)(a)–(c).
[76] SRMR, Art. 18(b) and BRRD, Art. 32(1)(b).
[77] SRMR, Art. 18(c) and BRRD, Art. 32(c); see also Jens-Hinrich Binder, 'Proportionality at the Resolution Stage: Calibration of Resolution Measures and the Public Interest Test (3 July 2017); also, 'The Principle of Proportionality and Its Applicability in EU Banking Regulation' (February 2017), available at SSRN: <https://ssrn.com/abstract=2990379>.
[78] See generally, Chapter 6, 'European Bank Insolvency and Liquidation Proceedings'.
[79] Chapter 6, 'European Bank Insolvency and Liquidation Proceedings', para 6.40.

same outcomes as resolution in line with the objectives and principles explored below. The Venato cases in some respects highlight that even relatively large banks can be placed in liquidation if the national insolvency-liquidation proceedings are conducive. This is contentious since resolution does not necessarily lead to a destruction of franchise value in comparison to insolvency-liquidation. Therefore, resolution is considered a more palatable option from the perspective of the bank. Moreover it very much depends on the scope and powers of national insolvency and liquidation law. The lack of predictability of outcomes is the principle concern that is naively focused on a case by case comparison of looking at apples if they were pears, which is always likely to identify inconsistencies.

The basis for triggering the decision of failing or likely to fail requires an assess of what could broadly be termed regulatory infringements either relating to the balance sheet or other requirements associated with authorization that could lead to the withdrawal of authorization, for instance evidence of financial crime.[80] However the primary reasons are either balance sheet or cashflow infringements that call in to doubt the bank's ability to meet prudential requirements on a continuous basis. In this respect, decision to intervene is made when the bank is balance sheet solvent but not according to prudential supervisory standards. This can be a point of contention if in normal insolvency proceedings the court decides the bank is balance sheet solvent and disagrees with the supervisory authority's outlook for the bank. The SRMR in Article 18(4)(c) requires consideration whether the entity will in the near future be unable to pay its debts or other liabilities as they fall due. In this respect the SRB will assess the speed with which the banks financial position is deteriorating, for instance the rate at which deposits are being transferred out of the bank. **5.45**

The cases primarily show how the courts have interpreted the position of the bank in national insolvency proceedings differently to that of the supervisory authority. This shows the need for harmonization and alignment of bank resolution and insolvency proceedings. As with administrative resolution-led proceeding, insolvency providing should also be couched within an administrative framework and require the courts to accept the administrative decision.[81] Rather than open up the administrative decision for review based on different criteria of whether the bank is failing and not necessarily taking in to the wider external factors that have likely been taken in to account to form the decision.[82] **5.46**

The notion of failing or likely to fail is a judgement call which requires considerable refection of both internal and external circumstances which could either lead to the bank or the group failing. The idea of failing is perhaps simpler since it requires assessment of the balance sheet and liquidity of the bank and indeed other requirements that could compromise authorization. The notion of likely to fail is couched in more discretion and requires the **5.47**

[80] SRMR, Art. 18(4)(a)–(d) and BRRD, Art. 32(4)(a)–(d).

[81] BRRD, Art. 85(4)(b): '[T]he decision of the resolution authority shall be immediately enforceable and it shall give rise to a Page 11 rebuttable presumption that a suspension of its enforcement would be against the public interest.'

[82] Jens-Hinrich Binder, Michael Krimminger, Maria J Nieto, and Dalvinder Singh, 'The Choice between judicial and administrative sanctioned procedures to manage liquidation of banks: a transatlantic perspective (2019)14(2) Capital Markets Law Journal 178–216; see also Sabino Cassese, A New framework of administrative arrangements for the protection of individual rights in ECB Legal Conference 2017, Shaping a new legal order for Europe: a tale of crises and opportunities, 4–5 September (2017) 239–55.

supervisory authority and the resolution authority to determine whether in the future it is going to fail. A critical element in this decision is ultimately the level of due diligence undertaken vis a vis the source of the problem. If consideration is given to the cases explored in this work relating to areas such non-performing loans then it can be difficult to gauge whether the extent of the problem is going to mean it is likely to fail. This is primarily reliant on the valuation process that is required to be undertaken to gauge the option of resolution or insolvency and the outcome of the no-creditor-worse-off in resolution than would be the case in insolvency. The time for the valuation has been a point of concern since it is reliant on when the problems surface. The three stage process for deciding how to resolve the bank requires months to complete but has been required to need to be done in a matter of weeks.

5.48 Valuation of assets and liabilities will play a critical role in the resolution process, since it will determine its success in terms of contributing to the decision regarding which resolution tool will achieve the resolution objective, conditions, and principles.[83] The process of valuation is not a perfect science and is primarily determined by the quality and accuracy of the information the institution holds and the timeliness of the information given to them. While considering the conditions for resolution the independent valuation will include the following matters: whether the conditions for write- down and conversation of capital have been achieved and the impact on the dilution of shares; the eligible debtholders of the outcome of the bail-in; which assets and liabilities are to be transferred to the bridge bank; and the decision on which assets and liabilities will be included in the sale of business tool.[84] A key factor in the success of the independent valuation will be the timing of intervention to ascertain value within the institution and the size of the losses. The valuation will need to be structured according to the priority of claims on the assets in the institution.[85] If the valuation cannot be done on time, then a provisional valuation is possible. This is perhaps the most critical aspect of the resolution process to determine the outcomes of the bank and the different stakeholder interests in both resolution and insolvency.

5.49 The no-creditor-worse-off is an integral outcome of the valuation process to ascertain the implications of the bank entering in to resolution in comparison to insolvency. If the resolution authority decides the bank is going to enter into domestic insolvency-liquidation then the principle becomes redundant. It would be left to the domestic proceedings to gauge what is therefore recoverable to cover creditor's claims. The resolution authority needs to try and decide as accurately as possible in the circumstance that no creditor of an entity in resolution shall incur greater losses than would have been incurred had the entity been wound up under normal insolvency proceedings. Since the resolution authority is exercising administrative discretion to intervene in the affairs of the bank to protect public interest objectives before it reaches balance sheet insolvency-liquidation. The no-creditor-worse-off principle provides a balance between the competing public and private interests to ensure the administrative decision is proportionate

[83] BRRD Art. 36.
[84] BRRD Art. 36(4)(a)–(g).
[85] BRRD Art. 36(8).

to its outcomes. The expropriation of private property requires appropriate due process to be followed to ensure compensation is payable if the outcome insolvency would have been better than that achieved in resolution.[86] While resolution is premised on consistent principles and objectives the counterfactual of insolvency-liquidation is far from consistent at the EU level.[87] In view of the fact that several models exist between corporate and some form of modified insolvency-liquidation proceedings. In part as was experienced in the Italian Venato cases modified proceedings can consist of resolution type options and the avoidance of a fire sale of assets can be a material part of the assessment of how best to deal with banks in such scenarios.[88] Moreover, in some jurisdictions the courts in insolvency proceedings can be more sympathetic to the interests of the bank and require a higher evidentiary burden to be reached to determine insolvency. In view of this, the courts can form the opinion that the resolution authorities decision was premature to the extent it did not allow the bank and its directors sufficient amount of time to orchestrate a private alternative to the proposed public solution. Moreover, the cases so far show that public assistance can play a significant role in a bank in distress which would need to be discounted in any potential assessment of compensation.[89] It would be important for the courts to consider all these factors when assessing such compensation claims.

In a group context it is likely the no-creditor-worse-off principle will lead to different outcomes for the creditors of the different incorporated entities. Since the counterfactual is different in each Member State the comparing treatment of stakeholders is not going to be possible. But this does not negate fact that domestic creditors Member State by Member State will assess how their interests have been affected in resolution and consider whether to peruse compensation. A resolution scheme is likely to consist of different resolution options in the different Member States for instance for the core and non-core entities of the group. In the former the bail-in tool and or the asset separation tool is likely to be utilized and in the latter the sale of business tool is a significant possibility. Since the aim of the resolution scheme is likely to restructure and recapitalize the core home country part of the group and the retrenchment from some hosts through the sale of business tool to recapitalize the home operations mean creditors interests will be affected differently. **5.50**

The cross-border dimension is equally important to consider in the contest of this decision and its timing. The position at the centralized level shows that the ECB and the SRB are well placed to address potential coordination risks between Member States participating in the Banking Union as is shown in the decisions regarding ABLV Latvia and Luxembourg.[90] At the national level each subsidiary is a separately incorporated authorized bank and so while some Member States may agree the group is failing or likely **5.51**

[86] Victor de Serière and Daphne van der Houwen, 'No Creditor Worse Off' in 'Case of Bank Resolution: Food for Litigation?' (2016) Journal of International Banking Law and Regulation, Issue 7, p. 376, available at SSRN: <https://ssrn.com/abstract=2856370 or http://dx.doi.org/10.2139/ssrn.2856370>.
[87] See Chapter 6.
[88] See Chapter 6, section 6.40.
[89] *Harbinger Capital Partner v Caldwell and Another* [2013] EWCA 492.
[90] See Chapter 6, The ABLV Case and the Cross-border Dimension, 6.31.

to fail some Member States may not agree with the decision and could base on their own assessment take a different decision about the subsidiary in their jurisdiction. In another set of circumstances the competent authority and resolution authority may be of the view the subsidiary independent of the group is failing or likely to fail. These scenarios highlight how an entity-by-entity-based approach is ultimately taken and a group based approach is quite possibly a voluntary affair.

Resolution Objectives, Conditions, and Principles

5.52 The resolution objectives are to ensure continuity of critical functions, avoid significant adverse effects on financial stability, protect public funds, protect covered depositors and investors, and protect client funds and client assets.[91] While regulation and supervision of financial services is implicitly mindful of these objectives, it is important to emphasize the importance of them being put in an explicit setting, coinciding with the wider concerns of financial stability, since it provides a clear expression of whose interests the competent and resolution authorities are primarily concerned about. Notwithstanding the hierarchy of interests, the resolution authority is required to evaluate the use of the resolution tools keeping in mind the importance of minimizing the costs of resolution and maintaining value within the institution or group to minimize unnecessary losses to shareholders and creditors. This is the case despite the fact that it does not explicitly make reference to those respective groups at this point. Therefore, while banks are traditionally considered to be special and require a special resolution regime, once the resolution and special insolvency regimes are in place to address the idiosyncratic risks of banks, their uniqueness is minimized. The reforms rightly address the importance of critical functions and the extent to which continuity of them is safeguarded through supervisory and resolution intervention rather than the institution undertaking such critical functions.[92]

5.53 The stabilization tools explained below provide the first line of defence when it comes to dealing with banks in distress either individually and/or in combination with one another. The directive sets out the resolution tools but does not imply one resolution tool or another is likely to take a dominant role, albeit the institution will need a sufficient amount of capital instruments that can be written down or converted so as to recapitalize the bank or fund the resolution measure. The more likely scenario is that this power will be exercised in conjunction with other resolution tools. Moreover, when there is a wider market-based situation of distress, governments may utilize market-wide tools so that critical functions and business lines can continue, and a sufficient amount of value can be retained to ensure creditors are not in a position where they are worse off than in a hypothetical insolvency proceedings. Notwithstanding the utility of the resolution tools and the central bank facilities and extraordinary facilities to resolve distress banks, they, on their own, may not be a complete panacea.

[91] SRMR, Art. 14 & 15; BRRD, Arts 31–34.

[92] Eva Hupkes, 'Protect functions, not institutions', The Financial Regulator (January 2004) pp. 43–99.

The Sale of Business Tool

The resolution authority is required to have in place the power to be able to transfer ownership and its assets and liabilities of the institution to a private purchaser.[93] The SRB would decide and then instruct the national resolution authority to execute the sale of business tool.[94] 5.54

The BRRD requires the resolution authority to follow a number of measures. The resolution authority will be required to take reasonable steps to get commercial terms and put in place a process of marketing the assets, rights and liabilities.[95] The latter is limited in terms of disclosure if it poses material risks to financial stability. The transfer or retransfer of shares, assets and liabilities will enable the resolution to assist with ensuring the commercial terms of the business. A particular issue associated with regulation and supervision of the purchaser is to ensure the acquirer has the appropriate authorization to undertake the business acquired.[96] This will require involvement of the competent authority to assess whether the acquirer is indeed fit and proper to undertake the acquired business. This is likely to be considered at the point of initiating interest in the acquisition. The BRRD does recognise that the need for speedy and orderly resolution may mean the due diligence to gauge whether the acquirer's authorization criteria is met runs the risk of the competent authority not agreeing with the authorization. In some respects it forms a kind of cooling off period for all parties involved. It is therefore important for the competent and resolution authority to work closely together at the point of assessing which resolution tool or combination of tools is the most appropriate to resolve the problems at the institution in distress. This would avoid circumstances where the resolution authority has to ask the acquirer to divest their ownership within the divestment period.[97] The new acquirer will need to be assessed for the purposes of membership of payment systems and clearing and settlement system, and compensation schemes.[98] The competent and resolution authorities will also need to minimize the risk of conflicts of interest in the way it evaluates the commercial terms between private sector bidders during the process of executing the sale and transfer of assets and liabilities.[99] 5.55

In the context of a cross-border group resolution the sale of business tool could be used to primarily assist the process of recapitalizing the parent entity. Therefore, foreign entities may well be the first to be sold to assist in restructuring the core business. While this makes perfect commercial sense from the host-home perspective the sale of business tool for an entity within a group resolution could lead to concerns about concentration risk within the market. This would particularly be the case for Member States that have a very high preponderance of foreign banks. The sale could lead to greater foreign bank concentration risks. It is argued that such issues do need considering by the group resolution authority when thinking about how best to restructure the group and not simply restructure in view of the interests of the home parent entity. 5.56

[93] BRRD, Art. 38(1).
[94] SRMR, Art. 24.
[95] BRRD, Art. 38(2)–(3).
[96] BRRD, Art. 38(7).
[97] BRRD, Art. 38(9)(a)–(f).
[98] BRRD, Art. 38(12)(a)–(b).
[99] BRRD, Art. 39.

The Bridge Institution Tool

5.57 The bridge bank tool has been an important tool in the resolution toolkit in a number of jurisdictions.[100] The bridge bank is expected to take responsibility of the critical function.[101] It will take responsibility by either a transfer of shares or instrument of ownership or assets and liabilities to the bridge bank.[102] The initiation of the bridge bank can be undertaken at the initiative of the resolution authority and does not require shareholder agreement.[103] This avoids the resolution authority seeking approval of the shareholders, which may not always be forthcoming, and enables the resolution authority to undertake the set-up of the bridge bank to achieve the resolution objectives and principles. The bridge bank will either be owned by a public authority or the resolution authority.[104] The bridge bank is not expected to be the bad bank. The balance sheet of the newly created bank needs to be regulatory compliant so the resolution authorities need to transfer and or reverse transfer assets and liabilities to ultimately improve its marketability.[105] This can have adverse consequences for those left in the residual bank since they can be tarnished with a reputation of holding non-performing loans or other bad assets. In two notable instances it has led to litigation in the UK and Ireland.[106] Since the bridge bank is publicly owned, such transfers can be undertaken during the life of the bridge bank. The bridge bank will undertake the regulated activity of the bank in resolution and so the new institution benefits from the franchise value of the business.

5.58 Once the assets are transferred, the shareholders or creditors have no further rights to the transferred assets.[107] The management of the bridge bank can have their liability configured so that it can be limited to an extent where they are exempted from liability unless the act or omission is one of gross negligence.[108] The resolution authority will set out the constitution of the bridge bank and it will craft its commercial strategy and its appetite for risk. However, the bridge bank is expected to cease existing when it merges with another bank by way of sale of the business to a third party.[109] The BRRD provides a timeframe for the life of the bridge bank of up to two years with the option for the resolution authority to extend the period in extraordinary circumstances.[110] The following cases highlight some of the challenges associated with using the bridge bank:

Goldman Sachs International v Novo Banco SA

5.59 The *Novo Banco* case was heard in the UK courts pursuant to a facility agreement entered into by the parties.[111] The facts concerned the resolution of distressed Portuguese bank

[100] SRMR, Art. 25; BRRD, Art. 40.
[101] BRRD, Art. 40(1).
[102] BRRD, Art. 40(1)(a)–(b).
[103] BRRD, Art. 40(1).
[104] BRRD, Art. 40(2)(a)–(b).
[105] BRRD, Art. 40(3).
[106] Hodge Malik and James Potts, 'The competing interests between bank and borrower when a bank in resolution sells debt' (2017) 32 Butterworths Journal of International Banking and Financial Law 268–70.
[107] BRRD, Art. 40(12).
[108] BRRD, Art. 40(13).
[109] BRRD, Art. 41(3)(a)–(e).
[110] BRRD, Art. 41(5)–(6).
[111] The agreement contained an express choice for English law in settling any disputes. *Goldman Sachs International v Novo Banco SA* [2015] EWHC 2371 (Comm), at 7.

Banco Espírito Santo SA (BES) through operating a bridge bank, 'Novo Banco', created by the Bank of Portugal in its capacity as resolution authority as per the BRRD.[112] As a resolution measure, the assets and liabilities of BES were transferred onto Novo Banco, with the exception of certain 'excluded liabilities'.[113] The point of contention was whether the liabilities arising out of the facility agreement (consisting of a $835 million loan granted to BES by a Luxembourg entity)[114] were to be considered in this category as well. The Bank of Portugal issued a ruling in December 2014 according to which the loan in question was not an 'excluded liability' and therefore remained in the residual bank, effectively negating the transfer.[115] However, the claimants, which included Goldman Sachs pursued Novo Banco as the borrower arguing it had replaced BES via a statutory transfer.[116]

Novo Banco applied to set aside the proceedings as well as to obtain a stay of the proceedings in accordance with Articles 86 and 66(3) of the BRRD. The latter provides, inter alia, that creditors and third parties affected by the transfer of assets or liabilities are not entitled to prevent, challenge or set aside the transfer 'under any provision of law of the Member State where the assets are located or of the law governing the shares, other instruments of ownership, rights or liabilities'. Novo Banco contended that the UK courts had no jurisdiction under Regulation (EU) 1215/2012[117] to hear the claims. Instead, it should be recognized that there had been no transfer of the liability according to the Bank of Portugal's ruling. Under Portuguese law, the latter was regarded as an administrative act which may only be reviewed by administrative courts.[118] On the contrary, the claimants argued that the ruling had no effect in English law, under which the facility agreement was concluded. They deemed irrelevant the Bank of Portugal's ruling status as a matter of Portuguese law.[119] 5.60

The UK High Court dismissed Novo Banco's application for three reasons. Firstly, Regulation (EU) 1215/2012 applied to civil and commercial matters, at the exclusion of administrative ones.[120] The court was persuaded by the claimants' argument that theirs was a private law (debt) claim based on rights contained in the facility agreement,[121] and therefore fell under the material scope of the Regulation,[122] as opposed to Novo Banco's interpretation.[123] Moreover, the defendant was not a public body, nor it did it exercise public powers.[124] Thus, the court held that it did indeed have jurisdiction to decide the matter. Secondly, the court stated that it would not pronounce on the validity of the Bank of Portugal's ruling, but rather on its effect in English law.[125] The non-justiciability or act of state doctrine[126] was further inapplicable due to the Bank of Portugal acting as a resolution 5.61

112 *Goldman Sachs International v Novo Banco SA* [2015] EWHC 2371 (Comm).
113 BRRD, C Mecklenburg, *supra* n 141, at 10.
114 BRRD.
115 Arguing instead, inter alia, a re-transfer to BES under BRRD, Art. 40(7). BRRD at 34.
116 BRRD.
117 Regulation (EU) 1215/2012 of the European Parliament and of the Council on jurisdiction and the recognition and enforcement of judgments in civil and commercial matters (recast) ('Recast Brussels Regulation').
118 *Goldman Sachs International v Novo Banco SA* [2015] EWHC 2371 (Comm), at 53(6).
119 BRRD at 61.
120 Recast Brussels Regulation, Art. 1(1).
121 *Goldman Sachs International v Novo Banco SA* [2015] EWHC 2371 (Comm) at 71.
122 Recast Brussels Regulation, Art. 25.
123 *Goldman Sachs International v Novo Banco SA* [2015] EWHC 2371 (Comm) at 73.
124 BRRD at 72.
125 BRRD at 109.
126 According to which adjudication on the 'validity, legality, lawfulness, acceptability or motives of state actors' is prohibited. BRRD at 110.

authority for BRRD purposes, as opposed to being an emanation of the Portuguese state.[127] Thirdly, the court clarified that a stay of proceedings would only be enforced in 'rare and compelling' circumstances,[128] which was not the case in *Novo Banco*.

5.62 The Court of Appeal overruled the High Court decision[129] and the Supreme Court unanimously upheld the Court of Appeal decision.[130] In many respects the decision was a relief in that it upheld the fundamental purpose of the BRRD of providing a coherent EU wide resolution strategy that recognizes the decisions of Member State national resolution authorities. An important element of the decision was to take in account the resolution decision as a whole rather than in a piecemeal fashion that ignored the wider administrative purpose of what is entailed in a resolution scheme as part of reorganization measures. The home Member State resolution authority and or the courts are expected to take the lead role in such decisions. Indeed the decision emphasizes the importance of other Member States taking 'active steps to enforce transfers of assets or liabilities made in the course of a reorganization in the home state and to prevent challenges to such transfers in their own jurisdictions'.[131] In view of this the English court did not have jurisdiction. Lord Sumption explained the Directive would be undermined 'if the acts of the designated national resolution authority were open to challenge in every other Member State'.[132]

Bayerische Landesbank v Hypo Alpe Adria Bank International AG (now HETA Asset Resolution AG) ('Heta')

5.63 The facts *Bayerische Landesbank v Hypo Alpe Adria Bank International AG* (now HETA Asset Resolution AG, 'Heta') related to the resolution of distressed financial institution Hypo Alpe Adria International AG ('Hypo').[133] This consisted of establishing a bridge bank, namely Heta, to which Hypo's assets and liabilities were transferred, save for 'excluded liabilities'.[134] In addition, the March 2015 administrative measure to initiate Heta's resolution was supported by a 15-month moratorium on its liabilities, issued by the Austrian Financial Market Authority (FMA). Acting as the resolution authority for the purposes of the BRRD and the Federal Act on the Recovery and Resolution of Banks (BaSAG),[135] FMA considered the temporary moratorium necessary to prevent Heta's insolvency.[136]

5.64 The administrative decision taken by the FMA was contested by certain creditors as it deferred the maturity of some of Heta's eligible liabilities, thereby postponing the payment due date (until 31 May 2016).[137] Bayerische Landesbank ('BayernLB') challenged the

[127] BRRD at 111.
[128] BRRD at 118.
[129] *Guardians of New Zealand Superannuation Fund & Ors v Novo Banco, SA* [2016] EWCA Civ 1092.
[130] *Goldman Sachs International v Novo Banco SA* [2018] UKSC 34.
[131] BRRD, para. 22.
[132] BRRD, para. 34.
[133] *Bayerische Landesbank v Hypo Alpe Adria Bank International AG* (now HETA Asset Resolution AG) (Az 32 0 26502/12) (8 May 2015).
[134] BRRD.
[135] The relevant legislation through which BRRD was transposed in Austrian law.
[136] DC Bauer, 'Resolving Austria's HETA—major milestone for the European bank resolution regime', 6 September 2015, <https://www.dlapiper.com/en/uk/insights/publications/2015/10/global-insight-15/resolving-austrias-heta/>.
[137] BRRD.

moratorium on the grounds of insufficient legal basis as well as its qualification as a BRRD measure.[138] In this sense, BayernLB argued that the objective of the Recovery Measures for Hypo Alpe Adria Bank International AG ('HaaSanG') and its Regulation on the Application of the Measures ('HaaSanV') were different as compared to those under the BRRD: whereas the former intends to terminate Heta's banking activities, the latter seeks to ensure their continuation. Furthermore, the moratorium cannot be qualified as a resolution regime for the purposes of Article 66 of the BRRD corroborated with Article 2 because the measures are applied against a bad bank (i.e. Heta) as opposed to a credit institution as required.[139] Heta's licence had been revoked and it was subsequently converted into an asset management firm.[140] Notwithstanding Heta being explicitly made subject to the BaSAG, the Munich court refused to recognize the moratorium, deciding that its application to Heta was outside the scope of the BRRD.[141] Consequently, German courts were not obliged to give effect to other resolution authorities' measures and Heta was ordered to pay Bayern around €2.3bn.[142] Heta appealed against this decision; the European Commission also initiated proceedings against the Republic of Austria for its failure to transpose the BRRD in an adequate manner. Therefore, highlighting the importance of the competent and resolution authorities to think through the implications of terminating authorization when the continuity of authorization is crucial for an orderly resolution. Moreover, the competent and resolution authorities need to clearly understand resolution is not a catch-all term to also include bank and insolvency administration. The directive is quite clear on this matter in particular what is a resolution tool and what is an insolvency tool for the purposes of managing the resolution process, and the residual bank for the purposes of winding up and liquidation of assets and liabilities.

Asset Separation Tool

The asset separation tool provides the mechanism to transfer and carve out rights, assets and liabilities to the asset management vehicle.[143] This approach gained significant prominence during the GFC and became known as the 'bad bank'. The Asset separation tool has been shown to be used to deal with non-performing loans of problem banks.[144] The main difference to the GFC however, and the other resolution tools, is that it cannot be applied alone but in conjunction with other resolution tools—most notably the bail-in tool. Once the institution is in resolution, the resolution authorities will need to work out how to improve the viability of the bridge bank and ensure the resolution objectives are complied with. The asset management vehicles contribute significantly to achieving that purpose. The asset management company will be separately incorporated but either partially or wholly owned as a public authority.[145] The assets and liabilities transferred to the asset management vehicle 5.65

[138] See Regulation (EU) No. 575/2013, Art. 4(1); Directive 2013/36/EU, Art. 2(5); *Bayerische Landesbank v Hypo Alpe Adria Bank International AG* (now HETA Asset Resolution AG) (Az 32 0 26502/12) (8 May 2015).
[139] BRRD.
[140] BRRD.
[141] BRRD.
[142] BRRD.
[143] SRMR, Art. 26; BRRD, Art. 42.
[144] Chapter 4, 'Regulation and Supervision of Non-Performing Loans and Loan Loss Provisioning, Public and Private Mechanisms to Reduce NPLs: A Portfolio-based Approach', para 4.40.
[145] BRRD, Art. 42(2)(a)–(b).

are more likely to be those deemed bad assets and liabilities—essentially non-performing, but attempting to execute the sale to maximize the value or ensure orderly liquidation.[146] This will place the asset management vehicle at arms-length and enable them to manage the winding-down of bad assets without institutional and political interference. The resolution authority is required to ensure the asset management vehicle is separately constituted but has the authority to appoint management and approve remuneration policy.[147] The resolution authority will need to work with the asset arrangement vehicle to work out its strategy and appetite for risk. More importantly, the resolution authority has the authority to limit the liability of the asset management vehicle to the shareholders or creditors of the rights, assets or liabilities transferred to it,[148] unless the asset management vehicle acts with gross negligence in the discharge of its responsibilities. The process of resolution is not static but a fluid relationship which will involve the various stakeholders in resolution to ensure assets and liabilities are transferred or re-transferred fully and or partially from the various parts of the institution in resolution, from the institution itself, the bridge bank and the asset management vehicle to ensure the objectives and principles of resolution are complied with.

The Bail-in Tool

5.66 The bail-in tool is the newest tool in the lexicon of bank resolution tools and is perhaps the most controversial given its purpose but part of the controversy appears to be that its viewed as a single solution and not part of a wider set of tools for bank recapitalization.[149] As Zhou et al explains, '[Bail-in] should supplement, not replace, other resolution tools that would allow for an orderly closure of a failed institution.'[150] In reality the bail—in tool is the private sector solution but as it's been shown in other parts of the work (Chapter 7) public assistance is equally available and necessary in the form of liquidity assistance, for example. Considering banks that have not been classed as a threat to financial stability have required public assistance in liquidation for those that are a threat to financial stability are possible likely to require public assistance to provide some implicit support to the initiative as a precaution to the market over reacting, if nothing else.[151]

5.67 The bail-in tool is equally perhaps the tool that deals in an administrative format with the home and host dilemma since it is an attempt *ex ante* to pre-commit to an administrative resolution strategy that is likely to recapitalise the group as a whole. This is likely to benefit the core material entities in the group. However other entities will be treated in such a

146 BRRD, Art. 42(3).

147 BRRD, Art. 42(4)(a)–(d).

148 BRRD, Art. 42(13).

149 Jianping Zhou, Virginia Rutledge, Wouter Bossu, Marc Dobler, Nadege Jassaud, and Michael Moore, 'From Bail-out to Bail-in: Mandatory Debt Restructuring of Systemic Financial Institutions', IMF Staff Discussion Note, April 24.

150 p. 3.

151 Rainer Palmstorfer, 'Bail Out or not to Bail Out? The current framework of financial assistance for Euro Area Member States measured against the requirements of EU Primary Law' (2012) European Law Review 771–84; Viral Acharya, Hyun S Shin, and Tanju Yorulmazer, 'Crisis Resolution and Bank Liquidity' (2011) 24 The Review of Financial Studies 21–66.

strategy is relatively unclear. It is likely the other parts of the group will be utilized through a sale of business strategy as mentioned before to assist with the process of recapitalization through bail in. Such a strategy is likely to gain support by the core part of the group since it will mean the extent of the bail in process is minimized. A particular challenge is connecting the simplicity of the concept with the complexity of the instruments it is attempting to utilise to recapitalize the bank. This essentially causes a pricing problem since the market can accurately calculate the risk. As Tröger rightly points out, '[d]esirable market discipline can only be induced if investors can predict the risk of their capital instruments being written-off or converted with reasonable certainty.'[152] The extent it will be used beyond the G-SIB and D-SIB constituency is also debatable. Therefore, the formulaic approach to its application in the EU framework causes in part the problems as well since not all banks have bail-in-able debt and more controversially retail customers are not prepared to be bailed in.[153] In more recent times concerns have arisen of subordinated debt held by retail consumers and the moral question of whether they are appropriate stakeholders to bail-in since they were not possibly aware they faced such a risk.[154] This risk of mis-selling would need to then feature in any potential valuation process if resolution is the preferred option.[155]

The bail-in power is primarily aimed at recapitalizing the bank and potentially turning its affairs around so that it complies with authorization requirements and can continue to undertake regulated activities or fund resolution measures.[156] The bail-in tool allows write-down of equity and certain debt instruments as well as the conversion of debt instruments into equity. The bail-in tool is perhaps the most sensible principle to start with in resolution but questions have equally been raised about its limits. This is partly, due to the complexity of bank finance and the unintended consequences of bail-in of certain instruments. The potential risk of contagion is equally raised as a concern in the market as a result of its announcement. The first mover problem is a concern on pricing in specific markets as a result of the potential risk of the power being exercised more widely in the sector.[157] Therefore, while the bail-in tool attempts to reduce the risk of moral hazard there is a need to assess the impact of adverse selection risk once the tool is administered and the market attempts to reprice liabilities. The trade-off between the two requires assessment at the point of execution, but the importance of privatizing losses is a critical policy position which should always be maintained and can be honoured even if the bail-in tool is not fully applied but partly applied and utilized with other techniques that attempt to distribute losses amongst **5.68**

[152] Too complex to work: a critical assessment of the Bail-in tool under the European bank recovery and resolution regime' (2018) 4 Journal of Financial Regulation 35–72 at 37.

[153] Rene Smits, 'Is my money safe at European banks? Reflections on the 'bail-in' provisions in recent EU legal texts' (2014) 9(2) Capital Markets Law Journal 137–56; Paul De Grauwe, 'The new bail-in doctrine: A recipe for banking crises and depression in the eurozone', CEPS Commentary, 4 April 2013.

[154] Silvia Merler, 'Four small banks: resolution via bridge bank and asset management vehicle tools to avoid full bail-in in World Bank, Bank resolution and Bail-in in the EU: selected case studies pre and post BRRD' (2016) pp. 36–44.

[155] Willem Pieter de Groen, 'Valuation reports in the context of banking resolution: what are the challenges?' European Parliament (2018) p. 12.

[156] Anna Gardella, 'Bail-in and the Financing of Resolution within the SRM Framework' in Danny Busch and Guido Ferrarini (eds), *European Banking Union* (Oxford: Oxford University Press) (2015) pp. 373–407; Jianping Zhou, Virginia Rutledge, Wouter Bossu, Marc Dobler, Nadege Jassaud, and Michael Moore, 'From Bail-out to Bail-in: Mandatory Debt Restructuring of Systemic Financial Institutions', IMF Staff Discussion Note, 24 April SDN/12/03 (2012).

[157] Emilios Avgouleas and Charles Goodhart, 'Critical Reflections on Bank Bail-ins' (2015) Journal of Financial Regulation 1(1) 3–29.

stakeholders of the bank that are best able to absorb them. Equally, the different levels of technical capacity of the supervisor also needs to be taken in to account to try and ensure it could work and the outcomes are appreciated for the entity and supervisor involved.

5.69 The Member State is required to work out in advance with the institution or group which liabilities are eligible for bail-in.[158] However, the resolution authority is prohibited from bailing-in a number of liabilities such as deposits covered by the DGS, secured liabilities, any liabilities held for a client that qualify as either client assets or client money, liabilities that arise from a fiduciary relationship, liabilities (to other institutions) with an original or, in certain cases, remaining maturity of less than seven days, employee remunerations and salaries with the exception of material risk takers, commercial trade creditors, tax and social security authorities, and the DGS. Nevertheless, the resolution authority does have some discretion in deciding which debt instruments are eligible for bail-in when considering the available time, market conditions, and the implications for financial stability. But this could be limited by the pre-designed depositor preference rule determining which deposits (retail or wholesale) are within or sit outside of the provision giving them priority over other claims.[159] However, the exclusion of otherwise eligible bail-in liabilities has to be proportionate and should not undermine safeguarding critical functions. The assessment of included and excluded liabilities in a write-down or conversion needs to be mindful of the principle that no shareholder or creditor is worse off than in a hypothetical insolvency proceeding. If only certain creditors within a creditor's class are subject to the bail-in, affected creditors should be compensated. The write-down and conversion of capital instruments needs to comply with the priority of claims set out in insolvency proceedings so that Common Equity Tier 1 instruments are written down in proportion to the losses incurred. Furthermore, necessary, the Additional Tier 1 and Tier 2 instruments must be either written down or converted into Common Equity Tier 1 instruments. Nevertheless, the resolution financing arrangement can be expected to make a contribution of up to 5% to the resolution of the institution provided that at least 8% has been bailed in by shareholders and those with eligible liabilities. The level of equity and liabilities bailed in needs to be proportionate so that the institution continues to meet the authorization criteria.

5.70 The bail-in tool requires institutions to have in place own funds and eligible liabilities at a percentage of total liabilities and own funds of the institution. In this respect, eligible liabilities need to be fully paid up, unsecured, with a maturity of at least one year, should not arise from a derivative or should not be a publicly insured deposit. The resolution authority and the competent authority are expected to work together to ensure the institution has sufficient eligible liabilities and is resolvable. This is likely to form part of the assessment to produce recovery and resolution plans at the preparation stage. The resolution authority and the competent authority will need to work together to work out the minimum requirement that institutions will need to hold at an institutional and group level. This requires them to also assess whether the DGS could contribute to the financing of the resolution. The move

[158] For a detailed technical analysis see Bart P M Joosen, 'Regulatory capital requirements and bail-in mechanism' in Matthias Haentjens and Bob Wessel, *Research Handbook on Crisis Management in the Banking Sector* (Cheltenham: Edward Elgar Publishing) (2015) pp. 175–235.

[159] Niall Lenihan, Maike Luedersen, and Martin Schulte, 'The hierarchy of creditor claims in bank insolvency' (2016) Forum Financier/Droit Bancaire et Financier 413–25; see Chapter 6, Creditors Interests in Insolvency—Depositor Preference, paras 6.45–6.51.

towards ensuring institutions meet minimum requirements will then form the basis of data submitted to the EBA so that it can report on the move towards compliance with these requirements to the European Commission.

The resolution authority will need to assess the amount of eligible bail-in liabilities to determine whether there is enough to convert into Common Equity Tier 1 capital. It needs to keep this under review to determine whether or not there is enough for the institution in resolution or a bridge institution. The resolution authority will also need to assess whether there are enough bail-in liabilities to meet the needs of the asset management vehicle, if that resolution tool is utilized in conjunction with bail-in. The level of bail-in liabilities varies considerably in light of the business and financing model of institutions, which means the institutions will need to change them to ensure they have enough. **5.71**

The resolution authority will also need to set out their treatment of shareholders so that they are informed about how their rights and interests will be impacted by the write-down and bail-in policy. The BRRD requires shareholders to be aware that the resolution authority can either cancel or transfer existing shares or other instruments to bailed-in creditors. This will comply with the principle that shareholders will bear the first losses in a resolution, and then creditors. The resolution authority during the process of write-down and transfer needs to review whether it is sufficient or not, as it could mean they will have to compensate or re-transfer. It will need to value the shares and liabilities to determine the possible rate of conversion and write-down depending on the class of instruments and in accordance with the predetermined sequence according to the Member State's insolvency law. Moreover, in circumstances where the resolution authority decides to exercise its resolution powers and only partly bail-in equity and liabilities, then the original shareholder and creditors will need to be compensated based on an estimation of the recovery rate in a hypothetical insolvency proceeding under normal insolvency law. **5.72**

The resolution authority will need to ensure that all administrative requirements such as registers and listing of shares are amended and changed to ensure the application of bail-in. It will also need to ensure that all procedural impediments to conversion are removed. The designated liabilities will require amendment to include a contractual provision to recognize bail-in. Thereby, liabilities governed or being otherwise subject to the laws of a third country become bail-in eligible in particular. In this respect, the contractual parties agree to abide by the write-down or conversion. The move towards complying with the provision is an onerous one and will require the EBA to assist with technical guidance to assist resolution authorities in devising a list of liabilities which are included and excluded from bail-in. **5.73**

The introduction of the bail-in tool as the option of 'first resort' poses a range of challenges for the respective authorities, leading to possible misalignment of incentives, which could leave the significant subsidiary in a rather vulnerable position. This is partly due to the fact that the bail-in is considered the tool of first resort if the bank exceeds the minimum 8% threshold. The guiding principle in these matters is that no shareholder or creditor should be worse off than insolvency, so ultimately this is a starting point rather than an end point with valuations and compensation claims considered during and after the resolution.[160] **5.74**

[160] BRRD, Art. 74(1)–(4) and Art. 75.

The narrow form of financing within many Member States means the subsidiaries are unlikely to be holding the right forms of debts to bail in. The move to changing the composition of financial markets is not likely in the short to medium term but it is a long-term outlook. In light of this, the option to get recapitalized in normal market circumstances is an unlikely one. The current vulnerabilities in the economies and financial markets are evident from the lack of ability of the respective central banks to introduce meaningful counter-cyclical and systemic risk capital buffers to improve the resilience of the financial systems. Moreover, the possibility of increasing these is problematic since it leads to lower levels of finance in the economy which is likely to have an impact on the speed of recovery. In the context of a counter-cyclical buffer, it is expected to be set at zero since in most regions there is little indication of excessive credit risk build-up but rather a considerable amount of non-performing legacy assets. It has been noted that the systemic risk buffer only addresses future expected losses rather than the existing legacy assets so offering limited protection. Moreover, the possibility of raising finance in the respective financial markets is likely to be limited or non-existent given the heavy reliance on a narrow form of bank finance. The existing problem of non-performing loans is also going to act as a heavy burden on these institutions. In light of the sheer size of these losses, in some cases the banks are exempted from complying with the systemic risk buffer. The level of concentration in the banking market as the primary form of finance is also likely to pose challenges since only a handful of foreign banks in the respective countries comprise around 60%–90% of the market.

5.75 The first losses will need to be absorbed by shareholders and, in this case, the significant subsidiaries are in many cases wholly owned by the group parent and so the group parent is inevitably going to bear the first losses in any write-down of equity. The incentive, therefore, for the parent is to try to ensure the liability structure of the subsidiary is such that the creditors of the significant subsidiary absorb a significant proportion of the remaining losses. To ensure this, the banks are expected to build up a solvency buffer, MREL, made up of liabilities that are expected to be in distress loss absorbing and so minimize the chances of relying on public funds to bail out the bank. The MREL requirements are applicable to all European banks, as opposed to the TLAC requirements which are applied to the G-SIB.

5.76 In the European context, the minimum threshold is set at 8% in the BRRD, but some Member States are expected to set considerably higher levels to act as a suitable buffer to absorb a significant proportion of the losses of a systemically importance institution. Despite this, some banks in the European Union will be exempt from holding MREL. Notwithstanding those banks, it is the case that the smaller Member States should move towards having such liabilities in place, since many of the banks rely heavily on deposits to fund their businesses and have little long-term unsecured debt. Since there is a lack of a developed debt market, it is likely that the subsidiaries in question are able to issue the appropriate debt instruments in the local market. A particular concern is the likelihood of them being issued to an overly concentrated financial sector which would cause its own risk of contagion.

5.77 The structure and prepositioning of bail-in-able debt has been a particularly important topic and it has required careful preparation between the resolution authorities to work with banks and their groups to address how bail-in could work. The prepositioning of bail-in-able debt does offer in many ways an *ex ante* answer to Herring's[161] home and host dilemma since the pre-commitment to it signals to the host authority a clear indication of its importance to the group and the parent regulator. While some may be disappointed with the outcome at least preparations could be put in place to prepare for a standalone resolution or insolvency-liquidation. However, such decisions could well see in the future the supervisory authority ensuring local banks are more capitalized (hoarding capital) than others in the market that maybe part of a bail-in strategy.

EU Member State Resolution Decisions

The cases of resolution actions in the EU highlight that a single one-size-fits-all approach has not been taken and a more purposive approach has been adopted. A reasonable number of cases now exist to evaluate the use of resolution tools and more importantly the combination of tools used. More controversially the question of consistency has been a concern in instances where bail-in has been avoided due to its implementation date being put forward, whereas in other jurisdictions banks were expected to exercise the right voluntarily. It is likely the bail-in tool will only play a limited role in small bank resolutions and in relatively small Member States in comparison to the other resolution tools explained above. Therefore, while it may be the tool of first resort for large complex banks, it is likely to play a limited role in cases relating to narrow banks reliant on deposits as a source of funds. **5.78**

In Hungary, the option utilized regarding Magyar Nemzeti Bank[162] was the sale of business tool and the asset separation tool to divest a portfolio of project finance loans. The sale of business tool requirements are set out in Article 42(2) of the Hungarian Resolution Act (transposing the BRRD into Hungarian law). With regard to the asset separation tool regarding state aid, MNB obliged the Bank to comply with the commitments approved by the European Commission based on the 'Commitments Letter'. Using the sale of business tool (divesting certain portfolio elements of the Bank), seven loan claims were sold to OTP Bank Nyrt (the biggest domestic bank in terms of total assets). The asset separation tool applied pursuant to decision SA.40441 2015/N of the European Commission. As a preparatory step, assets intended to be divested but which could not be sold to voluntary buyers on the market were transferred to MKB Pénzügyi Zrt to encourage the implementation of the asset separation tool. MNB transferred the shares issued by MKB Pénzügyi Zrt to the Hungarian Resolution Property Management Private Company Limited by shares (MSzVK) and the shares issued by RESIDEAL Zrt to MSzVK (RESIDEAL is a special company dealing with the real estate management). MSzVK paid real market value for the shares (above the market price), which entitled the bank to receive compatible State aid approved by the European Commission. MNB transferred all issued shares of the Bank to MSzVK (the provider of **5.79**

[161] R Herring, 'Conflicts between Home and Host Country Prudential Supervisors' in D D Evanoff, G G Kaufman, and J R LaBrosse (eds), International Financial Instability: *Global Banking and National Regulation* (New Jersey: World Scientific 2007) pp. 201–21.

[162] <https://www.eba.europa.eu/documents/10180/1460574/1+July+2016_Central+Bank+of+Hungary+notification+regarding+termination+of+resolution.pdf> [accessed 18 March 2019].

state aid) for a symbolic purchase price as compensation and as a precondition for the received state aid to comply with the rules of the internal market of the EU.

5.80 In Italy, a number of small banks opted for resolution.[163] With regards to Banca delle Marche, Banca Popolare dell'Etruria e del Lazio, Cassa di Risparmio di Ferrara, and Cassa di Risparmio della Provincia di Chieti, all assets and liabilities (including bad loans) of the banks were transferred under resolution to four bridge banks (Nuova Banca delle Marche, Nuova Banca dell'Etruria, Nuova Cassa di Risparmio di Ferrara, and Nuova Cassa di Risparmio di Chieti) and this was followed by the transfer of bad loans to an asset management vehicle (AMV). The Resolution Fund intervened in order to capitalise the four bridge banks, cover transaction losses and capitalise the AMV and provide guarantees if needed.

5.81 Portugal exercised resolution in the case of Banif-Banco Internacional do Funchal, SA.[164] Banif-Banco Internacional do Funchal, SA (Banif) and most of its assets and liabilities is being sold to Banco Santander Totta for €150m. Distressed assets will be transferred to a vehicle asset management. The voluntary sale involves a public support estimated at €2.255m intended to cover future contingencies, of which €489m comes from the resolution fund and €1.766m directly from the State as a result of the options agreed between the Portuguese authorities, the European institutions and Banco Santander Totta as regards delimiting the perimeter of assets and liabilities to be sold. This measure follows the European Commission's in-depth investigation of the State aid received by Banif, after the shareholders and the Banif Board of Directors initiated a sale of the institution to avoid the risk of it being declared illegal and subsequent demands for its restitution. Also in Portugal, in the case of Banco Espírito Santo (BES), SA, resolution was initiated.[165] A bridge bank ('Novo Banco, SA') was set up by the Bank of Portugal to transfer the assets and liabilities of BES with the exception of 'excluded liabilities' (certain issues of non-subordinated bonds issued by BES and intended for institutional investors). The original resolution decision provided that Bank of Portugal, as the Resolution Authority, may at any time re-transfer assets and liabilities between BES and Novo Banco. This measure was based on public interest reasons and was necessary to ensure that the losses of BES are absorbed by this institution's shareholders and creditors and not by the resolution fund or the taxpayers. In addition, Bank of Portugal made a final adjustment to the perimeter of the assets, liabilities, off-balance-sheet items, and assets under management transferred to Novo Banco. There was clarification that no liabilities have been transferred to Novo Banco that were contingent or unknown at the date the resolution measure was applied to BES. The shareholding in BES Finance was retransferred to BES, which is necessary to ensure full compliance with and application of the resolution measure as regards the non-transfer to Novo Banco of subordinated debt instruments issued by BES. There is clarification that it is the Resolution Fund's responsibility, upon the fulfilment of certain conditions, to make neutral for Novo Banco—through an appropriate measure—potential negative effects of future decisions resulting from the resolution process and giving rise to liabilities or contingencies.

[163] <https://www.eba.europa.eu/documents/10180/1890369/IT_notification_BRRD_5June2017.pdf/223a5aa0-12c4-48e8-b548-72750f7625fc> [accessed 18 March 2019].

[164] <https://www.eba.europa.eu/documents/10180/1315419/Comunicado+BdP_BANIF.pdf> [accessed 18 March 2019].

[165] <https://www.bportugal.pt/en-US/OBancoeoEurosistema/ComunicadoseNotasdeInformacao/Pages/combp20151229-2.aspx> [accessed 18 March 2019].

Denmark exercised resolution option in respect of Andelskassen J A K Slagelse.[166] Finansiel Stabilitet (FS) took over the management of Andelskassen to secure a controlled resolution of the bank. FS established a subsidiary (Broinstitut I A/S) which will take over the ownership of the bank. Existing contributed capital was written down to zero in the first instance. The Danish Guarantee Scheme for Depositors and Investors is required to contribute to cover the bank's losses (on first valuation). Additional measures have included the FS setting up a bridge institution (pursuant to s 21 of the Act and Article 40 of the BRRD) which shall contribute new capital to the institution and take over its ownership. A bail-in tool for loss absorption was carried out pursuant to s 24 of the Act (implementing Articles 43 and 46 of the BRRD) in respect of all other subordinated obligations of the institution, so that such obligations are written down to zero. 5.82

In the case of Greece and the resolution of Cooperative Bank of Peloponnese Coop Ltd,[167] the licence of the bank was withdrawn and its assessment indicated that the bank was failing or was likely to fail. In this case, the bank had no eligible liabilities for the purposes of recapitalization through a bail-in to convert into equity to reduce the capital shortfall. The bank was required to recapitalize once it was found to have a capital adequacy ratio of -7.02%. In this case, the sale of business tool was also utilized since, in comparison to the bridge bank, it was the least costly option to reduce the resolution costs and ensure minimum or no disruption to the continuity of critical functions. In the case of Panellinia Bank SA, the withdrawal of the bank's authorization without the simultaneous adoption of resolution measures would 'very seriously jeopardise the continuity of the banking operations of all cooperative banks and would thus negatively affect cooperative credit, and consequently, financial stability'. Panellinia Bank's property items (assets, liabilities, and contractual relationships) were transferred to Piraeus Bank SA to protect deposits. Emergency liquidity assistance (ELA) was provided by the Eurosystem. 5.83

Cross-border Group Resolution

The cross-border resolution of institutions and groups requires a significant degree of timely cooperation and coordination between the home and host Member State or between Banking Union participating and non-participating Member States. The SRB is expected to cooperate closely with national resolution authorities.[168] However, it has not, to date, set out the guidelines for cooperation and coordination. It is expected that the ECB and the SRB will publish an MoU with national resolution authorities in non-participating Member States. The national resolution authority will also assist with information to enable the SRB to formulate its decisions. The SRB will represent entities in participating Member States. In light of this, the SRB will represent the national resolution authority when working out how best to cooperate and coordinate with national resolution authorities 5.84

166 <https://www.eba.europa.eu/documents/10180/1413812/Resolution+of+Andelskassen+JAK.pdf> [accessed 18 March 2019]; <https://www.eba.europa.eu/documents/10180/1224279/Notification+-+BRRD+Article+83%284%29%20-+International+Authorities.pdf> [accessed 18 March 2019]; <https://www.eba.europa.eu/documents/10180/1321242/Andelskassen+JAK+press+release.pdf> [accessed 18 March 2019].

167 <https://www.eba.europa.eu/documents/10180/1486246/Bank+of+Greece.pdf> [accessed 18 March 2019].

168 SRMR, Art. 31.

of non-participating Member States. More specifically, the SRB is expected to enter into MoUs with non-participating Member States' national resolution authorities that have an institution which is part of one of the G-SIIs. The lack of success in ensuring binding commitments in the past where MoUs were present would lead one to conclude that such an approach is unlikely to get the binding results sought by the SRB.

5.85 It is expected that the SRB will communicate its plans, decisions, and/or measures with the national resolution authorities in non-participating Member States.[169] While this is a positive step forward, it is not very clear whether the documents will be provided or whether it will simply communicate the fact that they have been decided, leaving the national resolution authorities in the non-participating Member States with limited assistance with their resolution decisions. This should mitigate significant impediments to cross-border resolution for those banks considered significant. An equally important dimension is cooperation and coordination with third countries, in the capacity as either home state or host state supervisor.[170]

5.86 The BRRD requires Member States to work out in advance the role and responsibilities of competent and resolution authorities.[171] The process of cooperation and coordination between the various parties across borders will be partly assisted by the forward planning undertaken at the preparation stage with the recovery and resolution plans. However, these plans will form the starting point and the catalyst for early intervention and resolution may not necessarily arise from a scenario captured by the plans, although they will provide the authorities with a very good idea of the critical functions and business lines which will need to be considered during the resolution phase, and indicate which tools best address the problems experienced at the institution or group level.

5.87 In this respect, the BRRD identifies the broader hurdles relating to subsidiaries and branches located in other Member States; furthermore, and broader still, it seeks to minimize the adverse effects on financial stability in the EU and Member States.[172] Thus, 'due consideration is given to the objectives of balancing the interests of the various Member States involved and of avoiding unfairly prejudicing or unfairly protecting the interests of particular Member States, including avoiding unfair burden allocation across Member States'.[173] As noted earlier, the advance planning is likely to enable authorities to work out burden allocation rather than burden sharing equally, notwithstanding the uneven form it may take both from a supervisory, resolution, and liquidation perspective. In many respects, while the BRRD provides a legal framework to mandate cooperation, it primarily takes one Member State or third-country resolution authority to act in its own public interest and initiate insolvency proceedings to undermine the purpose of the BRRD. The broad powers and purposes of the resolution authority may resonate with other competent and resolution authorities but may not readily fit with the narrow approach taken by the courts. This is perhaps frustrating from the perspective of the resolution authority given that the purpose of the BRRD is to put in place a resolution process that minimizes costs based on the

[169] SRMR, Art. 8(2) and Art. 32.
[170] SRMR, Art. 32.
[171] BRRD, Art. 87(a)–(l).
[172] BRRD, Art. 34(2).
[173] BRRD, Art. 87(h).

resolution authorities' economic assessment, with the principle that shareholders and creditors take the first losses but no shareholder or creditor will be worse off with the application of the resolution tools than with liquidation.

Relations with Third Countries

A considerable amount of cross-border banking and finance exists within the EU and a proportion of it has significant origins or presence in third countries.[174] In the accession countries the presence of EU Member State banks is significant. The BRRD attempts to put in place a framework of cooperation and coordination between EU Member State competent and resolution authorities and third country counterparts so that the level of disruption to markets and impact on financial stability is minimized. The experience of those third countries considered in this report would suggest that the efforts fall short of the aspirations set out in the BRRD and the SRM. The incentives, it is argued, remain to promote self-serving interests so cooperation and coordination is likely to occur when it serves the interests of the home or serves the mutual interests of a select few home and host states. This could perhaps be improved if the EU resolution colleges and the international crisis management groups coordinated and cooperated better, with a super college arrangement for sharing information between members and observers. **5.88**

The BRRD provides a broad context for cooperation linked to crisis prevention and crisis management arrangements.[175] The crisis prevention tools, such as information sharing to complete recovery resolution plans, will involve the competent and resolution authorities separately. However, while the EU resolution framework advocates a separation of roles for supervision and resolution, their third-country counterparts may only consist of one authority that is both a supervisor and a resolution authority. Indeed, in some third countries, it is likely a resolution authority may not exist and a court-based system does exist, and coordination and cooperation with the competent authority is the first port of call. This is likely to result in the third country being unable to participate in the resolution college as well. This situation is likely to reduce with the introduction of special administrative led resolution regimes. In many respects the requests for information in the context of resolution exist within the broader supervisory mandates associated with techniques such as consolidated, supervision, and arrangements for information sharing in relation to financial conglomerates. This assumes the incentives in supervision are aligned for cooperation and coordination which is not necessarily the case in practice, as the study have shown earlier. While the information requests and data requests are honoured by third countries, the arrangements are not reciprocal in return and broad outcomes and decisions are shared without any meaningful dialogue. It is, therefore, not surprising to find the level of reciprocity in terms of information sharing regarding prevention or crisis management is also weak or non-existent. **5.89**

[174] Maria J Nieto, 'Third Country Relations in the Directive Establishing A Framework for Recovery and Resolution of Credit Institutions' in Jens-Henrich Binder and Dalvinder Singh (eds), *Bank Resolution: The European Regime* (Oxford: Oxford University Press 2016) pp. 137–56.

[175] BRRD, Art. 93.

5.90 The BRRD sets out the expected approach for those institutions or groups that have a parent located in a third country, a significant branch, or a subsidiary in a Member State.[176] In relation to these entities, the BRRD anticipates cooperation to inform the resolution process and sets out *ex ante* the expected role of the EU competent and resolution authorities. However, in practice, it is likely there are more incentives for the EU resolution authority to cooperate and coordinate with large systemically important third countries where perhaps the systemically important parent is incorporated. On the other hand, there are less incentives for the EU resolution authorities to cooperate and coordinate with host states with significant subsidiaries that pose little systemic risk exposure to the parent. The BRRD encourages Member States to enter into bilateral agreements with third countries to work out how they will attempt to work with one another in resolution. In practice, however, MoUs have not worked well and are likely to simply emphasize well-intentioned cooperation with third countries that pose larger systemic risk exposures to their interests. As a stopgap measure, the BRRD provides an interim measure to recognize and enforce third-country resolution proceedings until such agreements are made. The European resolution colleges are expected to play an important role in this regard, to provide a platform for coordination and recognition of proceedings emanating from a third country. As the study will show in the following section, the third countries are classed as observers on resolution colleges and there is not really an explicit commitment to share information with them in the resolution colleges unless it implicitly serves the group resolution authority's interests. Here, the group resolution authority can exploit its position by conferring better terms and conditions to some observers than others, provided it does not result in them having better terms than members. However since subgroups can also exist within the resolution colleges.

5.91 The BRRD offers limited assurance of third-country cooperation and coordination for resolution. It provides a number of eventualities that primarily mean at best that the resolution authorities will commit to a number of *ex ante* arrangements to recognize and enforce third-country resolution proceedings which will be dependent on Member States' own discretion. It could result in one Member State recognizing and cooperating with a third-country resolution authority and possibly in other Member States' resolution authorities not cooperating to the same extent.[177] In this respect, the BRRD expects Member States to give due consideration to such matters and the financial stability in those Member States. As a minimum, the Member States are required to be in a position where they can exercise their powers of resolution regarding:

- assets of third-country institutions in a Member State or governed by Member State law;
- rights and liabilities booked in a branch located in a Member State;
- transfer of shares;
- exercising contractual powers to support third-country resolution proceedings; and
- rendering enforceable rights to terminate, liquidate, or accelerate contractual rights that arise from resolution actions that relate to third-country resolution proceedings.[178]

[176] BRRD, Art. 93(1)(a)–(c).
[177] BRRD, Art. 94.
[178] BRRD, Art. 94(4)(a)–(d).

Taking into account the third countries considered in this project, the position is likely to be one where the resolution authority needs to be preparing for an MPE approach since it is unlikely to be involved in the group's possible pursuit of an SPE approach which is likely to apply to the more systemic parts of the group rather than the non-systemic parts. **5.92**

The BRRD does provide a basis for Member States to act in their own public interest when considering whether or not to recognize third-country resolution proceedings.[179] This is quite possibly the likely outcome of the reforms introduced by the EU for the very reasons highlighted above. For example, this may apply if: **5.93**

- the third-country proceedings would have an adverse impact on financial stability in the Member State;
- independent resolution of the branch is necessary;
- the third country would not confer the same treatment of creditors and depositors with similar legal rights;
- there would be material fiscal implications for the Member State; or
- it would be contrary in light of national law.

The lack of reciprocal information sharing and crisis simulation participation of these third countries means that on all fronts it is noteworthy to recognize that it is important for the third country in the accession region to develop their own crisis management arrangements which are fit for their own purposes. This is likely to take a considerable length of time since it needs to be developed at the crisis prevention level with recovery and/or resolution plans as well as the building up of the administrative arrangements for crisis management. The significant challenge is to try and ensure the LAC at the significant subsidiary level is sufficient for the local interests. **5.94**

In relationship to third-country branches located in a Member State, the authorities will need to decide whether third-country resolution proceedings or Member State resolution proceedings are to apply.[180] When the circumstances listed in BRRD, Article 95 are present, the Member State acting in the public interest, or when the third country is unable or unwilling to act in the wider interest, will need to be in a position to exercise resolution proceedings in accordance with the resolution's objectives, conditions, and principles. **5.95**

The BRRD also requires the EBA to consider entering into non-binding cooperation agreements with third countries to put in place their intentions *ex ante* to organize resolution of entities set up in the European Union. However, the cooperation agreements should be general and not made in reference to a particular third-country entity in the Member State. The BRRD explicitly provides that they are not legally binding on the Member State. Notwithstanding the non-binding nature of the agreements, they are expected to assist with: **5.96**

- recovery and resolution plans;
- assessment of resolvability impediments to resolution;
- early intervention measures; and
- the resolution powers and tools.

[179] BRRD, Art. 95(a)–(e).
[180] BRRD, Art. 96.

5.97 Moreover, the cooperation arrangements could include arrangements for sharing information, forming separate recovery and resolution plans, and the possible resolution tools to be expected to be used.

5.98 A particular problem identified by the GFC was the lack of a coherent cross-border resolution regime which primarily led to Member States taking action in their public interest, taking a territorial rather than a universalist approach. The extent to which the BRRD remedies this is debatable. The BRRD certainly enables the competent and resolution authorities to *ex ante* work out the possible options they are likely to initiate in resolution and to enter into non-binding cooperation arrangements. It appears to be dependent on a case-by-case basis. In some instances, the BRRD limits the Member State's authority when it sets out options for resolution of third-country entities. For example, when it requires two or more entities operating in the EU when it could be the case that an individual subsidiary or indeed significant branch could well pose risks to markets functioning efficiently and to the financial stability in the respective Member State and beyond.

5.99 The implications of the wider lack of coordination are material since a decision by a third country to trigger resolution before the EU group resolution authority does could have a detrimental impact on market confidence in the group and so undermine achieving its intended aims.

International Cooperation Arrangements

5.100 As part of the SRB's role to represent national resolution authorities, it is expected to enter in to cooperation arrangements with non-participating Member States and third countries to assist with the process of improving arrangements for cross-border resolution.[181] In respect of third countries, the SRB has entered in to a number of international cooperation arrangements with its counterparts, namely Canada (CDIC),[182] United States (FDIC),[183] Brazil (Central Bank),[184] Mexico (Mexico's Institute for the Protection of Bank Savings),[185] and Serbia, (National Bank),[186] and Albania (National Bank).[187] These soft law arrangements are in addition to formal membership of crisis management groups—the equivalent to resolution colleges. It expressly indicates that the cooperation arrangement does not create binding obligations or supersede domestic law. The commitments, therefore, are likely to be only as good as the relationship built up by the SRB and their respective counterpart, which is likely to be cemented better by the national resolution authorities and the

[181] SRM Regulation, Art. 32.

[182] Cooperation Arrangement Concerning the Resolution of Financial Institutions with Cross-Border Operations in Canada and The European Banking Union (2017).

[183] Cooperation Arrangement Concerning the Resolution of Insured Depository Institutions and Certain Other Financial Companies with Cross-Border Operations in the United States and The European Banking Union (2017).

[184] Cooperation Arrangement between the Banco Central Do Brasil and The Single Resolution Board (2018).

[185] Cooperation Arrangement between the Institute for the Protection of Bank Savings and The Single Resolution Board (2018).

[186] Cooperation Arrangement between the National Bank of Serbia and the Single Resolution Board (2018).

[187] Cooperation Arrangement between the Bank of Albania and The Single Resolution Board (2018).

relationship and confidence each jurisdiction has to each other. The important principle behind this initiative is the political will to work together for common ends which is primarily an orderly resolution with minimum disruption.

The cooperation arrangements share a common template, explaining the position and responsibilities of the SRB to its international counterparts in the arrangements. A significant part of the arrangement explains how the Banking Union reforms have introduced new relationships within the Eurozone and non-Eurozone Member States. It specifically explains the relationship between the SRB and national resolution authorities as points of contact for the Eurozone, namely execution of resolution schemes at the Eurozone regional level and at the national level, resolution planning, resolvability assessments, and determining levels of minimum levels of own funds and eligible liabilities respectively. It highlights the importance of cooperating to safeguard financial stability in the respective jurisdictions and so recognises the importance attached to working with one another to achieve that goal., the principle focus being 'their willingness to cooperate with each other in the interest of fulfilling their respective statutory objectives; enhancing communication and cooperation; assisting each other in the planning and the conduct of an orderly Resolution of an Entity'. Following on, this theme highlights that the decisions taken by resolution authorities duly consider the potential impact of their resolution actions on the respective financial stability of the named country and the EU. The arrangement goes significantly further in terms of a commitment, namely to essentially work together with other parts of the official safety net on matter relating to resolution: 'the Authorities seek to enhance cooperation in the analysis of Entities' Resolution issues, planning for potential Resolution scenarios, and appropriate simulations, contingency planning or other work designed to improve preparations of the Authorities for managing and resolving crises involving Entities'.[188] While there is no commitment to formal cooperation in resolution and who is likely to take the lead in resolution, the cooperation arrangement does indicate the importance of promoting efficiency and preserving value in the resolution entity and a commitment to maximize recoveries and minimize losses and moral hazard. From the third-country perspective a single point of contact is useful if it has a bank with multiple operations within the Eurozone. **5.101**

The principles of promoting efficiency and preserving value require good relationships regardless of whether the materiality of the interest is not necessarily mutual. This is dependent on whether there is recognition that both parties have a mutual interest in participating, in view of their risk exposure and indeed commitment *ex ante* to assist both parts to prepare for resolution in whatever form it may take. Nonetheless, in many instances it will be recognized that the risk exposure is not likely to be of mutual interest from a home and host perspective. In view of this, it is important to provide legitimacy to cooperation and coordination arrangements to show recognition that, despite **5.102**

[188] To the extent possible, in respect of any confidentiality and other restrictions, the Authorities intend to:
(i) discuss approaches to Resolution planning;
(ii) share ideas and strategies; and
(iii) facilitate mutual understanding of Resolution plan rulemaking, rules, practice and implementation in each other's jurisdiction.

unequal materiality of the entity, cooperation, and coordination arrangements are in place. For example, as shown in Chapter 1, the exposure of European banks in Serbia and Albania, potential accession countries, is very high. But these exposures may not be material to the group parent entity in the Member State; in many instances these are, Eurozone Member States, so within the umbrella of the Banking Union and SRB jurisdiction. In view of this, preparations for a resolution scheme, which may include, for the respective entity an MPE strategy, requires preparation in terms of managing, for instance, a decision to sell the business and so placing greater pressure on the country as a result of foreign bank concentration risk. Moreover, the resolution scheme for the Banking Union should enable a sharing of information, albeit at a strategic level, to prepare for dealing with disruption to intragroup funding, if the foreign third country entity is reliant on it for the purposes of liquidity. But, as shown in Chapter 1, the entities in those countries may be significantly reliant on local corporate and retail depositors for funding and less reliant on intergroup funding. This should insulate the entity in smaller third countries from the problems arising at the group level. But there may be a tug of war over the entities capital which could be well over the minimum levels and may lead to a position where it is reduced to improve the capital position of the parent or another material entity within the group. The argument that the entity is narrow and so likely to be dealt with in liquidation does not necessarily hold up from the country perspective, in view of the entities' critical importance of providing credit in the local market.

5.103 The SRM opens the door for the potential of an international agreement for recognition and enforcement of third-country resolution proceedings.[189] This is an important step, in principle, towards offering a route towards a binding obligation with third countries but at this juncture no agreement has been entered in to with a third country. The likelihood of a binding agreement is small, despite the recognition of how important it is to have clear commitments in such times to ensure orderly resolution on both sides. However, this requires something far more than the cooperation arrangement measures and indeed resolution colleges/ crisis management colleges are offering. The SRM Regulation would essentially require the exercise to be undertaken on a case-by-case basis, reviewing both sets of laws to determine what impediments exist for either the third country or the SRB to recognise such decisions. The SRM Regulation expects the SRB to refuse recognition or enforcement of resolution proceedings if, inter alia, they adversely affect the financial stability in a participating Member State or if the treatment of depositors or creditors is not the same. To reduce this risk, the role of colleges is critical but the outcomes for all members may not be equal in terms of commitments to share information.

Reconfiguring Home Bias for Significant Subsidiaries—The Resolution Perspective

5.104 The SRM and the BRRD provide a good starting point for effective coordination and cooperation in the resolution of cross-border banks. The SRM with the SRB at the helm

[189] SRM Regulation, Art. 33.

mitigates some of the conflicts of interests that can arise in cross-border resolution at the Eurozone level with the introduction of a single decision-making body. The move to a single, more consistent, approach to resolution of groups is likely to have a wider beneficial effect. The resolution framework does have a wider margin of discretion than its supervisory counterpart so there is a significant role for national resolution authorities to play in supporting the single resolution scheme adopted by the SRB. Moreover, there is a significant margin of discretion to enable resolution authorities that are non-participating Member States to exercise national discretion to formulate national resolution plans and schemes.

The significance of home bias remains present due to the approach, in practice, to resolution that is likely to be taken. In this respect, the dominance of the group resolution authority in the decision-making process means that it is expected that significant subsidiaries that are important to the viability of the group as a whole are likely to feature more importantly in the resolution scheme. The level of reciprocity in terms of building up resilience and information-sharing and decision-making is argued to be aligned in the interests of the group resolution authority and at the detriment of some small Member States and third countries that have significant subsidiaries from their financial system perspective. The resolution policy framework needs to be better aligned, in terms of proportionality, for significant subsidiaries from both the perspective of the group as a whole and the perspective of Member States. It is argued that a more coherent policy framework is likely to lead to a more orderly resolution from a group perspective and a single subsidiary perspective. Therefore, better aligning the interests of home and host Member States and third countries where a significant subsidiary is located. This would enable the resolution authorities of the significant subsidiary to work out whether there are potential impediments to resolvability such as cross-sharing of IT platforms and other back-office functions that the parent provides to the subsidiary. The level of discretion currently enables the group resolution authority to decide that it will not share such plans with a wider range of Member States and third countries. 5.105

The importance of improving the resolvability of a group and of a significant subsidiary that is not included in the group resolution plan cannot be underestimated. It is the starting point for orderly resolution. It would be important for an orderly resolution to have the resolution authorities that have been designated for the purposes of capital buffers to automatically be appointed onto resolution colleges as either members or observers. This would avoid a position where a subsidiary that is relatively small in comparison. The level of discretion at the resolution colleges needs to be better structured so that information is shared on a more reciprocal basis. This could improve group resolution as well as resolution of significant subsidiaries at the periphery of the group *ex ante*. It would be beneficial since it would enable both sets of authorities to work out the resolution plans in a more coordinated manner and minimize asymmetry of information, as well as Member States and third countries acting in their own self-interest. There are obvious challenges here from a group and from a single significant subsidiary perspective associated with building up the appropriate level of MREL and the associated issue of taking an SPE or MPE approach. In terms of the MREL, it will be important for the resolution authorities to decide what will constitute eligible 5.106

MREL. Moreover, the implications of including uncovered deposits of corporate and financial institutions on the wider economy should be considered as well. The wider implications of the principle of burden sharing and having 8% minimum own funds and eligible liabilities for write-down and conversion for the purpose of bail-in need to be assessed since they are closely related to access to resolution funds. The principle of burden sharing for subsidiaries in these respective Member States and third countries has a disproportionate effect on them, despite the fact that they have relatively high levels of own funds.

5.107 The policy framework needs to better explain its position on narrow banks for the purposes of resolution and insolvency. The idea of a narrow bank is a rather unhelpful term since the policy position appears to assume it is not systemically important. In a number of Member States, significant subsidiaries have been required to hold additional capital buffers based on criteria set by the EBA. In such cases, the O-SIIs have been determined to pose a systemic risk to financial stability. The O-SIIs are, to all intents and purposes, narrow banks, and if one were to apply the policy of resolution by way of insolvency this would limit the options the Member States are likely to want to use to act in their public interest, as is analysed in Chapter 6.

International Soft Law Instruments Focus on Home and Host Resolution Issues

5.108 The BRRD put in place equivalence requirements as well as reference to recognition of proceedings. The EBA Opinion on Argentina equivalence assessment of supervision mentions resolution but does not assess its equivalence to the BRRD.[190] This is quite surprising considering the critical importance of resolution and planning as a continuum of supervision. The principal international soft instrument in the field of resolution is the FSB Key Attributes of Effective Resolution Regimes.[191] These were originally endorsed by the G20 in November 2011 at the Cannes Summit.[192] The tone of the FSB Key Attributes does differ from its Basel Committee counterpart. This is perhaps because of the legal basis of resolution and liquidation of banks. An interesting emphasis in Annex 2 puts forward the idea of a 'presumption in favour of cooperation in the event of the firms resolution'.[193] The accession countries have put in place resolution powers and so there is a relatively high degree of functional equivalence. In part, this is due to the fact that reliance is placed on the BRRD as a template for such reforms. One avenue for third countries would be to seek information about resolution plans from the entity in their jurisdiction. The bank may complain that the request for information is duplicating information given to the parent entity authorities. Nevertheless, it is a recourse to ensure it can prepare for the resolution option

[190] EBA, Opinion of the European Banking Authority on the Equivalence of supervisory and regulatory requirements in relation to Argentina 22/05/19 <https://eba.europa.eu/documents/10180/2622242/EBA+Opinion+on+Third+Country+Equivalence+-+Argentina.pdf>; ANNEX—Republic of Argentina, <https://eba.europa.eu/documents/10180/2740473/Annex+to+EBA+Opinion+on+third+country+equivalence+-+Argentina.pdf>.

[191] FSB, Key Attributes of Effective Resolution Regimes for Financial Institutions, 15 October 2014, <https://www.fsb.org/wp-content/uploads/r_141015.pdf>.

[192] Communiqué, G20 Leaders Summit, Cannes, 4 November 2011.

[193] Ibid, Annex 2, p. 31.

that is proposed by the parent authorities. As shown in Chapter 1, a significant proportion of their banks have the ultimate owner that is a significant bank and so falls under the ECB supervision. The SRB would be the group resolution authority and so the chair of the resolution college, and it would be its decision whether these countries could participate as Observers. Since they have an Observer status within the supervisory colleges, it would be difficult to reject their participation in the resolution college. In this respect, the accession countries have a preferential relationship, which other third countries may not benefit from. In respect of observer status, it can attend meetings but not necessarily vote, yet it certainly can express its views on proceedings.

One of the most critical roles by home and host cooperation plays out in the execution of the resolution strategy. At the EU level, this is led by the parent entity resolution authorities. However, they will need to be mindful of those parts of the group located in third countries. The home and host may need to cooperate since critical services may be relied upon by the subsidiary in the third country. Equally, the options of resolution are likely to require the home to notify the hosts, with the possibility of cooperation likely to achieve more efficient and cost-effective ends. The resolution college and its third country participants should agree beforehand whether or not resolution measures are likely to be mutually recognized. This should in part ascertain whether the resolution authority of the parent will be recognized and accepted by the third country. Equally, concerning the parent entity resolution authority, in many of these cases the SRB will likely expect notifications of their possible intention to exercise resolution of a subsidiary that is part of a group. 5.109

Reflections on the Principal Issues

The chapter showed a number of challenges remain to address the asymmetry of information problems that can arise in resolution decision-making. The home and host dilemma remains albeit to a lesser extent. The formal processes of preparation exist in theory but in practice political will remains a critical obstacle. In view of this coordination and cooperation risks exist that are now pronounced in policy frameworks. It has been argued while not all will participate in the core parts of decisions it is imperative that all have at least sufficient information and data to prepare a standalone resolution or insolvency and liquidation. This is particularly acute in the third country perspective. However, it cannot be underestimated that it cannot exist even within centralized supervision and resolution. Since in part the ECB and SRB are reliant on national interpretations of EU law. A concern for some Member States will be the underlying policy assumption that narrow banks that provide credit finance are not critical and therefore will be resolved through national insolvency proceedings. This will inevitably lead to different outcomes when banks are failing or likely to fail with Member States likely to take a different view to the SRB about their banks. Another issue that has surfaced in the analysis is the sheer scale of technical expertise now required to operationalize so many new elements to execute orderly resolution. The role of resolution colleges is equally important to ensure preparations for resolution schemes. However, while Member States are members of colleges in substance some members have more of a role and ability to inform decisions than others. The level of 5.110

discretion in the instruments and the assessment of resolution colleges shows this. In part a significant problem faced by Member States is the complexity of the issues that require joint decisions. It is clearly evident that such pre-commitments are not present when it comes to third countries which will mean it will depend on the willingness of each party to be proactive. In view of the large presence of third country banks in the EU at a branch or subsidiary level this is likely to make it a challenge to undertake the task on a bank or country-by-country basis.

6
European Bank Insolvency and Liquidation Proceedings

Introduction

6.1 The fractured position of insolvency laws governing banks led to the introduction of the special resolution regime with the primary aim of safeguarding financial stability. It is important to note that not all banks are likely to be threats to financial stability, but the way in which bank failures can escalate because of regulatory gaps and weaknesses the risk from multiple small bank failures cannot be underestimated. In view of this, the presumption is that all 'small' banks are to enter winding-up proceedings as part of domestic insolvency law. The outcome of such a decision needs to be weighed carefully to ensure that once national insolvency–liquidation proceedings are initiated, the depositor interests are safeguarded and an orderly payout is made.[1] The Recital to the Bank Recovery and Resolution Directive (BRRD) supports the rationale of a resolution regime to safeguard the continuity of critical functions. As noted earlier, banks placed into insolvency-liquidations do not offer critical functions such that discontinuation of a bank's regulated activities is assumed not to threaten financial stability. While this informs the rationale for a resolution regime for banks undertaking critical functions, it is important that the wider ramifications of insolvency-liquidation proceedings are considered for those that are deemed not to undertake critical functions; particularly in view of the sheer number of banks (thousands) that fall under the public interest threshold within the participating and non-participating Member States. In view of this there is a clear contradiction between resolution and liquidation from a policy perspective between the BRRD approach and the Deposit Guarantee Schemes Directive (DGSD) approach. In the former the assumed premise is resolution as a last resort and in the latter the premise of resolution is assumed to be the first resort. In view of this the DGS policy assumes resolution limit its role in times of crises but this is unlikely to be the case and will expose the DGS and ultimately the state backstop to a potentially heavy burden.

6.2 The consistency in practice of deciding whether or not it is in the public interest to resolve or liquidate is lacking and so gives rise to concerns of predictability and certainty. In view of the dislocation of decision and execution of procedure, the cases in this chapter highlight

[1] 'However, liquidation under normal insolvency proceedings might jeopardise financial stability, interrupt the provision of critical functions, and affect the protection of depositors': Directive 2014/59/EU of the European Parliament and of the Council of 15 May 2014 establishing a framework for the recovery and resolution of credit institutions and investment firms and amending Council Directive 82/891/EEC, and Directives 2001/24/EC, 2002/47/EC, 2004/25/EC, 2005/56/EC, 2007/36/EC, 2011/35/EU, 2012/30/EU and 2013/36/EU, and Regulations (EU) No. 1093/2010, and (EU) No. 648/2012, of the European Parliament and of the Council Text with EEA relevance [2014] OJ L173/190 ('BRRD'), Recital.

European Cross-Border Banking and Banking Supervision. Dalvinder Singh, Oxford University Press (2020). © Oxford University Press.
DOI: 10.1093/oso/9780198844754.001.0001

the critical importance of authorities all working together during the period leading up to triggering the decision the bank is failing. To fulfil the principle of the decision namely insolvency in accordance with the national criteria. In this respect, the Single Resolution Board (SRB) decisions, albeit rather unhelpful, need to be scrutinized carefully to understand how the confidential valuation process informs the decision of whether resolution or insolvency is concluded. This is extremely challenging since the BRRD decision making process expects a static valuation when it is invariably difficult to quantify recoveries from long-dated instruments.

6.3 The challenge to the latter is that there is no consistent approach to bank insolvency and liquidation outside the remits of the resolution regime. This give rise to questions of consistency of practice and predictability of outcomes which are critical in a regional market place. The objectives and principles that reside in the special resolution regime do necessarily reside in domestic insolvency and liquidation. Therefore, the fractured nature of insolvency-liquidation law needs to be navigated Member State by Member State. An acute challenge here is the risk of a literal approach to liquidation leading to a fire sale of assets and time delays due to lack of coordination between the different parts of the official safety net when the decision of failing or likely to fail leads to bank liquidation. The trigger for the decision about a banks insolvency may reside outside of the administrative authorities mandate after deciding the bank is failing or likely to fail, in which case ordinary insolvency is triggered after an event such not being able to satisfy a creditors claim above a certain threshold within a predetermined timeframe. This is the case despite the utility of liquidation and insolvency being assessed during the decision-making process to determine whether the institution is failing or likely to fail. The underlying presumption in this aspect of bank failure is the idea of an idiosyncratic failure rather than a cluster of failures of similar types of institutions which could individually lead to a decision of liquidation and yet collectively pose a threat to financial stability. In the latter, the pressure is likely to be experienced by the deposit guarantee scheme since it may not have the funds to fulfil a timely payout, unless other insolvency techniques are utilized alongside a liquidation, such as transfer of covered and/or eligible deposits to another bank.

6.4 This chapter analyses the link between insolvency and liquidation, with the orderly protection of depositors as the principal point of analysis in this section. Most discussions have centred on the trigger and the ambiguity of what essentially amounts to winding-up in accordance with relevant insolvency proceedings rather than looking at how bank insolvency and liquidation supports depositor compensation proceedings. An observation by Enria highlights the difference in approach to safeguard the public interest at the regional and domestic levels which leads to inconsistent decision making across Member States.[2] This is partly a result of the jurisdiction of the two, namely the regional and national as a whole, rather than the national and sub-regional. The misalignment of domestic insolvency-liquidation law and depositor protection mandates is likely to lead to wider techniques being needed to effectuate an orderly insolvency-liquidation and payout to banks' depositors. This means the competent authority, the resolution authority and the management of the bank or administrator-liquidator will need to coordinate their responsibilities through

[2] 'Europe's top bank watchdog makes case for optimism', *Politico*, 7/5/17 <https://www.politico.eu/article/europes-top-bank-watchdog-makes-case-for-optimism/>.

a court-based process during the timeframe of failing or likely to fail to achieve an orderly payout to depositors. The potential disruption would need to be factored into the process outside of failing or likely-to-fail timeframe; the court's order of a creditor's moratorium also needs to be risk-assessed. In recent cases explored in this chapter, the administrative regime have operated outside the formal regime by orchestrating with existing bank liquidity a payout to covered depositors before formal legal proceedings have been triggered to manage the claims of the remaining eligible depositors. This cannot be always relied on and a more consistent approach is required.

The underlying challenges that led to the introduction of the EU special resolution regime need reassessment to review our understanding of how they are likely to apply in such circumstances. A significant expectations gap has arisen in the field of dealing with bank failures. One must ask, how do we deal with relatively small bank failures that are considered not to undertake critical functions? The view of the SRB is one of optimism: **6.5**

> [M]ost banks are now in such a shape that we can say with confidence that their failure would not endanger financial stability and that they can be resolved if they fail—like any other business in the market economy—through regular insolvency procedures.... The extra safety net of resolution is only for the few, not the many.[3]

The European banking sector consists of a significant range of medium-sized banks that are unlikely to be dealt with in resolution but rather wound up in normal insolvency proceedings according to national criteria. The necessity of a consistent approach to bank insolvency and liquidation is starting to surface, despite what appear to be decisions that are quasi-resolution as opposed to liquidation when dealing with the failing institution that is not considered important enough to be resolved. Indeed, one could go as far as to say that the majority of banks are not important enough in terms of providing critical functions in their respective economies and financial markets. In this respect, the competent authority and the resolution authority need to ensure the impediments for resolution equally address impediments to insolvency and payout to safeguard depositor interests. **6.6**

The existence of different approaches to bank insolvency and liquidation leads to criticisms in terms of the approaches adopted at the national level which appear to allow the authorities to circumvent the mechanism to protect the objectives of shareholders and creditors bearing the burden of losses first. In view of this, the concern is the creeping rise of national approaches that appear to be safeguarding local sub-regional 'champions' to the detriment of the credibility of the underlying principles of the Banking Union. The work so far has raised issues about a variety of matters, such as the construction of 'significance' and 'other systemically important institutions'. Consequently, challenges appear when it comes to dividing banks up for the purposes of resolution and insolvency-liquidation as to what is constituted as regional public interest and the national public interest. The business model of European banks is also problematic since it is orientated towards commercial banking. The work required to ascertain the quality of the loan book is therefore critical at the solvency and insolvency stages. In view of this, the ability of such institutions to raise capital privately and the lack of loss-absorbing instruments limit **6.7**

[3] Speech by SRB Chair, Elke König to Belgian Financial Forum (27 January 2017), <https://srb.europa.eu/en/node/193> [accessed 11 June 2019].

the ways such institutions can be dealt with when they experience distress. This is exacerbated by the lack of a coherent approach towards dealing with NPLs in the short- to medium-term. The underlying insolvency of small- and medium-sized banks is likely to surface during a potential second wave of economic decline, therefore leading to a situation where the EU and Eurozone will face its own secondary banking crisis. In view of this, a regulatory forbearance is likely due to the lack of a coherent approach to dealing with those banks that fall outside of the BRRD jurisdiction. National bias may surface in the decision-making process when national approaches are legitimately used to deal with banks that are deemed to be failing or likely to fail.

6.8 Cases explored below will illustrate the division from the perspective of the single resolution mechanism (SRM) and national resolution authorities (NRA) and the outcome of the public interest test. The decisions for failing banks moved into insolvency and liquidation. The common elements to the banking sector balance sheet of the EU, namely commercial banking and its significant levels of non-performing loans, suggest that the next crisis could well be a cross-border small- and medium-sized enterprise (SME) banking sector failure. The indiscriminate way contagion risk spreads and undermines market confidence indicates such an outcome would not be inconceivable in view of the risks (of a common balance sheet) within the real economy faced by the SME industrial marketplace. As such, there is a need for a consistent approach to bank liquidation to contain the spread of contagion risk. The possibility of forbearance or a lack of a conducive environment for liquidation is likely to lead to impediments to the movement of capital from 'unproductive economic activities' through the active pursuit of insolvency and liquidation proceedings. The move towards a coherent approach would enable the reduction of asymmetry of information in the less significant banking sector as well as the adverse selection and moral hazard problems associated with failing banks and potential fire sale of assets.

6.9 The concern about the home and host exists in these insolvency-liquidation and deposit protection issues as well and will be the focus of this chapter. The need for consistency is important at the European level, particularly in view of the questions that may arise from the sale of some instruments to consumers. The branchification and the existing approach of a mix of branches and subsidiaries pose their own challenges from a resolution and insolvency perspective. In the latter, the decision of the parent and its domestic approach to the resolution hierarchy between parent and branches would be one of the same, so leading to no discrimination between home and host. In the latter scenario, risks prevail. However, the home DGS will need to ensure the risk premium of the bank is fit for purpose to secure the payout to the branch depositors. Furthermore, who can initiate insolvency and liquidation becomes important so that the DGS is able to organize the payout to covered depositors as timely as possible. The ambiguous position associated with who can initiate insolvency proceedings is likely to lead to earlier intervention in the form of a covert operation to ensure an orderly payout of covered deposits immediately after a bank is announced to be failing or likely to fail. To achieve this, for instance, the Single Customer View file needs to be provided to the DGS, with its accuracy assessed prior to the payout. This process is also reliant on the payment method that the Member State adopts which vary and need to be tested in the context of insolvency proceedings to gauge the most reliable way to achieve a timely payout.

Bank Insolvency—Branches and Subsidiaries

The approach to bank insolvency has developed in a rather piecemeal fashion that does fall along corporate form: the credit institution and its branches. After the second wave of EU instruments to form the single market it was soon recognized that banks will fail and necessitated a common mechanisms to recognize insolvency proceedings with the adoption of the Reorganisation and Winding Up Directive (RWD).[4] The deficiency of the measures introduced by the RWD is it falls along the same fault lines as the other instruments discussed in previous chapters, namely the single entity level and its branches, rather than addressing the issues at the group level and other incorporated entities (subsidiaries) within the same group, which fall separately within national discretions. The RWD has formed the base for dealing with failing banks, albeit in limited circumstances, on numerous occasions, such as the imposition of requirements for reorganization purposes by the Irish authorities during the crisis.[5] 6.10

The RWD is equally centred on home Member State responsibilities for the incorporated credit institution, which is authorized to undertake the business of banking. The RWD provides some of the missing elements of the BRRD and SRMR, yet it is limited to mutual recognition of reorganization[6] and winding-up[7] proceedings. The reorganization measures are primarily aimed at coordinating proceedings and prevent the opening of secondary proceedings. Therefore allow the home country authorities to preserve or restore the financial position of a credit institution by inter alia putting in place a moratorium on claims. The RWD does not provide harmonized substantive provisions to construct domestic reorganization and winding up proceedings to ensure consistency of practice. Therefore, it provides the mutual recognition of 28 (or 27+1) different approaches to the law of bank insolvency relating to reorganization and winding-up by recognizing that such proceedings could be initiated by administrative or judicial authorities of the home Member State. In the Opinion of Advocate General Villalón, the designation of administrative and judicial authorities can equally infer from a functional perspective the role of the legislative authority. In view of the possible public assistance in the reorganization proceedings a wide interpretation to administrative and judicial authorities is given.[8] Therefore, the legislative measures, just as 6.11

[4] Directive 2001/24/EC of the European Parliament and of the Council of 4 April 2001 on the reorganization and winding up of credit institutions [2001] OJ L125/ 15. Further conflict-of-laws provisions exist within the Settlement Finality Directive and the Financial Collateral Directive. For an analysis see Gabriel Moss QC, Bob Wessels, and Matthias Haentjens, *EU Banking and Insurance Insolvency* (Oxford: Oxford University Press 2017) p. 61.

[5] Publication pursuant to Article 6 of Directive 2001/24/EC of the European Parliament and of the Council on the reorganisation and winding-up of credit institutions [2011] OJ C203/06. National Treasury Management Agency (NTMA), 'Direction Orders in Relation to Anglo Irish Bank Corporation Limited and Irish Nationwide Building Society pursuant to Section 50 of the Credit Institutions (Stabilisation) Act 2010' (8 February 2011), <https://www.ntma.ie/news/direction-orders-in-relation-to-anglo-irish-bank-and-irish-nationwide-building-society-under-the-credit-institutions-stabilisation-act-2010> [accessed 11 June 2019].

[6] Under the RWD, '"reorganisation measures" shall mean measures which are intended to preserve or restore the financial situation of a credit institution and which could affect third parties' pre-existing rights, including measures involving the possibility of a suspension of payments, suspension of enforcement measures or reduction of claims.'

[7] Under the RWD, '"winding-up proceedings" shall mean collective proceedings opened and monitored by the administrative or judicial authorities of a Member State with the aim of realizing assets under the supervision of those authorities, including where the proceedings are terminated by a composition or other, similar measure.'

[8] Opinion of Advocate General Cruz Villalón, Case C-85/12 *Société Landsbanki Islands HF v Kepler Capital Markets SA and Frédéric Giraux* (30 May 2013).

their administrative and judicial measures, require an equal recognition within the RWD. In the words of Advocate General Villalón:

> What we have, therefore, is not a legal provision subsequently put into effect by a court but a legislative provision which the legislature itself applies as the additional and automatic effect of a previous judicial decision.[9]

6.12 The home Member State for credit institutions incorporated in other Member States means each will be treated differently under the RWD. Notably, it will be the branches for those respective credit institutions that will be covered by the home Member State proceedings. In view of this, the single entity approach hinders a group-based approach. Wessel refers to Galanti, highlighting the limitations of such an approach from a crisis management perspective for the different credit institutions incorporated in different Member States.[10] It shows that the function of the resolution college would be reliant on legal cooperation of the Member State authorities, which may not always be forthcoming during the crisis. As is shown in Chapter 5 paras 5.28ff, there is no compulsion to legal compliance with the decision of the resolution college. The decision of the SRB can simply trigger the liquidation under normal insolvency, but this is based on the SRMR rather than the RWD. The SRB would then have to initiate different decisions for the respective subsidiaries that come under its jurisdiction.

6.13 The first critical aspect of the RWD is the reorganization measures set out in Title II of the directive. While it does not provide specific requirements of reorganization measures to ensure consistency of practice across the EU, the directive sets out the recognition requirements. The idea of reorganization measures is interpreted widely, including a variety of measures, such as public assistance in extraordinary circumstances involving the recapitalization of a bank.[11] The utilization of public assistance would come with the write-down of existing liabilities or wiping out of the existing shareholders.[12] Following the Opinion in the *Kotnik* case, a 'reorganisation measure' consists of three cumulative requirements. It must:

(1) be adopted by the competent administrative or judicial authorities of a Member State;
(2) have the purpose of preserving or restoring the financial situation of a credit institution; and
(3) potentially affect third parties' rights.

6.14 This means that burden-sharing measures constitute reorganization measures for the purposes of insolvency and liquidation proceedings.[13] It is further explained that shareholder rights are not the principle concern of the RWD. The home Member State's administrative or judicial authorities, once they are effective, have the sole discretion to determine the reorganization measures for a credit institution and its branches. The administrative

[9] Ibid.
[10] Wessel in Gabriel Moss QC et al (2017) 65.
[11] Extract from the decision on the opening of winding-up proceedings concerning the Banco Privado Português, S.A. under Article 9 of Directive 2001/24/EC of the European Parliament and of the Council on the reorganisation and winding up of credit institutions (Publication provided for in Article 13 of that Directive and in Article 21 of Decree-Law No. 199/2006 of 25 October 2006) [2010] OJ C138/07.
[12] Opinion of Advocate General Wahl, Case C-41/15 *Gerard Dowling Padraig McManus Piotr Skoczylas Scotchstone Capital Fund Limited v Minister for Finance* Notice parties: Permanent TSB Group Holdings plc and Permanent TSB plc (22 June 2016).
[13] Opinion of Advocate General Wahl, Case C-526/14 *Kotnik and Others* (18 February 2016).

or judicial authorities of the home Member States decision shall be recognized throughout the EU. In view of this, Wessel et al name three underlying norms concerning the scope of the home Member State that co-exist: the single entity, unity, and universality approach.[14] The home authorities are expected to communicate the reorganization decisions to their host counterparts and publicize them via the Official Journal of the European Union, so the respective stakeholders of the bank can understand the implications of the home Member State measures on their interests as creditors. For example, in 2013, the Bank of Slovenia exercised extraordinary measures to recapitalize Nova Ljubljanska Banka D.D. to comply with the capital requirements due to the risks present in the market.[15] In this decision the write-down and recapitalization impacted on existing shareholders rights. The authorities recognized that actions for damages could arise, but emphasized any lawsuit would also need to assess the potential damage if the extraordinary measures had not been taken. As such, the home Member State will have to put in place and publicize the procedures creditors will need to follow to lodge their claims. As is shown below, in the case requiring a DGS payout, the DGS will work with the resolution authority and the administrator or liquidator to orchestrate a payout for covered deposits, with the rest of the creditors required to lodge claims with the administrator or liquidator.

The home Member State administrative or judicial authorities responsible for the winding-up of credit institutions will apply to branches established in other Member States. The directive allows for both voluntary and forced winding-up proceedings. The decision to open up such proceedings is expected to be recognized in host Member States. The home Member State law will determine the practical execution of the procedures and how the insolvency estate of the credit institution will be realized together with how claims will be lodged and paid according to the hierarchy of creditors. If applicable, in respect of voluntary proceedings, the competent authority of the credit institution is expected to be consulted by the board of directors before winding-up proceedings can be initiated. Indeed, in most Member States such proceedings will require agreement from the competent authorities and result in the revocation of the bank authorization. The competent authorities could also withdraw authorization to force winding-up proceedings. Once authorization is withdrawn, the credit institution will no longer be able to undertake new business. However, the liquidator, for instance, is expected to ensure an orderly wind-down of the business and close out its obligations. The competent authority of the credit institution is likely to oversee this to ensure it is orderly and depositors or investors interests are appropriately managed. **6.15**

The RWD refers to third country banks that have two branches in the EU and thus fall within the perimeters of the requirements for the purposes of reorganization and winding-up proceedings. Table 6.1 in Appendix 6 shows the number of non-EU branches in the EU is significant in certain Member States. The UK has by far the largest number of non-EU branches at 94, followed by Belgium with 24, and Germany, France and Italy with sizeable numbers in the region of 20. As a proportion of the total number of branches these numbers are relatively low, with the exception of the UK, where it is 59%. For small Member States, such as Cyprus, the number of third country branches is disproportionately high, standing **6.16**

[14] Gabriel Moss QC et al (2017) 30–34.

[15] Publication pursuant to Directive 2001/24/EC of the European Parliament and of the Council on the reorganisation and winding-up of credit institutions: Summary of the Decision on Extraordinary Measures Imposed on Nova Ljubljanska Banka D.D. on 18 December 2013 [2014] OJ C38/09.

at 68% of the total number of branches. These figures emphasize the need for a separate approach to third country branches. Although the RWD does not indicate whether the two branch threshold from the same third country bank has been met. The reason why third country branches are treated separately is because each Member State can decide how it will exercise supervision of the branch and determine the level of capital, if any, it should hold in addition to complying with other prudential requirements; as if the branch were incorporated like a subsidiary. In practice, branches of overseas banks tend to be involved in wholesale banking business, which tends to limit the need for additional safeguards to coordinate a DGS payout. The DGS Directive requires the Member State to determine whether the third country provides equivalent protection for depositors at the branch. If the level of protection is not equivalent, then the branch can be required to become a member of the DGS. The supervisory and resolution authorities would need to work together to determine separate recovery and resolution plans for those designated significant branches and decide the options that can be used locally and how much confidence the supervisory and resolution authorities can place on the third country counterparts to coordinate and cooperate to equally protect the EU creditors. In this respect, reliance is be placed on the third country resolution or insolvency proceedings set out in the resolution plan to manage the branch proceedings.

6.17 The position for subsidiaries is a separate matter for each Member State, where they are incorporated as credit institutions, and would initiate their own proceedings. The proceedings in the home country that is the consolidated supervisor of the parent and the group does not lead to recognition of proceedings in respect of a subsidiary as it would for the respective parent branches. Therefore, concerning the home-host Member State of the subsidiary, the directive does not provide the same requirements for recognition and coordination of proceedings. While it is broadly presupposed that cross-border banks are likely to be resolved through resolution where safety measures are in place to ensure the continuity of critical functions even across borders, formal recognition of the home Member State, where they are initiated, is respected. The *ABLV* decision highlights that a number of relatively small banks do have overseas operations in the form of a subsidiary that could lead to a position where creditors are considered to have been treated unequally. This is explored separately in the chapter.

6.18 The RWD requires that Member States have some common requirements in place that recognize a number of minimum features for both reorganization and winding-up proceedings. The provision to respect certain contracts and rights essentially attempts to assert recognition of the governing law in relation to contracts of employment and where the immovable property is located or registered in a public register. In relation to third parties' rights *in rem*:[16] the right exists for the authorities to dispose or realize assets in accordance with any lien or mortgage or respect of any guarantee. There is also the expectation that the two proceedings will respect the transfer of title in both purchases and sales contracts in accordance with the law it is adopted or proceedings are open. The two proceedings are not expected to effect the right of creditors to set-off against the credit institution in accordance with the law of the Member State. This allows differing treatment in respect of the right of

[16] Whilst the RWD refers to right *in re*, it is more commonly referred to *in rem* in today's common legal practice.

set-off since it is applicable in some Member States but not in others. Contractual set-off will be in accordance with the governing law of the agreements.[17] Finally, a requirement is included that netting agreements are expected to be governed by the same law which governs the contract.

The BRRD and SRMR and the 'Normal Insolvency Procedure' in Context

The EU has not gone as far as what has been prescribed for credit institutions and investment firms, which is a rules-based insolvency and liquidation regime applicable in each Member State. The political and economic will existed to put in place a special resolution regime. Since it was evident during the GFC that insolvency regimes were not entirely effective for the purposes to safeguard the public interest concerns. Through an orderly procedure that would minimize the banks failure on financial stability and safeguard depositor and client funds. But also reduce the reliance on taxpayer bailouts at the same time.[18] The need for a coherent group resolution strategy is emphasized as well, since risk of contagion from an insolvency of group entity can spread to other parts of the group, so putting the viability of group as a whole in jeopardy.[19] 6.19

The EU leaves in place national approaches to insolvency and liquidation for banks that do not meet the resolution threshold. This leads to different administrative and judicial barriers to either liquidation or rehabilitation that encompass depositors and clients. The political perception of what winding-up under normal insolvency proceedings entails clashes with the benefits of what can be achieved in a coherent insolvency—administration regime that rehabilitates corporations and reduces costs associated with recovering debts. As explained by McCormack et al, 'An insolvency regime that encourages more debt restructuring may in turn enhance the creditworthiness of viable companies by facilitating their deleveraging'.[20] In view of this, the economic incentives for workouts are wider since they are likely to safeguard viable business and employment and prevent value destruction from costly liquidation proceedings. Workouts refer to collective action which is sanctioned by court and outside of normal insolvency proceedings. 6.20

Normal Insolvency Proceedings

The BRRD provides a special resolution regime for credit institutions and investment firms. It is an institution-specific insolvency regime as opposed to a general insolvency regime. The definition of 'normal insolvency proceedings' is wide. The BRRD defines it in the following terms: 6.21

[17] Art. 23 and Art. 25.

[18] BRRD, Recitals 1 and 4.

[19] IMF, An overview of the legal, institutional and regulatory framework for bank insolvency, 17 April 2009.

[20] Gerard McCormack, Andrew Keay, and Sarah Brown, *European Insolvency Law* (Cheltenham: Edward Elgar Publishing 2017) p. 5.

> [N]ormal insolvency proceedings mean collective insolvency proceedings which entail the partial or total divestment of a debtor and the appointment of a liquidator or an administrator normally applicable to institutions under national law and either specific to those institutions or generally applicable to any natural or legal person.[21]

6.22 In view of this definition, a variety of insolvency proceedings could co-exist, such as specialist or corporate insolvency proceedings. Moreover, reference to normal insolvency proceedings in the BRRD is occasionally qualified by 'winding-up' under normal insolvency proceedings. However, 'winding-up' is not defined in the BRRD. Elsewhere, the RWD provides a definition:

> '[W]inding-up proceedings' shall mean collective proceedings opened and monitored by the administrative or judicial authorities of a Member State with the aim of realising assets under the supervision of those authorities, including where the proceedings are terminated by a composition or other, similar measure.[22]

6.23 The SRB considers the lack of harmonised bank insolvency law a challenge to creating a 'level playing field' and a 'fully-fledged' Banking Union.[23]

Bank Liquidation and Moratoria

6.24 The BRRD and the SRMR leave what constitutes normal insolvency and liquidation within the discretion of the Member State. This leaves the position in a precarious state, which is likely to lead to criticism as Member States will ultimately reach different outcomes. In many respects, the national authorities and the SRB will need to coordinate with a number of stakeholders in the insolvency and liquidation proceedings leading to time inconsistency problems. While the bank resolution regime is the primary approach to dealing with bank failures, Member States will have in place either specialist insolvency and liquidation proceedings or a corporate insolvency regime by its side. The former specialist insolvency regimes are designed to ensure the right to petition the court or to open insolvency proceedings in relation to banks is the reserve of the administrative authorities.[24] This contrasts with the insolvency proceedings for corporations which can be initiated by creditors by petitioning the court to initiate proceedings without requiring the consent of the administrative authority. In part, this also influences the role of the courts and the role of the administrative authority in such proceedings. A particular problem that can surface in the latter discussion is the threshold that needs to be satisfied to trigger insolvency, since in modified or special insolvency proceedings the administrative authority is likely to determine it based on regulatory requirements. However, the courts may view the balance sheet position

[21] BRRD, Art. 2(47).

[22] RWD, Art. 2.

[23] Public hearing with Elke König, Chair of the SRB Supervisory Board, presenting the SRB Annual Report 2017, 11 July 2018.

[24] Sabino Cassesse, A new framework of administrative arrangements for the protection of individual rights' in ECB Legal Conference 2017, *Shaping a new legal order for Europe: a tale of crises and opportunities,* December 2017, pp. 239–55; Silvia Merler, Bank liquidation in the European Union: clarification needed, Bruegel Policy Contribution, January 2017. Jens-Hinrich Binder, Michael Krimminger, Maria J Nieto, and Dalvinder Singh, 'The Choice between Judicial and Administrative Sanctioned Procedures to Manage Liquidation of Banks: a Transatlantic Perspective' (2019) 14(2) Capital Markets Law Journal 178–216.

differently and conclude the bank is not insolvent because it has not reached the point of negative net worth.[25] In this respect, the administrative approach of triggering insolvency may be resisted by the courts.

The rationale of insolvency and liquidation equally need to be considered.[26] Indeed, an expectations gap between resolution and insolvency-liquidation can easily arise, as shown below. Most notably does it consist of a process of bank restructuring as a going concern? or the process of collecting assets to distribute the proceeds from the sale of assets to creditors in accordance with the hierarchy of creditors' claims and the *pari passu* principle (albeit it does not have a generally accepted meaning) between creditors in each class? In both instances time is required to achieve the most appropriate outcomes, since, in the former situation of insolvency, conservation of value as a going concern is important and, in the latter situation of liquidation, the best return on the sale of assets in a gone-concern scenario. The outcome of such a step is likely to be significant externalities in the market and possible risk of contagion to other banks. This can arise because market participants may lose confidence in the legal process and seek to act in their own self-interest, leading to possible adverse selection problem due to the collapse in prices and a moral hazard problem due to risk shifting. It is important to emphasize sale and distribution of proceeds of the bank with haste is not necessarily synonymous with either insolvency or liquidation proceedings. **6.25**

The need for time in both insolvency and liquidation to realize the right outcomes is of the essence. The administrative authority or the courts may seek a moratorium managed by the administrator or the liquidator.[27] In liquidation, a moratorium is likely to be put in place; especially if the bank's authorization is revoked and it can no longer seek new business. The moratorium will contain the bank's financial problems and retain value, so that the bank's assets and claims against the estate can be worked out.[28] Since depositor finance is a principle source of finance for a bank, the loss of access to their accounts is likely to cause economic hardship and political backlash. The role of deposit insurance in such circumstances becomes critical to stave off problems. In these circumstances the law normally allows special consideration for depositors so that their claims are transferred and completed ahead of the moratorium. In view of the serious implications of putting in place a moratorium, the form it can take varies on a case-by-case basis. **6.26**

The BRRD empowers the national resolution authority to suspend any payment or delivery obligations to which the bank is a party.[29] In resolution the suspension may not last more than two working days. In the case of the resolution the suspension specifically excludes a range of counterparties, such as eligible deposits, obligations to certain payment and settlement systems and central counterparties or eligible claims to deposit and **6.27**

[25] Patrizia Baudino, Antonella Gagliano, Edoardo Rulli, and Ruth Walters, FSI Insights on policy implementation No.10, How to manage failures of non-systemic banks? A review of country practices, October 2018.

[26] IMF, An Overview of the legal, institutional and regulatory framework for bank insolvency, April 17, 2009. For an international and comparative analysis of resolution and insolvency see Michael Schillig, *Resolution and Insolvency of Banks and Financial Institutions* (Oxford: Oxford University Press 2016); see also Andrew Campbell and Rosa Lastra, 'Definition of Bank Insolvency and types of bank insolvency proceedings' in Rosa Lastra (ed.), *Cross-Border Bank Insolvency* (Oxford: Oxford University Press 2011) pp. 26–56.

[27] IMF (2009) pp. 44–55.

[28] Eva Hüpkes, 'Insolvency: Why a Special Regime for Banks, Current Developments in Monetary and Financial Law', Vol. 3 (Washington DC: International Monetary Fund 2003) p. 17.

[29] BRRD, Art. 69.

investor compensation schemes. The use of moratoria in resolution is controversial, hence its limited duration, since it counters the objective of resolution, namely the continuity of critical functions.

6.28 In insolvency and liquidation proceedings the timeframe can be set in law and managed by the courts; it can also be extended since purpose of the moratoria in insolvency and liquidation proceedings differs.[30] Moratoria generally restricts the bringing of legal action, disposition of assets or acquisition of sizeable assets, or the opening of insolvency proceedings.[31] The suspension of contractual rights does not usually form part of any such provision in relation to collateral arrangements since it is overridden by the Financial Collateral Directive.[32] Arguably, the application of the moratoria in insolvency and liquidation proceedings presupposes the bank poses little risk to financial stability, so the wider repercussions are not so significant. However, the exposure of those with operational liabilities and commitments in the payment and settlement system need particular consideration.[33] A common moratorium arrangement is called the 'debt-service moratorium', which enables the liquidator to continue to honour the banks' obligations to service certain debts. This type of moratorium does have benefits since it retains the reputation of the bank, so a potential acquirer can be sought; it also retains a willingness in the market to continue doing business with the bank in the future provided it is implemented correctly. According to Asser,[34] the use of a moratorium causes a paradox, since it is likely to be viewed as a sign of weakness—time is given to the bank to return to viability, yet it undermines the bank's ability to raise market funding to restore viability and continue essential services and transactions. In the case of the Icelandic bank Glitnir banki hf, the courts granted a moratoria and it was decided, once the moratoria expired, it was automatically to enter into winding-up proceedings.[35] In this case, the bank's assets amounted to ISK 783bn and its liabilities ISK 2838bn and it was decided it was insolvent and unlikely to experience payment difficulties. In view of this, the grounds for moratoria vary significantly. As will be shown below, the debt service moratorium can vary depending on the objectives of the proceedings. During uncertain times, a moratoria could have destabilizing effects on market confidence and the banks' franchise value. In this respect, the rationale of a moratoria could hinder the valuation process that is required to take place in order to determine resolution or insolvency.[36] The inconsistency of practices and scope could may well lead to flight to quality domestically from one bank to another or capital flight from one jurisdiction to another.

[30] See also Andrew Campbell and Rosa Lastra, 'Definition of Bank Insolvency and types of bank insolvency proceedings' in Rosa Lastra (ed.), *Cross-Border Bank Insolvency* (Oxford: Oxford University Press 2011) 26–56, 34–6. See also Eva Hüpkes, *Legal Aspects of Bank Insolvency: A Comparative Analysis of Western Europe, the United States and Canada* (London: Kluwer International 2000).

[31] IMF (2009), p. 48.

[32] Directive 2002/47/EC of The European Parliament and of The Council of 6 June 2002 on financial collateral arrangements.

[33] Ross Leckow, Tomoas Laryea, and Sean Kerr, 'Operational Issues' in Rosa Lastra (ed.), *Cross-Border Bank Insolvency* (Oxford: Oxford University Press 2011) pp. 315–44.

[34] Tobias MC Asser, *Legal Aspects of Regulatory Treatment of Banks in Distress* (Washington DC: IMF 2001) 95–6.

[35] Extract from the Decision concerning Glitnir banki hf pursuant to Directive 2001/24/EC of the European Parliament and of the Council on the reorganisation and winding-up of credit institutions [2011] C22/03.

[36] Tobias MC Asser, *Legal Aspects of Regulatory Treatment of Banks in Distress* (Washingtson DC: IMF 2001) pp. 99–100.

The decision in *ENEFI*[37] sheds some light on the opening of cross-border proceedings and as to whether they are enforceable in another Member State. In this case, Directive 1346/2000 on Insolvency Proceedings was applicable but the RWD has similar provisions that were utilized to aid the interpretation of the pending lawsuit and whether it equated to proceedings on the substance rather than enforcement of proceeding. ENEFI is registered in Hungary and has an establishment in Romania. The case relates to the registering of claims in insolvency outside the deadline which are essentially forfeited if done so. The Romanian Public Finance division was notified of the proceedings and sought to undertake an assessment of the tax liability of the subsidiary in Romania. The Romanian Public Finance division specifically asked the court to review the consequences of not lodging the claim during the insolvency proceedings. The court reviewed the requirement of equivalence by deciding whether the creditors were subject to less favourable treatment compared to domestic creditors regarding registering of claims. Equally, the requirement of effectiveness is important. A Member State is prevented from making the exercise of rights to lodge claims conferred by EU law practically impossible or excessively difficult. The underlying assessment focused on whether this was an intrinsic feature of cross-border insolvency proceedings that falls into the category of obstacles of geographical distance or linguistics. The designation of a time limit on insolvency proceedings is by its nature not incompatible with the principle of effectiveness. A particular concern in these proceedings was the principle of maintaining unity of the insolvency estate until the end of the insolvency proceedings. The court decided Hungarian law governs the effects of the opening of insolvency proceedings and its forfeiture rights is not in violation of the directive. 6.29

A critical observation that can be made during the following analysis is what constitutes liquidation varies between Member States. The use of moratoria in liquidation proceedings shows that for larger institutions a longer duration is provided. However, in the case of the smaller institutions discussed later, it is primarily triggered once authorization is revoked and covered depositors are reimbursed, to manage the creditors' remaining claims. 6.30

The *ABLV* Case and the Cross-border Dimension

ABLV Bank, AS is not a typical narrow commercial bank but part of a financial conglomerate consisting of subsidiaries with business lines in asset management and capital markets. In 2018, the European Central Bank (ECB) as the supervisor decided that ABLV Bank, AS was failing or likely to fail following the announcement of the US Department of the Treasury's Financial Crimes Enforcement Network (FinCEN) that the bank was a 'primary money laundering concern',[38] in accordance with s 311 of the Patriot Act 2001. [39] In view of 6.31

[37] Case C-212/15 *ENEFI Energiahatekonysagi Nyrt v Direcţia Generală Regională a Finanţelor Publice Braşov (DGRFP)* (9 November 2016).

[38] Department of the Treasury, Financial Crimes Enforcement Network, 31 CFR Part 1010, RIN 1506–AB39 'Proposal of Special Measure Against ABLV Bank, AS as a Financial Institution of Primary Money Laundering Concern' <https://www.fincen.gov/sites/default/files/federal_register_notices/2018-02-16/2018-03214.pdf> [accessed 11 June 2019].

[39] ECB Notice, '"Failing or Likely to Fail" Assessment of ABLV Bank, AS' <https://www.bankingsupervision.europa.eu/press/pr/date/2018/html/ssm.pr180224.en.html> [accessed 11 June 2019]; <https://www.bankingsupervision.europa.eu/ecb/pub/pdf/ssm.2019_FOLTF_assessment_ABLV_Bank_AS~48046b4adb.en.pdf> [accessed 11 June 2019]; <https://www.fincen.gov/sites/default/files/federal_register_notices/2018-02-16/2018-03214.pdf> [accessed 11 June 2019].

this, the US authorities decided to prohibit it from completing transactions in US dollars or holding US assets for its own or customer accounts. Consequently, the decision led to the withdrawal of deposits. In view of this, the ECB concluded that the bank was cash flow insolvent and unlikely to be able to pay its debts or other liabilities as they come due. As such, the ECB ruled to withdraw the authorization of ABLV Bank, AS as a credit institution and instructed the Latvian Financial and Capital Market Commission to put in place a moratorium on all payments.

6.32 The decision is recognized as significant for the Latvian banking market, since ABLV was the third largest bank and considered an O-SII by the national central bank. The primary business of the bank also involved a significant proportion of non-resident account holders.[40] The US authorities concluded that ABLV had 'institutionalised money laundering as a pillar of the bank's business practices'. [41] According to ABLV, 90% of its customers are classed as high risk and their legal form is one of a shell company following its own risk methodology.[42] The depth of the problem is also illustrated by the conclusion that non-resident business accounted for 0.8–1.5% of Latvia's GDP. The ABLV Bank Luxembourg SA subsidiary was equally exposed to the non-EU business clients and so experienced the same reputational damage.

6.33 Following the ECB's ruling, the SRB had to decide on the resolution technique it would consider the best to deal with the failed bank. The opinion of the SRB was that the bank did not pose public interest concerns to justify resolution; the bank could, therefore, be dealt with by the national authorities.[43] This was based on the conclusion that the bank did not undertake critical functions in terms of deposit taking or lending activities that would, if discontinued, lead to disruption to the services in the real economy or cause financial instability. In view of the size of the non-resident business of the bank, it is not so surprising that a significant bank, which was required to hold additional capital buffers, was considered to not have significant interconnections with the Latvian financial system and the real economy. Indeed, after the decision, in a talk by Elke König of the SRB, it was disclosed that the bank had, in its resolution plan, agreed its fate: if it were to fail, it would go into insolvency-liquidation rather than resolution.[44] In many respects, the concerns about the bank's involvement in money laundering, in view of previous supervisory interventions, appear to be the underlying reason for opting for insolvency proceedings:

[40] <https://srb.europa.eu/sites/srbsite/files/20180223_summary-decision_-_luxembourg.pdf> [accessed 11 June 2019]. The Single Resolution Board does not take resolution action in relation to ABLV Bank, AS and its subsidiary ABLV Bank Luxembourg SA (24 February 2018). See further US Department of the Treasury, 'FinCEN Names ABLV Bank of Latvia an Institution of Primary Money Laundering Concern and Proposes Section 311 Special Measure', <https://www.fincen.gov/sites/default/files/federal_register_notices/2018-02-16/2018-03214.pdf> [assessed 11 June 2019]; Department of the Treasury, Financial Crimes Enforcement Network, 31 CFR Part 1010, RIN 1506–AB39 'Proposal of Special Measure Against ABLV Bank, AS as a Financial Institution of Primary Money Laundering Concern', <https://www.fincen.gov/sites/default/files/federal_register_notices/2018-02-16/2018-03214.pdf> [accessed 11 June 2019].

[41] Department of Treasury, n 38.

[42] EU Parliament Briefing, 'Latvia Cracks Down on Unscrupulous Banking' (December 2018), <http://www.europarl.europa.eu/RegData/etudes/BRIE/2018/631027/IPOL_BRI(2018)631027_EN.pdf> [accessed 13 June 2019].

[43] SRB, 'Notice summarising the decision taken in respect of ABLV Bank, AS' <https://srb.europa.eu/sites/srbsite/files/20180223-summary_decision_-_latvia.pdf> [accessed 13 June 2019].

[44] SRB Press breakfast—Speech of Elke König, Chair of the Single Resolution Board, Thursday 5 April 2018.

> [I]n the 2016 Resolution Plan, it was also stated that normal insolvency proceedings would seem feasible and credible in situations where the failure of the Institution would be due to the non-sustainability of its business model, reputational damage (e.g. due to fraud), and poor internal governance.[45]

The summary decision does not explicitly state the option of insolvency-liquidation. It **6.34** simply concludes:

> Therefore, it was decided that the Bank is not put in resolution. The decision is addressed to the National Resolution Authority in Latvia, the Financial and Capital Market Commission, which should implement it in accordance with the national law.[46]

The Financial and Capital Market Commission decided to apply a voluntary liquidation **6.35** plan under its supervision.[47] The conclusion does not refer to what the national authorities are expected to do in contrast to the press statement. Yet, it is implied that the summary decision would be more authoritative than a press statement, so the former should be considered of greater legal validity. It is likely to be best practice for such decisions to be published to improve the understanding of the complexity of the process. If it is left to the national authorities, then, in view of the BRRD and SRMR, normal insolvency proceedings would be an option that they could take. In this situation, the SRB assessed the implications of the bank being resolved under Latvian insolvency proceedings and determined the outcomes and impact on the local DGS. The SRB assessment included consideration of the payout to depositors and the feasibility of the Latvian DGS raising more contributions through extraordinary contributions. In view of the payout, it also included the recovery rate that could be achieved using its domestic insolvency procedures and concluded that it was high. The SRB evaluated the resources required to achieve the payout and concluded that, while a significant amount of the pre-fund would be exhausted, options existed to raise additional funds either through contributions with the members of the DGS or by entering into a loan agreement with the state.

The cross-border dimension of the case includes the decision by the ECB and SRB that **6.36** ABLV Bank Luxembourg SA would also be resolved through insolvency.[48] The fact that both Latvia and Luxembourg take a single entity approach in insolvency has meant separate proceedings have taken place rather than it being coordinated through unified proceedings by the parent entity courts. The ECB concluded the subsidiary was likely to fail since it was reliant on the parent entity for financial support. In conjunction with the ECB instructions to the Latvian authorities, the Luxembourg *Commission de Surveillance du Secteur Financier* (CSSF) (the Luxembourg Financial Sector Monitoring Commission) was also instructed to put in a moratorium on payments. The Resolution Plan concluded, 'liquidation

[45] Decision of the Single Resolution Board of 23 February 2018 concerning the assessment of the conditions for resolution in respect of ABLV Bank, AS (SRB/EES/2018/09) <https://srb.europa.eu/sites/srbsite/files/decision_srb-ees-2018-09_ablv_lv_non_confidential_version_final_0.pdf> [accessed 13 June 2019].

[46] Notice summarizing the decision taken in respect of ABLV Bank, AS <https://srb.europa.eu/sites/srbsite/files/20180223-summary_decision_-_latvia.pdf> [accessed 13 June 2019].

[47] Extract of a winding-up measure decided under Article 9 of Directive 2001/24/EC of the European Parliament and of the Council on the reorganisation and winding-up of credit institutions [201] C272/04 <https://eur-lex.europa.eu/legal-content/EN/TXT/?qid=1482278181891&uri=CELEX:52018XC0803(01)> [accessed 13 June 2019].

[48] Notice summarizing the decision taken in respect of ABLV Bank Luxembourg SA <https://srb.europa.eu/sites/srbsite/files/20180223_summary-decision_-_luxembourg.pdf> [accessed 13 June 2019].

of the Group and its entities under normal insolvency proceedings is credible and feasible'. The subsidiary equally experienced loss of reputation and mass withdrawals of deposits which it could not stave off through market means to improve its liquidity position. The opportunity for a private sector solution passed, marked by the lack of interest in the business of the subsidiary. As such, the SRB formed the view that a private sector solution was not an option. The SRB assessed the outcomes of using Luxembourgish insolvency proceedings accordingly:

> The 2015 Law provides for two distinct proceedings:
> (a) the judicial liquidation procedure ('*liquidation judiciaire*'), which is laid down in Articles 129-152 of the 2015 Law: This procedure is ordered by the court which discharges the management body from its duties, appoints a supervisory judge and one or more liquidators. It will automatically result in the withdrawal of the banking licence.
> (b) the procedure of suspension of payments ('*le sursis de paiement*'), which is laid down in Articles 120 to 127 of the 2015 Law. This procedure allows for the suspension of any of the institution's payment obligations unless provided otherwise by law (e.g. for covered deposits). Its aim is to evaluate the situation and to either propose a plan to restore the financial situation of an Institution, or to put the institution into liquidation.[49]

6.37 The SRB concluded that, since a private solution experienced little interest, the option it thought likely was judicial liquidation, albeit it recognized the rights and powers of the NRA to exercise its responsibilities in accordance with applicable national law, meaning an alternative could equally be utilized.

6.38 The SRB recognises that the discretion lies with the Member State to undertake procedures according to normal insolvency law despite the BRRD and the SRMR alluding to liquidation. The CSSF as the resolution authority applied for judicial liquidation in the Luxembourg Commercial Court.[50] The CSSF requested both an order for the liquidation of ABLV Luxembourg SA and stay of proceedings procedure. It was therefore for the court to decide which it thought was the most appropriate in these circumstances. The decision explains that the potential acquirer of ABLV Luxembourg SA would need to negotiate with the US authorities to lift the ban and comply with any potential sanctions. The CSSF put its position forward to the court, saying that 'there is no realistic prospect of avoiding liquidation and in in any event, in the circumstance, the suspension of payment is fully justified'.[51] The bank itself justified its position to avoid such a decision based on its capital position and coverage ratio. In addition to the balance sheet position, the bank was confident it could secure a buyer and so would no longer be part of ABLV Latvia. In view of the negative press, the bank requested the court to order a stay of proceedings to give it enough time to orchestrate a takeover. The court informed that it needed to decide the order based on whether the 'the financial institution is no longer able to meet its commitments to all debt and equity rights'.[52] As such, the Court confirmed that it is not bound by the assessment by the authorities. The Court concluded that the CSSF assessment that the bank does not have

[49] Decision of the Single Resolution Board of 23 February 2018 concerning the assessment of the conditions for resolution in respect of ABLV Bank, AS (SRB/EES/2018/09) (n 45 above).
[50] Judgment commercial n° 2018TALCH06/00285.
[51] Ibid.
[52] Ibid.

sufficient liquidity is proven. The Court however found the application for the procedure of suspension of payment admissible and well founded and decided the suspension should last for six months. The temporary administrators applied to the court on 5 October 2018 for an extension; four months were granted for the sale of the bank to proceed. But this still remains 'negotiations with several interested parties' continue.[53]

The case of ABLV highlights how a bank group in a cross-border insolvency can lead to different legal outcomes and, critically, unequal treatment of creditors. It is important to note the rights depend on governing law of the instrument and not only the location of the debtor. The level of administrative discretion to determine the outcomes of insolvency-liquidation is set within the national parameters. The SRB clearly recognizes that in view of the assessment of resolution or insolvency. Indeed, the SRB assesses the outcome up to the point of a potential payout to depositors and investors. The case acutely highlights problems of consistency of outcomes for the Latvian and Luxembourg entities. It also illustrates how the courts could interpret the balance sheet position of a bank literally rather than from the regulatory perspective. The Luxembourg Court's decision to allow a stay of proceedings was not necessarily a surprise but the basis of the decision, that, in its view, the bank was not likely to be insolvent, went against the administrative opinion of the local resolution authority and the ECB and SRB. Since the SRB's conclusion was based on its inability to secure market access as a result of the US decision and impending financial penalties for a potential breach of the decision. But more importantly, the lack of an acquirer of the Luxembourg entity to date. The inconsistency of outcomes strongly indicates an unequal treatment of legal persons as a result of the two differing decisions. 6.39

Veneto Banca and Banca Populare di Vicenza

The two banks, Banca Popolare di Vicenza and Veneto Banca, were established in Italy and located in the Veneto Region. Outside Italy, the former had limited presence, only in third countries through representative offices, while the latter had subsidiaries in Croatia, Moldova, Albania, as well as branches in Romania. The institutions are not by any stretch of the imagination small banks. In 2015, the banks reported a breach of capital requirements and, following the ECB's request, submitted a capital plan providing for an IPO of €1bn. Consequently, Atlante, an Italian private equity fund, became the main shareholder of the banks. However, the banks continued to face liquidity outflows from customers, high levels of NPLs, increased needs for provisioning due to escalation in lawsuits, and a sharp decline in core revenues. In 2016, the Atlante fund invested approximately €3.5bn in the banks, but it was not enough to hinder the deterioration of their financial position. Further breaches of the capital requirements and liquidity needs forced the ECB to renew its request for capital conservation and capital raising plan. However, the effective and timely implementation of the new plan proposed by the banks was deemed implausible by the ECB. As a result, on 23 June 2017, the ECB determined that both banks were failing or likely to fail. It should be noted that by that time the banks were not deemed as systemically important 6.40

[53] 'ABLV Bank Luxembourg, S.A. Looks Forward to Complete Sales Process' (Riga, Latvia, 10 October 2018) <https://www.ablv.com/en/press/2018-10-10-ablv-bank-luxembourg-s-a-looks-forward-to-complete-sales-process> [accessed 13 June 2019].

institutions as their assets had decreased significantly, having experienced large deposit outflows, which were absorbed by other institutions in Italy, and their bond yields became even more disconnected from the rest of the Italian and European markets. Veneto Banca 'lost around EUR [5–10]bn or [30–40]% of its deposits between June 2015 and December 2016. In the first three months of 2017 VB lost a further EUR [0–5]bn in deposits. In total, VB lost around [40–50]% of its deposit funding base in less than two years.'[54]

6.41 Banco Popolare di Vicenza, 'lost around EUR [5–10]bn or [30–40]% of its deposits between June 2015 and December 2016. In the first three months of 2017 BPVi lost further EUR [0–5]bn. In total, BPVi lost around [40–50]% of its deposit funding base in less than two years.'[55] In view of this deterioration of the size of the individual banks over several years, the conclusions reached in the respective Resolution Plans in 2016, namely that the bank should be resolved through resolution, were no longer viewed as necessary. As such, a liquidation under Italian law became a feasible option. This change highlights that Resolution Plans are not static and may become redundant in light of new developments. As such, the reconsideration of the initial decision draws attention to the importance of examining the current circumstances of the institution.

6.42 The SRB decided the conditions for resolution were not met and the banks should be wound up under normal insolvency proceedings. It concluded that the condition of Article 18(1)(c) (public interest) was not satisfied because the banks no longer provided critical functions, were unlikely to cause financial stability due to the lack of interconnections and, more importantly, Italian insolvency proceedings would afford comparable protection to depositors and investors. Consequently, the SRB concluded that resolution action is not warranted in the public interest and the banks should be wound-up under normal Italian insolvency proceedings. The insolvency proceedings set out in (the Italian Decree-Law 99) involved the splitting of the banks into 'good' and 'bad' banks. The good assets of both banks were sold to Italy's largest retail bank, Intesa Sanpaolo, with the Italian Government contributing about €5bn as part of the deal. The lenders were then liquidated. In regard to the 'bad' bank, the asset management company, Società di Gestione delle Attività (SGA) took on NPLs of €10–20bn. The Italian government had to provide state guarantees worth up to €12bn to cover potential losses. The assessment of the outcomes under Italian insolvency law shows that the SRB decision is not devoid of a clear recognition that national insolvency laws differ and it does not have jurisdiction to determine a specified insolvency liquidation strategy but should respect the national approach that is adopted. For banks outside of resolution, the Italian Compulsory Administrative Liquidation provides orderly insolvency-liquidation proceedings that co-exist with the Special Administration. The former designates the winding-up procedure and the latter that of reorganization. According to the liquidation procedure, once the bank's licence is revoked, a purchase and assumption strategy is put in place. Indeed, the orderly application of the compulsory administrative liquidation (CAL) leads to the retention of value; this is contrary to a strategy of piecemeal sales that would lead to a destruction of value in a disorderly manner.

[54] State Aid SA. 45664 (2017/IN)—Italy—Orderly liquidation of Banca Popolare di Vicenza and Veneto Banca—Liquidation aid (Brussels, 25 June 2017) (C(2017) 4501 final), para. (12), <http://ec.europa.eu/competition/state_aid/cases/264765/264765_1997498_221_2.pdf> [accessed 13 June 2019].

[55] Ibid, para. (17).

The size of the banks and the regional concentration of the banks' business activities created a significant dilemma in the debate about resolution and insolvency proceedings. The assessment of the Italian insolvency regime and the outcomes it provided were viewed as appropriate to safeguard the interests of depositors and investors as well as the national financial stability. The SRB's mandate under the SRMR is required to consider a regional and or national threat to financial stability. National authorities are likely to consider sub-regional impacts as well, which in some respects they had already done but considered it to be manageable. It is notable that the Croatian authorities took the opposite view when faced with a bank failing and its potential impact at the sub regional level. Following the resolution decision of Jadranska Banka d.d. Šibenik €300m in assets it held below 1% of total share market in Croatia. However, from a regional perspective it accounted for 34% of total deposits and 50% of finance to the regions business sector and operated over half the ATM machines.[56] **6.43**

The case clearly highlights the concern raised by Enria of a two-track public interest set of criteria operating at the eurozone and Member State levels.[57] However, the changing importance of the two Italian banks (assets in the region of €30bn each) led to a change in resolution strategy. While there is no one-size-fits-all approach, the words of Enria also highlights the surprise that banks of this size could not be placed into resolution.[58] The assessment by the SRB raises questions: can the national insolvency regime provide similar outcomes? Would the banks have remained intact if they were moved into resolution or would a sale of business and asset separation techniques have led to similar outcomes, since shareholders and certain creditors would be wiped out through the burden sharing process? In part this was not achieved since senior bondholders avoided being bailed in under the interpretation of national law. The controversial part of the decision is the need for liquidity assistance in insolvency-liquidation. While the summary assessment is silent on this, it would have been useful to have articulated whether the SRB would have had to factor in resolution funding if resolution was the preferred option. This would have mitigated in part the political backlash that arose after the decision was publicized, which appears to be fixated on liquidation in the strictest sense. **6.44**

Creditors Interests in Insolvency—Depositor Preference

The lack of consistent treatment of creditors in insolvency across the EU leads to specific challenges as noted in Chapter 5 and the application of the no-creditor-worse-off principle as the counterfactual when it comes to comparing the outcomes between resolution **6.45**

[56] Notification of Resolution Decisions to the EBA (9 October 2015) <https://eba.europa.eu/documents/10180/1227439/Letter+to+the+EBA.pdf> [accessed 13 June 2019].

[57] Europe's top bank watchdog makes case for optimism, Politico, 7/5/17 <https://www.politico.eu/article/europes-top-bank-watchdog-makes-case-for-optimism/>.

[58] 'The Commission said rules have been strictly applied. And I am convinced this is the case, but some questions remain and might have to be looked at in more detail when the dust settles," he said. "The decision that there was no EU public interest at stake in the crises of two ECB-supervised banks that were hoping to merge and operate in the same region with combined activities of around €60 billion sets the bar for resolution very high.' in Europe's top bank watchdog makes case for optimism, Politico, 7/5/17, <https://www.politico.eu/article/europes-top-bank-watchdog-makes-case-for-optimism/>.

and insolvency.[59] The difference in treatment is primarily a result of the lack of modified insolvency and liquidation proceedings in addition to the resolution regime for banks across the EU. The interests of depositors are of particular concern when it comes to creditor interests since they traditionally rank under secured creditors, and so are at the lowest levels of the creditor hierarchy.[60] This is despite the fact that they could provide a significant proportion of a bank's finance. For example, DeYoung and Rice, in their study focussing on the US found that 'about 57% of the banking industry's assets, and about 82% of the typical banking company's assets, were financed with deposits in 2003'.[61] The figures they provide reflect a position of decline, with the increasing use of subordinated debt and equity financing; they do, however, show the significant contribution to their business. Earlier, the levels of subordinated debt issuance in the EU and limited forms of financing, such as capital markets, were analysed, which leads to the conclusion that the EU might be even more reliant on deposit finance than previously thought. The risks associated with fractional reserve banking have equally led to concerns about the vulnerability of depositors in debates about bank safety and soundness. In view of this, the mechanisms to protect depositors have obviously been of concern, namely, the need for deposit protection schemes and, more recently, the introduction of depositor preference in addition to such schemes.

6.46 The hierarchy of creditors' claims in insolvency is of critical importance when determining the priority in which claims are ultimately paid from the estate of the liquidated firm. Depositor preference rule formally places their claims ahead of unsecured creditors in a bank insolvency. The depositor preference rule is not however a single homogenous rule but has been interpreted in a variety of ways. Neither is it without costs to other unsecured creditors, because priority for depositors will lead to greater potential losses for unsecured creditors. In view of their risk exposure, unsecured creditors may consider improving their claims on a firm by seeking collateral or structuring their exposure through securitization against their exposures.[62] According to the International Association of Deposit Insurers (IADI), '[t]hese actions could have profound implications for bank funding and could offset any positive benefits of depositor preference',[63] since other unsecured creditors recognizing their exposure can also decide to run on the bank.

6.47 The synergies between the role of deposit insurance and depositor preference are clearly articulated by IADI Core Principles 2014, which explain the importance of depositor preference to the deposit insurance scheme. The utility of depositor preference arises by reducing the costs of the deposit insurer in achieving its wider functions in supporting resolution options by having sufficient funds to achieve either a timely payout or assist with the transfer of deposits to another bank. According to Hardy:

[59] V P G de Serière and DM van der Houwen, 'No creditor worse off in case of bank resolution: ford for litigation?' (2016) 31 Journal of International Banking Law and Regulation 376–84.

[60] Niall Lenihan, Maike B Luedersen, and Martin Schulte, 'The hierarchy of creditor claims in bank insolvency' (2016) Forum Financier/Droit Bancaire et Financier 413–25.

[61] DeYoung and Rice, 'How Do Banks Make Money? The Fallacies of Fee Income' (2004) 28(4) Economic Perspectives–Federal Reserve Bank of Chicago, 35–51 at 40.

[62] Daniel Hardy, 'Bank Resolution Costs, Depositor Preference, and Asset Encumbrance' (IMF Working Paper No. 13/172, July 2013), available at SSRN <https://ssrn.com/abstract=2307415> [accessed 17 June 2019].

[63] IADI, 'IADI Core Principles for Effective Deposit Insurance Systems (November 2014), p 17 < https://www.iadi.org/en/assets/File/Core%20Principles/cprevised2014nov.pdf> [accessed 17 June 2019].

When there is no depositor preference, the DGS is normally required to find a solution that ensures that other unsecured creditors are made no worse off than depositors, which can be difficult to achieve without delaying resolution and destroying more value.[64]

This is critically important, as explained below, since the role and resources of the DGS in the European context are limited, therefore, to achieve outcomes that protect depositors, in its widest sense, sufficient funds need to be in place to mitigate the impact of executing such operations on their resources and capabilities. More specifically, the ECB has emphasized the importance of depositor preference during the liquidation phase, since national law may have not provided preference to eligible deposits in the liquidation phase as would be provided for covered deposits. Notably, such disparity of treatment of depositors could lead to a scenario where eligible depositors would seek to run on the bank to secure their deposits, while covered deposits would remain confident that they need not run on the bank as their deposits are fully protected. **6.48**

Directive 94/19/EC[65] provided for the first time in EU law the right of the DGS to subrogate the rights of depositors in liquidation proceedings for an amount equal to the payment it made, so conferring on the DGS a higher priority than other unsecured creditors. Article 9 of the DGS Directive as recast in 2014[66] further extends the protection of the DGS in resolution in view of its role to assist resolution options such as bridge bank and deposit transfers. In this respect, the DGS would have a claim against the bank equal to the amount of its payments, which would rank equal to the level of covered deposits under the national law governing normal insolvency. However, in view of the vulnerability of eligible deposits above the coverage limit, risks remained regarding their interests. Regarding this risk exposure, the BRRD in Recital 111 and, specifically, Article 108 introduce the need for Member States to put in place a formal depositor preference rule to mitigate the risk of eligible deposits being exposed to bail-in during the loss absorbency exercise and minimize potential losses in resolution, while ensuring the continuity of critical functions.[67] Therefore, a tiered depositor preference law was introduced that provides protection to natural persons, micro-, small- and medium-sized enterprises. The importance of carving out the protection in law for covered and eligible depositors is to avoid their claims distorting the assessment of resolution or normal insolvency options. As a result of the no-creditor-worse-off principle being applied in resolution when comparing outcomes between resolution and normal insolvency, parity for depositors in both those scenarios is critical to minimize compensation claims ensuing from other unsecured creditors, whose losses have thereby increased. **6.49**

Depositor preference can take a number of different forms according to IADI. For example: **6.50**

- national (or domestic) depositor preference gives priority to deposit liabilities booked and payable within the domestic jurisdiction and does not extend to deposits in foreign branches abroad;

[64] Hardy (n 62 above).

[65] Directive 94/19/EC of the European Parliament and of the Council of 30 May 1994 on deposit-guarantee schemes [1994] OJ L135/5.

[66] Directive 2014/49/EU of the European Parliament and of the Council of 16 April 2014 on deposit guarantee schemes [2014] OJ L173/149.

[67] SBR, Annex 3—Insolvency Ranking in the jurisdictions of the Banking Union, <https://srb.europa.eu/en/file/ldr-annex-insolvency-ranking-2018-clean>.

- eligible depositor preference gives preference to all deposits meeting the eligibility requirements for deposit insurance coverage;
- insured depositor preference gives preference to insured depositors (and the deposit insurer under subrogation);
- a two-tiered depositor preference concept, in which eligible, but uninsured deposits have a higher ranking than claims of ordinary unsecured, non-preferred creditors, and insured depositors have a higher ranking than eligible depositors; and
- general depositor preference, in which all deposits have a higher ranking than claims of ordinary unsecured, non-preferred creditors, regardless of their status (insured/uninsured or eligible/not eligible).[68]

6.51 In view of the IADI Core principles, the EU has adopted a tier depositor preference rule. In this respect, deposits up to the EU coverage level of €100,000 are given a higher priority or 'super priority' to the reimbursement of their claims in liquidation proceedings. A second priority or 'simple priority' is then conferred on eligible depositors with deposits exceeding the €100,000 coverage level.[69] The EU therefore adopts, in line with the IADI examples, the two-tiered depositor preference approach. However, some Member States have introduced additional provisions to safeguard certain other instruments in line with the bail-in tool. For instance, Slovenia included interbank liabilities equal to guaranteed deposits, which is in compliance with the BRRD, if interpreted broadly.[70] In Italy, the depositor preference rule applies to all depositor claims and gives priority over other unsecured claims.[71] The argument in favour of such a rule is that the application of the bail-in tool is significantly simpler as it will cover remaining unsecured debt instruments. The additional benefit of the all-encompassing depositor preference rule is the liability ensuing from the application of the no-creditor-worse-off is likely to be minimal, with reliance on the resolution fund also likely limited. The ECB argued that clear delineation of senior unsecured bank debt instruments reduces the contagion risk than depositor liabilities.

The Role of the Deposit Guarantee Scheme

6.52 The principal rationale of a special resolution regime for banks is the protection of financial stability which includes the protection of depositors and those creditors entrusting assets with banks. The importance of ensuring the continuity of critical functions, such as deposit taking, is a key consideration when determining the fate of a bank. In many respects, the tools to ensure continuity of access to deposit taking minimize the burden on the deposit insurance schemes, since the restructuring of the bank takes on the burden rather than the authorities shifting the risk and burden onto the deposit insurance scheme to ensure a payout. This reflects the view fact deposit guarantees schemes play a limited role in

[68] IADI Core Principles, (n 63 above), p. 8.

[69] Ibid.

[70] Opinion of the European Central Bank of 3 May 2016 on the resolution and winding-up of banks, (CON/2016/28), pp. 7–8.

[71] Opinion of the European Central Bank of 16 October 2015 on recovery and resolution of credit institutions and investment firms (CON/2015/35), pp. 4–5.

crises. This point is premised on the assumption that the national authorities wish to avoid replacing an explicit coverage level in normal times with an implicit or explicit government guarantee higher than the previous coverage level. The two should be viewed separately from a policy perspective, albeit the end goal is protecting depositors. The political decision to implement the former is primarily an indication of a poorly designed safety net and tools that cannot contain the impending crisis. It is important to emphasize, the tools for resolution and insolvency and liquidation need to be fit for purpose to ensure the integrity of the deposit guarantee scheme's ability to fulfil its function. In view of this, deposit protection systems, according to the IADI, are designed to safeguard against one medium-size bank failure or a cluster of smaller bank failures. This would lead to the conclusion that the deposit protection scheme plays a different role that might be limited during a systemic crisis. The use of resolution tools bridges the gaps that exist between the different pieces of the official safety net, especially when it comes to minimizing public bailout or the onerous task of a large payout by the DGS.

The Member State DGS's differ in terms of resources, albeit there are common minimum features in each, such as funding and coverage level. This section will explore the challenges the DGS is likely to face in case of a bank closure and the possibility of it having cross-border implications when such an event arises. The underlying infrastructure for a seven-day payout needs to be considered from the perspective of insolvency procedures that could inhibit achieving this outcome, thus leading to either reliance on the DGS and utilizing national funds to step in or delays to a payout. While this is possibly containable on an idiosyncratic basis, in the circumstances of multiple failures it is likely to lead to unreasonable delays that could exasperate a small bank failure, therefore undermining financial stability. Of particular concern here is the reliance on the existence of accurate data files that can be utilized to orchestrate a payout. This requires coordination between the competent authorities and the designated authority for depositor protection to work together *ex ante* to ensure that eligible depositors' accounts (commonly referred to as the Single Customer View file) are identifiable at short notice to orchestrate a payout. 6.53

The misalignment of dealing with failing banks and the protection of depositors was all too clear during the GFC. The ill-designed coverage levels and non-existent funding inevitably led to serious moral hazard risks. The (recast) 2014 DGS Directive implements further reforms to the national approaches to try and ensure the guarantee scheme is fit for purpose. It is argued that the risk of misalignment between insolvency-liquidation is a material risk to safeguarding depositors and will likely require public assistance to fulfil the DGS's responsibility to depositors. All the decisions notified by resolution authorities and the DGS to the EBA are published. An analysis of those notifications illustrates the decisions taken when a failing bank is dealt with in liquidation proceedings.[72] It attempts to extrapolate common elements from the cases to form conclusions about the use of liquidation as a procedure to deal with a failing institution. A review of notifications of 6.54

72 Decision of the European Banking Authority on notifications to the EBA relating to Directive 2014/49/EU on deposit guarantee schemes (EBA/DC/2018/243, 23 July 2018) <https://eba.europa.eu/documents/10180/16082/EBA+DC+2018+243+%28Decision+on+DGS+Notifications%29.pdf/6e6eec29-a1ba-49f4-af4f-cb7b8f92fe9d> [accessed 17 June 2019].

resolution decisions do not make reference to DGS assistance during the restructuring of the bank therefore supporting the argument that resolution minimizes reliance on the DGS.

DGS Funding and Target Coverage Level

6.55 The level of confidence in the deposit guarantee scheme in the banking system is primarily reliant on a variety of factors, with perhaps the level of pre-existing fund to cover depositor reimbursements being the principle factor. While the BRRD and the SRMR are in place for those institutions that undertake critical functions, greater reliance on resolution tools to limit the use of the DGS is deemed to be the expected approach according to the DGSD. The EBA equally claim:

> The new bank resolution regime provides the authorities with an alternative mechanism to deal with a failing bank, called 'bank resolution'. The likelihood that a DGS is used has been reduced because of the existence of bank resolution tools. The existence of 'bank resolution' means that some banks are likely to be dealt with using these new mechanisms, and thus limiting the need for DGS support. The existence of the bank resolution regime means that (i) DGSs are less likely to be used; and (ii) even if used, are likely to recover more of the money spent than it would have been the case in the past.[73]

6.56 Current practice would appear to suggest that resolution is likely to be the exception rather than the rule in line with the BRRD as well. In view of that, orderly and timely normal insolvency—liquidation is absolutely necessary to ensure there are sufficient assets at the bank to minimise the impact on the DGS fund and the likely need for a payout once reimbursement is decided. The reliance on domestic approaches to bank liquidation assurances in minimizing the use of the DGS fund. The super priority of the DGS means it will be paid back before other creditors but this is after utilizing the fund. If the limits of DGS in a crisis are put into the equation, namely to be able to deal with one or two small bank failures or a medium bank failure, then the expectation is such that the DGS is not likely to have a significant role in a systemic crisis. Indeed, the IADI recognize that during a systemic crisis the DGS, as well as other parts of the official safety net, are to play a significant role. Therefore, the level of available means to cover possible payouts is important to consider.

6.57 The DGSD expects Member States to have in place a target level fund of 0.8% of covered deposits and in exceptional cases it can be as low as 0.5%.[74] Therefore, DGS's are required to build up their funds whether from pre-existing levels or from a position of no pre-existing fund to one where the fund of 0.8% of covered deposits is in place by 2024. However, the DGSD does not prescribe an approach to raise this fund other than through banks contributing risk-based premiums. The level of the fund 0.8% is indicated. The data in Table 9.1 (Appendix 9) shows that the target coverage level for DGS does vary and not all Member States have opted for the 0.8% level. The Table shows that the vast majority of Member States—64%—to date

[73] EBA, DGS data-2015-2016-2017, <https://eba.europa.eu/regulation-and-policy/recovery-and-resolution/deposit-guarantee-schemes-data>.

[74] DGSD, Art. 2 (11): 'target level' means the amount of available financial means which the DGS is required to reach in accordance with Article 10(2), expressed as a percentage of covered deposits of its member'.

have opted to have a target level of 0.8%. Only one has opted for the lowest target level of 0.5%, France.[75] The IADI research paper highlights that a target level of 1.15% was proposed, however this met opposition based on the view that resolution techniques and the resolution fund would reduce the burden on the DGS.[76] France has opted for the lowest level of 0.5% target level. France has therefore set it at the lower level because it views their banking system as highly concentrated and so normal insolvency is not likely to be the option it will resort to, but resolution instead.[77] This position appears to be untenable and suggests it is underestimating its needs when for its significant banks the SRB will decide whether a bank moves in to resolution or insolvency and it cannot be assumed the former option will be always confidentially taken. The rest of the Member States have opted for a higher target level ranging from 1.19% (Portugal) to the highest 3.43% (Romania). In order to calculate the fund, target covered deposits are used. However, other factors could also be included, namely, eligible deposits. In this respect, the DGS primarily calculates its loss exposure with reference to covered deposits rather than include eligible deposits. The other factors DGS could use to calculate the target ratio can vary according to the IADI. The primary factors include: financial system structure and characteristics, legal framework, prudential regulation, supervision and its effectiveness, and failure resolution regime, macro-economic conditions, availability, and accessibility of emergency/back-up funding.[78] Notwithstanding these primary factors, historical losses experienced by the DGS can equally be considered. Therefore, it is recommended the target level is reviewed periodically to ensure it is fit for purpose. While it is beyond the scope of this study to explore individual rationales, it suffices to say a range of factors can be incorporated rather than simply the level of covered deposits and indeed what is expected by the DGSD.

Table 9.1 (Appendix 9)[79] also shows the current funding level and the extent to which it meets the target ratio. The DGSD expects Member States to build up the fund, so it meets the target level. However, the size of the fund is important to consider to try and gauge what in the vast majority of cases is the shortfall. The Table 9.1 (Appendix 9) shows that 67% of Member States are experiencing a shortfall in meeting the target fund ratio level. The range of the shortfall does vary considerably from 0.04%–1.09%, which is a sizeable shortfall. The shortfall is not simply a feature of any particular size of Member State, which shows the challenge ahead is not just based on the relatively smaller Member State experiencing problems. However, 32% indicate that they already either meet the target ratio or exceed it. This is not just a feature of those that have set it at the 0.8% level but also those that have set a much higher funding target ratio. In these cases, it must be a positive sign and perhaps one that is more cautious, considering the likelihood of utilizing the DGS fund is possibly higher. The IADI research paper indicates that some states decide to either reduce or reimburse funds back to member institutions in such circumstances. However, in view of the **6.58**

[75] DGSD, Art. 10(6)(b).

[76] IADI, Deposit Insurance Fund Target Ratio, Research Paper, Prepared by the Deposit Insurance Fund Target Ratio Technical Committee, Core Principles and Research Council Committee International Association of Deposit Insurers, July 2018: <https://www.iadi.org/en/assets/File/IADI_Research_Paper_Deposit_Insurance_Fund_Target_Ratio_ July, 2018.pdf>.

[77] DGSD Recital 28.

[78] IADI (2018) p. 11.

[79] Authors own analysis based on EBA data, Aggregated DGSD data: <https://eba.europa.eu/regulation-and-policy/recovery-and-resolution/deposit-guarantee-schemes-data>; see also <https://eba.europa.eu/regulation-and-policy/recovery-and-resolution/dgs-data/additional-information-on-dgs-data>.

uncertainty of how many banks are likely to be put in to insolvency—liquidation than resolution, then it is arguable the target level is currently set too low. The expectations that the DGS is less likely to be used is unsubstantiated considering the position taken in the BRRD. In many respects, this can only be assessed once the resolution planning process is complete and the true picture of the proportion of banks likely to go in to resolution and insolvency is discovered. It will be important when resolution plans are drawn up that Single Customer View (SCV) files and payout scenarios are assessed when liquidation is proposed by the SRB or the national resolution authorities. The evidence so far would suggest it is likely to be more of the latter. These decisions needs to be coordinated alongside the DGS decision making to ensure the target level for the fund is fit for purpose. Otherwise, it will fall on the state to provide loans to the DGS which is counter intuitive to the aims of minimizing the burden on the state. The rules could grid lock the SRB and the national resolution authorities in a systemic crises of multiple bank failures and undermine the credibility of the planning process.

Liquidation Cases with DGS Payouts and Other DGS Interventions

6.59 The cases notified by the Member States' designated authority to the EBA between 2016 and 2019 (listed in Table 9.2 in Appendix 9)[80] provide insights into what kind of institutions have been put into liquidation.

6.60 In the notifications there are several notable absences (*ABLV Latvia, Veneto Banca*, and *Banca Popolare di Vicenza*) which are considered above. Table 9.2 (Appendix 9) shows the use of liquidation for failing banks and credit unions. DGS responsibilities are brought into play in such circumstances when either an administrative or a judicial authority has decided that deposits are unavailable, which means that the deposit is due and payable but not paid by the credit institution. The administrative authority needs to determine the 'credit institution is unable for the time being, for reasons which are directly related to its financial circumstance to repay the deposit and the institution has no current prospect of being able to do so';[81] or 'the judicial authority has made a ruling for reasons which are directly related to the credit institutions financial circumstances and which has the effect of suspending the rights of depositors to make claims against it'.[82] The administrative authority has the discretion to gauge before a bank is balance sheet insolvent as to whether the credit institution has no current prospect of being able to pay, which links in with the discretion the competent authority and the resolution authority have to determine whether the institution is failing or likely to fail. A jurisdiction where the decision has to be made or requires approval by a judicial authority is stricter, since the court is required to only look at the credit institutions' financial circumstances directly causing the unavailability of the deposit. In view of this, the administrative authority can form an opinion whether the credit institution is likely to

[80] Authors own analysis based on EBA Notifications on resolution cases and use of DGS funds, <https://eba.europa.eu/regulation-and-policy/recovery-and-resolution/notifications-on-resolution-cases-and-use-of-dgs-funds>.

[81] Directive 94/19/EC of the European Parliament and of the Council of 30 May 1994 on Deposit-Guarantee Schemes [1994] OJ L135/5, Art. 1(3)(i).

[82] Ibid, Art. 1(3)(ii).

be insolvent in the future, whereas the court will essentially have to determine if the institution is insolvent. It would be difficult to envisage a situation where a court forms a view opposite to the administrative authority, as long as there is sufficient evidence to support the decision that the bank is failing or likely to fail. The evidence, depending on the standard of proof, will have to be sufficient to satisfy the objective (failing) and subjective (likely to fail) decision of the administrative authority. In such circumstances, the bank may be of the view it was not given a sufficient amount of time to orchestrate a deal to rescue itself, and so convinces the court that more time is needed to avoid balance sheet insolvency as opposed to regulatory insolvency. The latter would be triggered once the bank breaches capital or liquidity requirements. In this respect, the objectives of bank insolvency need to be workout in advance. A special insolvency-liquidation procedure would also be helpful to assist with the decision-making process and ensure alignment between the administrative and judicial authority. However, the objectives within resolution would need to be replicated in insolvency-liquidation.

The competent authority and the resolution authority would need to work very closely with the DGS to ensure an orderly payout. In fact, the DGS would need to be forewarned to prepare for such an event. In view of this, time is critical since, as will be shown, the timing is linked to the different methods DGS use to execute payment. The Member State would need to ensure sufficient resources are in place and they are tested to assess any impediments that could cause a delay. If judicial authority is required to provide confirmation of insolvency of the bank, then potential timing for their decision needs to be factored in as well. The size of the institution is relative, depending on the capacity of the DGS, so it cannot be assumed the DGS will be able to manage in a relatively short timeline. **6.61**

The cases so far show that the preponderance of decided cases is with Eastern European Member States in comparison to other EU Member States. Overall, the size of the institution is evident from the number of depositors paid and the size of the DGS payout. The smallest number of depositors recorded is seven depositors and the largest is 39,575 depositors. In terms of DGS payouts, the smallest payout is €1.63m and the largest is €66.1m. These figures illustrate that the institutions placed in liquidation are extremely small. As such, currently, they are not listed as O-SIIs in their respective jurisdiction to require capital buffers for the purposes of macroprudential regulation.[83] In such circumstances, the institutions listed in Table 9.2 (Appendix 9) are not likely to cause significant impact on financial stability. In this respect, all the cases indicate that the bank is balance sheet insolvent or cash flow insolvent but, for a range of reasons, not necessarily as a result of balance sheet losses. Two cases, notably Malta (*Nemea Bank Plc*) and in Estonia (*Versobank AS*), indicate other regulatory reasons for the revocation of the bank licence. In the latter case, the CRD IV requirements for the withdrawal of authorization are referred to alongside other regulatory reasons, which include primarily reporting and governance failures. This indicates that other reasons can be used to put banks into liquidation. The principal trigger to make deposits unavailable then is revocation of authorization, since the business will not be able to trade without a licence. For instance, in the case of Lithuania and the Baltija Credit Union, the supervisory authority intervened after concerns about dissipation of high-value assets **6.62**

[83] See notifications on the ESRB, Systemically important institutions, at <https://www.esrb.europa.eu/national_policy/systemically/html/index.en.html> [accessed 26 November 2019].

but then decided it was insolvent. In view of these cases, it is evident the revocation of a bank's authorization results in the initiation of insolvency-bankruptcy proceedings, and so essentially terminates business to new clients.

6.63 The repayment of deposits has been a controversial area of the EU deposit protection since the original 1994 DGS Directive, as it provided the authorities with a very wide repayment timeframe that did not comply with international best practices at the time. Indeed, the repayment was likely to exasperate problems at banks, unless governments or banks were not merged to protect depositors' access to their bank accounts. In view of this, the DGS Directive moves towards a position where DGSs are expected to have the repayable amounts available within seven working days. The directive indicates that this should start on the date the administrative authority makes a determination that deposits are unavailable. The repayment period is relatively short, but to achieve this outcome a considerable level of resources have to be in place. In view of this, the DGS allows Member States to transition to the seven-day payout until 2023—from 20 working days by 2018, 15 working days by 2019–20, and 10 working days by 2021. As noted earlier, a principal source of information needed is the SCV file for the particular bank to orchestrate an orderly repayment. In respect of repayments, the credit institution is expected to transmit information about depositors as soon as the DGS makes the request. This column also shows that the reimbursement period can be open for a considerable length of time. This allows cases to be dealt with outside the covered depositors but those who are eligible but required to lodge claims or have their claims assessed for the purposes of know-your-customer identification for the purposes of excluding cases of money laundering. From a cross-border perspective, all creditor claims from different Member States are expected to be treated equally, according to the same ranking as claims in the home Member State, where proceedings have been initiated.[84]

6.64 A recent study by the European Forum of Deposit Insurers (EFDI) 2018 identifies a number of impediments to the achievement of a seven-day payout.[85] For example, the primary one is the accuracy of the SCV file and the ability of the DGS to accurately identify covered and eligible depositors. The other impediment is the alignment of decision-making and preparation prior to the closure of the bank. This would provide the DGS with the opportunity to request the SCV file in advance of the closure of the bank, and so the larger the institution, the more time needed to improve the accuracy of payouts. The other impediments could be the need to draw up cheques, provide new account details or visiting the agent bank that is assisting with the reimbursement and verifying their identify. As shown in Table 9.2 (Appendix 9), the vast majority of the Member States used an agent bank to make the disbursements to depositors. In some jurisdictions the liquidator can request that set off is applied before payout, which is likely to lead to potential delays that also need to be factored into the timing of payouts. Furthermore, this may have an impact on the seven-day commitment for a payout.

[84] Opinion of Advocate General Szpunar delivered on 26 May 2016, Case C-195/15 *SCI Senior Home, in administration, v Gemeinde Wedemark Hannoversche Volksbank eG* [2017] OJ C6/14.

[85] EFDI Non-Binding Guidance Paper, 'Pay-Out In 7 Working Days' (12 April 2018) <https://www.efdi.eu/sites/default/files/publications/efdi_non-binding_guidance_paper_-_pay-out_in_7_working_days-12_april_2018.pdf> [accessed 17 June 2018].

6.65 The cases provided in Table 9.2 (Appendix 9) show the determination date (in column 5) and the reimbursement period (column 9). The expectation, since all these cases are prior to 2019, is that the 20-day repayment period is complied with during the transitional period. Indeed, in all the cases the repayment period was significantly shorter than 20 days, with the quickest being three working days: the Croatian bank only had seven depositors. In the case of Maltese bank Nemea Bank Plc, the administrator of the bank put in place interim measures for depositors to access limited amounts on a daily basis, ranging from €250 to €2,500 per depositor per day, to ensure the bank's maturity policy on accounts was maintained. However, these measures were soon replaced with a full reimbursement scheme, once the licence was revoked. In the UK, Southsea Mortgage and Investment Ltd, another very small institution,[86] was closed as a result of its poor balance sheet position (case outside of the BRRD timeframe). The appointed liquidators were able to submit the SCV to the Financial Services Compensation Scheme (FSCS) by the close of business on the first day of the bank liquidator's appointment. The FSCS was then able to pay compensation to 80% of depositors by the close of business the next day. In this way, it managed to minimize disruption and provide access to funds by paying out as quickly as possible.

6.66 Table 9.2 (Appendix 9) also provides information on the techniques used to execute the reimbursement of deposits. The administrative hurdles associated with repayments can be onerous and, on occasions, centre on depositors being proactive in their efforts to have the compensation reimbursed. While this may be manageable for a relatively small institution with a few depositors, it can be onerous for a medium-sized bank, albeit non-systemic. The initial delay is likely to involve waiting for the SCV file and ensuring it is accurate, so the DGS can complete a payment instrument file. It is to be hoped that a part of this work has been done through routine assessments of the SCV files and checks for possible impediments to reimbursements, which are addressed *ex ante*. While the DGS requires the repayable amount to be made available without a request to the DGS, in practice, from the review of the cases, not all will be treated in this way. The EFDI explains that this is rather ambiguous, since some steps are likely to be needed by the depositor and can, as noted above, act as impediments to a seven-day payout. ABLV initiated a disbursement of €480m for covered deposits before the commencement of liquidation proceedings.[87] In this case, covered deposits did not need to lodge claims for their deposits; however, those with deposits above the coverage level of €100,000, such as SME enterprises and individuals, were required to lodge claims.

6.67 The EFDI study also identifies a number of techniques that are utilized by DGS in the EU to orchestrate a payout. In many respects, the different techniques illustrate the design limits of a local DGS as a result of constrained resources and their mandate that influence the use of one or another technique. There are three primary techniques: the use of internet-based solutions, payout agent, or financial instruments. Each has its own challenges. The internet-based approach necessitates a sophisticated IT support platform and it will also require the depositor to provide their new account number online. The identification of the depositor

[86] Malcolm Cohen and Shane Crooks, Bank Failures under the Banking Act 2009, 9(2) International Corporate Rescue, pp. 127–9.

[87] ABLV, General Terms of Liquidation of ABLV Bank, AS in Liquidation, 05/05/2019; ABLV Bank, AS in Liquidation, Operation report, March 2019 pursuant to Part 4 Art. 136 of the Credit Institution Law of the Republic of Latvia.

can be a risk that needs to be managed. Another issue is the compatibility of the SCV file and the platform and its ability to read the information and distribution accurately. As such, the internet-based solution could be resource intensive, unless the DGS can use the internet platform of the bank in question. The other method used is the payout agent. Table 9.2 (Appendix 9) shows that this is the most frequently-used method. The main benefit of this method is that the cost of a 'one-off' disbursement is limited to the outsourcing cost of using an agent bank. As with all outsourcing activities, the reliability of the agent needs to be ensured. According to the EFDI, difficulties include:

> security and logistical challenges related to cash payments of large sums of cash; know-your-customer issues in the account opening process; geographical location of the agent branch offices; number of depositors to be compensated.[88]

6.68 The final payment method is by way of cheque or pre-payment card, which poses its own challenges as well. In this approach securing accurate depositor data is a risk that needs managing, with the additional requirement of validating identity of the depositor. The EFDI highlights that a one-size-fits-all approach involving the adoption of a single method has inherent risks, and so the DGS should consider the use of as many methods as possible and risk assess the most suitable one depending on the case.

The Role of the DGS and Cross-border Challenges

6.69 The DGS Directive provides requirements for Member States to cooperate when dealing with depositors at a branch set up by a credit institution from another Member State. The DGS Directive sets out how the home and host authorities are expected to work together when a cross-border bank fails. It explains that depositors at a branch will be repaid by the DGS in the host on behalf of the home Member State DGS. The host is expected to make repayments according to the home DGS instructions. In view of the challenges posed in coordinating payouts across borders, a waiver for the need to comply with seven-day payout commitment has been introduced. The EFDI, however, in their non-binding recommendations have urged Member State DGSs to comply. This matter is important, since the EU market has been shown to have a significant number of EU foreign bank operations of which the majority are branches. It is particularly acute, since the policy of branchification is likely to lead to a concentration of risk and reliance on the home DGS to orchestrate payouts. This would be less of a concern with the previous diversification of risk and reliance on the local DGS to which the subsidiary would be a member. In the former, the incorporated entity would be a member of a separate DGS in the home and host. This section will finally gauge whether separate cooperation arrangements should be extended to foreign subsidiaries of groups as well, if the local DGS finds itself with a lack of funds to compensate eligible deposits with covered deposits.

6.70 The EBA Guidelines set out the minimum content expected in cooperation agreements that are required between home and host DGS to fulfil a payout to branch depositors.[89] Notably,

[88] EFDI Non-Binding Guidance Paper, 'Pay-Out In 7 Working Days' (n 85 above), p 7.
[89] Directive 2014/49/EU of the European Parliament and of the Council of 16 April 2014 on deposit guarantee schemes [2014] OJ L173/149.

the EBA Guidelines are a non-binding instrument that puts forward a number of recommendations to Member State DGS and designated authorities to develop written cooperation agreements. The EBA advocates the use of their multilateral framework to form the basis of cooperation agreements. These cooperation agreements are an attempt to minimize agency problems in times of a payout that could arise if the DGS in the home and host have not worked out how they expect to prepare and cooperate to execute a payout to branch depositors. In view of these responsibilities, the home and host DGS are expected to work in accordance with the principle of 'best efforts', which 'means taking such steps and performing in such manner as a well-managed deposit guarantee scheme would undertake where such deposit guarantee scheme was acting in a determined and prudent manner to achieve particular desired results for its own benefit.'[90]

The EBA Guidelines recognize that the EU DGS in respective Member States are set up in a variety of ways within the official safety net and have a number of mandates in resolution and insolvency to fulfil, such as financial stability and the protection of depositors. In view of this, the EBA Guidelines focus on three key areas to ensure ex ante consistent practice between the home and host DGS authorities. The DGS can put in place additional requirements in their respective cooperation agreements between their home and host counterparts in view of their different exposures and/or synergy in terms of mandates. The cooperation agreements as a minimum should cover the following points. **6.71**

The agreements require that the announcement concerning repaying the depositors by the host DGS at branches of a credit institution headquartered in other Member States should be specified. In this respect, the two designated authorities need to determine the size of the expected payout. Once that is done, they will need to identify the number of covered deposits and eligible deposits. The DGS directive also enables protection in different currencies, so the exchange rate will need to be calculated. The timing of notifications is particularly important, so issues, such as language of any communications, need to be worked out in advance. **6.72**

The agreements should also refer to information and data that are likely to be exchanged between the home and the host. Timing and deadlines for the exchange of information are expected to be within two working days. The type of information that should be included is timing of repayment and deadlines for reimbursement. The most critical potential impediment, however, is the lengthy preparation of the SCV account information by the home which is essential for the host to then execute reimbursement. Other critical information includes the date funding is expected to be transferred by the home to the host, so the latter has sufficient amount of time to orchestrate a payout. In view of the burden on the host, the costs for reimbursement need to also be determined. The home DGS will need to ensure that depositors eligible for 'cost of living payout' and 'temporary high balances' are separately identified when the SCV is being produced. In order to instil confidence in the arrangement, the agreement opens the door to external audit of DGS procedures to ensure they can fulfil a payout before a cooperation agreement is entered in to. This could overcome barriers associated with confidentiality and security arrangements as well. **6.73**

[90] Ibid.

6.74 The requirement that the cooperation agreement should outline the circumstances in which DGS's are likely to lend to one another is perhaps the most controversial aspect of the agreement, but equally the most critical, if such a need arose. The GFC highlighted the problems and fallout from the Icelandic crisis and the cross-border consequences of the inability of the Icelandic authorities to provide compensation to branch depositors in the UK and the Netherlands. This led to a position where the host authorities had to step in to prevent the fallout of the failure spilling over to other parts of the banking system. Indeed, the problem led to the UK authorities needing to put in place blanket guarantees to stave off depositor panic, which is difficult to quantify, let alone compensate. It was only recently that the full funds used to cover the compensation payout were finally repaid. The episode highlights the need for agreements ex ante that would enable Member States to gauge whether assistance would be provided in times of crisis. While agreements may be in place, the circumstances of the failure are likely to lead to a position of self-interest playing a role in whether support is provided or not. A critical feature of this episode is the need to undertake contingency planning to determine whether sufficient funds are available which will be dependent on the reliability of a risk-based premium system in place to adequately raise funds to build up the DGS fund.

6.75 The DGS Directive does enable DGS to borrow funds from one another on a voluntary basis.[91] In many respects, unlike Article 14 which is linked to the EU foreign bank branches, Article 12 is silent on whether it relates to solely supporting branches. In view of this, the ability to borrow could extend to support a foreign subsidiary which is a member of the local DSG, but the loan is required to support the foreign subsidiary depositors. The provision leads to a sensible opportunity to share the burden between the Member States, albeit voluntary, and so is likely to be requested when incentives are aligned between the home and host. The rationale of such reforms is to minimize the spillover effects of bank failures. It is therefore not surprising that it is not specifically linked to branches as the other wider cooperation measures are, which is set out in the DGS. The repercussions of an idiosyncratic subsidiary bank run could well spill over to undermine the confidence of the parent entity and other group entities, if there are delays to payout depositor reimbursements. This is obviously assuming that the resolution or liquidation proceedings of a bank were not implemented in an orderly manner. The incentives for support lie in the incentives on the home to contain the crisis and ensure an orderly payout as soon as possible. This is particularly relevant since in some jurisdictions identified in this work foreign entities' subsidiaries and branches do play a dominant role in their respective banking markets.

6.76 The EBA guidelines recommend for the home and host authorities to assess whether domestic law enables lending to other DGS in the first place. The home and host will also need to agree on the circumstances when a DGS is likely to lend, such as at a point of crisis or a large bank failure that requires additional financial resources to support payouts to branch depositors. In some jurisdictions, subsidiaries have had their legal form changed to branches. In those jurisdictions, branches can be very large and play a dominant role in the domestic banking market. In view of this, the branch is likely to provide critical functions and feature in the resolution plan. However, assistance is likely to be triggered after the

91 DGS Directive, Art. 12.

home DGS can demonstrate that they have exercised the powers at their disposal before a request for a loan is made, namely, instructing its members for extraordinary contributions. In order to calculate the size of the loan, it will be necessary to ensure the accuracy of the SCV file, which will form the basis of the reimbursement commitment. Notwithstanding the opening of the door to request a loan from a host DGS, it is capped according to the DSG Directive and the total request cannot exceed 0.5% of covered deposits of the borrowing DGS. This is a sizeable proportion of the fund, considering Member States are expected to build a DGS fund that is at least 0.8% of the amount of covered deposits.

Insolvency, Liquidation, and DGS Third Country Perspective

The RWD provides little reference to third country measures. Recital 21 states that the branches located in a Member State are expected to be overseen by the competent authorities of that Member State. Other than this, there is no provision referring to the equivalence within the RWD. The DGS Directive, on the other hand, does include provisions for branches of banks whose parent entity is located in a third country. In this area, it is the responsibility of the Member State to admit the branch to its DGS. The DGS Directive confers responsibility on the branch to ensure depositors are fully aware of the guarantee arrangements. The DGS Directive also requires the DGS to assess whether the third country provides equivalent guarantees. If the third country is found not to provide equivalent guarantees, the DGS is expected to require the branch to join its scheme as a member. The DGS would then have to work with the competent authority to agree on the premium it would be expected to pay based on the risk profile of the branch's business. Furthermore, the DGS Directive requires the assessment of the coverage level and scope of the protection. As such, the branch is expected to provide the information to the DGS about the guarantee arrangements. **6.77**

It is highly likely the local DGS will contact the third country deposit insurer, so that some form of communication and coordination channels and arrangements must be put in place to effectuate a potential payout. However, the DGS is silent on this matter. Other issues that would need to be considered are the timeliness of funds to be passed to the Member State to orchestrate a local payout. The DGS Directive indicates the need for agreements between DGS to better understand the designated responsibilities and undertake due diligence to provide confidence in one another's ability to undertake the tasks. However, the European Regional Committee (ERC) and IADI assessment recognize this as a gap in the DGS Directive. Therefore, the DGS directive should provide provisions for EU foreign branches and non-EU foreign branches.[92] While the DGS Directive does not require an agreement with third country counterparts, it does not mean that the two cannot ensure the necessary arrangements are in place if the parent entity was to fail. The resolution authority could assist by assessing whether the branch is of an appropriate size to require a separate resolution plan and cooperate with the parent entity resolution authority through the crisis management group to understand the resolution strategy and how it will impact the branch business. **6.78**

[92] IADI-ERC Subgroup, 'Mind the Gap: A Comparative analysis between the IADI CPs and the DGSD' (December 2017), p. 25.
<https://www.iadi.org/en/assets/File/Papers/.../Mind_the_Gap__Final.pdf> [accessed 17 June 2019].

International Soft Law Instruments Focus on Home and Host Deposit Protection Issues

6.79 The IADI Core Principles 2014 focus on the mandate of the deposit insurer and the efficiency with which it can execute its responsibilities to support financial stability and depositor protection. A significant challenge for the deposit insurer has been one of how it can best be included in the official safety net decision-making to ensure it can execute its responsibilities in a timely manner. The Core Principles recognize the possibility of the home and host acting in their own interests to safeguard their depositors over and above those of their respective counterparts. The responsibilities of the deposit insurer essentially emanate from the membership of the individual bank, so its focus is not necessarily on the relationship between home and host authorities cooperating and coordinating as configured in the DGSD. In many jurisdictions the responsibilities of the deposit insurer can be very narrow, namely a simple paybox system (reimbursement of insured deposits) that is reliant on funding and loss minimizing decisions (involved in deciding resolution options and minimizing the use of its resources) being taken by other parts of the official safety net.

6.80 In view of the dominant role played by foreign banks in the accession countries, it is critical that efforts are made to put in place measures to assist with the local deposit insurer executing its mandate by being given information in a timely manner to ensure a payout is made without causing disruption in the local market. Table 6.1 (Appendix 6) shows that the number of EU foreign branches in the accession countries is non-existent amongst the top-five institutions in each market, so reliance on the need for cross-border cooperation and coordination from their perspective is limited since the vast proportion of the entities are subsidiaries and so likely to be members of the local deposit insurer. Nonetheless, information sharing is critical for the deposit insurer to execute their responsibilities and to ensure a disruptive payout does not lead to spillover risks. Principle 5 of the Core Principles advocate that formal information sharing arrangements are put in place and agreements are entered into that outline the division of responsibilities between the home and host authorities. Such provisions for information sharing at the supervisory and resolution would assist the deposit insurer, especially if the SCV file is held centrally and would need to be shared with the third country deposit insurer to ensure an orderly payout. Indeed, in some cases the accession countries have simulated stress-testing exercises in accordance with EBA criteria, for instance, sharing of the SCV file and its delivery to the deposit insurer within the allocated time. The multilateral agreement put in place in the EU could be a template for assisting with coordination and cooperation commitments with third countries as well, but that will need political will. This then would also extend to calculating risk premiums and contingency planning for reimbursements. For example, a critical area would be the coverage level expected to be in place that is credible. Comparing the coverage level of the EU with those of accession countries could be a point of contention since the accession countries are unlikely to be able to provide coverage levels equivalent to the EU's €100,000 level or its equivalent in the local currency.[93] Another important element would be to set the correct expectations in view of the possible deposit insurance mandates. For instance,

[93] IADI, Principle 8.

a clear recognition that a deposit insurer, according to international expectations, is able to manage payouts for a medium-sized bank or a cluster of small banks, therefore limiting expectations of its role in any potential systemic crisis, where political decisions are taken to put in place some form of public guarantee at the institutional level or sectoral level. Limited available funds to cover potential payouts is equally an important aspect of the dialogue between home and host to ensure the right techniques are used to try and minimise the burden on the deposit insurer to execute a payout.[94] For instance, one must ask, do the authorities have a propensity for liquidation or resolution? If it is the former, then reliance on the deposit insurer is likely to be almost immediate and reimbursements would need to be made in a timely manner, whereas in the latter, the resolution techniques are likely to reduce the burden of a payout and ensure continuity of access to deposits. Equally important is the confidence in the authorities to act in a timely manner to minimize potential shortfall to payout covered depositors. These matters should be discussed by the resolution authorities, if they exist, and form part of the dialogue when preparing resolution plans at the college level.

The importance of contingency planning is set out in Principle 6 of the Core IADI principles.[95] It is of critical significance for the preparation for executing the deposit insurance mandate. In part, timely information is needed to be shared between home and host authorities. In view of the EU accession countries, deposit protection powers do exist and are relied on to deal with failing banks. The mandate for accession countries does vary from paybox to paybox-plus systems, where in the former the mandate is simply reimbursements, as in the case of Albania and Montenegro, and, in the latter, it can consist of resolution functions as well, such as in Serbia, where it is responsible for overseeing the transfer of assets of banks in resolution. There have been coordinated meetings within the region to better understand their roles and functions. In part, MoUs are in place and there is willingness to enter agreements, but in most instances cross-border agreements are not necessary to cover foreign deposits in view of the little or non-existent cross-border presence of their domestic banks. 6.81

Reflections on the Principal Issues

The analysis of bank insolvency and liquidation shows how contradictions are exposed by the different approaches. While the RWD essentially provides conflicts of law provisions, it enables Member States to use administrative and judicial authorities to execute decisions. A number of issues need to be considered in order to improve consistency such as the role of moratoria in bank insolvency and liquidation proceeding and the scope of depositor preference and the priority it confers. This enables the co-existence of administrative and judicial authorities and unless there is alignment with public interest objectives there is a potential chance of the judiciary exercising decisions about bank insolvency and liquidation on a different criteria. The cases such as ABLV Luxembourg 6.82

94 IADI, Principle 9.

95 IADI, Principle 6; see also IADI, Deposit Insurers' Role in Contingency Planning and System-wide Crisis Preparedness and Management Guidance Paper (Consultation version) 6 March 2019, <https://www.iadi.org/en/assets/File/Public_Consultation/IADI_Guidance_Paper_contingencyplanning_crisismanagement_public_consultation060319.pdf>.

SA illustrate this problem well, when the resolution authorities' opinion about the bank's insolvency was rejected by the court. Moreover, the cases of the Venato region equally show how the SRB's public interest assessment of whether the bank enters resolution or insolvency does differs with national approaches as indicated with the use of the Croatian decision. A stricter view is not necessarily the concern what is a concern is the inconsistency of interpretation. Since it could lead to *ex post* burdens on other parts of the official safety net like the DGS or the state itself in order to support an orderly liquidation and possibly a payout to covered deposits. The lack of harmonized bank insolvency and liquidation regime within the EU leads to a case-by-case approach that is likely to lead to comparisons of potential outcomes which is expected to lead to delays or require more time to organize the different parts of the proceedings to ensure a timely payout of covered deposits. A key problem with the current arrangements is the lack of funding of DGS systems in view of the relatively low target level. This is likely to lead to significant reliance on other lines of funding such as state loans which should be minimized considering such cases are not supposed to threaten financial stability. A clear line of cases at the national level indicate the national authorities have generally put banks that are relatively small with a few thousand deposits at the most in to liquidation. The policy narrative of resolution clearly contradicts that of deposit guarantee schemes.

6.83 The practice at the cross-border level requires better alignment since it is not likely to be efficient to share data with the host when a payout from the home DGS is perfectly feasible and could be potentially delayed due to incompatibility of data systems and processes. This is particularly likely where banks have executed a corporate decision to branchify their foreign operations in Member States and the SCV file is centrally managed or exists via an internet platform. In respect of the branchification policy serious questions need to be asked whether the home Member State DGS has sufficient available funds and whether the risk premium system is robust to ensure sufficient funding can be generated. A high level of optimism exists within the cooperation arrangements. In view of the lack of funds available it is unlikely for DGS systems to cooperate with funding. A high degree of self-interest exists in terms of assisting with funding to another DGS, and where there is a high level of exposure of your own banks then financial stability is equally important to both parties.

7

EU Financial Crisis Management and Containment

Introduction

The critical asymmetry of information problem that can arise during a cross-border crisis is whether the parties will cooperate and coordinate their efforts to minimize the spillover effects of a crisis. The legal provisions and expectations are geared towards co-operation and coordination of responsibilities along pre-determined lines. The ultimate challenge is likely to be who will fund the necessary costs of dealing with a potential resolution or insolvency-liquidation of a bank and are there sufficient funds in place to ensure such decisions give rise to orderly outcomes and minimize the costs of resolution and liquidation.[1] The process of mutualization and centralized funding may well improve greater confidence for integration. Two principal techniques to contain a financial crisis, namely resolution and insolvency liquidation, exist. However the need for financial assistance will be shown to be necessary to provide orderly outcomes. The principal instruments paradoxically do not prohibit public support but provide administrative structures around such decisions to improve the transparency of decisions but not necessarily the accountability of those decisions to provide public assistance. The mechanisms to contain crises during the global financial crisis (GFC) coexist at the bank and sovereign levels. In part the centralization of the SRF and the European Stability Mechanism (ESM) assist with burden-sharing but do not tackle the root problem. It will ask whether a system should at every turn in—pre-solvency to resolution and liquidation—enable public assistance and or state aid. This is important to consider if we view the GFC as a liquidity crisis and the provision of large scale liquidity would have adverted some of the failures that materialized. The necessity to provide public assistance was to contain the spread of the crisis and minimize it, albeit once it reached systemic proportions. The measures analysed in this chapter look at the mechanism to minimize the risk of contagion and the chances of another systemic crisis. **7.1**

[1] For a historical perspective see D Mayes and J Vesala, 'On the Problems of Home Country Control' (Bank of Finland Discussion Papers, 20/98 (1998)); R Herring, 'Conflicts between Home and Host Country Prudential Supervisors' in D Evanoff, G Kaufman, and J R LaBrosse (eds), *International Financial Instability: Global Banking and National Regulation*, Vol. 2 (New Jersey: World Scientific Publishing Co Pte Ltd 2007), at 201–21. For a more recent perspective see K Pistor, 'Host's Dilemma: Rethinking EU Banking Regulation in Light of the Global Crisis', ECGI Working Paper Series in Finance (No. 286/2010); see also K D'Hulster, 'Cross Border Banking Supervision: Incentive Conflicts in Supervisory Information Sharing between Home and Host Supervisors' (World Bank Policy Research Working Paper No. 5871, 1 November 2011), <https://ssrn.com/abstract=1955108> [accessed 20 March 2019]; G Ferrarini and L Chiarella, 'Common Banking Supervision in the Eurozone: Strengths and Weaknesses' (Working Paper No. 223/2013, ECGI Working Paper Series in Law, August 2013), pp. 6–10; see also, E Avgouleas, *Governance of Global Financial Markets: The Law, the Economics, the Politics* (Cambridge: Cambridge University Press 2012), 422–3.

European Cross-Border Banking and Banking Supervision. Dalvinder Singh, Oxford University Press (2020). © Oxford University Press.
DOI: 10.1093/oso/9780198844754.001.0001

7.2 This chapter analyses the decentralized and centralized mechanisms to support crisis management. The decentralized mechanisms reside at the national level. The centralized mechanisms reside at the Eurozone level for participating and Eurozone Member States. The decentralized and centralized mechanisms can cause political frictions when there are concerns about the lack of consistency between Member States and the vexed issue of public assistance in a world that views this as an issue of the past. The first part of the chapter analyses the role of national powers to provide assistance through recapitalization initiatives and/or liquidity assistance. Ultimately, these responsibilities fall along national lines and where there has been coordination it is essentially *ex post* once a crisis has materialized with a cross-border bank. The techniques to minimize the moral hazard risk, namely through approval of public assistance by the Commission, is considered separately and again shows such decisions fall along national lines. However what is evident in these cases is the focus is on the distortion of the home market and decisions about other markets is primarily one of sale of business to recapitalize the entity in question. The consideration of the European Central Bank (ECB) to provide liquidity assistance is the first step to explore how centralization deals with home and host dilemmas. The next part of the chapter explores the formal centralized mechanisms to fund resolution and the proposal for EDIS. It will be argued that EDIS is critical to the success of the Banking Union, especially if liquidation is the option of first resort. Since it is argued the national deposit guarantee schemes (DGSs) are unlikely to be able to support the liquidation of multiple banks at any one time, without resorting to national financial lines of support. Considering that narrow banks have limited or no loss absorbing capacity the need for public assistance is likely to be greater to address potential shortfalls. It is suggested that EDIS, like the SRF, is equally provided a backstop to improve its credibility. These are considered as principal measures to address home and host dilemmas. It is argued the funding of these initiatives through private means is an important contributing factor. It is an important step to minimize moral hazard risks through levies calibrated according to bank risk as opposed to supervision addressing the problems of public support mechanisms and the risks they give rise to. If these are calibrated properly they should go some way to address the political anxiety from Member State concerns about subsidizing risky banking in other Member States. It will be argued that these measures have not been properly tested with a crisis of multiple bank failures. The backstop to these measures resides with the European Stability Mechanism (ESM). This is distinct at two levels firstly it is funded by sovereign Member States and secondly it aims to minimize the risk associated with the nexus between banks and sovereigns. Finally, the third country dimension is explored and the Financial Stability Board (FSB) guidelines on temporary funding needs in resolution.

Central Bank, Emergency Liquidity Assistance, and Extraordinary Financial Support

7.3 The role of the central bank during the GFC was at the heart of containing problems at the institutional and market level. The primary central bank intervention at the institutional level with good collateral has traditionally been the function of lender of last resort, or in more modern terms, emergency liquidity assistance. But the complexity of the task of containing a systemic crisis involves both the central bank and the state. Since the central bank may not have the autonomy to exercise such decisions and will ultimately require the go ahead from the state. During the GFC, states have initiated techniques such as nationalization of banks, guarantees (institutional or market, implicit or explicit, partial or blanket guarantee), or asset purchase schemes. A critical aspect of containing the GFC, in hindsight, was the need for sufficient liquidity in the market to ensure it could continue despite the rumours about the level of bad assets. In hindsight, the problem for some banks was more akin to cashflow insolvency. This is nowhere more pertinent than in the case of Lehman Brothers in bankruptcy, with the administrators presiding over a surplus as opposed to huge losses way above all expectations.[2] In view of this case it is important to have in mind the current situation, and whether it is one of balance sheet insolvency, or cashflow insolvency, or both? In view of the dominance of credit finance in the EU market as shown earlier, the failures explored in this chapter indicate a combination of short term balance sheet problems rather than cashflow problems experienced by highly leveraged investment banks.[3] Therefore, the EU in view of the prevalence of balance sheet losses is not likely to see the kind of return on its public assistance as was seen in the United States.

Currently, the national central banks still retain the discretion to provide emergency liquidity assistance. In view of the fractured nature of decision making, at critical points the partial centralization gives rise to national discretion that may not always get the consensus amongst the regional members. There will be concerns about consistency and fairness in treatment of banks across different Member States in such circumstances, especially when there are situations of under- and over-accommodation of problem banks. The following section analyses the two principle forms of pre-insolvency assistance that are provided in the Bank Recovery and Resolution Directive (BRRD). But it is important to emphasize that these measures operate outside of the requirements of formal resolution. In view of this position the criteria of burden-sharing falls within the criteria of state aid which are explored below. It is evident the criteria in the latter differs significantly to that residing in the BRRD. Since in the BRRD the criteria for precautionary recapitalization and liquidity assistance require capital and liquidity plans that may implicitly include burden-sharing amongst the principal shareholder. The use of public assistance in liquidation is also considered but again the criteria for burden-sharing resides outside of the BRRD in the national insolvency-liquidation proceedings and the state aid criteria to minimize abuse of position and the distortions in the market. Nonetheless it is, important to critically evaluate their use since it highlights the vexing 7.4

[2] 'Lehman Brothers administrators left with £5bn surplus after creditors paid', *The Guardian*, <https://www.theguardian.com/business/2014/mar/05/lehman-brothers-administrators-surplus-creditors-paid> [accessed 5 March 2014].

[3] Christopher Gandrud and Mark Hallerberg (2017), 'How not to create zombie banks: lessons for Italy from Japan', Bruegel Policy Contribution, No. 2017/6, Bruegel, Brussels; see also Lorenzo Codogno and Mara Monti, 'Is Italy's recent support to its banks the start of a new wave of public intervention in the EU?', <https://blogs.lse.ac.uk/europpblog/2017/01/16/italy-support-banks-start-of-new-wave-eu-intervention/>.

question of whether the Member State is simply supporting insolvent banks as they are likely to fail.

Precautionary Recapitalization

7.5 The EU resolution framework takes a rather pragmatic view and incorporates the possibility of the Member States government or central bank offering assistance *ex ante* while the financial institution is experiencing capital or liquidity problems that can be addressed by short-term assistance. The first exception to the general prohibition to provide extraordinary public assistance is the precautionary recapitalization and the second is emergency liquidity assistance. In part this is the first area where national bias can filter in to decisions. It is argued the delegation of responsibility to the national level leads to claims of inconsistency of practice. Where there is centralized decision-making such as assessing resolvability, resolution planning, and resolution schemes on the one hand, there is the decentralization of decision-making to national competent and resolution and designated authorities in areas such as support during the pre-insolvency support initiatives on the other. These are explored in the following section.

7.6 A prohibition on the use public funds is an important signal to minimize the risk of moral hazard that can ensue from state support. The dilemma the official safety net authorities face, however, is one where some public support may be useful and may actually assist in either avoiding the unnecessary resolution being triggered or risk loss of market confidence in the institution by placing the bank at the mercy of the markets to decide whether it can raise the necessary funds from private sources of liquidity. The controversial element in this respect is perhaps what is precautionary and to what extent is it likely to be temporary, which leads to a degree of uncertainty as to the length of time if such support is provided. In view of the decision to provide precautionary recapitalization, a principal risk to consider is the perception support is evidence of resolution forbearance. It could be considered a signal the public support was given prematurely and triggering resolution is a signal the public funds have been wasted.

7.7 The kinds of market disruption that come to mind, when thinking about whether precautionary recapitalization is provided, are difficult to perceive since they are either based on a lack of confidence in the bank's balance sheet, or they are a market disruption which is experienced by a set of banks in a particular sector, and so are market-wide. What is evident is the speed with which markets react, highlighting the acute need for some access to public support to avoid the loss of confidence and so risking contagion in the sector. The supervisory measures used to identify difficulties ahead, such as stress testing of adverse plausible scenario testing or asset quality review, are the potential triggers for precautionary recapitalization. It ultimately leads to a position where triggering the options of either formal resolution or insolvency is avoided. In this respect the supervisory intervention is critical, albeit it is partly within the mandate of the macro-prudential authority to be involved since it is also linked to potential outcome of a stress test scenario. The challenge here is that, while capital is the ultimate cushion to weather shocks, it is generally considered a time lag indicator, which means the deterioration of a bank's capital level as a result of asset write down may transpire once it is too late. The BRRD in this respect is unhelpful since Recital 41 does not mention cashflow (liquidity) requirements, so it primarily addresses one potential form of insolvency, balance sheet rather than as debts fall due. Notwithstanding the fact that the conditions set out below include guarantee for liquidity support.

The challenge here is whether a common approach is taken, considering the discrepancies highlighted in terms of the quality of data and information from one Member State to another being different. The approval for the purposes of state aid of such assistance is perhaps the only real assurance that decisions made by national competent and designated authorities will be 'independently' scrutinized and ensure consistent treatment. From the perspective of the Banking Union, the ECB would be responsible for such decisions after the stress test. The move towards a consistent approach to non-performing loans, which is a likely trigger for the potential capital shortfall, is likely to assist this process of deciding precautionary recapitalization since the national discretion to write down the value of assets or write off assets is critical to this decision. This calls into question the requirement that public assistance 'shall not be used to offset losses that the institution has incurred or is likely to incur in the near future'.[4] Moreover, precautionary recapitalization is not akin to a form of open bank assistance either, which can consist of 'direct loans, an assisted merger or purchase of assets'.[5] The position for precautionary recapitalization is no different to the provision of emergency liquidity assistance, albeit it is focused on capital shortfalls as opposed to liquidity problems of solvent banks in both instances. 7.8

The decision of applying precautionary recapitalization to the plausible outcome of a stress test or asset quality review and failing, or likelihood of failing, is somewhat linked, since in both scenarios the bank is likely to be technically solvent but not necessarily regulatorily solvent.[6] In the former, it is necessary to establish that the bank does not meet the conditions for resolution although the outcome of the stress test indicates a capital shortfall is evident. The techniques within the precautionary capitalization that are listed are not new but were commonly used during the GFC.[7] These include a state guarantee for liquidity support facility or issue of new liabilities or injection of own funds or purchase of capital instruments. In the latter context, these need to be proportionate to address shortfall of capital. It is then qualified by indicating that the techniques can only be used for solvent institutions and not to offset losses that the institution is likely to incur. In view of the difficulty of providing an accurate picture of the size of the problem and then the size of the capital injection and the likely success of private investment, an overly optimistic picture is likely to lead to an overly pessimistic outcome and so consequently require a greater level of need than first anticipated. Nonetheless, the BRRD expects that the assistance does not provide the institution 7.9

[4] See the critique by N Véron, 'Precautionary recapitalisations: time for a review' (provided in advance of the public hearing with the Chair of the Single Resolution Board in ECON on 11 July 2017), <http://www.europarl.europa.eu/RegData/etudes/IDAN/2017/602090/IPOL_IDA(2017)602090_EN.pdf> [accessed 15 March 2019].

[5] <https://www.iadi.org/en/core-principles-and-research/publications/glossary/open-bank-assistance/> [accessed 15 March 2019].

[6] Recital 41: 'The fact that an institution does not meet the requirements for authorisation should not justify per-se the entry into resolution, especially if the institution is still or likely to still be viable.'

[7] D Singh and J R LaBrosse, 'Developing a Framework for Effective Financial Crisis Management', in Financial Crisis Management and the use of Government Guarantees, OECD Journal: Financial Market Trends, No. 101, Vol. 2011–12, 1–30, Table 1, p. 13.

with an advantage which is difficult to count out unless the competitive advantage is eliminated by the process of applying state aid requirements to ensure the assistance is temporary and proportionate to fulfil this requirement. This is explored later in the chapter.

7.10 The case of Monte Paschi di Siena (MPS) is an interesting one which illustrates the use of precautionary recapitalization, albeit although its problems were ongoing long before the BRRD during the height of the GFC.[8] The findings of the 2016 EBA stress test found MPS was the worst performing of 51 banks across the EU. In this respect the stress test result was not a serious disturbance that warranted such intervention. In this case the exogenous serious disturbance in the economy was not the trigger for the intervention. As a result of the findings, the bank undertook the task of putting together a capital plan which was subsequently approved by the ECB, which required MPS to raise capital in the market and shrink its balance sheet by disposing of a portfolio of bad loans to improve its capital position. The initial efforts were not sufficient and several rounds of working out a revised capital plan and an additional state injection of capital led to finally a position where 'MPS booked losses of EUR 14.3 billion, raised private capital for EUR 8 billion, and repaid EUR 2 billion of State aid'.[9] As a result of this MPS divested €26.1bn and ultimately 'reduced its balance sheet by 37%, its branches by 34%, and its staff by 23%'.[10]

7.11 In view of these figures it is difficult to conclude how MPS could ever have been simply experiencing a 'capital shortfall,' rather than a persistently poor balance sheet. In view of this, it could be argued that the initial findings of the stress test did not identify the true extent and severity of the legacy problems otherwise it would not have found itself in need of several rounds of capital planning to improve its final capital position. It also highlights that, despite its position, it did not command the position in the market in the market to initiate market-based solutions to resolve its problems. The case shows the very close proximity between precautionary recapitalization and the decision of 'failing or likely failure' for the purposes of deciding resolution or insolvency. Moreover, as Hellwig also explains, the scope for precautionary recapitalization ultimately delays the inevitable and possibly increases the costs of such interventions.[11]

7.12 Do the findings from the stress test or asset quality review illustrate a bank that is likely to fail? The competent authority's discretion within the space of supervision with powers of early intervention powers highlights the extent to which the supervisory competent authority can extend its involvement in the bank before the decision of resolution needs to be triggered. In many respects the MPS case shows the use of quasi-resolution of restructuring decisions outside of a formal resolution decision being taken. This point is illustrated by the problems experienced by Deutsche bank, highlighted by Véron in his discussion of precautionary recapitalization, albeit that it is not required or officially acknowledged to be put forward.[12] The different cases do not lend themselves to garnering

[8] 'The precautionary recapitalisation of Monte dei Paschi di Siena': <http://www.europarl.europa.eu/RegData/etudes/BRIE/2017/587392/IPOL_BRI(2017)587392_EN.pdf> [accessed 15 March 2019].
[9] Ibid.
[10] Ibid.
[11] Martin F. Hellwig, 'Precautionary Recapitalisations: Time for a Review' (July 2017) MPI Collective Goods Preprint, No. 2017/14, available at SSRN: <https://ssrn.com/abstract=3000951> or <http://dx.doi.org/10.2139/ssrn.3000951>.
[12] Véron (n 4), p. 13.

what is common in the use of precautionary recapitalization, since the timeline of the decisions for recapitalization differ significantly both before and after the introduction of the BRRD. The convoluted requirements certainly necessitate the need for a review, as suggested by, inter alia, Olivares-Caminal and Russo.[13] The difficulty of what is proposed by Olivares-Caminal and Russo of a clear definition of serious disturbance or financial stability when such a task has been avoided or deemed unhelpful by legislative authorities since it could constrain the administrative discretion of the competent authority or the national designated authority. It is likely to be simpler to emphasize stress-testing or asset quality reviews as a better trigger for deciding whether precautionary recapitalization is useful to address the problems at a solvent bank. To then deal with the banks' capital shortfall despite the fact that the exogenous factors could expose the capital shortfall and the need for such intervention which is verified by the asset quality review. It is also difficult to isolate the effect of the intervention to offsetting losses that the institution has incurred or likely to incur in the near future. It would imply this is done after the capital injection. In the case of MPS, it could have been undertaken simultaneously and hence the need for additional levels of intervention.

Emergency Liquidity Assistance

Liquidity assistance during periods of distress for solvent banks in periods of financial instability is of the utmost importance. The reliance on short-term wholesale markets was unsustainable prior to the GFC. Central bank assistance in the form of exceptional emergency liquidity assistance was ramped up to step into the market and assist with the provision of liquidity. However, the reforms introduced by the BRRD place emergency liquidity assistance in a different position, as a 'pre-resolution' technique to the traditional position it held during the GFC. When the market mechanism faltered, the state and central bank acted as the backstop to intervene and stabilize market panic to alleviate serious adverse selection problems and, perhaps more controversially, moral hazard problems by cushioning banks from adverse risks.[14] More specifically, the central bank assistance provided during the GFC consisted of a number of techniques that are placed in more formalized administrative arrangements and decision-making processes, rather than the opaque position in which such would traditionally have been placed to ensure constructive ambiguity and thereby minimize the risk of moral hazard.[15] But transparency does not always lead to an improved position if the rule is couched in broad terms and provides a significant degree of administrative discretion to evaluate options. As noted earlier, what was undertaken broadly under the umbrella of lender of last resort (LOLR) and state assistance has been split into capital-based assistance, as explained in the previous section, and here in the form of liquidity assistance and state guarantee support to such facilities. 7.13

[13] R Olivares-Caminal and C Russo, 'Precautionary recapitalisations: time for a review' (provided in advance of the public hearing with the Chair of the Single Resolution Board in ECON, on 11 July 2017): <http://www.europarl.europa.eu/RegData/etudes/IDAN/2017/602092/IPOL_IDA(2017)602092_EN.pdf> [accessed 15 March 2019].

[14] K Kirabaeva, 'Adverse Selection and Financial Crises', Bank of Canada Review (Winter 2010–2011) pp. 11–19.

[15] R M Lastra, 'Emergency Liquidity Assistance and Systemic Risk', in A Anand (ed) *Systemic Risk, Institutional Design, and the Regulation of Financial Markets* (Oxford: Oxford University Press, 2016) pp. 175–206.

7.14 In view of the more formalized approach, the BRRD introduced emergency liquidity assistance (ELA)[16] for banks in distress. Emergency liquidity assistance is placed in a position that enables the central bank to intervene with liquidity assistance in instances where the financial institution or group of financial institutions are solvent but not at the point where the financial institution is or will be unable to pay its liabilities, or where it will form the basis of such a decision. This indicates that assistance is not expected to be a trigger to decide whether a financial institution is failing or likely to fail. In view of this, ELA is placed in a distinct position and not in the vicinity of traditional LOLR, in view of the possible negative reactions to this likely to be experienced in the market once a bank announces that it has sought ELA. In respect of solvency, ELA provides a distinct definition of solvency to assist central banks in their decision-making process.[17] In part this is not classed as extraordinary public finances if the state guarantees to support the liquidity facilities by the central bank. The positioning of ELA in the BRRD is central bank liquidity assistance before a financial institution is considered failing or likely to fail for the purposes of deciding resolution or insolvency. This does not necessarily imply during resolution and insolvency that liquidity to support the restructuring process is not needed, but reliance at this juncture on liquidity support is placed on the resolution fund and potentially the deposit guarantee fund for additional support. Despite this repositioning the stigma associated with accessing it is likely to lead to a position where banks will refrain until there is no other option in case it risks undermining market confidence.

7.15 The central bank assistance through liquidity assistance can be provided for two different purposes: to assist with normal monetary policy operations, and in the form of emergency assistance outside of monetary policy operations when a financial institution or group of financial institutions are experiencing liquidity problems.[18] The European Central Bank ELA procedures explain that the national central bank is expected to use national central bank money or provide other assistance reliant on the central bank to solvent financial institutions facing temporary liquidity problems with high-quality collateral.[19] The emphasis on the burden being placed on the central bank balance sheet is rather symbolic, since it attempts to provide distance from the state balance sheet, though one could argue that they are both one of the same. The relatively small size of national central banks in comparison to financial institutions in the market suggests its role could potentially be limited unless it gained state support as well.[20] The central bank's exercise of its discretion to provide

16 BRRD, Art. 2(1) and (29): 'emergency liquidity assistance' means the provision by a central bank of central bank money, or any other assistance that may lead to an increase in central bank money, to a solvent financial institution, or group of solvent financial institutions, that is facing temporary liquidity problems, without such an operation being part of monetary policy.

17 'ELA solvency criterion for credit institutions: A credit institution is considered solvent for ELA purposes if: (a) its Common Equity Tier 1, Tier 1 and Total Capital Ratio as reported under CRR on an individual (if applicable) and consolidated (if applicable) basis comply with the harmonized minimum regulatory capital levels (namely 4.5%, 6% or 8%, respectively); or (b) there is a credible prospect of recapitalization—in case (a) is not met, ie the Common Equity Tier 1, Tier 1 and Total Capital Ratio, on an individual and/or consolidated basis, do not comply with the harmonized minimum regulatory capital levels (namely 4.5%, 6% or 8%, respectively)—by which harmonized minimum regulatory capital levels would be restored within 24 weeks after the end of the reference quarter of the data that showed that the bank does not comply with harmonized regulatory minimum standards; in duly justified, exceptional cases the Governing Council may decide to prolong the grace period of 24 weeks.'

18 ECB, 'Agreement on emergency liquidity assistance' (17 May 2017): <https://www.ecb.europa.eu/pub/pdf/other/Agreement_on_emergency_liquidity_assistance_20170517.en.pdf> [accessed 15 March 2019].

19 Protocol on the Statute of the European System of Central Banks and of the European Central Bank: <https://www.ecb.europa.eu/ecb/legal/pdf/en_statute_2.pdf> [accessed 15 March 2019].

20 C A E Goodhart, *The Regulatory Response to the Financial Crisis* (Cheltenham: Edward Elgar 2010), p. 66.

emergency liquidity assistance is not in all instances its sole decision and in some Member States it does require government approval. At the Eurozone level, the Statute of Central Banks and of the European Central Bank, Article 14.4 provides the Governing Council of the ECB with responsibility for restricting emergency liquidity assistance if it considers it would interfere with the objectives and tasks of the Eurosystem.[21] The attempt to distance itself from concerns about the viability of the financial institution is more controversial since it could be a signal of impending failure. To counter the sensitivity of the stigma about temporary liquidity assistance, Goodhart suggests a reassessment of disclosure to desensitise its possible use and reduce stigma.[22] This is possibly more in line with the disclosure of findings from stress-testing, which could be equally sensitive. However, liquidity management is perhaps significantly more difficult than capital and balance sheet quality since it can be exposed to more volatility of loss of confidence in the market, with the market withdrawing support at critical moments. For example, in instances of market-wide need for assistance the stigma is perhaps less of a concern, particularly because the assistance is in line with support of monetary policy operations. Whereas, disclosures in the case of an individual bank in need of emergency liquidity assistance may be met with less sympathy.

The central bank has the discretion to disclose emergency liquidity assistance; if it does decide to do so then it needs to orchestrate a plan with the individual plan to publicise the news and ultimately be ready to deal with any potential reaction. In the case of the ECB and its concerns about wider financial stability implications of such announcements, the Governing Council could express its objection to publicizing such information. The markets could technically review the balance sheet of the central bank to gauge whether assistance has been provided, but recent reforms have attempted to address this. To mitigate the risks of disclosure and the stigma associated with such assistance being provided, the EBA guidelines take a cautious approach and require modification to the rules on asset encumbrance to prevent the markets detecting assistance provided by the central bank for its refinancing purposes.[23] For example, a supervisory authority may exercise its discretion to stop disclosure to avoid detection of the liquidity assistance provided by a central bank both in **7.16**

[21] ECB, Agreement on emergency liquidity assistance (17 May 2017). As a rule, NCBs inform the ECB of the details of any ELA operation, at the latest, within two business days after the operation was carried out. The information needs to include, at least, the following elements: 1. the counterparty to which the ELA has been/will be provided; 2. the value date and maturity date of the ELA that has been/will be provided; 3. the volume of the ELA that has been/will be provided; 4. the currency in which the ELA has been/will be provided; 5. the collateral/guarantees against which the ELA has been/will be provided, including the valuation of, and any haircuts applied to, the collateral provided and, where applicable, details on the guarantee provided and the terms of any contractual safeguards; 6. the interest rate to be paid by the counterparty on the ELA that has been/will be provided; 7. the specific reason(s) for the ELA that has been/will be provided (ie margin calls, deposit outflows, etc.); 8. the prudential supervisor's assessment, over the short and medium term, of the liquidity position and solvency of the institution receiving the ELA, including the criteria used to come to a positive conclusion with respect to solvency; and 9. where relevant, an assessment of the cross-border dimensions and/or the potential systemic implications of the situation that has made/is making the extension of ELA necessary.
The Agreement provides thresholds (€500m and €2bn) over which the decision to be evaluated in terms of their impact.

[22] C A E Goodhart, *The Regulatory Response to the Financial Crisis* (Cheltenham: Edward Elgar 2010) p. 66.

[23] EBA Guidelines, on disclosure of encumbered and unencumbered assets (27 June 2014) <https://eba.europa.eu/documents/10180/741903/EBA-GL-2014-03+Guidelines+on+the+disclosure+of+asset+encumbrance.pdf/c65a7f66-9fa5-435b-b843-3476a8b58d66> [accessed 15 March 2019]: 'The EBA believes that disclosure by institutions about encumbrance is vitally important as it allows market participants to better understand and analyse the liquidity and solvency profiles of institutions. Specific modifications have been made to the draft guidelines to ensure that the level and evolution of assets encumbered to central banks and the amount of liquidity assistance given by central banks cannot be detected, as recommended by the ESRB', p. 3.

the present and in the future, for instance when collateral swaps are undertaken to access liquidity assistance.[24]

7.17 The information the national central bank is required to provide to the ECB provides some interesting changes to the traditional role played or expected to be played by the central bank. While one could claim this is a criterion which is more transparent, critical elements of it remain couched in administrative discretion. The responsibility of devising the criteria and assessing the solvency of the financial institution resides with the supervisory authority and its assessment is given to the ECB. Finally, the cross-border dimension of the need for ELA needs to be provided if it is a reason for such assistance. More importantly, there is reference to a penalty rate of interest. This does not highlight a move away from the principle of not applying a penalty rate. The argument for a penalty rate is that it potentially reduces the moral hazard risk of providing such assistance. The removal of a penalty rate would move to a position advocated by Goodhart as a step to remove the stigma in part of needing temporary liquidity assistance and place it in the traditional position.[25] The national central bank position may differ from Member State to Member State. The ECB guidelines indicate the assistance can continue for 10 months, but if it exceeds 12 months Governing Council permission is required.

7.18 The case of Banco Popular, the sixth largest bank in Spain, illustrates the difficulties of applying the policy of providing emergency liquidity assistance in practice when the quality of the balance sheet is over-optimistic and the bank is deemed solvent at the juncture of requesting emergency liquidity assistance but its balance sheet soon deteriorates as result of market reactions and downgrading by the credit rating agencies. The Banco Popular Group consisted of a number of cross-border operations, a Spanish banking group with its parent entity established in Spain and with a wholly owned subsidiary in Portugal in the Eurozone. It also had a wholly owned subsidiary TotalBank in the United States and partially owned Group Bx+ in Mexico. Its business was primarily within the Banking Union (98.4%), with 1.6% in the third countries.[26]

7.19 The problems at Banco Popular surfaced in view of higher capital requirements expected by the ECB and in view of its SPREP review which found it in need of additional capital. The bank initiated a €2.5bn rights issue. This intervention in the market did not instil confidence in the bank and led to investor confidence in other banks also faltering. Underlying problems with non-performing loans meant its capital position was only likely to deteriorate further, leading to under-provisioning for non-performing loans. It was able to access emergency liquidity assistance from the Bank of Spain to stave off the bank run it started to experience due to a complete loss of confidence in the market and depositors. The central bank would have considered it solvent at the time and experiencing a temporary liquidity problem. According to the accounts of 31 December 2016, its CET 1 ratio was 12.14%, T1 ratio 12.14%, and total capital ratio 13.13%, which are well above the minimum provided to determine solvency for the purposes of emergency liquidity assistance but soon deteriorated

24 Ibid, p. 14.

25 C A E Goodhart, *The Regulatory Response to the Financial Crisis* (Cheltenham: Edward Elgar 2010) p. 6.

26 Banco Popular Group Resolution Plan (2016) <https://srb.europa.eu/sites/srbsite/files/bpe_2016_resolution_plan_updated_on_30_10_2018.pdf> [accessed 15 March 2019].

by 21.2%, 11.7%, and 10.2% respectively by 31 March 2017.[27] While such information is not disclosed to prevent exacerbating the problems at a bank, it was nonetheless reported in the national press that the bank received €2 billion and immediately following up with a further €1.6bn, and recently noted in the updated resolution press release of the emergency liquidity assistance with the amounts redacted.[28] In a matter of a day the ECB lost confidence in the bank's attempts to turn its own affairs around with a private sector takeover, decided the bank was failing or likely to fail and placed into resolution, leading to the conclusion that the initial ambitions for it to turn its affairs around were overly optimistic.

The case highlights the difficulties of determining the extent of the problems at Banco Popular, a significant bank supervised by the ECB. There is also evidence of the authorities forbearing on the decision to decide it was failing or likely to fail in view of the quality of its balance sheet and its expected losses indicating insolvency rather than experiencing a temporary liquidity problem. The Single Resolution Board (SRB) provisional valuation indicated its problems at a conservative estimate in the region of €2bn and in the region of €8bn in the adverse scenario. This is after the write-down and conversion of equity and debt instruments to ensure the first losses are borne by the shareholder and then conversion of the subordinated debt instruments in accordance with the principle that no shareholder or creditor is worse off than in liquidation.[29] The timeline between the initial capital assessment and the decision to place the bank into resolution appears to be relatively short. The outcome for the SRB was a satisfactory one, with Santander intervening to purchase the bank, inter alia, initiating the assignment of 51% of Banco Popular real estate business to Blackstone Fund.[30] However, this case brings to the fore when the resolution authority should initiate its valuation process: should it be at the point when the competent authority notifies its view about the financial institution, or when the financial institution seeks emergency liquidity assistance, or when it seeks precautionary recapitalization or much earlier, relying in part on the outcome of the stress test? The trigger of such a decision would need to be carefully evaluated and its confidentiality secured since it could trigger a bank run itself which would be self-defeating. If the competent authority has acted prudentially then theoretically the bank remains solvent but if it is likely to fail this is not always possible. In this case the initial valuation by the SRB was initiated in May 2017 based on relevant public and non-public supervisory information.[31] An over-optimistic picture from the liquidity perspective is also present in the Resolution Plan, which indicates a sense of confidence about its ability to raise finance within the short and medium term. But more specifically, 7.20

[27] <https://srb.europa.eu/sites/srbsite/files/valuation_1_report_updated_on_30_10_2018.pdf> [accessed 15 March 2019].

[28] <https://srb.europa.eu/sites/srbsite/files/resolution_decision_updated_on_30_10_2018.pdf> [accessed 15 March 2019].

[29] FROB, '7 June 2017 Resolution of the FROB Governing Committee adopting the measures required to implement the Decision of the Single Resolution Board in its Extended Executive Session of 7 June 2017 concerning the adoption of the resolution scheme in respect of Banco Popular Español, S.A., addressed to FROB, in accordance with Article 29 of Regulation (EU) No. 806/2014 of the European Parliament and of the Council of 15 July 2014 establishing uniform rules and a uniform procedure for the resolution of credit institutions and certain investment firms in the framework of a Single Resolution Mechanism and a Single Resolution Fund and amending Regulation (EU) No. 1093/2010' (7 June 2017): <http://www.frob.es/en/Lists/Contenidos/Attachments/419/ProyectodeAcuerdoreducido_EN_v1.pdf> [accessed 15 March 2019].

[30] <https://www.santander.com/csgs/Satellite/CFWCSancomQP01/en_GB/pdf/HR080817en.pdf> [accessed 15 March 2019].

[31] <https://srb.europa.eu/sites/srbsite/files/valuation_1_report_updated_on_30_10_2018.pdf> [accessed 15 March 2019].

this surprisingly identifies the possible need to access emergency liquidity assistance rather than simply rely on private means.

7.21 Banco Popular submitted a tailored resolution plan for its US subsidiary TotalBank, which is a wholly owned subsidiary.[32] The US bank in Florida was subsequently sold after the announcement of its acquisition by Banco Santander. The subsidiary essentially financed its business from the local market and so was not reliant on its parent for inter-company finance. In view of this, the resolution plan explains that Banco Popular does not pose a risk or threat to TotalBank. Indeed, putting the two resolution plans together, the emphasis on sale of business as a mechanism to improve Banco Popular's position is quite striking in its restructuring phase, albeit names are redacted. In respect to its Portuguese subsidiary, this entity (amongst four others) consists of a centralized relationship with the parent entity and the resolution strategy adopted would be a single point of entry with Banco Popular Spain at the helm as the operating company.

The Financial Support Measures and the State Aid Perspective

7.22 The moral hazard implications of such assistance in pre-insolvency or in liquidation are significant and inevitably have a distorting impact on the functioning of markets. The need for a single resolution regime was recognized early on in the crisis but equally the important role played by the Commission in executing state discipline through its state aid decisions.[33] These support operations can constitute State aid which is incompatible with the internal market unless it is approved by the Commission.[34] The European Commission Communication on the application of State aid rules has been in place since 2013.[35] The 2013 Communication is the more recent and provides guidelines on a range of support techniques that can constitute state aid. The Communication is a soft law measure but offers another important approach to the problems of failing institutions by allowing public assistance to them to 'remedy a serious disturbance in the economy'.[36] Bodellini identifies an important issue about the provision which is referred to in Recital 41 of the BRRD that Member States have linguistically refer to 'avoid' rather than 'remedy' 'a serious disturbance in the economy', as with the United Kingdom.[37] The difference is significant since the latter is an *ex ante* exercise to attempt to stop it from causing disruption and the latter is *ex post* after the disruption to manage the impact of the restructuring. This is likely to legitimately lead to differences of treatment between Member States. The aid is not for the benefit of the bank per se but to prevent and mitigate the wider spillover effects of the problems spreading to other banks and the

[32] 'Banco Popular Español, SA Totalbank Tailored Resolution Plan' (31 December 2016), <https://www.fdic.gov/regulations/reform/resplans/plans/popular-165-1612.pdf> [accessed 15 March 2019].

[33] Mathias Dewatripont, Gregory Nguyen, Peter Praet, and André Sapir, 'The Role of State Aid Control in Improving Bank Resolution' in *Bruegel Policy Contribution* (2010).

[34] Art. 107(1)–(3) TFEU.

[35] Kotnik Case C-526/14.

[36] Point 3. See also Maria R Miserendino, 'State Aid for the Banking Sector: What has Changed after the New BRRD and SRM Regulation?', 17(2) European State Aid Quarterly, (2018) 204–11.

[37] Marco Bodellini, 'Greek and Italian "Lessons" on Bank Restructuring: Is Precautionary Recapitalisation the Way Forward?' (2017) 19 Cambridge Yearbook of European Legal Studies 155.

adverse impact on the real economy.[38] Whether the provision is interpreted strictly is debatable in the Italian Veneto cases the sub-regional considerations were accepted by the Commission for the purposes of state aid.[39] This section will focus on the requirements to mitigate the distortions of financial assistance analysed above. The criteria of the BRRD and the Commission Communication are aligned (yet providing different effects) so the latter provides additional avenues for Member States to provide assistance to safeguard the economy by remedying or avoiding a serious disturbance to it. In these cases, the emphasis should be on avoiding linguistically speaking in the Italian, Spanish and French contexts.[40] In this respect the provision in the Commission Communication is more akin to the public interest test as well relating to impact on the real economy. But the notion of 'serious disturbance' is wider and other aspects such as sustaining the real economy filter in to the decision making process and so provides Member States more discretion to exercise public support. Kokkoris argues the number of measures approved by the EU Commission has essentially led to view that the EU Commission largely 'rubber-stamped' all requests for approval to grant state aid.[41] Nevertheless, the implications on the state have not been considerably serious since the banks have paid back the assistance provided but the return remains relatively poor in comparison to the amount provided to the banks.[42]

The recapitalization and asset guarantees when banks are experiencing a capital shortfall are covered by the Commission Communication.[43] Similarly to the BRRD, the Commission requires the Member State to provide a capital raising plan[44] followed by a restructuring plan to show how the bank will attempt to address the shortfall and return the assistance it has received.[45] A critical part of the process is the asset quality review which will need to be undertaken by the supervisor. While the capital raising plan is likely to be prepared by the bank the review may show evidence of further deterioration of assets leading to a position where the bank may have underestimated the amount of capital it needs to raise.[46] For instance, in the case of Banca Monte dei Paschi di Siena[47] the bank was expected to sell off at least 30% of its branches and reduce staff by 22% and more critically to either sell or wind down its cross-border operations in Belgium and France by placing them in run-off so they are required to not enter in to new business but to close out its commitments to its existing customers. Equally, pertinent is the need for it to dispose of its non-performing loans (NPLs) through techniques such as securitization to reduce its loan loss provisioning and improve its capital level. The Member State had to demonstrate to the Commission the 7.23

38 Point 7.

39 For background see, Chapter 6, 'European Bank Insolvency and Liquidation Proceedings', paras 6.40ff.

40 See Bodellini (n 37), p. 155.

41 Ioannis Kokkoris, 'Competition Law in Financial Markets', in Jonathan Galloway (ed.), *The Intersections of Antitrust*, Oxford University Press (2020).

42 Lorenzo Codogno and Mara Monti, Is Italy's recent support to its banks the start of a new wave of public intervention in the EU? 16/1/17, p. 6, <https://blogs.lse.ac.uk/europpblog/2017/01/16/italy-support-banks-start-of-new-wave-eu-intervention/>.

43 Point 28.

44 Point 35(a)–(g).

45 U Soltesz and C Kockritz, 'From State Aid Control to the Regulation of the European Banking System—DG COMP and the Restructuring of Banks' (2010) 6 European Competition Journal 285.

46 Point 30.

47 State Aid SA.47677 (2017/N)—Italy New aid and amended restructuring plan of Banca Monte dei Paschi di Siena, 4/7/2017, <http://ec.europa.eu/competition/state_aid/cases/270037/270037_1951496_149_2.pdf>.

measures were proportionate and the minimum in terms of minimizing risks to financial stability in terms of inter alia minimizing its impact.[48] Indeed the assistance also needs to be effective and not lead to frequent requests in which case the Commission has been known to require the bank to reduce the balance sheet by up to 50% and even 70% as a punitive measure for such requests.[49]

7.24 The techniques to provide liquidity assistance to banks fall between ordinary activities (monetary operations) and extraordinary activities (emergency liquidity assistance) falling outside of ordinary central bank operations.[50] Liquidity assistance falls outside of normal central bank operations and so it does amount to state aid.[51] The assistance is expected to be for a maximum period of six months. The period of six months is not long, considering how poorly supervisors have estimated the quality of bank assets it may well be additional assistance is needed. In the case of Greece in 2008, as the crisis worsened, the banks required further liquidity assistance to address the liquidity shortfall from the Central Bank of Greece.[52]

7.25 Guarantees can only be provided for specific purposes as well such as issuances of senior debt but not for subordinated debt.[53] The instruments can only be dated between 3 months and 5 years and in some cases limited to one-third of the total issuance and the guarantee is capped at 5% of total liabilities or an amount not exceeding €500 million. The competent authority also needs to certify that the bank is not experiencing a capital shortfall. This is within the realm of the supervisor since in many cases banks that have attempted to raise capital multiple times and failed, it has been left for the central bank to intervene to provide the necessary liquidity,[54] as shown in Chapter 5. The ongoing monitoring of the Commission is focused on the possible benefits the bank has gained from the state aid.[55]

7.26 The cross-border dimension of a banking group in need of liquidity assistance or government guarantees to support at the parent level and at other subsidiary levels are not controversial since a number of central banks offered liquidity assistance simultaneously to contain the crisis. The use of government guarantees, as explained by Christine Cummings, during the GFC, highlighted a notable benefit of using guarantees to ensure continuity of critical relationships within the banking system, since the guarantee is 'about protection against failure to meet financial obligations that is, against default and insolvency.'[56]

[48] Points 32–34.

[49] Case C 14/2008—*Northern Rock*, Commission decision of 18 October 2009; see Commission Press Release IP/09/1600, State aid: Commission approves restructuring package for Northern Rock (28 October 2009); Case C 15/2009—*Hypo Real Estate*, Commission decision of 13 November 2009 (decision to extend proceedings and temporary approval of capital injections) [2010] OJ C 13/58, para. 68, stating that the proposed balance sheet reduction of around 70% is sufficient in light of the 'extremely large amount of aid' that the bank has received.

[50] For an extensive analysis of ELA and the ECB monetary policy and financial stability functions see Armin Steinbach, 'The Lender of Last Resort in the Eurozone', Common Market Law Review 53 (2016) 361–84 at p. 370.

[51] TFEU Art. 107.

[52] State aid SA.42215 (2015/N)—Greece Prolongation of the Greek financial support measures (Art. 2 law 3723/2008) Brussels, 29.06.2015 C(2015) 4452 final, <http://ec.europa.eu/competition/state_aid/cases/259088/259088_1673296_86_2.pdf>.

[53] Points 56–61.

[54] Point 60(a).

[55] Point 61.

[56] Christine M Cumming, 'Managing crises without government guarantees: How do we get there?' in J R LaBrosse and R Olivares-Caminal (eds), *Financial Crisis Containment and Government Guarantees* (Cheltenham: Edward Elgar 2013) p. 7.

Cummings also recognizes the importance of supervision, resolution, and crisis management arrangements to mitigate the need to use guarantees. In many respects, the use of guarantees is likely to restore access to liquidity that prior to this may have been limited. However, lessons from the crisis equally highlight the fine balance needed when using government guarantees, if one reflects on the Irish experience in 2009.[57] A principal lesson from the GFC is that a combination of solutions is required to restore confidence in a bank. The introduction of many tools explored in various parts in this work show that they do exist now within a formal rules based system.[58]

The coordination risks of multiple central bank assistance to provide liquidity support for a banking group is not explored in any great detail. The example of Dexia is a useful case in point about the cross-border coordination of liquidity assistance by a set of multiple central banks.[59] The seriousness of the impact on the economy as a whole was assessed in view of the respective damage it could cause in each Member State. It is illustrative of the fact that central banks have opted for different techniques. For example, Belgium announced liquidity assistance to Dexia Group (parent entity Dexia SA), France put in a place a guarantee for Dexia Group, and Luxembourg provided Dexia Banque Internationale Luxembourg SA a guarantee.[60] While Belgium and France highlighted the urgency of the aid to improve its capital position but falling outside state aid. In the case of Luxembourg, on the other hand, objections were raised that the assistance was not state aid in view of its implementation of a liquidation plan. The guarantee put in place was a joint and non-several guarantee in the following proportions: Belgium (60.5%), France (36.5%), and Luxembourg (3%) for six months and then extended by mutual agreement. In this case, either Member State can be sued but the Member States then have to repay each other. The Commission viewed the guarantee as sufficiently limited and proportionate to ensure the continuation of Dexia's activities. In order to minimize the distorting effects, Dexia agreed to curtail parts of business and not utilise its position of a state-backed bank in terms of pricing its products. The Commission concluded, '[t]he penalising rate of the LA operation means that the measure is an expensive source of liquidity which is therefore unlikely to give Dexia an undue advantage for its operations.'[61] 7.27

[57] Charles Enoch, 'Crisis management and guarantees in Europe' in J R LaBrosse and R Olivares-Caminal (eds), *Financial Crisis Containment and Government Guarantees* (Cheltenham: Edward Elgar 2013) p. 63.

[58] Charles Enoch, Gillian Garcia, and V. Sudararajan, 'Recapitalizing Banks with Public Funds' January *IMF Staff Papers*, (2001) 48(1), 58–110.

[59] State aid NN 49/2008—Belgium NN 50/2008—France NN 45/2008—Luxembourg Emergency aid to Dexia in the form of a guarantee for bonds and liquidity assistance, Brussels, 19 November 2008 C(2008)7388 final, <http://ec.europa.eu/competition/state_aid/cases/227704/227704_944159_114_1.pdf>.

[60] According to information from the Belgian authorities, the €6 billion capital increase by the Belgian and French shareholders, consisting of the issuance of ordinary Dexia SA shares, became definitive on 3 October 2008. The underwriting of this reserved capital increase is broken down as follows: (a) Belgium: the Belgian State is investing €1 billion in Dexia SA; the Flemish Region is investing €500 million in Dexia SA; the Walloon Region is investing €350 million in Dexia SA; the Bruxelles-Capitale Region is investing €150 million in Dexia SA; Holding Communal SA is investing €500 million in Dexia SA; Arcofin SC is investing €350 million in Dexia SA; Ethias is investing €150 million in Dexia SA. (b) France: the French State is investing €1 billion in Dexia SA. This contribution will be managed by the Agence des Participations de l'Etat; the Caisse des Dépôts et Consignations (CDC) group is investing €1.71 billion in Dexia SA; CNP Assurances is investing €228 million in Dexia SA. The Luxembourg State has undertaken to invest €376 million in Dexia Banque Internationale Luxembourg SA in the form of convertible bonds with a maturity of three years, interest of 10% a year and conversion to ordinary shares on terms to be agreed.

[61] State aid NN 49/2008—Belgium NN 50/2008—France NN 45/2008—Luxembourg Emergency aid to Dexia in the form of a guarantee for bonds and liquidity assistance, Brussels, 19 November 2008 C(2008)7388 final, at p. 16.

Liquidation Aid

7.28 In the context of liquidation aid, while the institution, from the perspective of the BRRD, is not a threat to financial stability, the disorderly liquidation of the bank could pose a wider threat to the Member State. The Commission criteria sits outside the BRRD and is significantly wider in terms of state aid within the criteria of recapitalization of banks pre-insolvency. Indeed it could equally be the case if the Commission or the Council object to the resolution scheme a bank is placed in to national winding-up proceedings. Theoretically, this move ironically would not prohibit the state from providing public assistance to ensure an orderly liquidation and remedy or avoid a serious disruption to the economy which could amount to state aid and need approval from the Commission.

7.29 The criteria is premised on the need to liquidate banks that are not viable, but recognizes the need for this to be done in an orderly manner when 'institutions cannot credibly return to long-term viability'.[62] In part, this is couched within the RWD regime in view of the date of implementation of the instrument. The cases from the Veneto region raised concerns about the impact on the regional economy of the decision to liquidate them. These decisions highlight the fractured nature of deciding how banks that fail are dealt with in regard to multiple dimensions to assess the 'importance' of banks and their risk to financial stability, and how best to contain the risks of banks, small or large. In part, the incoherency of the approaches is primarily due to the existence of multiple sets of criteria classifying banks for different purposes, rather than inconsistent application of individual sets of rules serving different purposes.[63] Notably, this leads to a position where the consistency of practice raises questions about the outcomes of the decision in resolution or normal insolvency-liquidation. The need for state aid for institutions in the latter case, that are considered not a risk to financial stability, appears to be rather at odds with the reforms introduced by the BRRD to put into resolution only those banks that do pose a risk to financial stability and include the possibility of using resolution funds. In these two cases of resolution and normal insolvency, another dimension to the importance of banks transpires relating to the right of states to provide public funds to support failing banks in resolution and indeed liquidation. While the backlash has been significant, the legal basis is such that the cases raised significant concerns if an orderly liquidation did not take place.[64] Indeed, if decisions associated with failing institution give rise to the need for state aid another criteria exists for burden-sharing amongst the different stakeholders of banks.

7.30 The Commission identifies the need for possible support with the liquidation proceedings, provided it meets the following criteria: there is a cessation of business and new business; the orderly winding down of the business is possible, provided the aim is to reduce liquidation costs.[65] The aim of the liquidation includes the possibility of sale of

[62] Point 65.
[63] See Chapter 3; Kotnik Case C-526/14, 11.
[64] See Italy tests EU's new bank rules, again, Politico, 26 June 2017 quote: 'Since the financial crisis, through the development of the banking union, we have striven to ensure that taxpayers' money would no longer be used to bail out banks', said Petr Ježek, Czech MEP who belongs to the centrist Alliance of Liberals and Democrats for Europe. 'This decision is blow to that intention'. In Italy Rattles Europe's Post-Crisis Banking Doctrine, Bloomberg Opinion, 17 January 2019; EU Commission Approves Billions in Aid for 2 Italian Banks, New York Times, 25 June 2017.
[65] Point 66.

business assets through a competitive process rather than simply a fire sale of assets. In order to ensure compliance with liquidation aid and to minimize the moral hazard risk, the Member State is required to submit a plan for the orderly liquidation. The primary aim is to ensure an effective winding up of the bank.[66] The liquidation aid is there for a limited period to ensure it does not distort competition.[67] The receiver of liquidation aid cannot compete for new business.[68] Moreover, the terms of business need to be about winding down the business and relinquish its relationship with its customers by pricing itself out of market to force its customers to find new banks in the market offering the services they have just relinquished. Finally, these measures attempt to address the moral hazard risk by minimizing the benefits of granting state aid and the resulting distorting effects.

The Commission Communication could also assess support for the sale of a bank in an orderly liquidation as state aid.[69] The Commission will review the sale process and assess whether it was based on an open and unconditional competitive tender based on market terms and so maximizing the sale price for the assets.[70] If, on the other hand, aid has been considered to have been provided, then the Commission will need to decide on a set of measures to minimize the distorting impact of the state aid. This will need to take in to account what advantage it has gained by acquiring the business, in terms of its size and strength, as a result of the purchase.[71] **7.31**

The more controversial aspects of the Commission Communication is the burden-sharing criteria it requires Member States to comply with. This is notwithstanding the Communication 2013 which goes beyond the previous expectations that existed, where limited burden-sharing went on. The position of the BRRD is premised on a relatively strict requirement of burden-sharing of 8% minima, for up to 5% maximum level of resolution funding. In this respect, it needs to be recognized (as examined extensively in this Chapter 6) that normal insolvency criteria are not harmonized in line with the expectations set by the BRRD. In view of this, the criteria for state aid highlight the need for losses to first of all fall on the shoulders of shareholders and subordinated debt holders during the liquidation proceedings. The Commission Communication equally requires their interests not to continue and to absorb losses first. The Communication more controversially allows Member States to exempt bondholders and other senior debt holders from contributing to minimize losses. However, since the purpose of liquidation aid is to provide orderly liquidation, then their interests are equally likely to be wiped out eventually. The rules in existence were clearly devised at a time before the new burden-sharing criteria was put forward by the BRRD and what was considered politically acceptable to ensure burden-sharing is equitable across the different stakeholders of banks. The recapitalization and impaired asset measures where the state aid is the counterfactual in a no-creditor-worse-off scenario can be assessed by looking at the outcome of not providing state aid and the alternative for the bank in insolvency. **7.32**

[66] Point 67.
[67] Point 67.
[68] Points 73–76.
[69] Point 79.
[70] Point 80.
[71] Points 83–86.

In liquidation aid the alternative would be whether the creditors would receive more or less by not adhering to the burden-sharing requirements for state aid, with the bank entering normal liquidation proceedings.

ECB and Centralizing Liquidity Assistance

7.33 The principal debate about emergency liquidity support has been whether the ECB should be given the mantle to be responsible for the removal of potential coordination risks that can be experienced if assistance in one Member State is not forthcoming. The position it has from a home and host perspective would provide it with a wider set of tools as well as it could combine liquidity assistance with other interventionist supervisory techniques such as voluntary bail-in and sale of business to improve the capital position of the group. This is important considering central banks may take decisions on a case-by-case basis with little obligation to coordinate. This would combine the traditional problem surfacing during the GFC of central banks not having supervisory information at hand to improve decision-making in such delicate matters. From a wider macroprudential perspective centralizing it could minimize the bank and sovereign doom loop that damages the credit rating of the bank and the sovereign simultaneously.

7.34 A long-time advocate of centralized liquidity assistance has been RM Lastra for the ECB to take on the mantle of provider of centralized emergency liquidity assistance.[72] It has been recognized as a wide interpretation of Article 18.1 Statute which opens up the possibility of the ECB taking on such a responsibility. Indeed, as Borger explains, one can say that this 'wider interpretation has prevailed during the financial crisis, as several measures of the Eurosystem's "enhanced credit support" are widely seen as lender of last resort actions, including by the ECB itself.'[73] The move towards centralization of supervision and resolution would logically lead to the need to centralize additional support mechanisms, such as emergency liquidity assistance. The principal rationale being the ability to minimize information asymmetries between the different tasks that can exist when functions are separated and there is lack of information-sharing to make consistent decisions. As was explained in Chapter 5, liquidity assistance can be provided to solvent institutions that may be in breach of minimum capital requirements. However, current thinking is indicating this is not enough. Russo and Lastra,[74] explain that the risk sharing mechanism at the level of monetary policy is shared amongst the 19 Member States, whereas for the purposes of emergency liquidity assistance the onus falls on the national central bank. The advantage the ECB would have for pure Eurozone banks is to provide a more accurate approach to the level of liquidity across a bank group within the Eurozone Member States. Unlike the case of Dexia, where the individual liquidity supported was provided by Belgium, France, and Luxembourg, the level of transparency and equitable sharing of the burden would be an important consideration. As noted by Lastra, the ECB would be

[72] R M Lastra, 'Banking Union: An Incomplete Building' in Franklin Allen, Elena Carletti Joanna Gray, and Mitu Gulati (eds), *Filling the Gaps in Governance: the Case of Europe* (Florence: European University Institute (2016) 169–85.

[73] Vestert Borger, 'Outright Monetary Transactions and the stability mandate of the ECB: Gauweiler' (2016) 53 Common Market Law Review 139–96 at 150.

[74] Costanza Russo and Rosa Lastra, 'The financing of bank resolution—who should provide the required liquidity?', ECON Committee, June 2018.

most appropriately positioned to identify the risk of contagion.[75] This is explored in a separate section below. Therefore, it is not just that the ECB would have more financial resources at hand and eliminate the bank sovereign doom loop, it would also benefit those Member States that have significant cross border exposures but less political bargaining power to influence burden-sharing in a way that safeguards there interests. For example, smaller Member States may well be faced with the options of sale of business which could distort competition by further concentrating the banking market in foreign hands in view of their dominance in such markets.

The risk shifting from the ECB to the NCA at the most critical point serve little benefit for overall Eurozone financial stability. This is especially the case if insufficient support (at the critical point) means it is unlikely to serve its purpose of staving off the panic but leads to an exasperation of panic in the markets. The limitations in many respects exist as a result of the necessity for good collateral, which may not be present in sufficient quantities at the time of greatest need. **7.35**

The Eurogroup in 2018 recommended that the ESM should provide a backstop to the Single Resolution Fund in the form of a revolving credit line to further strength its credibility in the financial markets.[76] It is recognized that the SRF is underfunded and is likely to be insufficient when it is even fully funded to provide large scale support to multiple banks in resolution.[77] The insufficiency of funding at critical times could only lead to destabilizing effects contrary to Bagehot's principle (explained above) that insufficient liquidity support is likely to not stave off a panic. It is envisaged a permanent backstop would be put in place by 2024, when the other risk reducing measures come in to play. The ESM commitment would be equivalent to the size of the SRF. The commitment by States to contribute the backstop is an interesting dichotomy considering it is funded by industry levies. **7.36**

The mutualization of financial arrangements of resolution and the future protection of depositors among those participating in the Banking Union embodies in many ways the European solidarity principle.[78] This is because it goes some way to show a commitment to centralized decision-making and financing of resolution when it comes to containing a cross-border bank failure. This is evident at two broad points: at the resolution stage to support restructuring the bank and safeguard critical functions, and at the point of liquidation of a bank to support and compensate depositors up to the coverage limit. Both elements that are privately funded minimize the moral hazard risk through adjusted premiums and the utilization of a Member States resources in the first instance.[79] The commitment to the continuity of critical functions of a failing bank at the Banking Union level means that the **7.37**

[75] R M Lastra, 'Emergency Liquidity Assistance and Systemic Risk' in Anita Anand (ed.), *Systemic Risk, Institutional Design, and the Regulation of Financial Markets* (2016) p. 198.

[76] Eurogroup, The President to Mr Donald Tusk, President of the Euro Summit, Brussels, 25 June 2018; for more information about the Eurogroup see <https://www.consilium.europa.eu/en/council-eu/eurogroup/>.

[77] Speech by Yves Mersch, Member of the Executive Board of the ECB, 'The limits of central bank financing in resolution', IMFS Distinguished Lecture Series Goethe Universität Frankfurt, 30 January 2018, <https://www.ecb.europa.eu/press/key/date/2018/html/ecb.sp180130.en.html>.

[78] Carlos Closa and Aleksandra Maatsch, 'In a Spirit of Solidarity? Justifying the European Financial Stability Facility (EFSF) in National Parliamentary Debates' (2014) 52(4) Journal of Common Market Studies 826–42.

[79] Maria J Nieto, Bank Resolution and Mutualization in the Euro Area (15 September 2006). European Economy, Banks, Regulation, and the Real Sector 2016-2. Available at SSRN: <https://ssrn.com/abstract=3057503 or http://dx.doi.org/10.2139/ssrn.3057503> at pp. 142–3.

support to safeguard critical functions needs to be spread more widely due to the significant amount of funds required for the resolution and liquidation stage and to minimize the scope for bank failure leading to a sovereign debt crisis.

Single Resolution Fund

7.38 The cost of resolving cross-border banks is the principal hurdle in any decision to share the burden of resolving a bank in distress.[80] It is important to assess the moves towards centralized funding of resolution through the mutualization of contributions to the Single Resolution Fund.[81] As a result, this line of defence of providing regional resources for matters at the national level gave cause for concern for some Member States, as it would risk moral hazard in the market. The following section will explore the administrative discretion encapsulated in the decision-making process to gauge whether centralization minimizes the agency problems at the Member State and cross-border level and succeeds in an attempt to reduce or eliminate actions based on pure self-interest of the Member State.

7.39 The need for funding is always going to be a controversial aspect of any negotiations about how best to construct burden-sharing. The issue of the resolution fund was no exception as highlighted by Howard and Qualia.[82] They highlight how Germany proposed a model based on a network of national funds perhaps similar to the current DGS approach.[83] It was the Dutch compromise position that gained support of utilizing the national portion of the resolution fund in the first instance and then access the wider fund.[84] The apparatus to put in place *ex ante* and *ex post* mechanisms to provide financing for resolution through contributions by eligible financial institutions, essentially including banks and investment banks (including branches), provides three mechanisms at the 'microprudential' level to minimize the agency problems that arise in resolution and crisis management.[85] The first element of minimizing the agency problems between Member State and banks attempts to move towards a position where contributions to resolution are provided by private sources rather than through public taxpayer bailouts. The starting point of the rule on write-down and conversion has the aim of privatizing the benefits and costs of their commercial endeavours. The second is ensuring banks and financial institutions that pose the greatest risk contribute more than those that pose the least risk to financial stability. The third part of the apparatus attempts to align the incentives between Member States to

[80] D Schoenmaker, *Governance of International Banking: The Financial Trilemma* (Oxford: Oxford University Press 2013), pp. 68–89.

[81] Regulation (EU) No. 806/2014 of The European Parliament and of The Council of 15 July 2014 establishing uniform rules and a uniform procedure for the resolution of credit institutions and certain investment firms in the framework of a Single Resolution Mechanism and a Single Resolution Fund and amending Regulation (EU) No. 1093/2010; SRMR Recital 19.

[82] David Howarth and Lucia Quaglia, 'The Steep Road to the European Banking Union: Constructing the Single Resolution Mechanism' (2014) 52 Journal of Common Market Studies 125–40.

[83] See Chapter 6, 'European Bank Insolvency and Liquidation Proceedings', Role of the Deposit Guarantee Scheme, para. 6.52.

[84] David Howarth and Lucia Quaglia, 'The Steep Road to the European Banking Union: Constructing the Single Resolution Mechanism' (2014) 52 Journal of Common Market Studies at 134.

[85] Commission Delegated Regulation (EU) 2017/747 of 17 December 2015 supplementing Regulation (EU) No. 806/2014 of the European Parliament and the Council with regard to the criteria relating to the calculation of *ex ante* contributions, and on the circumstances and conditions under which the payment of extraordinary *ex post* contributions may be partially or entirely deferred [2017] OJ L113/2.

minimize spill-over effects damaging the stability of other financial systems. In this respect, the mutualization of resolution funds should minimize the conflicting incentives between home and host Member States by disconnecting in part the national fiscal position from the outcomes of resolution decisions. This section will review whether the reforms will address the dilemma between home and host Member States to act in their self-interest when the apparatus for cooperation and mutual support lends itself to managing cross-border spill-over effects of a banking group entering distress and requiring access to resolution funds to restructure the banking group. All in all, it will be important to gauge the benefits of the two approaches to minimize the asymmetry of information problems noted above but also, considering the fact the division between home and host is challenged, in light of the large bank and small subsidiary paradigm as well.

The SRB acts as the resolution authority within the Single Resolution Mechanism (SRM) **7.40**
and as it stands in 2016 it is responsible for 142 banks, including 129 banking groups.[86] The SRB administers the Single Resolution Fund (SRF),[87] which forms a crucial part of the SRM as it is the mechanism for providing a centralized financial platform to reduce the implicit support Member States may or may not be able to offer between the Member States and their banking sector. In part, the centralization of funding for resolution provides a basis for minimizing benefits in terms of reduction of the cost of finance and the size of the fiscal backstop that some banks gain from the jurisdiction of the home Member State and which other Member States cannot provide to their banks.[88] The move to a single fund also means home or host bias in terms of access to support funds is reduced. The agreement to mutualize contributions to the single resolution fund reside in a separate intergovernmental agreement.[89] Nonetheless, Zavvos and Kaltsouni recognize the introduction of the SRF as a critical element in the efficient workings of the single resolution regime.[90]

The SRM Regulation puts in place the aims and objectives of the SRF in terms of the target **7.41**
fund for its participating Member States.[91] The Board of the SRM is required to decide the annual contributions to finance the fund based on a percentage of the amount of covered deposits of all credit institutions in the participating Member States.[92] In order to achieve this, the participating Member States are expected to raise *ex ante* annual contributions and *ex post* contributions from a range of institutions.[93] These are not just banks but also investment banks and central counterparties in order to achieve the above level and, more importantly, to maintain the Fund at such a level after parts of the fund are utilized for the purposes of resolution in participating Member States. With this in mind, the contributions

[86] Banks within the remit of the SRB: <<https://srb.europa.eu/en/content/banks-under-srbs-remit > [accessed 25 November 2019].

[87] SRMR, Art. 67(2); Art. 75.

[88] Willem Pieter De Groen and Daniel Gros, Estimating the Bridge Financing Needs of the Single Resolution Fund: How expensive is it to resolve a bank?, CEPS Special Report, No. 122, November 2015.

[89] Agreement on the transfer and mutualization of contributions to the Single Resolution Fund, 14 May (2014); for a constitutional perspective see, Federico Fabbrini, 'The Intergovernmental Agreement on the Single Resolution Fund in Context' (2014) 21(3) Maastricht Journal of European and Comparative Law 444–63.

[90] George S Zavvos and Stella Kaltsouni, 'The Single Resolution Mechanism in the European Banking Union: Legal foundation, governance structure and financing' in Matthias Haentjens and Bob Wessel (eds) *Research Handbook on Crisis Management in the Banking Sector*, (Cheltenham: Edward Elgar 2015) p. 139.

[91] SRMR, Art. 67.

[92] SRMR, Art. 75.

[93] SRMR, Art. 68.

within participating Member States are to be proportionate to the aim of achieving the target level.[94] To ensure proportionality is fulfilled, the size of the contributions is based on conditions explored below. The number of eligible financial institutions required to contribute to the respective domestic funds is in line with a risk-based premium system. Moreover, the variety of institutions contributing highlights an important point about the broader benefits that an 'official back stop' offers to the wider financial system, not simply those who are the likely beneficiaries of such funds, namely banks and depositors.

7.42 The resolution authority can utilize the funds for a variety of purposes, such as putting in place a guarantee, or providing loans or purchasing assets or making contributions to the bank in resolution, a bank subsidiary, a bridge bank, or an asset management vehicle, either individually or in combination with one another.[95] The requirements explain that the resolution authorities will be working towards utilizing the financing arrangements to restructure the banks as a mechanism to safeguard depositors' interests and as a last resort insolvency and liquidation. Notwithstanding this access to the SRF, there is a requirement that shareholders and some creditors have to bear at least 8% of the losses and this limits the contribution of the SRF to a maximum of 5% of total liabilities. More specifically, it can assist, on the basis of mutualized funds, with financing the resolution of a group in participating Member States.[96]

7.43 The contribution to the Fund is based on a flat contribution and risk-based contribution system which is calculated in conjunction with the competent authority based on the institution's liabilities, covered deposits and its risk profile.[97] Howarth and Quaglia explain the move to a more risk-sensitive approach was also contentious with the large German banks opposed to the idea of it based on risk based activities over and above deposits.[98] This methodology should enable the resolution authority to work out the contribution so that it is proportionate to the size and risk profile of the institution and the potential systemic risk it could pose. In this respect, the requirements enable the Board to put in place a separate approach to work out the contributions for institutions designated as small institutions whose assets are equal or less than €3m. This enables small institutions to contribute a single lump sum to the target fund as opposed to a risk-based approach calculated for large institutions. This links the policy aim of resolution to the public interest rationale interpreted narrowly of an institution posing inter alia a threat of systemic risk to the financial system if it were to fail. Whereas for smaller institutions, where it is not considered in the public interest to resolve it by using the resolution options, liquidation is the first option and therefore resolution fund support will not be used to support that decision. It is rather contradictory but it could well be the case more support is required for banks entering liquidation in view of the national discretion that exists to allow for the use of state aid. This is notwithstanding the fact that the DGS, as set out below, may well require formal intervention to safeguard covered deposits.

[94] SRMR, Art. 69.
[95] SRMR, Art. 76.
[96] SRMR, Art. 78, referring to BRRD, Art. 107(2)–(5).
[97] SRMR, Art. 70.
[98] David Howarth and Lucia Quaglia, 'The Steep Road to the European Banking Union: Constructing the Single Resolution Mechanism' (2014) 52 Journal of Common Market Studies, at 133–4.

The risk profile of an institution is based on information from both the competent and resolution authorities and, in particular, in accordance with that information, the recovery and resolution plans. The risk profile of institutions is assessed according to the following pillars which are accorded different risk weights to calculate the annual contribution:[99] 7.44

(1) risk exposure;
(2) stability and variety of sources of funding;
(3) importance of an institution to the stability of the financial system or economy; and
(4) additional risk indicators to be determined by the resolution authority.

The risk pillars require information which is likely to be provided in the recovery and resolution plans. The risk exposure pillar is expected to include, inter alia:

(a) information on the level of own funds;
(b) leverage ratio; and
(c) the net stable funding ratio and the liquidity coverage ratio.

The provision also includes a requirement based on the 'importance of an institution to the stability of the financial system or economy',[100] which is likely to mean institutions classed as Global Systemically Important Institution (G-SIIs) and Other Important Institutions (O-SIIs) are included but perhaps others that may not meet the thresholds of such categories but nevertheless should be included. The additional risk indicators concerning the institutions can include information about the importance of trading activities and off-balance sheet activities, the size of derivatives exposures and those centrally cleared, membership of a protection scheme, complexity of the business, and past public assistance provided to the institution. The resolution authority is also required to work out the probability of an institution failing and requiring funds from the resolution fund. This is ultimately going to be based on factors such as the resolvability assessment of the institution and likely options to be used to resolve it if it is likely to fail. 7.45

The qualitative and quantitative information generated under the different risk pillars for calculating contribution to the fund are then conferred different weightings: '(a) Risk exposure: 50%; (b) Stability and variety of sources of funding: 20%; (c) Importance of an institution to the stability of the financial system or economy: 10%; (d) Additional risk indicators to be determined by the resolution authority: 20%.'[101] The risk exposure pillar is further calibrated into the following proportions: (a) Own funds and eligible liabilities held by the institution in excess of MREL: 25%; (b) Leverage ratio: 25%; (c) Common equity tier 1 capital ratio: 25%; (d) Total risk exposure divided by total assets: 25%. In terms of additional risk indicators, the following proportions are set: (a) Trading activities and off-balance sheet exposures, derivatives, complexity and resolvability: 45%; (b) Membership in 7.46

[99] The significant amount of discretion within the BRRD is structured and fleshed out in the Delegated Regulation 2015/63 since it will be the resolution authority that determines how the adjustment is calculated: Commission Delegated Regulation (EU) 2015/63 of 21 October 2014 supplementing Directive 2014/59/EU of the European Parliament and of the Council with regard to ex ante contributions to resolution financing arrangements [2015] OJ L11/44. The technical requirements to calculate the annual contributions exclude intragroup liabilities provided the institution is established in the EU and falls within consolidated supervision of the group, liabilities relating to clearing activities, liabilities from holding client assets, and client money.

[100] Delegated Regulation (EU) 2015/63, Art. 6(1).

[101] Delegated Regulation (EU) 2015/63, Art. 7(1).

an Institutional Protection Scheme: 45%; (c) Extent of previous extraordinary public financial support: 10%. A separate method is adopted to work out contributions for small institutions which is simpler, based on total liabilities less own funds and covered deposits and a set range of total assets. Small institutions fall into six categories depending on the size of the institution.[102] Based on the categorization the annual contribution ranges from €1,000 to €50,000.

7.47 The decision to categorise banks to determine their contribution to the fund is essentially based on a risk-based approach to ensure contributions are proportionate. However, the resolution authority does have the discretion to move institutions from one category to another category if the risk profile of the bank changes. The contributions system assumes the resolution authority is competent to decide contributions from central counterparties, notwithstanding the challenges posed by banks and investment banks. This is very important since it means the categorization is not static and enables the resolution authority to change the contribution accordingly. This decision is likely to require a significant input from the competent authority in view of the information and the supervisory view they have of the institution's risk appetite. Regarding this, the regulation does envisage creating a sub-category for small institutions so that the resolution authorities can delineate based on risk profiles which sub-category banks should be placed in. The small institutions category will then enable the resolution authority to taper the lump sum contributed by such institutions accordingly. In the short to medium term, resolution authorities are likely to experience significant challenges until the system of deciding contributions is refined.

7.48 In circumstances where institutions do not think the resolution authority has taken a proportionate approach with its qualitative and quantitative indicators to work out the annual contribution, institutions have sought to appeal against the decision. Where the Resolution Board of the SRM is the resolution authority, a few banks have taken action against the contribution the bank is expected to make to the Fund, highlighting also some of the challenges faced by the SRB and Member State resolution authorities who are required to execute the decision of the SRB. The principal argument in *Banco Cooperativo Espanol v SRB*[103] is that

[102] Delegated Regulation (EU) 2015/63, Art. 10(1)–(6).

1. Institutions whose total liabilities, less own funds and covered deposits, are equal to or less than EUR 50 000 000, and whose total assets are less than EUR 1 000 000 000, shall pay a lump-sum of EUR 1 000 as annual contribution for each contribution period.
2. Institutions whose total liabilities, less own funds and covered deposits, are above EUR 50 000 000 but equal to or less than EUR 100 000 000, and whose total assets are less than EUR 1 000 000 000, shall pay a lump-sum of EUR 2 000 as annual contribution for each contribution period.
3. Institutions whose total liabilities, less own funds and covered deposits, are above EUR 100 000 000 but equal to or less than EUR 150 000 000, and whose total assets are less than EUR 1 000 000 000, shall pay a lump-sum of EUR 7 000 as annual contribution for each contribution period.
4. Institutions whose total liabilities, less own funds and covered deposits, are above EUR 150 000 000 but equal to or less than EUR 200 000 000, and whose total assets are less than EUR 1 000 000 000, shall pay a lump-sum of EUR 15 000 as annual contribution for each contribution period.
5. Institutions whose total liabilities, less own funds and covered deposits, are above EUR 200 000 000 but equal to or less than EUR 250 000 000, and whose total assets are less than EUR 1 000 000 000, shall pay a lump-sum of EUR 26 000 as annual contribution for each contribution period.
6. Institutions whose total liabilities, minus own funds and covered deposits, are above EUR 250 000 000 but equal to or less than EUR 300 000 000, and whose total assets are less than EUR 1 000 000 000, shall pay a lump-sum of EUR 50 000 as annual contribution for each contribution period.

[103] Case T-323/16 *Banco Cooperativo Español v SRB* (2016/C 296/39) [2016] OJ C296/30: <https://eur-lex.europa.eu/legal-content/EN/TXT/?uri=uriserv:OJ.C_.2016.296.01.0030.01.ENG&toc=OJ:C:2016:296:TOC> [accessed 20 March 2019].

the contribution is not commensurate with its view about the risk profile of the bank, which is lower than the risk profile on which the SRB has based the expected annual contribution. In *Credito Fondiaro v CRU*,[104] the need for resolution authorities to explain how the annual contribution has been calculated is identified in the claim in order to ensure the institution is able to understand how the calculation has been made to produce the risk profile. It has been argued that the contribution is not proportionate and infringes the principle of equal treatment and legal certainty.

The mutualization of resolution funds into a single resolution fund does address some of the important challenges faced by Member States home and host dilemma by delocalizing the costs and benefits of supporting the resolution of financial institutions. Indeed, the non-participating Member States recognize the benefits of mutualization but raise concerns about the transition to mutualization as a hurdle for entering close cooperation.[105] The possibility of Member States opting into the mutualized arrangements if a Member State seeks to enter close cooperation in the Banking Union is a significant benefit even during the transition to full mutualization. The decision by Bulgaria to enter close cooperation shows its commitment by initiating legislation to mutualize its resolution fund.[106] This holds true, provided there is a single decision-making body, with responsibility to apply the rules and principles of resolution rather than decision-making, residing in a multiple number of Member States if a cross-border bank is potentially failing. It also partly goes towards depoliticizing the decision-making process with decision-making being conferred to resolution authorities rather than political agencies. Member States are arguably likely to opt for a co-operative approach to resolution and so minimizing the chances of resolution authorities acting in their own self-interest, which could create obstacles for the group competent authority to execute a wider resolution strategy. **7.49**

The cost of resolution of cross-border banks, as mentioned earlier, is a central obstacle to the willingness for cooperation between Member States. In the national setting, the ability to provide resolution funds is always going to be dependent on a range of political and economic factors. Moreover, the risk of forbearing or delaying and/or hesitating to use funds in sufficient quantity for resolution is likely to lead to a position where more is needed in case of a crisis spreading nationally or even regionally. The size and complexity of banks in the EU has brought to the fore the realization that individual resolution support is not likely to be sufficient to ensure orderly resolution. As explained, while a target level for funding is generally accepted, it is likely to be still deficient for possibly multiple bank failures.[107] In view of this, the position of large banks from large home Member States and located in small host Member States, as set out earlier, leads to exposure to risks that the small host may not be able to manage if a crisis was to ensue. This could be the case based on the possibility that such banks are either liquidated and so reliance is on the local DGS to orchestrate a payout when it could have limited funds to do so and so relies on the state for a loan to support the **7.50**

[104] T-661/16 *Credito Fondiario v CRU* (2016/C 402/71) [2016] OJ C402/59: <http://eur-lex.europa.eu/legal-content/EN/TXT/PDF/?uri=CELEX:62016TN0661&from=EN> [accessed 20 March 2019].

[105] National Bank of Poland, 'The Economic Challenges of Poland's Integration with the Euro Area' (Warsaw 2015), p. 93.

[106] See Chapter 2, 'The ECB's Supervision and SRB Resolution—Participating and Non-Participating Member States', Bulgaria and the Application to Enter Close Cooperation, para. 2.47.

[107] Ioannis G Asimakopoulos, 'International law as a negotiation tool in Banking Union; the case of the Single Resolution Fund' (2018) 21(2) Journal of Economic Policy Reform 118–31 at 120.

reimbursement of depositors. Finally, the mutualization of the resolution fund, once it is realized, enables the resolution board to act in the interests of the EU and with its financial integrity and stability in mind rather than a scenario where a resolution authority acts in the interests of an individual Member State; therefore reducing even further the home and host dilemma. As highlighted by 'some Member States with fairly strong banking sectors expressed concern that they would be required to subsidise weaker banking sectors in other member states'.[108] However the GFC clearly highlighted that the principal culprits where the Member States with the largest banking sectors. Indeed if a review of the main recipients of state aid is done (as noted earlier) it is clearly evident that they were the principal culprits of the crisis.

The Move Towards the Third Pillar: The Proposed European Deposit Insurance Scheme

7.51 Deposit protection has been shown to be crucial in minimizing the spill-over effects of a bank in distress. During such times of crisis, governments take political decisions to stave off the ensuing panic by extending explicit legal levels of coverage and putting in place government guarantees to safeguard a bank or sector of banks.[109] The cross-border nature of banking within the EU and the significant interests in the respective countries explored in this study highlight the importance of understanding the role and expectations attached to the EU DGS. Moreover, it highlights the expected benefits of a Eurozone European Deposit Insurance Scheme (EDIS) for Eurozone Member States and those Member States opting into the Banking Union and benefiting from it.[110] In this context, the important principle is consistency of approach to ensure a level playing field. The different levels of actual funding of Member States do vary and would in some cases place a considerable burden on the state or banks *ex post* to contribute to the DGS fund at a time perhaps when funds are not so readily available. The long-term aim of pooling funds would improve the resilience of the Banking Union. However, this is not without its objectors on the grounds, once again, the concern about subsidizing poor banking behaviour in other jurisdictions. In view of this objection the proposal has been towards improved 'risk—reducing rules'.[111]

[108] Rosalind Z Wiggins, Mihael Wedow, and Andrew Metrick, 'European Banking Union B: The Single Resolution Mechanism', Yale Program on Financial Stability Case Study 2014-5B-V1, March 2015, p. 12: available at SSRN: <https://ssrn.com/abstract=2577347 or http://dx.doi.org/10.2139/ssrn.2577347> [accessed 20 March 2019].

[109] See C Enoch, 'Crisis Management and Guarantees in Europe', in JR LaBrosse, R Olivares-Caminal, and D Singh (eds) *Financial Crisis Containment and Government Guarantees* (Cheltenham: Edward Elgar 2013) pp. 57–74.

[110] Proposal for a Regulation of the European Parliament and of the Council amending Regulation (EU) 806/2014 in order to establish a European Deposit Insurance Scheme (COM(2015) 586 final, 2015/0270 (COD)); Communication from the Commission to the European Parliament, the Council, the European Central Bank, the European Economic and Social Committee and the Committee of the Regions 'Towards the completion of the Banking Union' (COM(2015) 587 final); Opinion of the European Central Bank of 20 April 2016 on a proposal for a Regulation of the European Parliament and of the Council amending Regulation (EU) No. 806/2014 in order to establish a European Deposit Insurance Scheme (CON/2016/26); Opinion of the European Economic and Social Committee on the 'Proposal for a Regulation of the European Parliament and of the Council amending Regulation (EU) No. 806/2014 in order to establish a European Deposit Insurance Scheme' (COM(2015) 586 final—2015/0270 (COD)). The Five Presidents' Report of 22 June 2015 on 'Completing Europe's Economic and Monetary Union', available on the Commission's website at <www.ec.europa.eu>.

[111] Shawn Donnelly, 'Advocacy coalitions and the lack of deposit insurance in Banking Union' (2018) 21(3) Journal of Economic Policy Reform 211.

As noted by Donnelly, the risk premium is calculated in a way to 'prohibit' poor banking.[112] The mandate of the EU DGS is wider with some Member States adopting a loss-minimizing imperative and a wider role in supporting resolution with possible financial support.[113] Moreover, the introduction of EDIS is argued to 'increase the resilience of the Banking Union against future crises'[114] by moving the decision to safeguard depositors away from the national level to the Banking Union as a whole. It should be recognized that the risk-based premium system could well mitigate national concerns if it is calibrated correctly to be a force for reform and modify Member State and bank behaviour. In order to ensure those that are putting more risk in to the system are duly penalized with higher risk premiums making such behaviour prohibitive. In many respects the argument that the DGS is likely to be less used based on the resolution aiming to avoid access to it has not materialized. Moreover, if the underlying basis of DGS funding is inadequate and insolvency-liquidation is the option of first resort then the ability of the DGS to manage multiple bank liquidations is likely to be difficult without resort to the sovereign for assistance, which arguably should be minimized and placed on private shoulders. According to Enoch, as a result of the first IMF Financial Sector Assessment Program (FSAP) of the EU as whole argues 'The DGS in a particular country may exhaust its funding and its borrowing limits ... thus rendering the backstop not credible.'[115] According to Constâncio, 'depositors would be treated in a uniform way across countries, independently of their location and the location of the bank to whom they have entrusted their savings'.[116] This is critical, as observed in Chapter 6, and the outcomes of ABLV Latvia and Luxembourg and implicit is the need for an EU single insolvency-liquidation regime, as advocated by Binder, Krimminger, Nieto, and Singh.[117]

The high coverage level means it is unlikely depositors will panic if a bank was found to be failing. Its credibility nevertheless is likely to be tested if the underlying funding it is based on is shown to be weak. If insolvency is *ex ante* decided to be the fate of a bank, the deposits will be curved out before the announcement and depositors would have continuity of service of their bank accounts via a new bank or transferred to a competitor bank in the market. The shortfall, if any, in theory would then be covered by the DGS and it would have a super priority in terms of claims in the administration of the bank. In this respect, the DGS has a wider mandate concerning financing resolution rather than simply dealing with the post-insolvency payout. This is possibly minimized by the obligation to initiate write-down and conversion of own funds and eligible liabilities. However, it could be argued that the reliance on the DGS is greater in those jurisdictions where there is a significant level of 7.52

[112] Ibid, p. 214.

[113] Giuseppe Boccuzzi, *The European Banking Union: Supervision and Resolution* (Basingstoke: Palgrave Macmillan 2016) p. 131.

[114] Proposal for a Regulation of The European Parliament and of The Council amending Regulation (EU) 806/2014 in order to establish a European Deposit Insurance Scheme, 2015/0270 (COD) at p. 3.

[115] Charles Enoch, p. 67 para. 3.22, 'The Bank Recovery and Resolution Directive: An International Standard Perspective' in Jens-Hinrich Binder and Dalvinder Singh (eds) *Bank Resolution: The European Regime* (Oxford: Oxford University Press 2016).

[116] Vítor Constâncio, Banking Union and European Integration Speech at the OeNB Economics Conference, Vienna, 12 May 2014, <https://www.ecb.europa.eu/press/key/date/2014/html/sp140512.en.html> [accessed March 19 2019].

[117] Jens-Hinrich Binder, Michael Krimminger, Maria J Nieto, and Dalvinder Singh, 'The choice between judicial and administrative sanctioned procedures to manage liquidation of banks: a transatlantic perspective' (2019) 14(2) Capital Markets Law Journal 178–216.

depositor-based funding but limited and, in some cases, non-existent where there is 'bail-in-able' debt. Thus, one of the drawbacks of a narrow form of finance is the greater possibility of DGS intervention.

7.53 The reformed DGS to mutually support one another in times of need is the precursor to the proposed EDIS. This is referred to as the third pillar of the Banking Union, the first being the Single Supervisory Mechanism (SSM) and the second being the SRM. The pillar attempts to minimize the conflicts of interests at the point of bank closure and so payouts to depositors, shifting the burden from the national to the Eurozone as a whole. The SRM Board would be responsible for resolution and deposit insurance, therefore, combining the roles in a similar fashion to the Federal Deposit Insurance Corporation (FDIC) in the United States. The EDIS project builds on the DGS directive by gradually moving towards a centralized administrative regime to oversee deposit protection. In this respect, the powers at the local level would be exercised centrally similarly to the ECB exercising supervision over significant banks and the SRB exercising decisions conferred to national resolution authorities. The ECB have highlighted in their Opinion on the proposal for EDIS the Board would 'shield [EDIS] from political influence and will ensure access to the DIF on equal terms for all DGSs'.[118]

7.54 The third pillar is expected to be fully operational following three distinct stages by 2024. The first stage is titled 'reinsurance', where the EDIS would bridge local funding gaps if a bank was to be placed into insolvency and a shortfall is found to cover a payout to depositors or the local DGS is expected to contribute to the resolution of the bank. In the latter case, it would be the liquidity shortfall which would be bridged by EDIS to fulfil the DGS mandate in resolution. The second stage is titled the 'co-insurance' stage. During this period, EDIS co-insures the participating DGSs and provides joint funding in an event of a payout. The expected shared contribution is to increase over time. By 2024 full insurance is expected to be operational with the DGS in Eurozone and participating Member States completely insured by EDIS and, therefore, covering payouts and support needs for resolution and liquidation.

7.55 The DGS Directive provides for the basic mechanism for mutual support to ensure deposit protection is achieved. The branch and subsidiary dichotomy plays out in the approach to DGS since levels of preparedness could have a bearing on internal capital flight from subsidiary to branch of a bank of another Member State, despite a single supervisory approach and resolution approach being in place. The EDIS could also mitigate the risk of 'foreign banks' in the respective Member States. The incentives to opt into close cooperation in the SSM and SRM would be higher by including the EDIS in the equation as well. The introduction of EDIS is also likely to lead to a position where in the Eurozone the home and host Member State dichotomy is further reduced. The mutualization of funds may lead to some interesting outcomes. Those Member States with a significant foreign bank presence, which is primarily constituted by European banks both at the branch and subsidiary levels, could well benefit through mutualization. Moreover, they could benefit from the introduction of a 'cost neutral' model, whereby the bank's contributions to the individual

[118] Opinion of the European Central Bank of 20 April 2016 on a proposal for a Regulation of the European Parliament and of the Council amending Regulation (EU) No. 806/2014 in order to establish a European Deposit Insurance Scheme (CON/2016/26) at p. 4.

funds in the home and host Member States are pooled and theoretically eliminate home or host bias within the Eurozone. It is not quite clear what synergies would be harnessed by the execution of the resolution fund and the deposit insurance fund when both are funded by contributions based on covered deposits. The conferring of responsibility of discharging the resolution fund and the deposit insurance fund by the SRB enables it to execute both its resolution entity and insolvency entity approach, albeit it has the authority to decide the resolution scheme for significant Eurozone banks. This could well include both options, which the national authorities would need to execute. Whether Member States are willing to accept their decisions is another matter. The proposal includes the instrument to iron out the different levels of funding and funds in place by incorporating a co-insurance mechanism. The proposed mechanism will further diminish the home and host dilemma and bias, since, in the short to medium term, EDIS would provide liquidity support to the DGS and bridge the different levels of funds at the local and central levels.

The banks in many Member States are narrow and essentially financed by local deposits and offer credit finance to the local economy. However, this does not diminish the importance of these institutions and in fact makes them acutely more important considering they are foreign as opposed to domestic banks since they provide critical credit finance in the local economy. That being said, it will not always be automatic that such institutions are likely to be dealt with through resolution. In view of this, the importance of an effective DGS is all-important to safeguard the interests of depositors. At the liquidation stage this is more important since the deposit guarantee scheme can play a critical role in ensuring timely compensation to the depositors. Under the current circumstances, the risk of an underfunded DGS is a significant risk, as is the risk of the Member State reneging on the responsibility to safeguard depositors of branches in host Member States. This is a material risk when the significance of the host operations is not material to the group. Hindrances at the insolvency level will still remain as shown in Chapter 6. The eventual move to a mutualized financing arrangement for compensating depositors minimizes those risks and, more importantly, is likely to provide the appropriate resources to compensate depositors of a large or significant bank, therefore minimizing the large and small home-host Member State dilemma. **7.56**

The introduction of a more robust risk premium system of raising private finance for deposit insurance is critical for the credibility of EDIS. It is equally necessary moving forward that legacy issues associated with bad banking behaviour is reflected in the risk premium approach so that it minimizes the contribution of those that were not culpable in such adverse risks-taking. According to the recent study undertaking by the ECB the risk premium system is seriously considered as an important component to give legitimacy to EDIS. The study argues 'adjusting the indicators in the risk based contributions would make it possible to take in account the relative riskiness of the banking sectors while the [Deposit Insurance Fund] DIF is being built up and while risk reduction measures are implemented'.[119] A critical finding of the work is the limited cross-subsidization between the Member States, which means the larger Member States with low bank risks are not overall contributing to cover **7.57**

[119] Jacopo Carmassi, Sonja Dobkowitz, Johanne Evrard, Laura Parisi, André Silva, and Michael Wedow, 'Completing the Banking Union with a European Deposit Insurance Scheme: who is afraid of cross-subsidisation?', No. 208/April (2018) p. 4.

the risks of Member States with high bank risks. It has been raised in the past whether some individual Member States can realistically cover deposits up to €1,000,000 during a multiple bank failure without sovereign support, since the coverage level could lead to markets raising concerns about the ability of the sovereign to credibly support it. Whether these findings will appease the politicians is a completely different matter but it certainly highlights important evidence to suggest the concerns raised can be addressed through a better-designed risk-based premium system. The target level for covered deposits remains at 0.8% in the proposal and, as shown in Chapter 6, Member States currently have different target levels either below or above. Indeed the relatively smaller Member States have generally taken a more cautious approach and aim to have a higher level. This could also be because it is now generally considered a significant proportion of their banks will enter insolvency-liquidation rather than resolution proceedings. Other research would suggest the 0.8% target level is relatively low to produce a sufficient fund.

7.58 The move towards separating resolution and insolvency-liquidation is a critical feature of the Banking Union. The separation of the two approaches is normally supported by one fund (as in the USA) rather than two funds with separate aims and objectives.[120] This simply dilutes the funding base and is likely to lead to a scenario where funds are likely to be depleted quicker than having one centralized fund for both purposes. The EU resolution policy assumes that banks that are not offering critically important functions in the market will be moved in to national liquidation proceedings which are currently not harmonized. The few cases analysed in this chapter highlight how they can lead to the need for public assistance in liquidation. While it was certainly the case covered deposits were paid out or carved out in an orderly manner it could not always be assured in a scenario where a number of banks fail in multiple Member States. Indeed it is evident that DGSs are relatively underfunded and quite possibly the 0.8% target is insufficient to produce an appropriately funded deposit protection scheme at the Eurozone level. In view of this it arguable that EDIS equally requires a backstop as is the case for the SRF. The credibility of EDIS to ensure it can fulfil its aims is predicated on sufficient funds as well. If it were to function as an equal footing with the SRF then it requires a backstop by ESM as well to support its credibility. The alternative would be to potentially bailout EDIS in the future if a scenario of insufficient funds were to materialise. If the EU or Eurozone were predicated with a coherent liquidation regime then the need for liquidity in insolvency-liquidation proceedings to support a payout to covered deposits would equally address a significant home and host dilemma. It is arguable smaller Member States that may have more banks theoretically assigned for bank insolvency-liquidation are likely to face a greater budgetary burden than banks assigned for resolution.

The European Stability Mechanism

7.59 The European Stability Mechanism (ESM) was established in 2012 in response to the banking and sovereign debt crisis that unfolded amongst the Member States in the

[120] J Deslandes, C Dias, and M Magnus, 'Liquidation of Banks: Towards an "FDIC" for the Banking Union?' Directorate-General for Internal Policies, February 2019, <http://www.europarl.europa.eu/RegData/etudes/IDAN/2019/634385/IPOL_IDA(2019)634385_EN.pdf>.

Eurozone. The ESM replaced the tools used on an ad hoc basis to address the unfolding crisis in Greece, Ireland, Portugal, and Spain, by placing the support mechanism on a permanent centralized basis. As explained by Constâncio in his analysis of the risk of contagion between sovereigns, 'when the sovereign crisis became more severe again and Moody's downgraded Portugal on 5 July 2011, it cited—among other factors—developments in Greece. Moody's believed that contagion from a default of Greece made it more likely that Portugal would require a second round of official financing.'[121] Most notably, ESM minimizes the agency problem between Member States large or small that can threaten the integrity of the European project when national taxpayer bailout is not sufficient to address the localized problems, or where the inability of the Member State to raise finances through normal market channels creates a set of perverse incentives between Member States to aid the financially stricken Member State(s). Therefore dealing in part with the political tensions that can exist during a sovereign debt crisis.[122] The pre-commitment to build up *ex ante* a financial fund and mechanisms of support at the Member State level provides a foundation to ensure all Member States in ESM have a financial interest in minimizing adverse conflicts of interest on national lines which undermine the integrity of the Eurozone.

The establishment of the ESM is contentious from an EU constitutional perspective since it required exercise of the simplified revision procedure in Article 48(6) of the Treaty on the Functioning of the European Union (TFEU) which led to the introduction of an additional paragraph in the TFEU—Article 136(3)—enabling the establishment of the ESM to safeguard the stability of the Euro area as a whole by providing financial assistance subject to strict conditionality.[123] The ESM is a Treaty-based legal entity that sits in a distinct place outside the EU legal framework. The ESM is formed as a separate intergovernmental organization under public international law with 19 members. Originally, the ESM had 17 founding members; this increased to 19 with the accession of Latvia and Lithuania to the ESM when both Member States joined the Euro, on 13 March 2014 and 3 February 2015 respectively. The ESM is not a fiscal backstop in the true sense, but it is as far as one can get without a fiscal union to support the financial stability of the region while respecting principles of sovereignty. The primary aim of the ESM is to provide financial assistance to its members that have lost or are possibly going to lose the traditional means of raising finance through the international financial markets at normal market rates. As highlighted by Adam and Parras, the Court in the *Pringle* case highlighted ESM as a financing mechanism and not one influencing economic policy.[124] These financing needs are then to be 7.60

[121] Vítor Constâncio, 'Contagion and the European debt crisis', Banque de France, Financial Stability Review, No. 16 April (2012), p. 111, <https://conference.nber.org/conferences/2012/SI2012/GFCs12/Constancio-Contagion%20and%20the%20European%20Debt%20Crises.pdf>.

[122] Christian Hoffman, 'Greek Debt Relief' (2017) 37(1) Oxford Journal of Legal Studies 1–30 at 26–7.

[123] The following is the additional text to Art. 136 TFEU: 'The Member States whose currency is the Euro may establish a stability mechanism to be activated if indispensable to safeguard the stability of the Euro area as a whole. The granting of any required financial assistance under the mechanism will be made subject to strict conditionality.' For a comprehensive analysis see Bruno de Witte and Thomas Beukers, 'The Court of Justice approves the creation of the European Stability Mechanism outside the EU legal order: *Pringle*' (2013) 50(3) Common Market Law Review 805–48; Susanne K. Schmidt, 'A Sense of Déjà Vu? The FCC's Preliminary European Stability Mechanism Verdict' (2013) 14(1) German Law Journal 1–19; Michael Schwarz, 'A Memorandum of Misunderstanding—The doomed road of the European Stability Mechanism and a possible way out: Enhanced cooperation' (2014) 51(2) Common Market Law Review 389–423.

[124] Stanislas Adam and Francisco Javier Mena Parras, 'The European Stability Mechanism through the legal meanderings of Union's constitutionalism: Comment on Pringle' (2013) European Law Review 848–65 at 854.

provided to the member by the ESM to minimize the adverse impact on the sustainability of public finances.

7.61 The ESM voting procedure is based on the seriousness of the matter.[125] In circumstances where a member requires financial assistance, the ESM requires 85% of the votes to initiate it.[126] This, however, is not so straightforward due to the way the voting rights are attached to the sovereign-shareholder contribution to the ESM.[127] The shareholder contribution is calculated on the basis of the particular Member State's proportion of the total EU population and its contribution to the EU GDP. In this respect, it is not surprising, therefore, that Germany, France, and Italy have the largest proportion of shares and are the largest contributors to the ESM. In light of this, general decisions associated with annual accounts require 80% of the vote.[128] However, for financial assistance a qualified majority is required of 85%. Considering the proportion of shares held by Germany, France, and Italy, 27.0716 (26.96%), 20.3297 (20.24%), and 17.8643 (17.79%),[129] respectively, it means that either of the three members of the ESM could veto financial assistance requested by one of the other members. As highlighted by Schwarz, the voting power translates in to a 'structural bias' that 'translates the economic power of most creditor States into formal voting rights attributing more weight to them relative to their economic power and thus cements the status quo'.[130] The Eastern European members of the ESM contribute the least to the ESM based on the criteria and, therefore, are likely to be in a position where their votes will contribute little to the ultimate decisions taken by the Board of Governors of the ESM when it comes to providing financial assistance.

7.62 The ESM has a total subscribed capital of €705bn, of which €80bn is paid-up capital, with the additional ability to call up capital up to €625bn from its members. It is expected that the capital level will be maintained at 15% between paid in capital and that disbursed to a member. In this case, the Board of Directors has the authority on a simple majority basis to call up capital to maintain the 15% level.[131] There is also an emergency capital facility to provide assurance to its bondholders that there is a sufficient degree of liquidity on call which can be paid up within seven days.

[125] Treaty Establishing the European Stability Mechanism Between the Kingdom of Belgium, the Federal Republic of Germany, the Republic of Estonia, Ireland, the Hellenic Republic, the Kingdom of Spain, the French Republic, the Italian Republic, the Republic of Cyprus, the Republic of Latvia, the Republic of Lithuania, the Grand Duchy of Luxembourg, Malta, the Kingdom of The Netherlands, the Republic of Austria, the Portuguese Republic, the Republic of Slovenia, the Slovak Republic, and the Republic of Finland, T/ESM 2012-LT/en 1; European Stability Mechanism By-Laws (2014), 'These By-Laws of the European Stability Mechanism (the "ESM") are adopted under the authority of, and are intended to be complementary to, the Treaty Establishing the European Stability Mechanism signed in Brussels on 2 February 2012 (the "Treaty"); they shall be construed accordingly.'

[126] ESM Treaty, Art. 4(4). The governance of the ESM is critical to its role and it is important to be aware how it will make its decisions. The governance of the ESM is set out in the form of a Board of Governors made up of Ministers of Finance of the respective members and the Board of Directors each appointed by the respective Ministry of Finance. For the purposes of financial assistance to a member, the Board of Governors takes the role and for such a decision unanimity is required. With respect to the Board of Governors, the President of the ECB and the European Commissioner for Economic and Monetary Affairs participate as observers.

[127] ESM Treaty, Annex II, Subscriptions to the authorized capital stock.

[128] ESM Treaty, Art. 4(5).

[129] ESM Treaty, Annex, II Subscriptions to the authorized capital stock.

[130] Michael Schwarz, 'A Memorandum of Misunderstanding—The Doomed Road of the European Stability Mechanism and a Possible Way Out: Enhanced Cooperation' (2014) 51 Common Market Law Review 389–424 at 393.

[131] ESM Treaty, Art. 41(2).

The ESM, with support from the ECB and the Commission, assesses a request for assistance by evaluating the risk to financial stability of the Euro.[132] Once the support is provided, then it is the responsibility of the Commission to assess compliance with the conditions attached to the financial assistance. In the process of assessing the needs of the Member State, the IMF also works alongside the Commission.[133] The Member State would be expected to put in a request for assistance to the IMF alongside its request to the ESM.[134] Equally important is the need for private sector involvement in the support through compliance with conditionality requirements.[135] The impact of the conditions imposed would require confidence that the structural reforms in the form of spending adjustments and tax reforms will lead to sustainable repayment of the financial assistance. The ESM has the authority to stop additional support if the structural reforms are not introduced in line with the Memorandum of Understanding.[136] 7.63

The ESM can assist a member in several ways.[137] The first option is a stability support loan which requires compliance with strict conditionality to enable disbursement of the financial assistance. The terms of the loan can vary in length of repayment and costs of the loan. However, the cost is principally calculated on the base rate (calculated based on what the ESM can raise) and a commitment fee which is applied *ex post* based on the difference between the cost of raising the funds and disbursement until maturity. Additional fees can also apply such as a service fee and a margin. The other option is the precautionary financial assistance which is a credit line to the member to reduce the chances of it losing access to international financial markets. It is suggested that this, in many respects, acts as a signal that the macroeconomic credentials of the Member State are sound, but it could also trigger a more negative reaction, highlighting that they are correctly considered unsound, thus precipitating a further run on their debt. This facility can be in a form of a loan or it could be provided through a bond purchase scheme. In respect of these facilities, the member will be subjected to enhanced surveillance. The primary market support facility is to provide an additional safety net during the initial public offering in order to secure investment community's confidence in the Member State's ability to raise funds in the international market place. The secondary market support facility attempts to maintain adequate liquidity to continue investment and refinancing in the secondary market and ensure interest rates on such debt are sustainable. The purchased debt instruments would then be sold back in the market when the price and appetite has normalized. 7.64

The ESM introduces facilities to address the fiscal burden of a bank failure either directly or indirectly.[138] The fiscal burden of the financial assistance has led to the introduction of 7.65

[132] ESM Treaty, Art. 13.

[133] ESM Treaty, Art. 13(7); see also Memorandum of Understanding on the working relations between the Commission and the European Stability Mechanism, 27 April 2018, <https://www.esm.europa.eu/sites/default/files/20180427_esm_ec_mou.pdf>.

[134] ESM Treaty, Recital 8.

[135] ESM Treaty, Recital 12.

[136] ESM Treaty, Art. 13(7); see also Memorandum of Understanding on the working relations between the Commission and the European Stability Mechanism, 27 April 2018.

[137] ESM Treaty, Art. 14, ESM Precautionary financial assistance; Art. 15, Financial assistance for the recapitalization of financial institutions of an ESM Member; Art. 16, ESM Loans; Art. 17 Primary market support facility; Art. 18, Secondary market support facility.

[138] European Stability Mechanism, Guideline on Financial Assistance for the Recapitalisation of Financial Institutions (Indirect bank recapitalization).

a direct recapitalization facility. Its purpose is to avoid a situation where the financial assistance to the Member State is specifically for a bank in distress. The adverse implications for the member once it is announced by the Member State it is seeking to support it. In this case, the distress at the financial system level places pressure on the Member State. Yet, the direct support avoids placing undue pressure on the Euro area. This support facility will only be initiated if it is shown that the means to address the problems of the distressed bank have been exhausted. The Member State is likely to find itself in this position when the bank is of systemic importance based on 'their size, interconnectedness, complexity, and substitutability.'[139] In this case, the ECB is likely to be the supervisor and will be in a very good position to assess the systemic importance of the bank and the state it is in after the required stress test. Moreover, the ESM board of governors will be expected to liaise with the European Commission to evaluate the forthcoming restructuring plans to fulfil the criteria for state aid support and the implications of such aid.

7.66 The other approach introduced is direct recapitalization of financial institutions.[140] In this scenario, the financial assistance is provided after the resolution tools have been exhausted and there remains, nevertheless, a need for financial assistance to minimize an adverse impact on the Eurozone as a whole. The direct recapitalization technique is to avoid a situation where the indirect financial assistance via the Member State itself puts the Member State in a precarious position and so exacerbates the banking crisis in to a sovereign debt crisis once the markets are sensitive to the news of the sheer size of the losses incurred. This tool is devoted to the credit institutions of systemic relevance. The contribution is calculated based on the following criteria—insufficient equity capital less than 4.5% of tier 1 Capital.

7.67 The ESM is a form of risk sharing at the regional and Member State level by minimizing the agency problems: at the Member State level between the state and taxpayers and the banking industry, but also in a cross-border setting by reducing spill-overs from externalities that could arise in a Member State from the significant cross-border banking activity that exists within the Eurozone. As noted above, the ESM attempts to minimize the fiscal implications of another banking crisis morphing into a sovereign debt crisis. The backstop it provides forms the line of defence, provided the appropriate level of burden-sharing has been exercised at the national level to minimize as far as possible the support required. In this setting the ESM needs to play a crucial role in assessing the culpability of the Member State and the banking industry and try to reduce the spill-over effects from the ensuing negative externalities. The role of the European Commission and the ECB in exercising authority by advising the managing director is crucial to ensure that decisions are not simply made in a Member State's self-interest but rather in the interests of avoiding a threat to the economic and financial sustainability of the Euro area. The largest contributors have the ultimate decision since a qualified majority is required of 85%. So while the ESM is premised on the solidarity principle like its predecessor concerns nevertheless remain. As Closa and Maatsch explain, '[t]he proponents also pointed to the fact that the effects of the financial crisis had spilled

[139] Dalvinder Singh, 'Recovery and Resolution Planning' in Jens-Hinrich Binder and Dalvinder Singh (eds) *Bank Resolution: The European Regime* (Oxford: Oxford University Press 2016) pp. 12–13.

[140] European Stability Mechanism Board of Governors Resolution, Meeting of 8 December 2014, Establishment of the instrument for the direct recapitalization of institutions, <https://www.esm.europa.eu/sites/default/files/20141208_establishment_of_the_instrument_for_the_direct_recapitalisation_of_institutions.pdf>; Guideline on Financial Assistance for the Direct Recapitalisation of Institutions, 8 December 2014.

over to other Member States and that the finances of the Eurozone states had proved to be more dependent on each other than previously assumed'. [141] In view of this the commitment of Bulgaria to entering close cooperation within the SSM and SRM will be limited in ways as it will not benefit from the wider sovereign level part of the safety net that is currently the exclusive benefit of Eurozone participating Member States. As was shown the mutualization of resolution funds and eventually the common deposit insurance scheme show an important step to contribute to the other burden-sharing aspects of the Banking Union.

The likelihood of a systemic crisis within a small Member State spilling over to large Member States is small due to the lack of interconnection between them. There are exceptions of course, such as Ireland and Greece. The small Member State may nevertheless experience a significant idiosyncratic bank shock which could lead it to require ESM support. The evidence from the precursor of the ESM is that large Member States as well as small Member States can threaten the financial stability of the region and threaten the credibility of the Euro. **7.68**

The decisions made by the ESM could either align or not align with national interests, depending on the extent to which national financial stability threatens regional financial stability. Leading to a position observed by Ban and Seabrooke by 'giving each member a veto can worsen the brinkmanship and expose members in need of financial assistance to blackmail'.[142] The large bank presence in the small Member States from France, Italy and to a less extent Germany means that it is possible the respective Member State could be incentivized to either vote for or to veto financial assistance to such a small Member State, or indeed to veto financial assistance to a larger Member State which would have direct implications on smaller Member States due to the cross-border nature of the banking relationship. For example, this scenario could arise in decisions associated with direct recapitalization of a financial institution that has cross-border exposures in terms of assets and liabilities. Small host Member States are also particularly vulnerable where a European bank's exposure is considerable and, in many instances, classed as one of the three largest banks. In such countries it likely the recapitalization of the parent will lead to a sale of business strategy in the non-core parts of the group leading to greater foreign bank concentration risk within the Member State. **7.69**

International Soft Law Guidance on Temporary Public Funding

The evidence from the recent failures highlight the importance of some form of public or private assistance to support orderly restructuring of banks. The EU and Eurozone measures are in place to provide some coherency to a policy space that has been neglected. The principal instruments provide little or no guidance on how they extend to third countries. Financial assistance to support an orderly restructuring or liquidity assistance is **7.70**

[141] Carlos Closa and Aleksandra Maatsch, 'In a Spirit of Solidarity? Justifying the European Financial Stability Facility (EFSF) in National Parliamentary Debates' (2014) 52(4) Journal of Common Market Studies 826–42 at 829.

[142] Cornel Ban and Leonard Seabrooke, 'From Crisis to Stability: How to make the European Stability Mechanism Transparent and Accountable' (2017) p. 7 <https://transparency.eu/wp-content/uploads/2017/03/ESM_Report_DIGITAL-version.pdf>.

the principal barrier between home and host that eclipses all the hard law and or soft law supervisory measures that may be negotiated. In view of this, the international literature recognizes now sufficient liquidity to banks is likely to minimize the possible social costs of a disorderly resolution. The importance of formulating policy and guidance in this area is to ensure public assistance is worked in to the national policy space *ex ante*. This is particularly important in the accession countries where there is a significant presence of European banks. The formulation of policy for cross-border banks from the host perspective should provide the accession countries the opportunity to prepare for potential resolution or insolvency-liquidation decisions emanating from European Member States or by the SRB. The role played by such countries may be limited but reciprocal arrangements may minimize unintended consequences of a separate resolution decision that works against both sides.

7.71 The FSB in 2015 developed guiding principles on temporary funding needs in resolution through public and or private means.[143] It is an attempt to develop guidelines in line with the FSB Key Attributes to understand the risks and benefits when providing temporary assistance in resolution. While the guiding principles focus on Global Systemic Important Banks (G-SIB), the principles are arguably wide enough to apply to domestically important banks regardless of the systemic importance of the state in question. They therefore could be utilized by both large and small states. The significant subsidiary is prevalent in the accession countries as shown in Chapter 1.

7.72 The principles place specific importance on private funds as the first port of call if temporary financial assistance is needed.[144] This can come in the form of private liquidity assistance through a consortia of banks in the market or utilizing resolution funding from other banks and hedge funds that attempt to orchestrate a restructuring of the bank. The public sector guiding principle is interpreted widely to include formal assistance through either the deposit insurance fund or resolution funds as well as central bank emergency liquidity assistance or through the ministry of finance.[145] In the former, the funds are or should be ultimately privately funded through risk-based premiums and in the latter through taxpayers, which is more politically controversial. The support provided from the latter needs to be evaluated from three perspectives: the potential size of the fund need to be credible; liquidity assistance needs to be timely; and the funds should be provided on a short-term basis but for long enough to allow an orderly restructuring. The risk of moral hazard is expected to be evaluated *ex ante* to minimize the adverse important on competition.[146] Ultimately, it will require close cooperation with the resolution authority when the resolution plan is being put together. The techniques to mitigate moral hazard are set out in the next guiding principle relating to recovery of losses. These would require a significant amount of legal review of the judicial and national insolvency and liquidation laws to ensure losses are recoverable in a timely manner.[147] The penultimate principle is the importance of robust resolution planning to recognize the complexity and needs for an orderly resolution.[148] From the accession country perspective it would be important to know what

[143] FSB, Guiding principles on the temporary funding needed to support the orderly resolution of a global systemically important bank ('G-SIB') (August 2016).
[144] Ibid, Principle 1.
[145] Ibid, Principle 2.
[146] Ibid, Principle 3.
[147] Ibid, Principle 4.
[148] Ibid, Principle 5.

temporary funding the group is likely to secure for its core parts and what funding it would need to provide to stabilize the local entity.

The last principle focuses on cross-border cooperation between the home and host authorities to assist to formulate a temporary funding policy with its other counterparts at the group level and or the institutional level.[149] It advocates the importance of effective cooperation between the home and host in working out the resolution scheme and the liquidity needs that is expected to be used to deal with the cross-border group in resolution. The guidance implicitly emphasizes the importance of the home authority in its policy. The guidelines suggest the crisis management group is used to work through the policy challenges the home and host authorities could face. The key challenge for the accession country is it is unlikely to feature in a Single Point of Entry strategy. 7.73

The guidelines fall short in a number of respects from the host perspective. It would have been useful to have work in to the guidance the importance of the home and the host working to assist the host for instance. In this respect it is likely that the small host is likely to opt for a standalone Multiple Point of Entry (MPE) strategy to safeguard its own interests. For the small host, local funding maybe sufficient. The home authority may be reliant on the host entity upstreaming profits which may not be forthcoming if the local authorities feel they are responsible for their own risks and exercise ringfencing. From the host perspective the upstreaming of profits may lead to a larger package of temporary assistance at the local level than would otherwise be needed. A particular challenge the host could also face is the fire sale of the entity to safeguard the home rather than the host interests, which could be left through the sale a larger and more vulnerable bank to stabilize. 7.74

Reflections on the Principal Issues

The analysis of the co-existence of decentralized and centralized crisis management and financial crisis containment measures within the Eurozone highlight how potential frictions remain at the national and regional level. The poor attention to matters at the decentralized level are likely to make potential bank problems worse unless there is clear evidence of early intervention in the affairs of banks at the pre-insolvency stage. It is evident the reforms have not prohibited the use of public assistance. It is obvious that such mechanisms are necessary to minimise potential crises in particular liquidity assistance. The important contribution is the formal nature they now exist and the mechanisms of accountability that reside within the state aid approval process to curb moral hazard risks. Provided the assistance is short-term and paid back, then there is less of a concern. However, the success has not been as apparent as the experience in other jurisdictions notably the United States. This is partly as a result of the composition of banks' balance sheet in the EU and reliance on loans and deposits as a core form of finance. Exposed to risks of non-performing loans along the lines of an economic decline in the real economy. In view of this, while idiosyncratic failures have been contained by national actions in resolution and liquidation proceedings it may be a different picture if multiple banks were to fail putting pressure on national lines of defence which could only be contained by centralized support. The reforms associated 7.75

149 Ibid, Principle 6.

with mutualizing financing go a long way to minimize the conflicting incentives between home and host when it comes to supporting the costs of resolution and containing a crisis to safeguard financial stability.[150] Therefore, the asymmetry of information between large and small home and host Member States is further minimized by pooling the funds and sharing responsibilities. The critical concern is the level of funds is likely to be insufficient and in view this the ESM will act as the backstop to the SRF. The backstop is fiscally neutral since support is recovered from the banks through the risk premium contributions to the SRF. It has also been suggested that EDIS should also be covered by the backstop if the strategy of insolvency-liquidation is going to be a credible one. The DGS does have a potential role in resolution as well. It is already evident liquidity assistance to ensure orderly liquidation has been necessary in cases of idiosyncratic bank failures, let alone for multiple bank failures during a systemic crisis.

[150] R A Eisenbeis, 'Home Country Versus Cross Border Negative Externalities in Large Banking Organization Failures and How to Avoid them' in D D Evanoff, G G Kaufman, and J R LaBrosse (eds), *International Financial Instability: Global Banking and National Regulation*, Vol. 2 (Singapore: World Scientific Publishing Co Pte Ltd 2007), pp. 181–200 at p. 190.

APPENDIX 1

Loans, Deposits, and Securities

The source of this data is the BIS Statistics Explorer on International Banking which is compiled from data provided by various national authorities. The data has been analysed and amended by the Author. Any translation of this work is not an official BIS translation with regard to this data.

Group 1

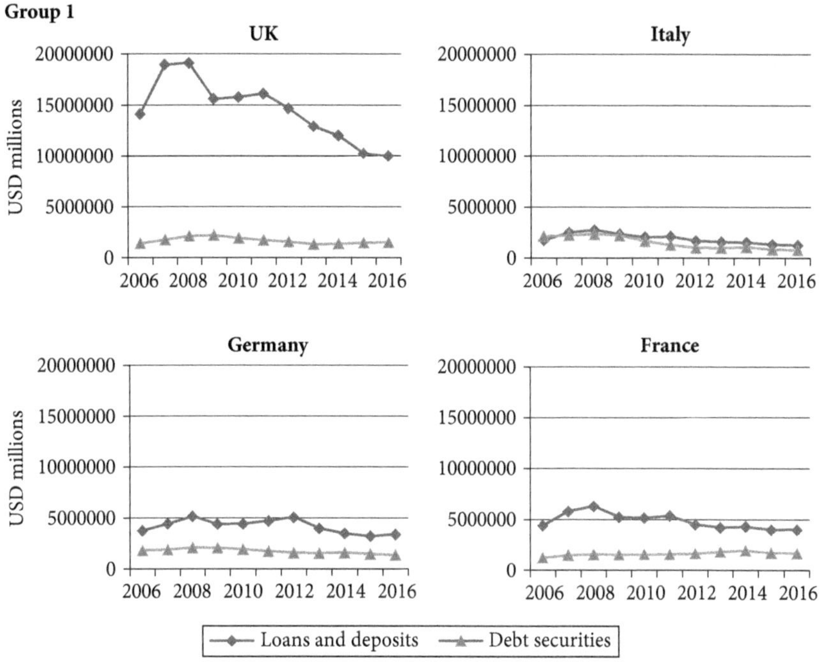

Group 2

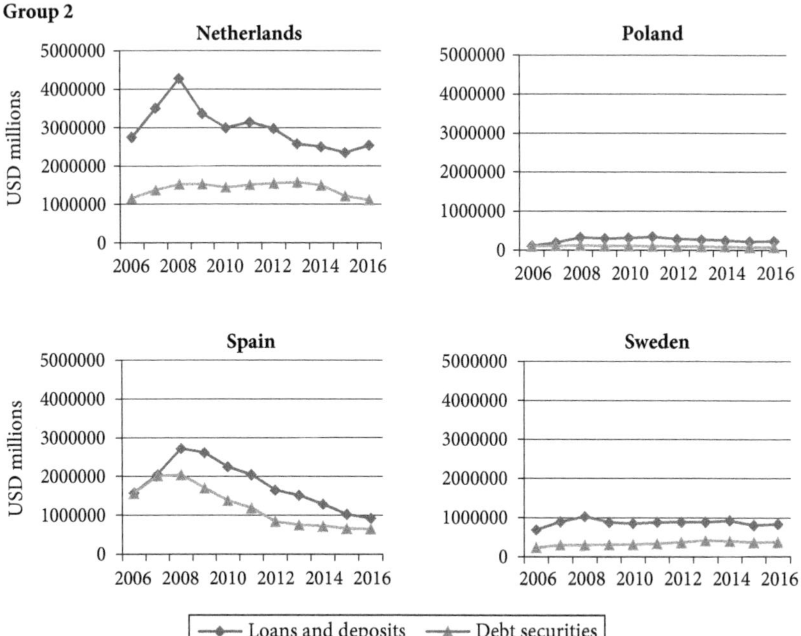

Group 3

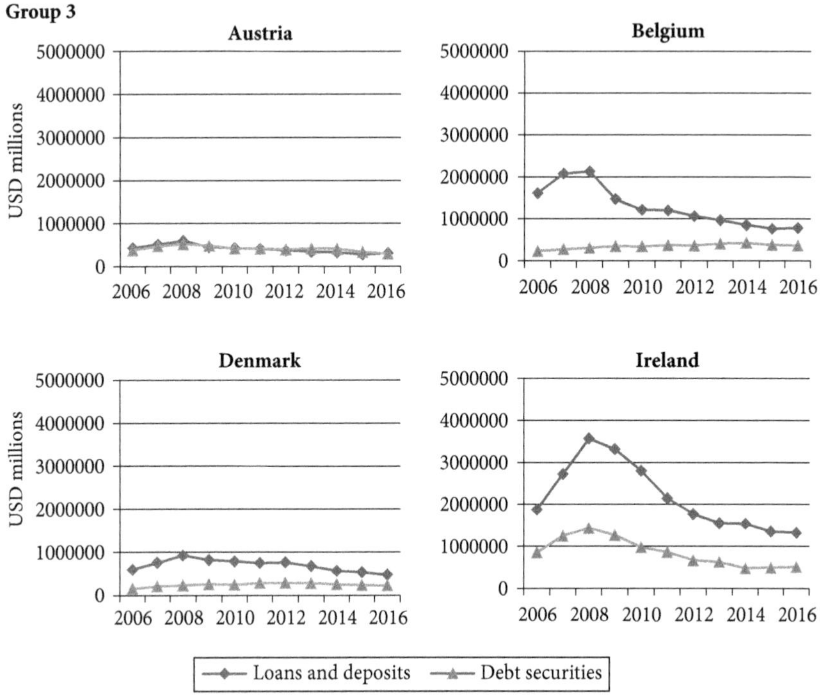

Group 4

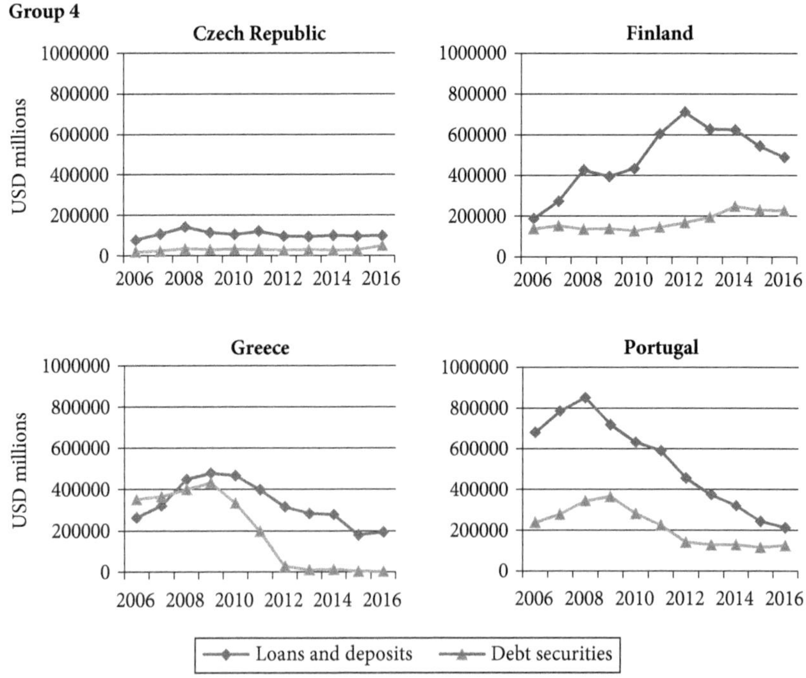

Group 5

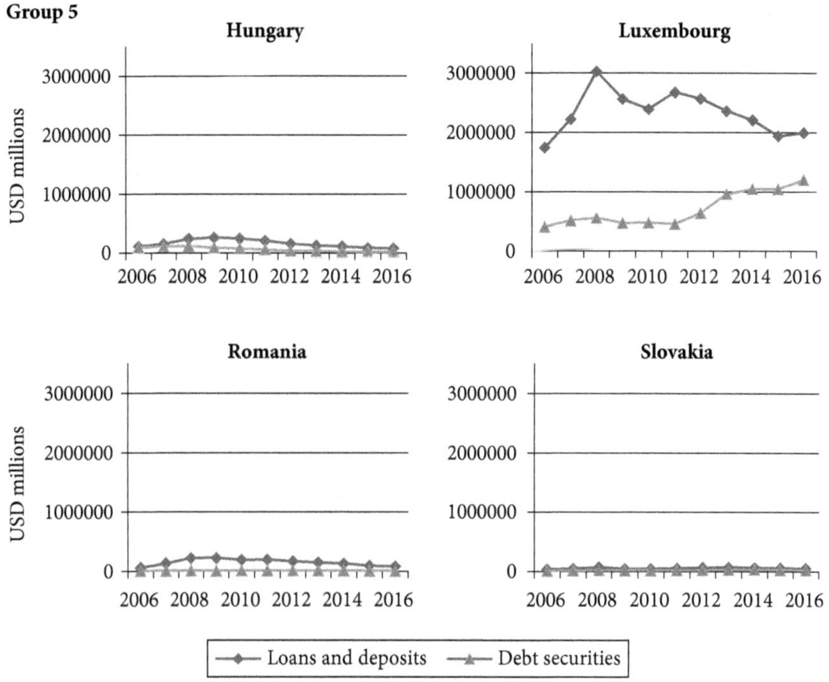

Group 6

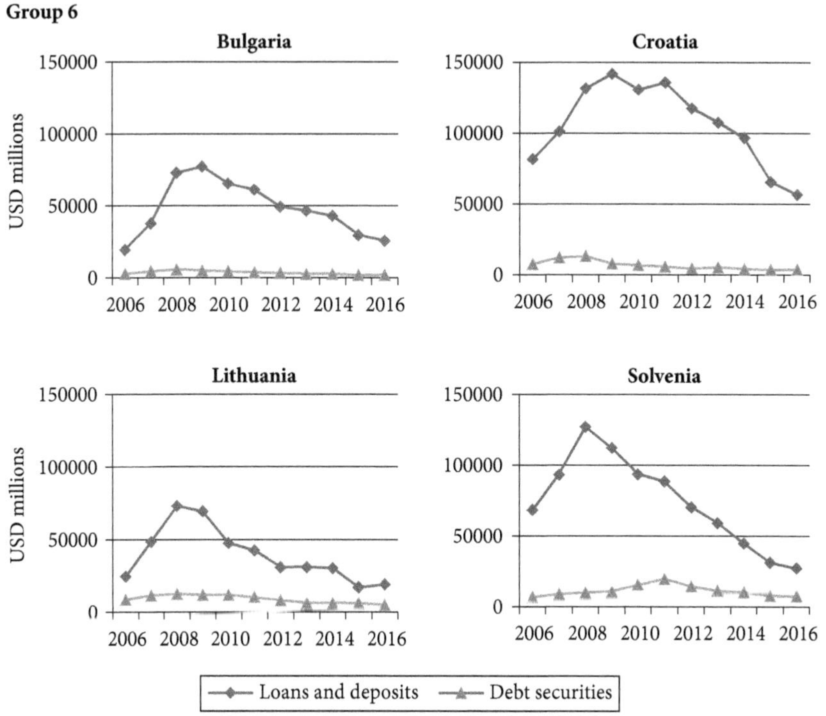

Group 7

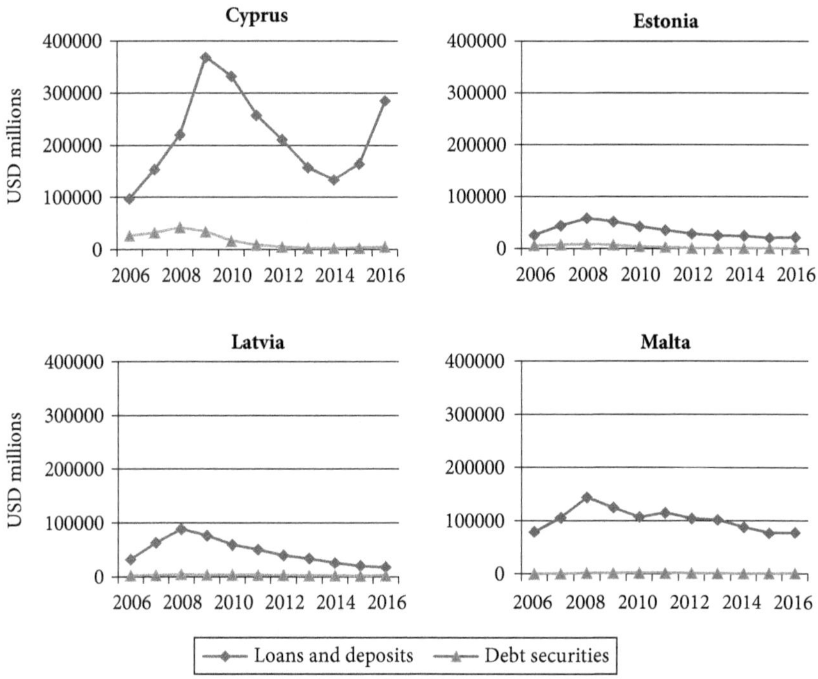
Cyprus
Estonia
Latvia
Malta
USD millions
400000
300000
200000
100000
0
2006 2008 2010 2012 2014 2016
Loans and deposits
Debt securities

APPENDIX 2

Country Exposure (USD)

The source of this data is the BIS Statistics Explorer on International Banking which is compiled from data provided by various national authorities. The data has been analysed and amended by the Author. Any translation of this work is not an official BIS translation with regard to this data.

Group 1

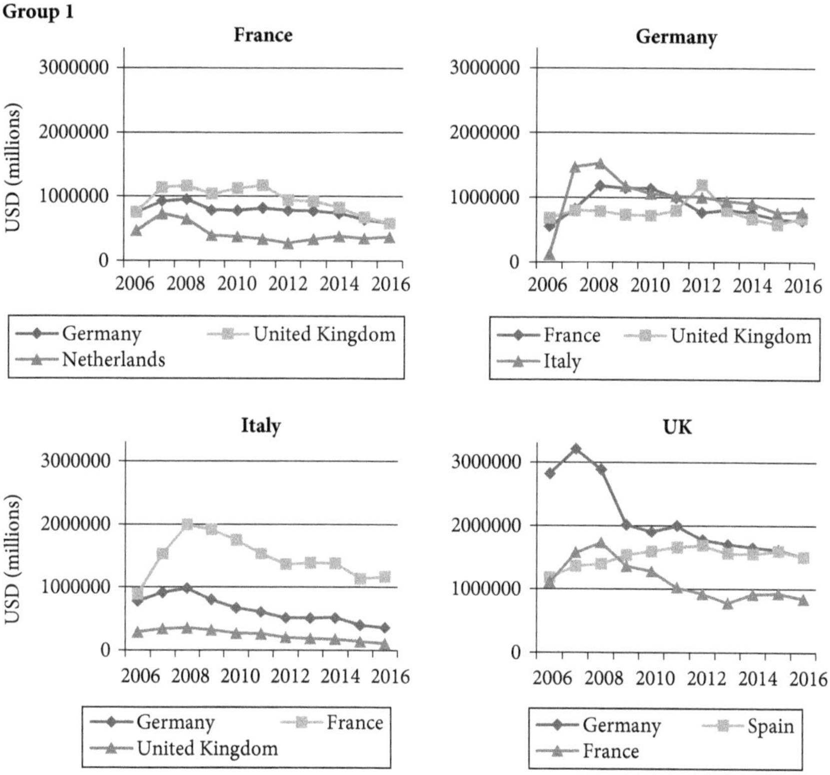

Group 2

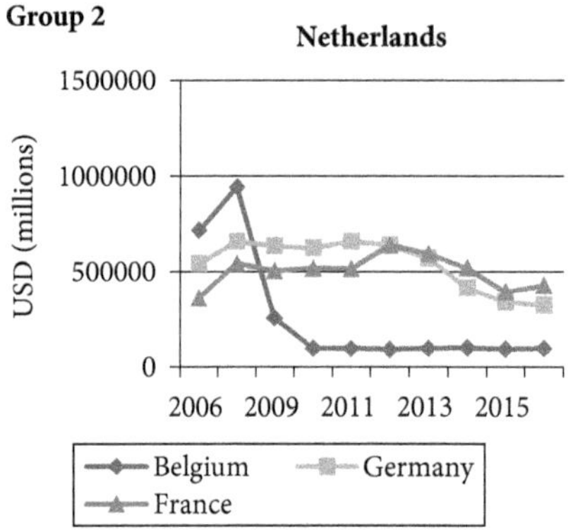

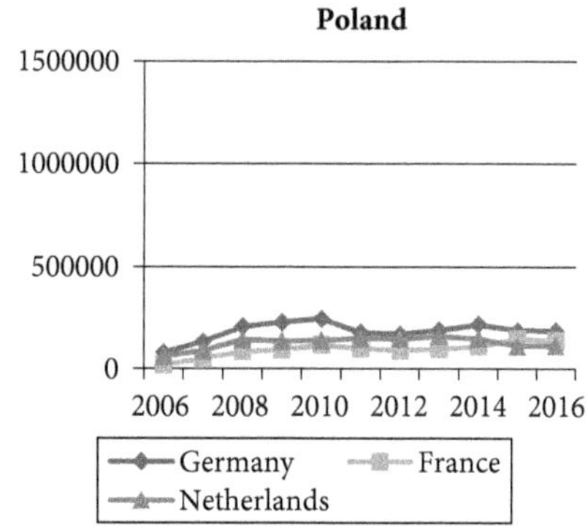

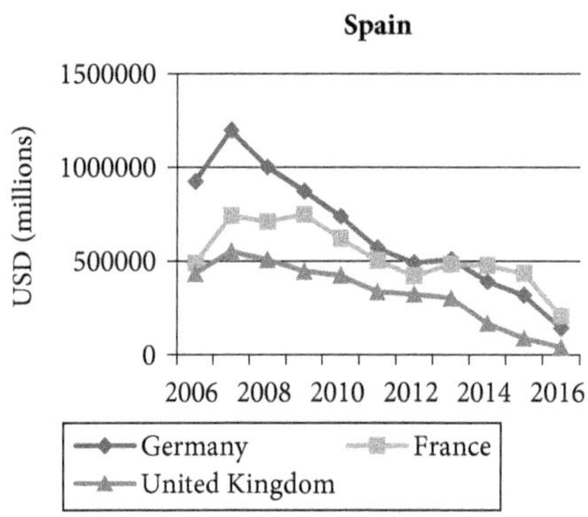

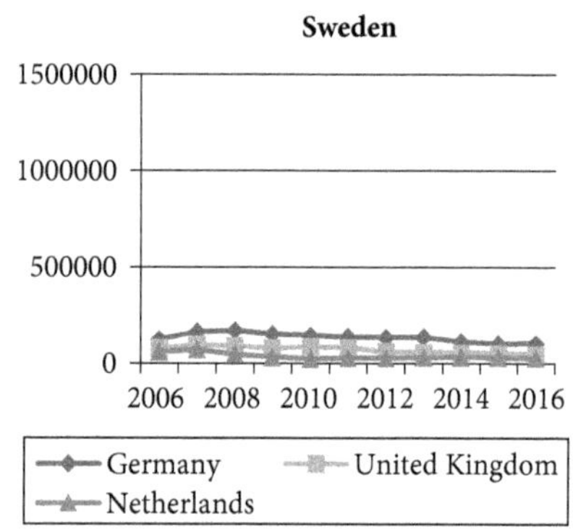

Group 3

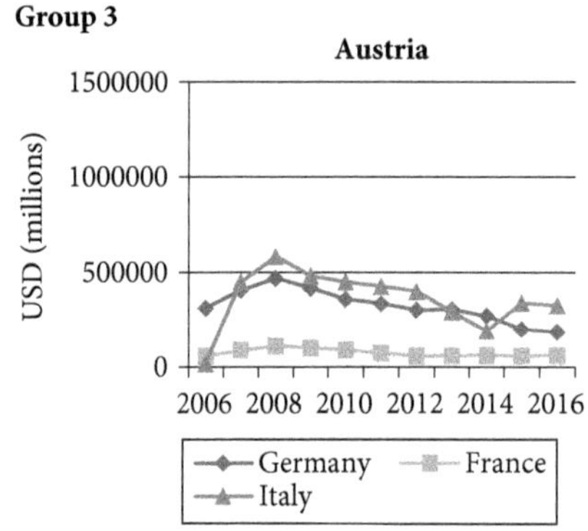

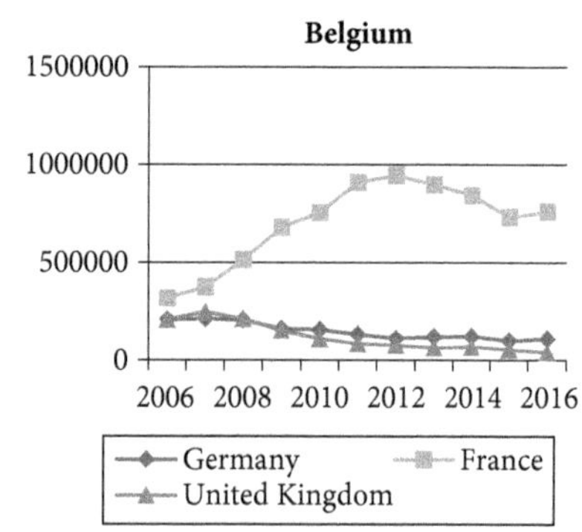

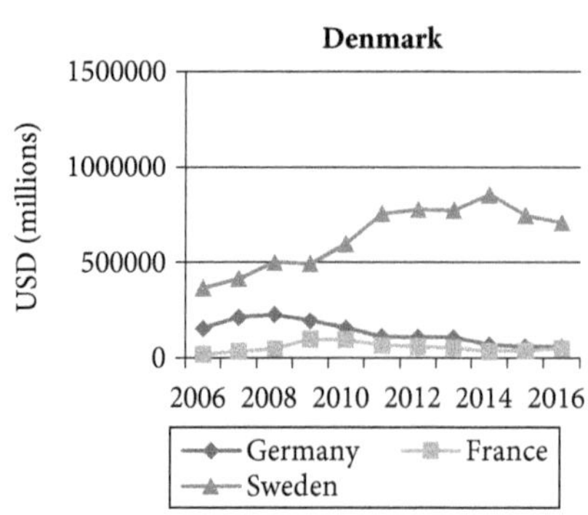

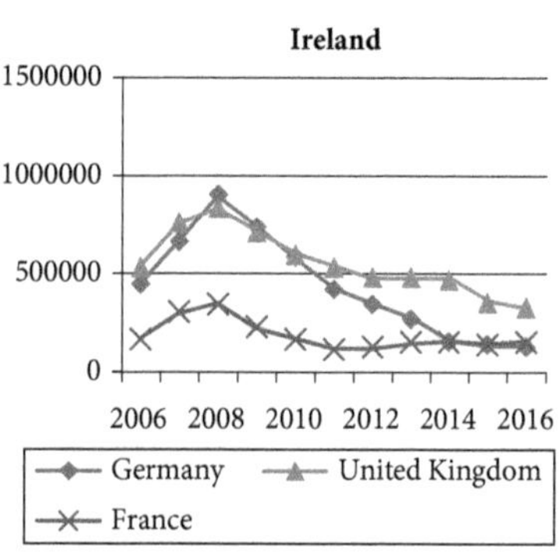

Group 4

Czech Republic

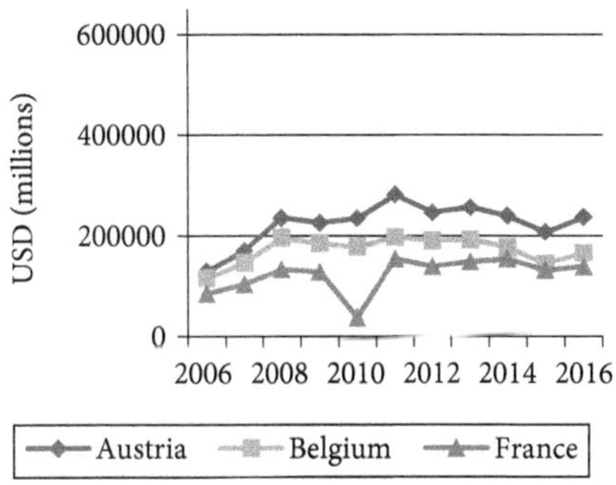

Finland

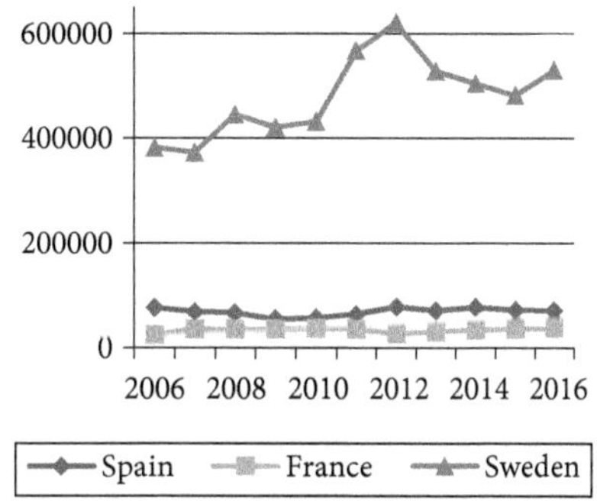

Greece

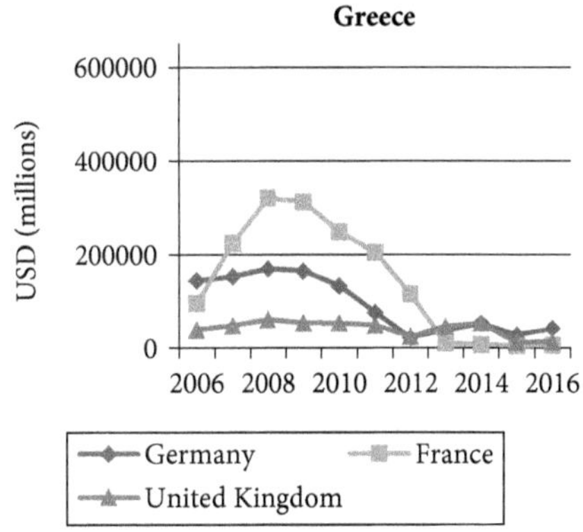

Portugal

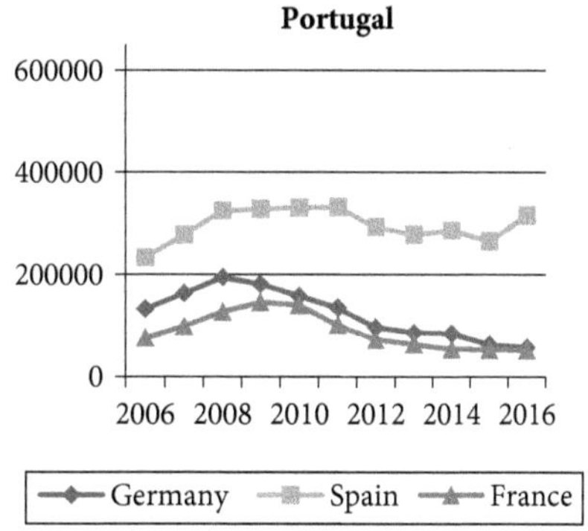

Group 5

Hungary

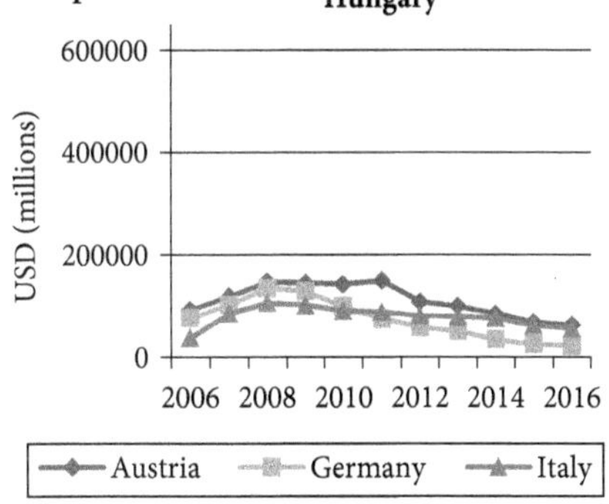

Luxembourg

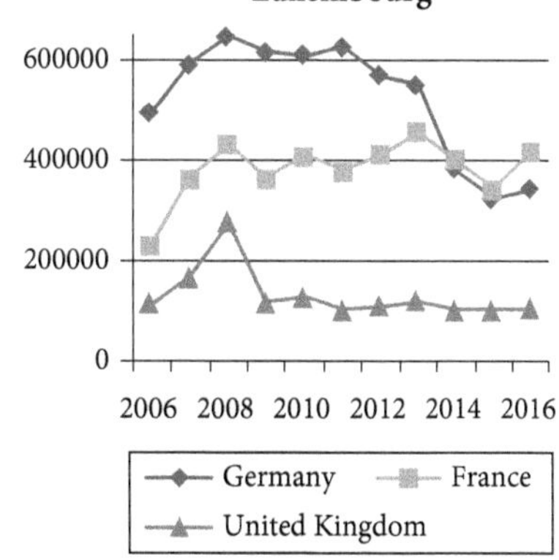

Romania

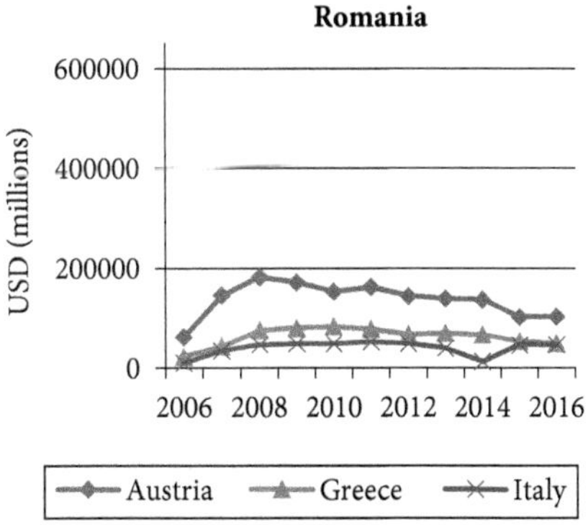

Slovakia

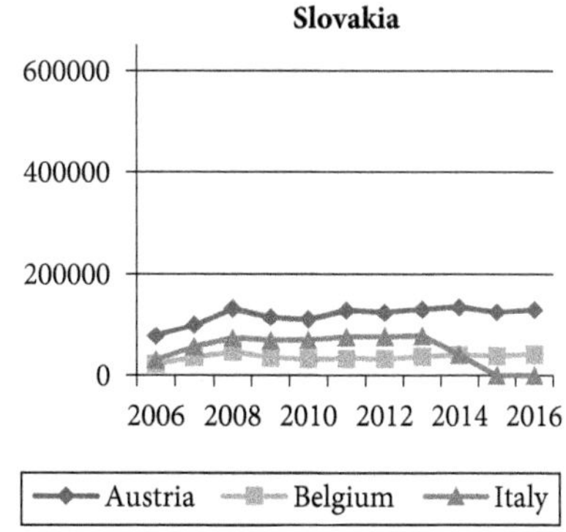

Group 6

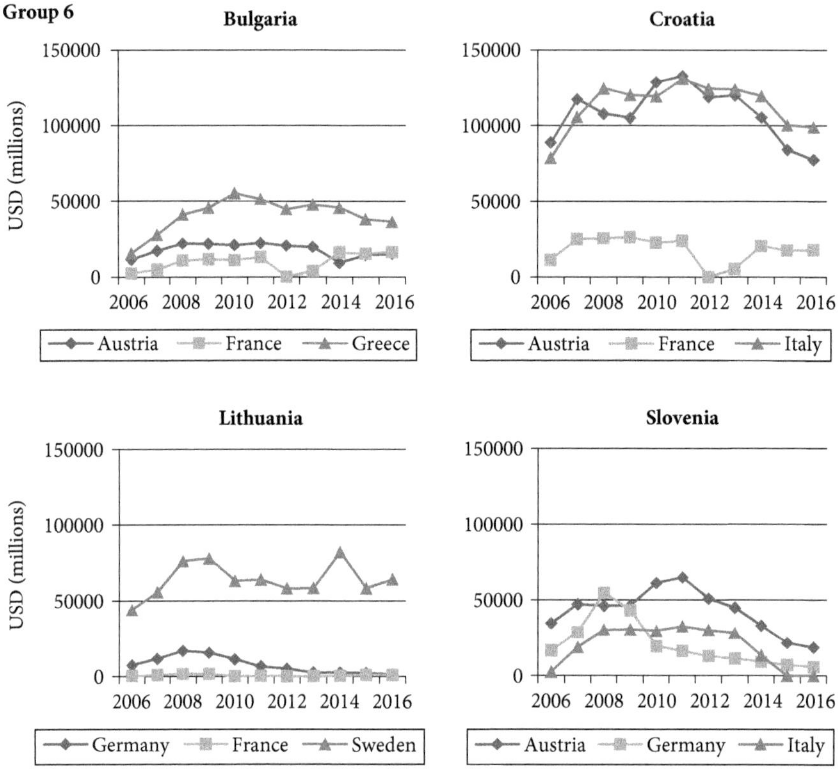

Group 7

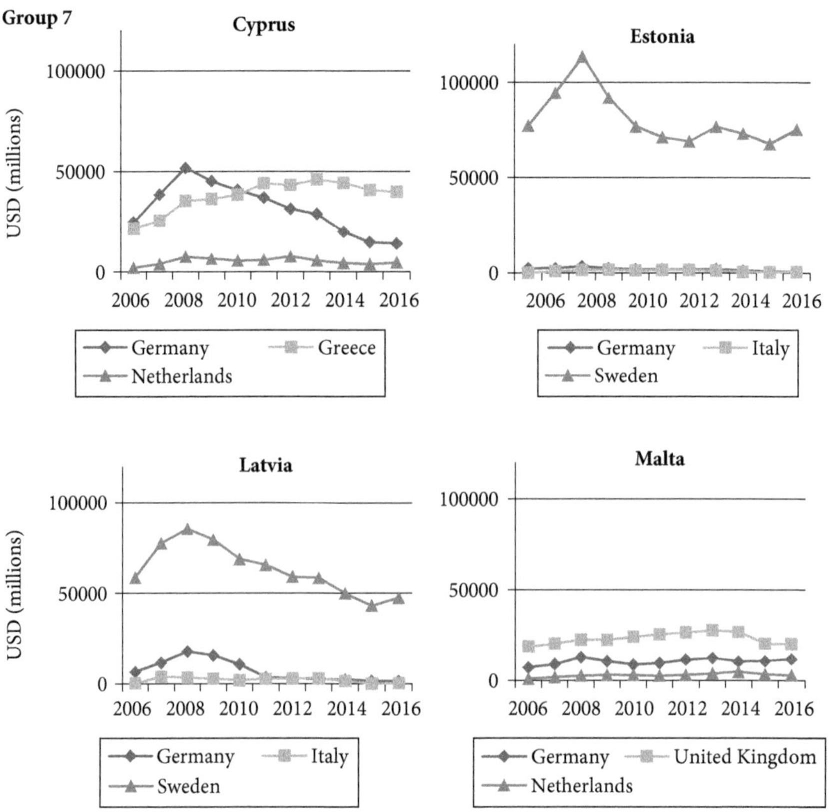

Group 8: Accession Countries

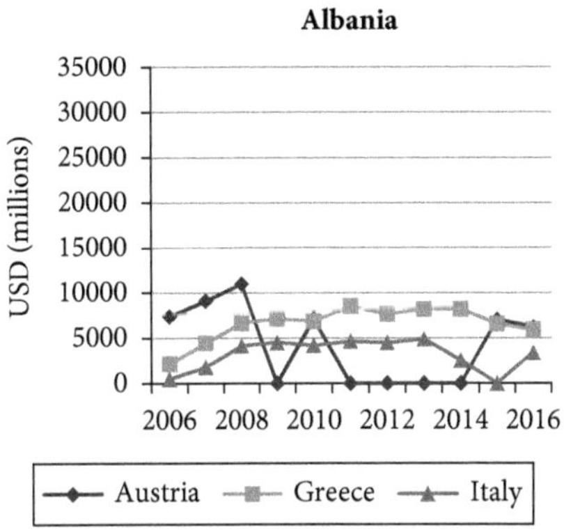

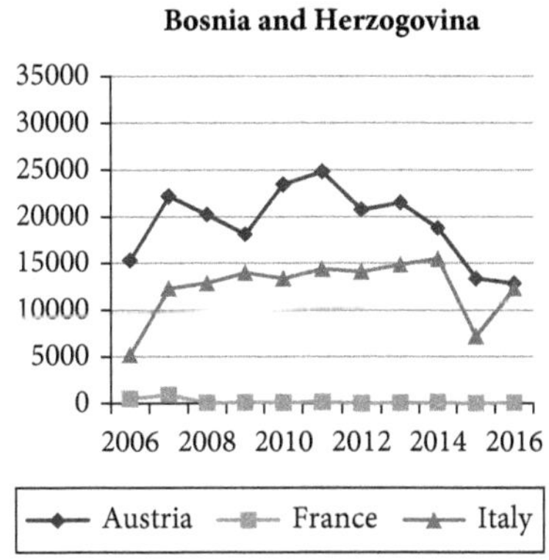

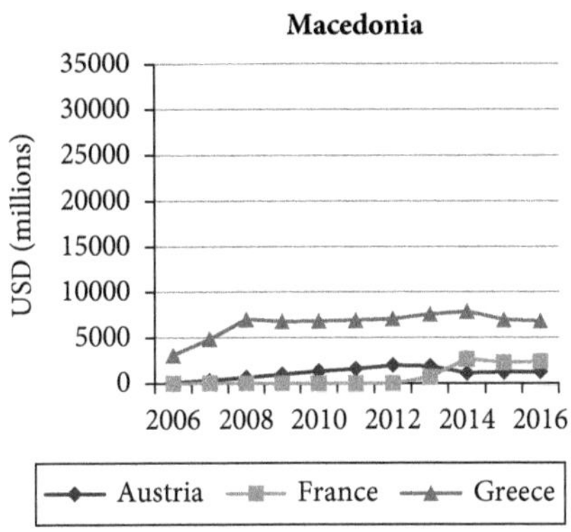

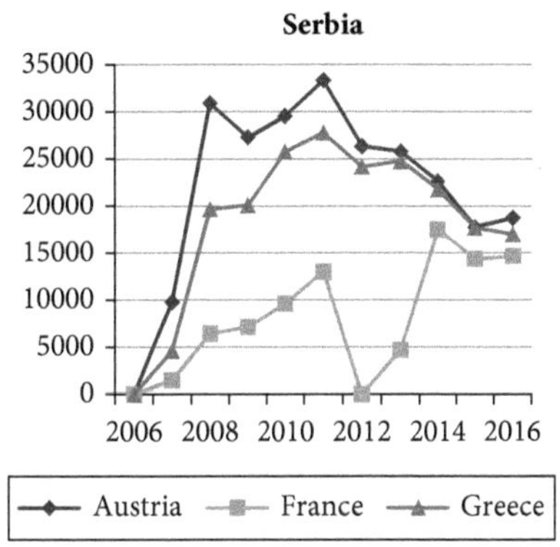

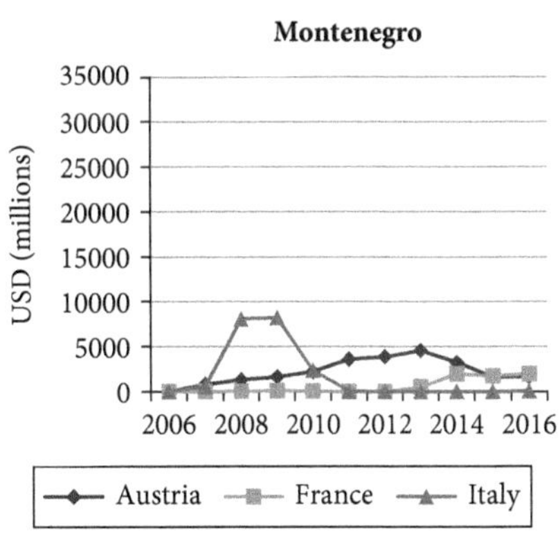

APPENDIX 3

Country Exposure (%)

The source of this data is the BIS Statistics Explorer on International Banking which is compiled from data provided by various national authorities. The data has been analysed and amended by the Author. Any translation of this work is not an official BIS translation with regard to this data.

Group 1

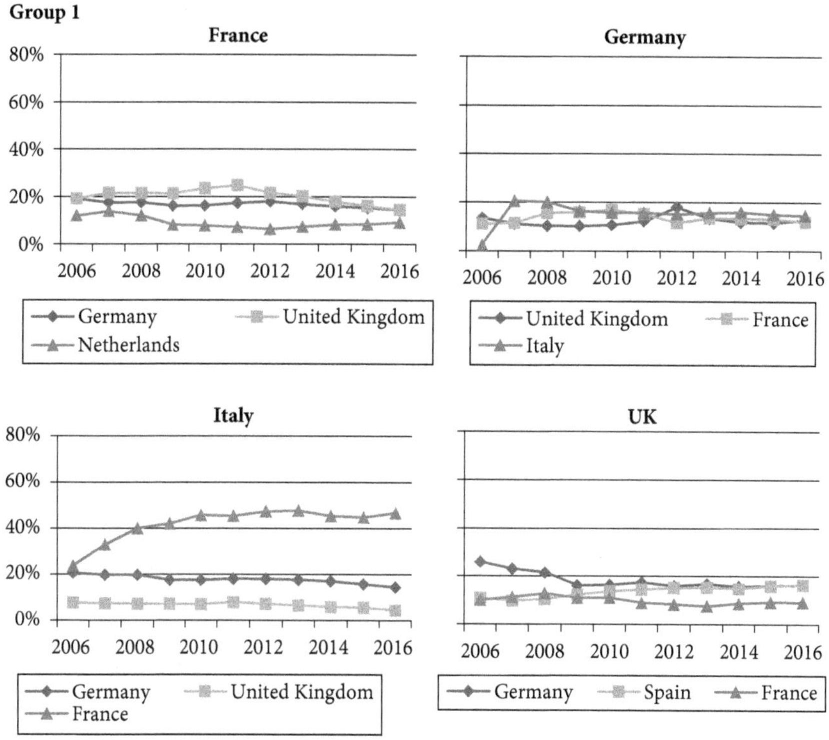

Group 2

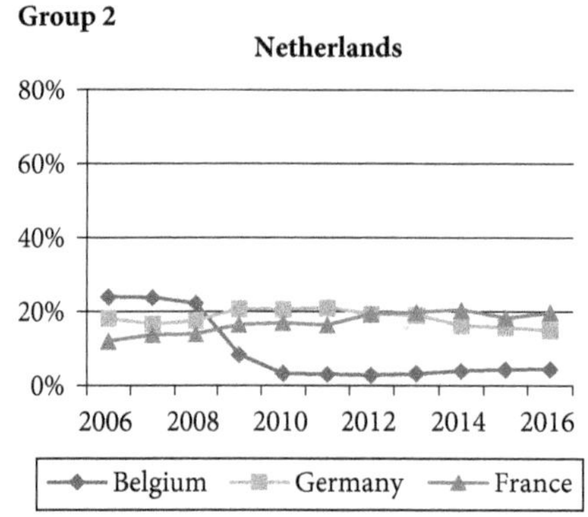

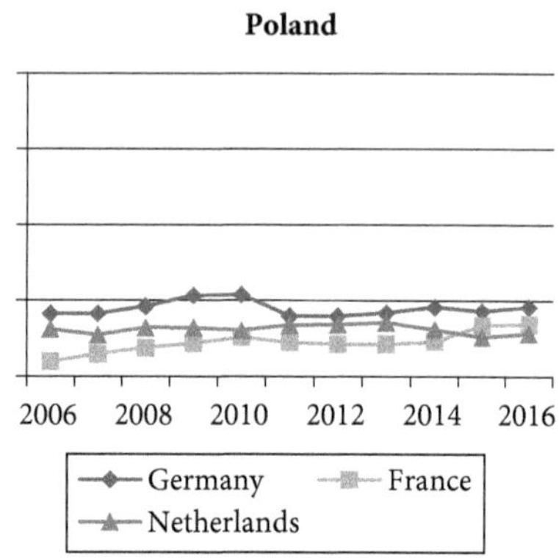

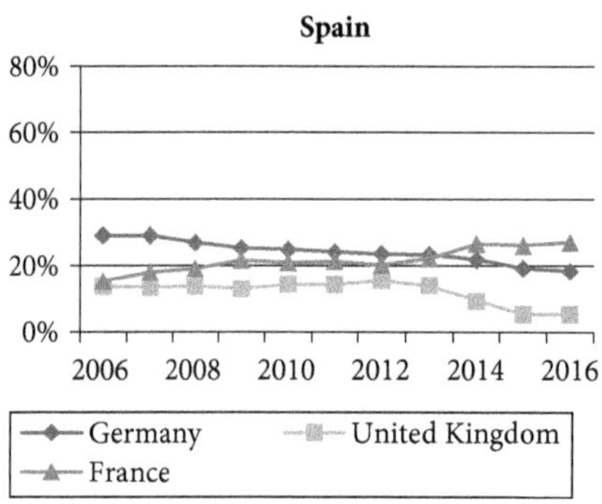

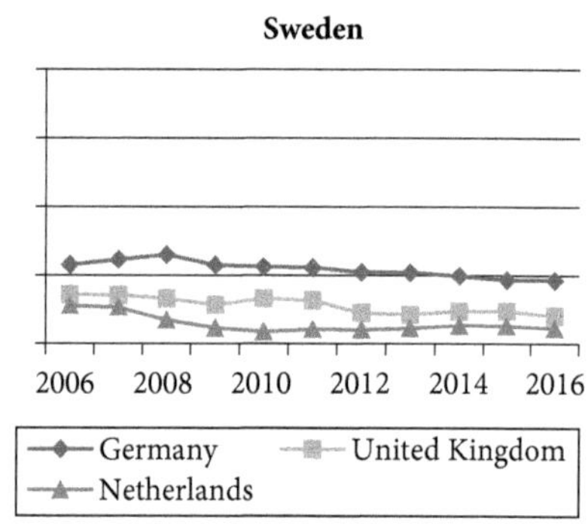

Group 3

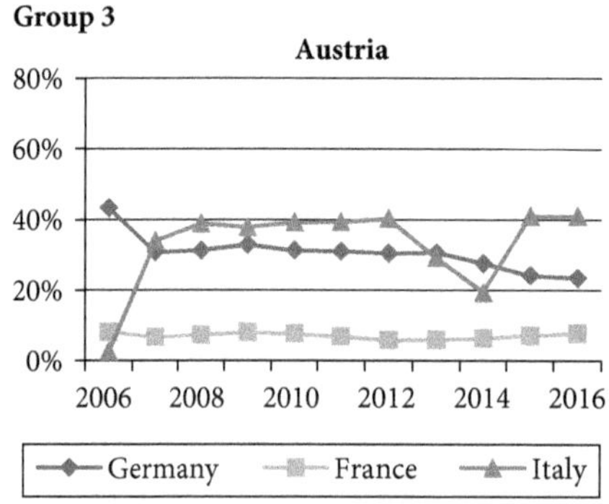

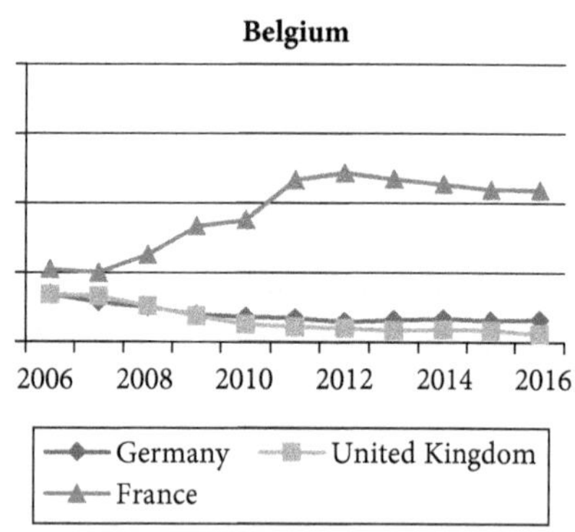

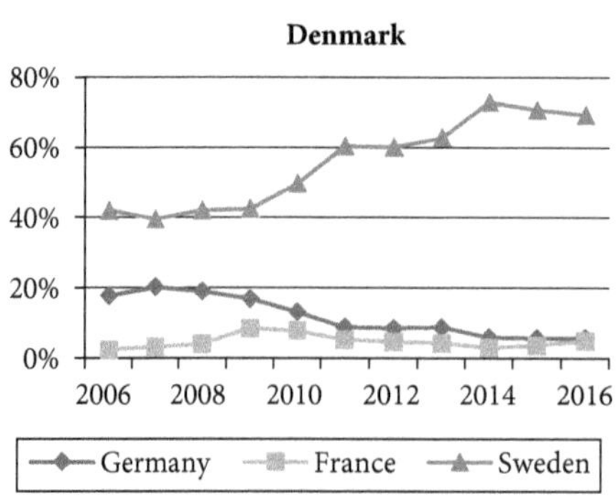

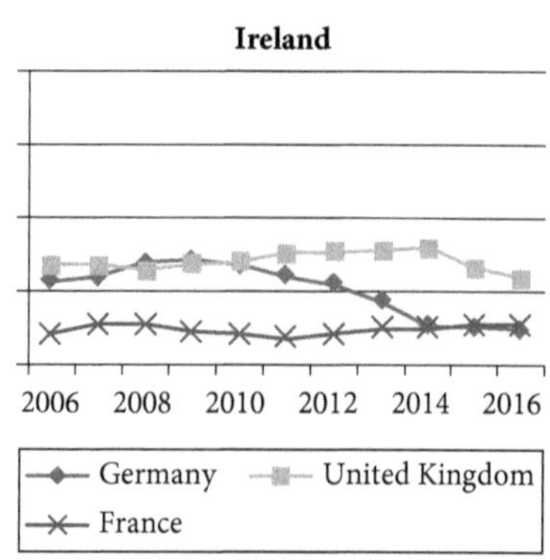

Group 4

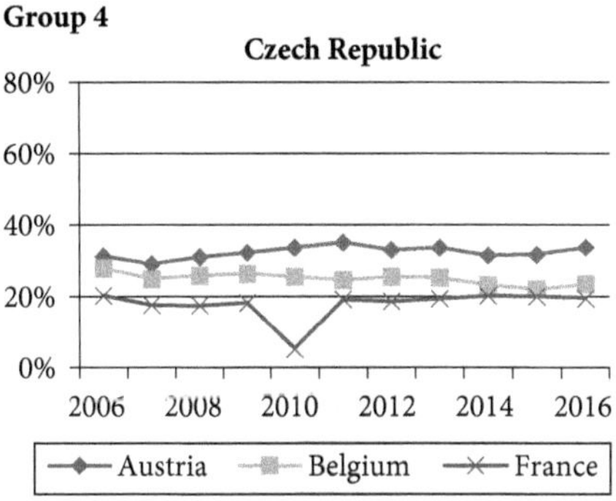

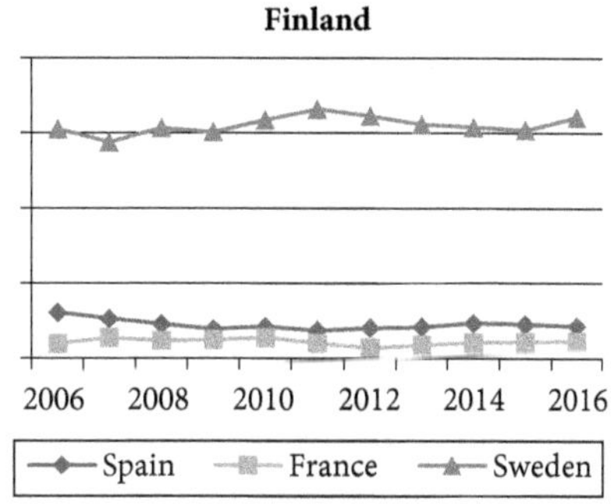

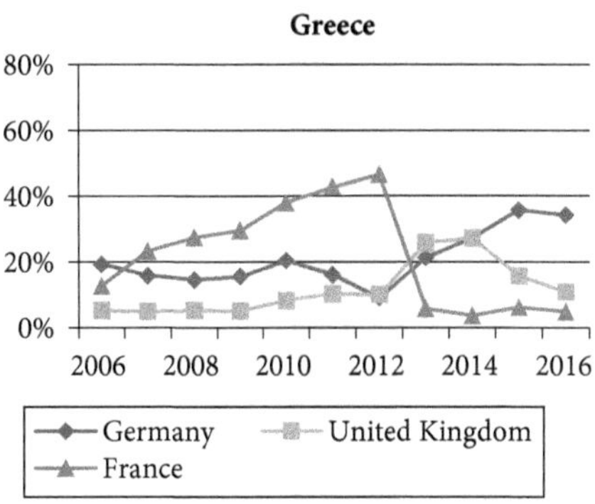

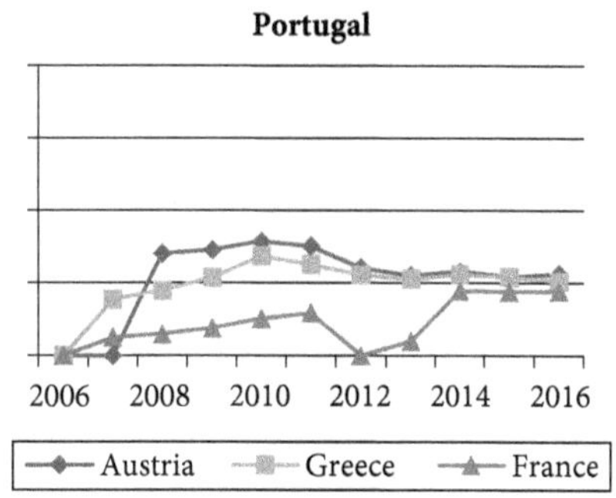

Group 5

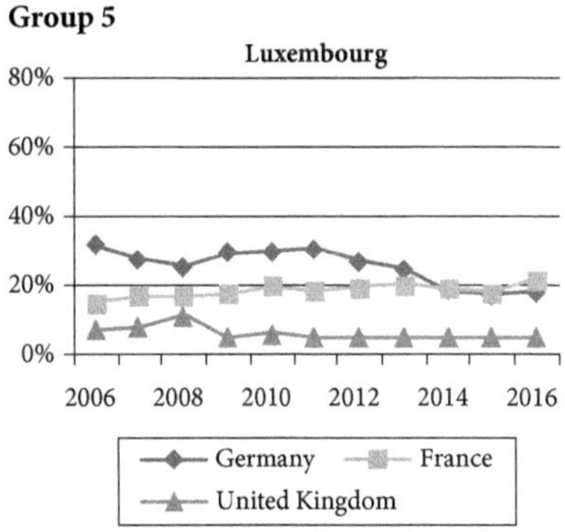

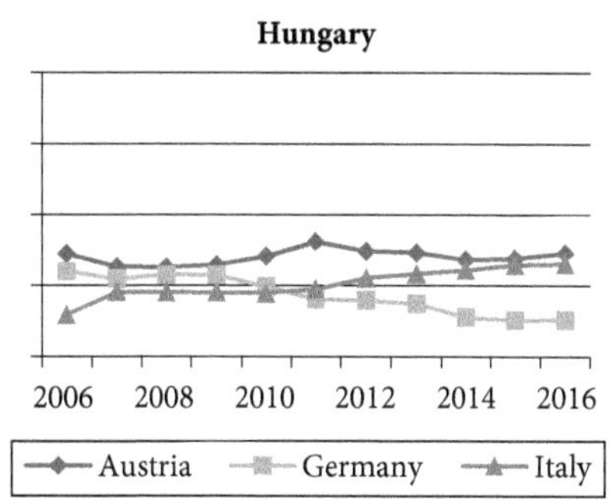

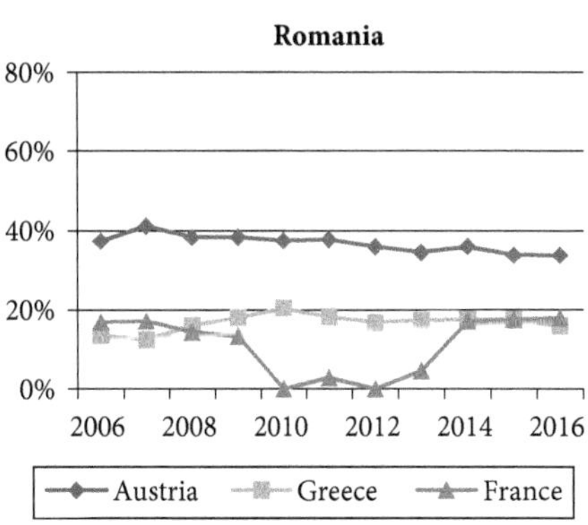

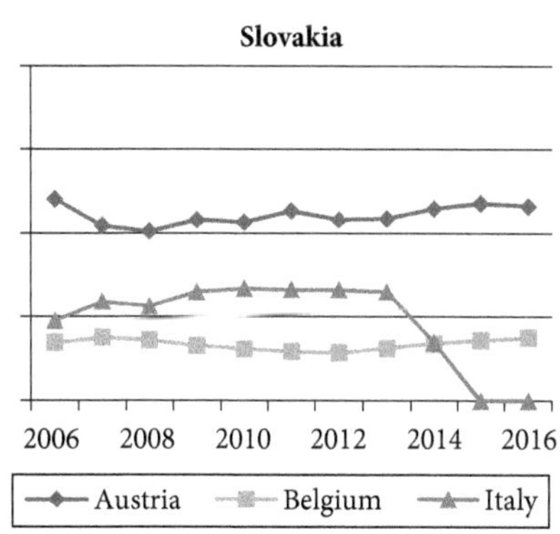

Group 6

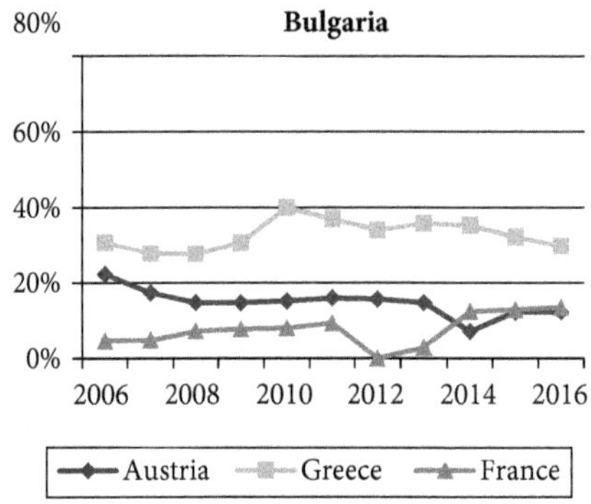

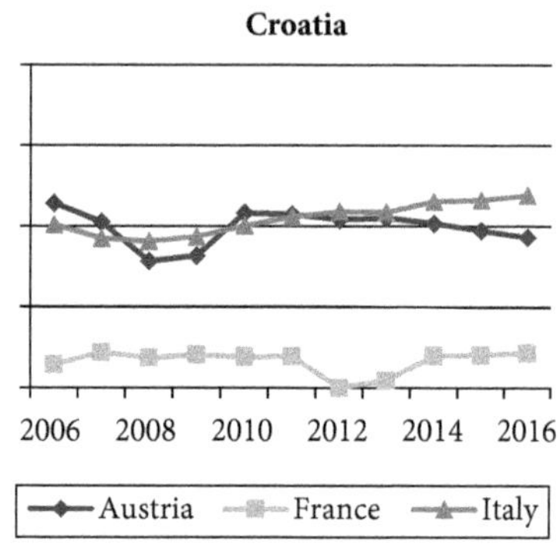

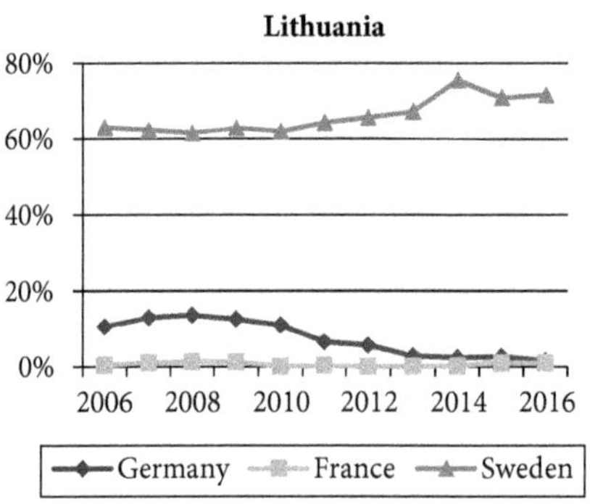

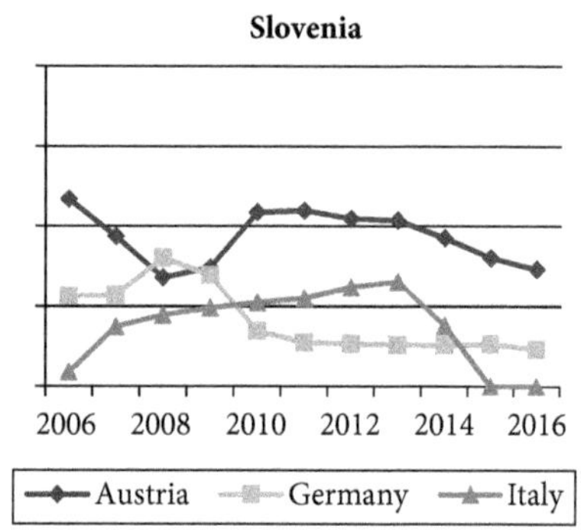

Group 7

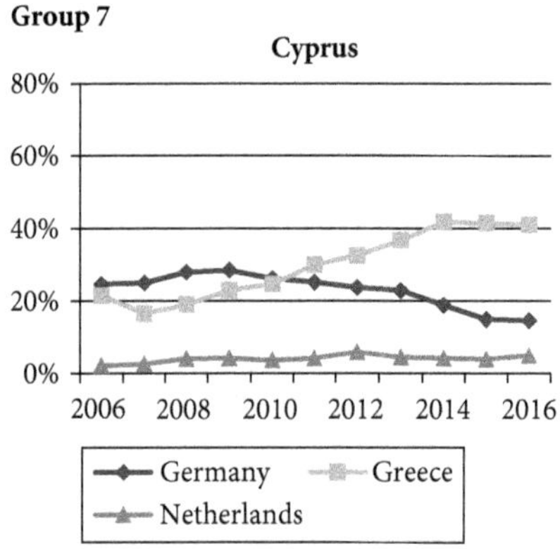

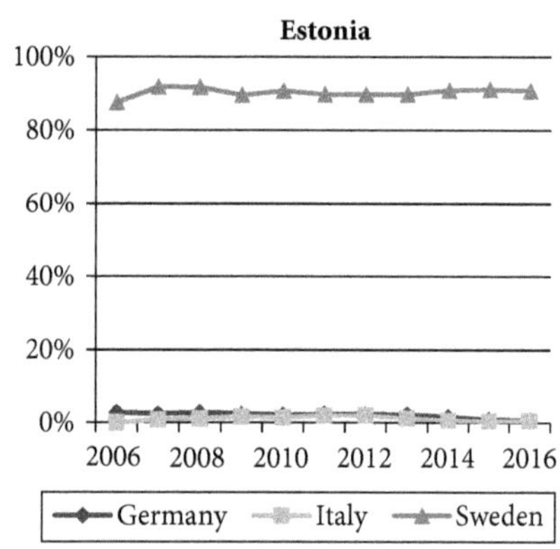

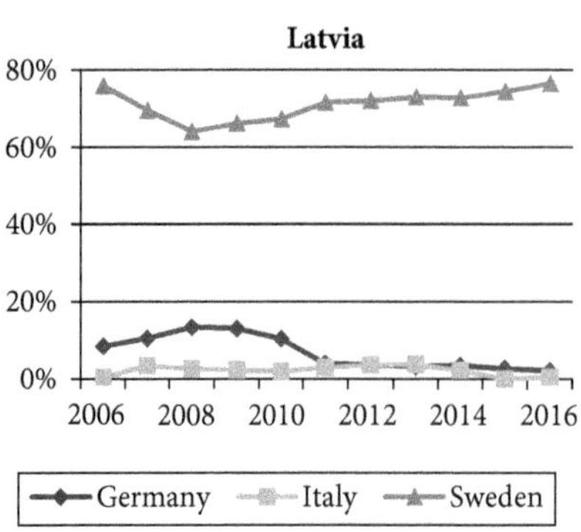

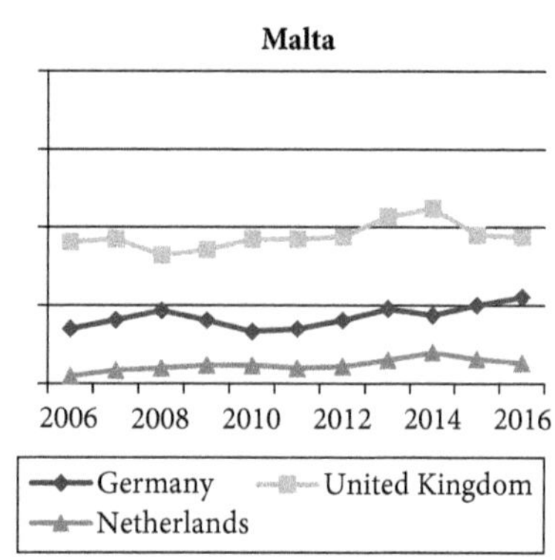

Group 8: Accession Countries

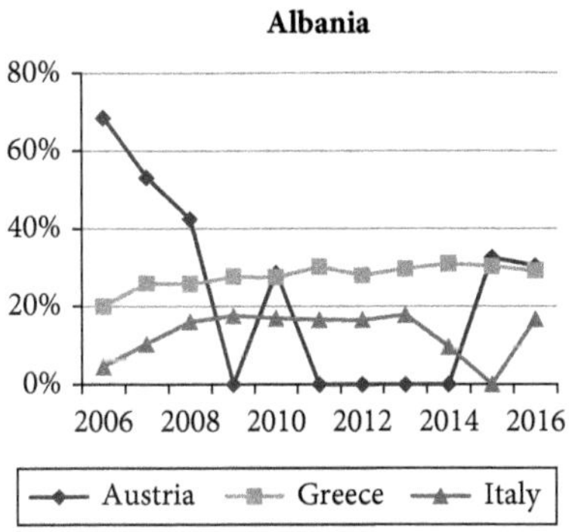

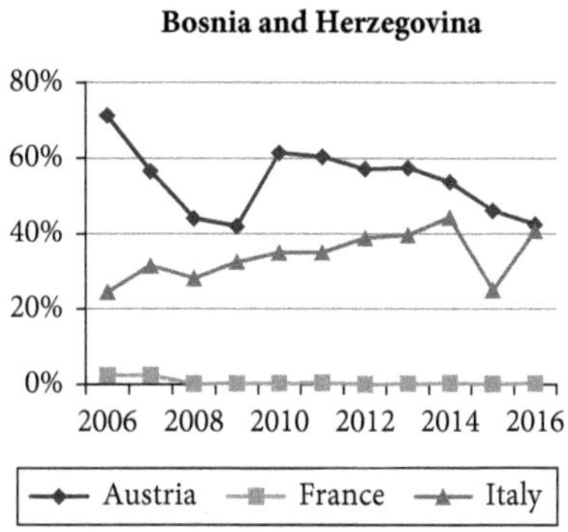

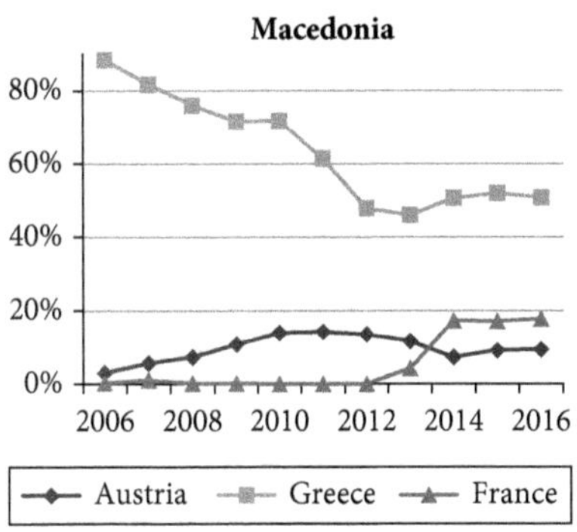

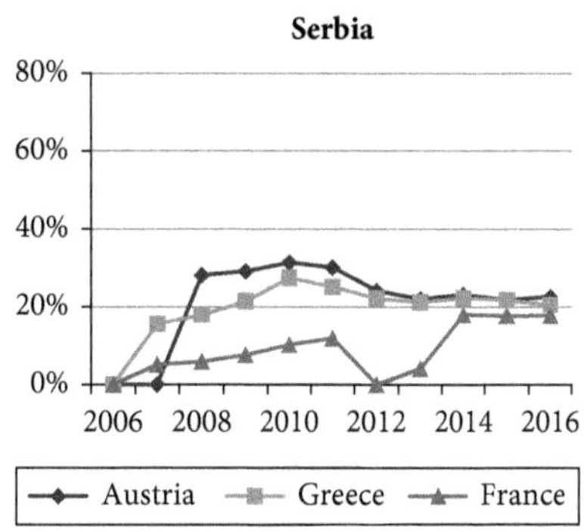

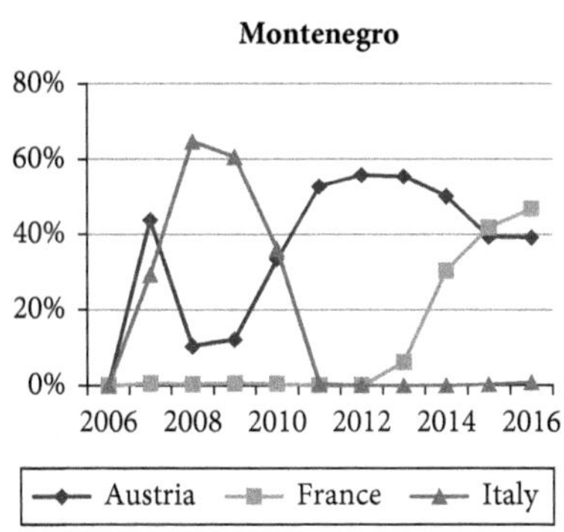

APPENDIX 4

Local Position Data

The source of this data is the BIS Statistics Explorer on International Banking which is compiled from data provided by various national authorities. The data has been analysed and amended by the Author. Any translation of this work is not an official BIS translation with regard to this data.

Group 1

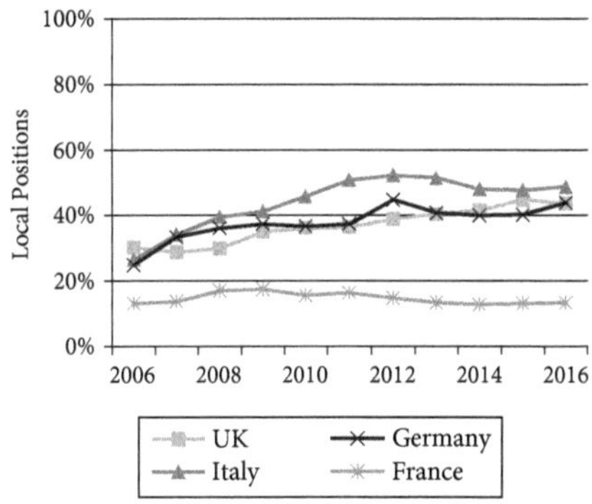

Group 2

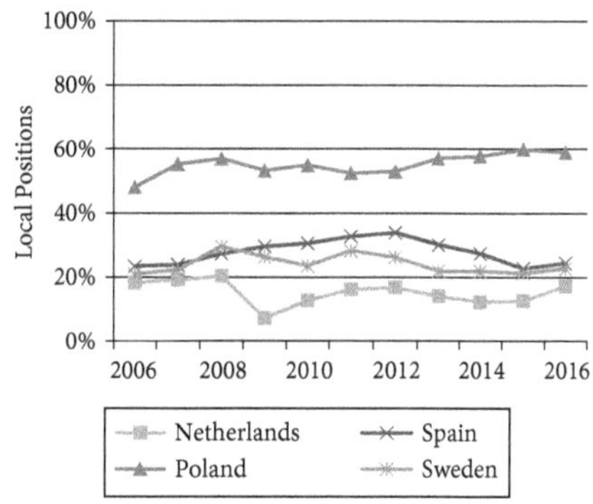

Group 3

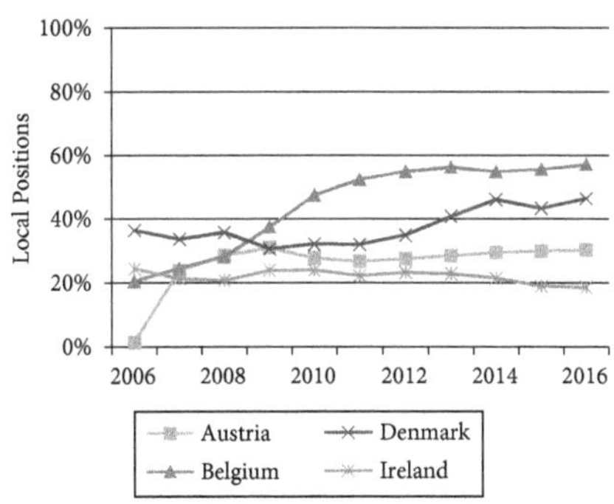

Group 4

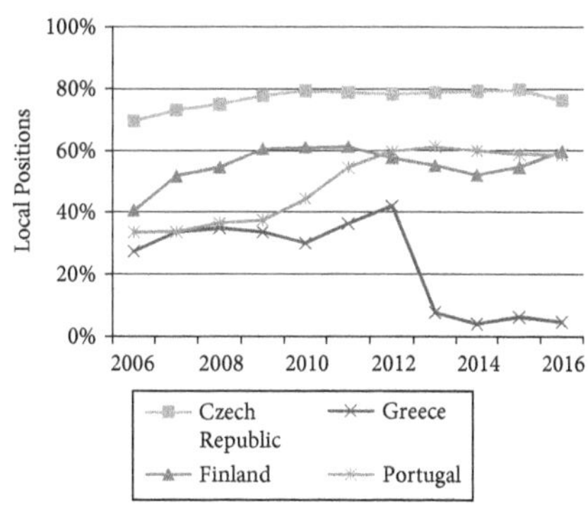

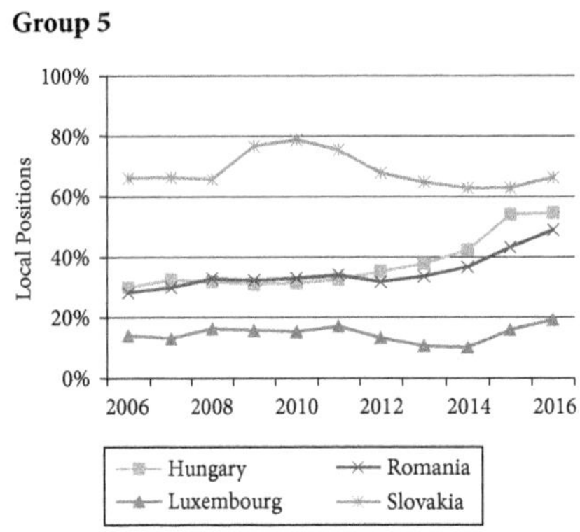
Group 5
100%
80%
60%
40%
20%
0%
Local Positions
2006
2008
2010
2012
2014
2016
Hungary
Romania
Luxembourg
Slovakia

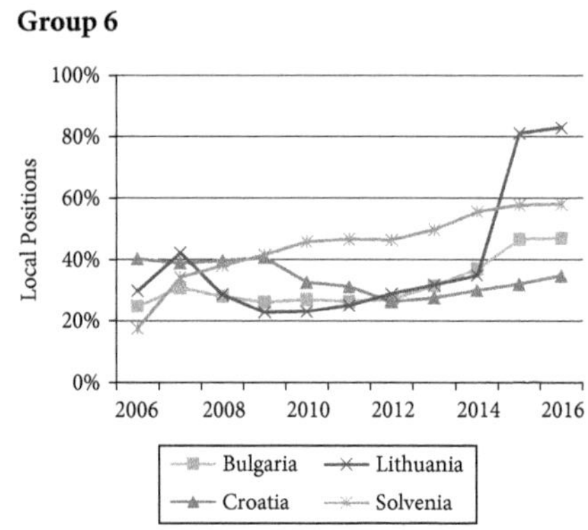
Group 6
100%
80%
60%
40%
20%
0%
Local Positions
2006
2008
2010
2012
2014
2016
Bulgaria
Lithuania
Croatia
Solvenia

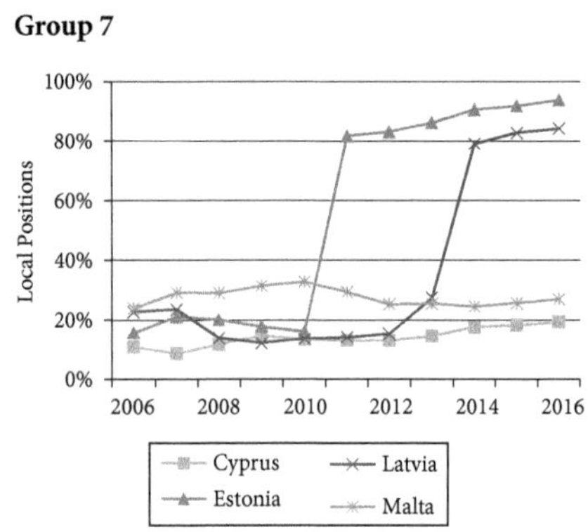
Group 7
100%
80%
60%
40%
20%
0%
Local Positions
2006
2008
2010
2012
2014
2016
Cyprus
Latvia
Estonia
Malta

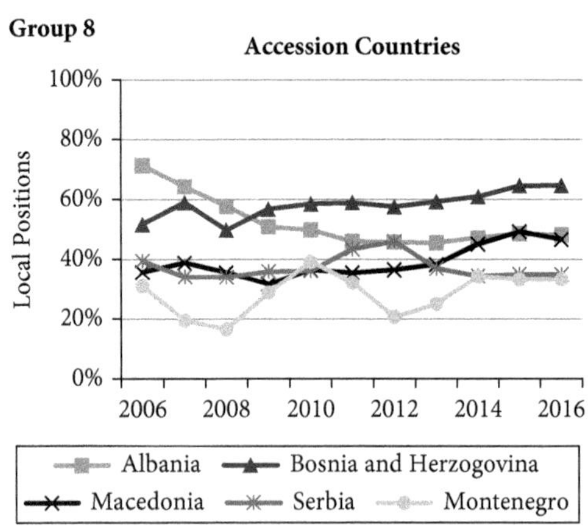
Group 8
Accession Countries
100%
80%
60%
40%
20%
0%
Local Positions
2006
2008
2010
2012
2014
2016
Albania
Bosnia and Herzegovina
Macedonia
Serbia
Montenegro

APPENDIX 5

Liabilities

The source of this data is the BIS Statistics Explorer on International Banking which is compiled from data provided by various national authorities. The data has been analysed and amended by the Author. Any translation of this work is not an official BIS translation with regard to this data.

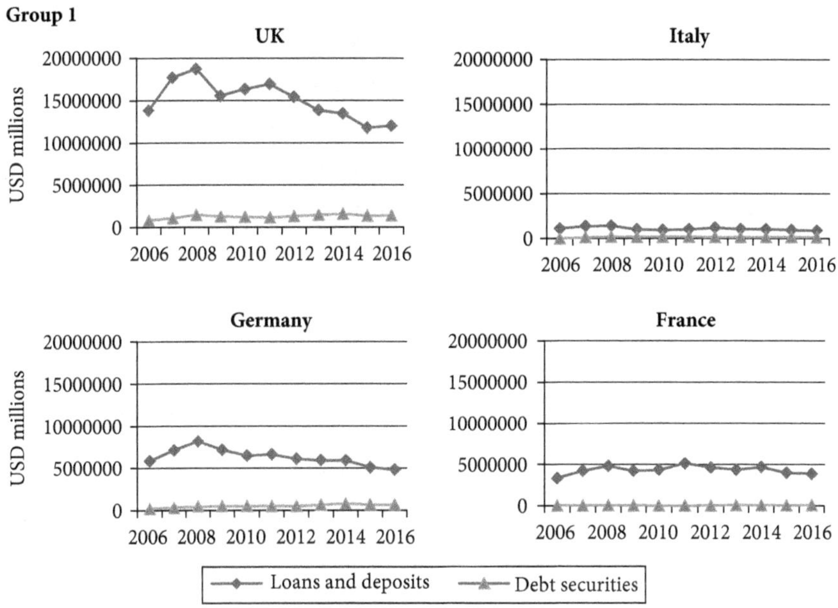

Group 2

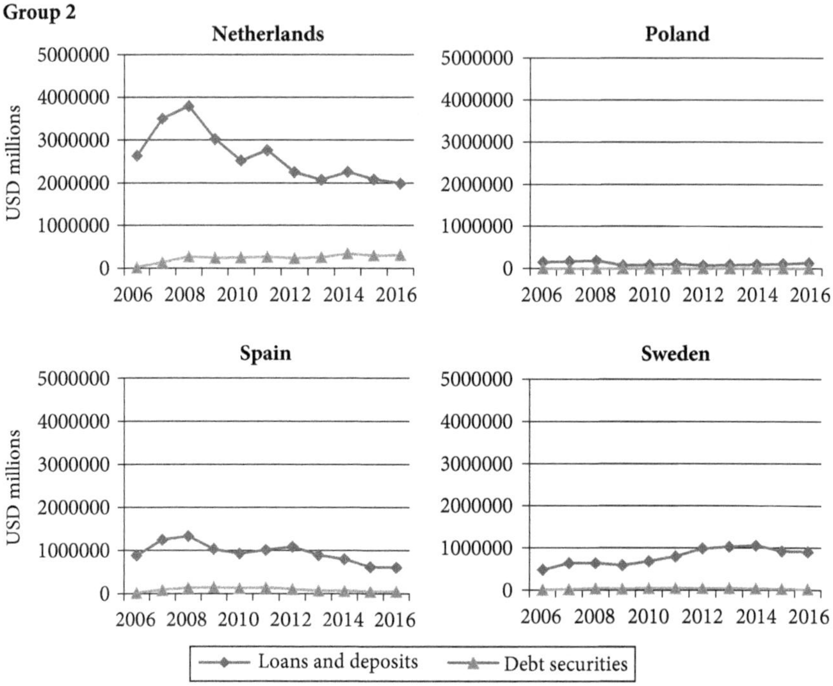

Group 3

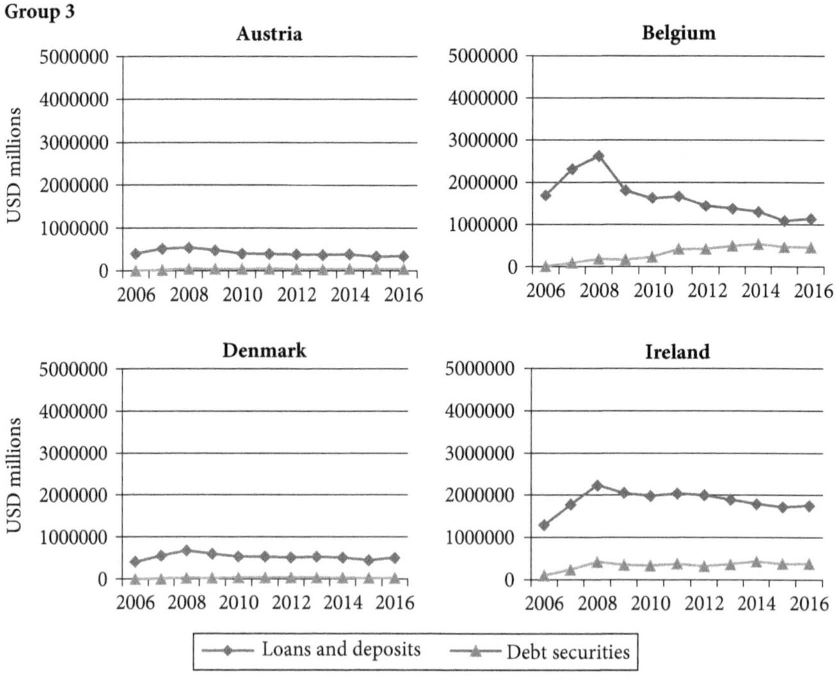

Group 4

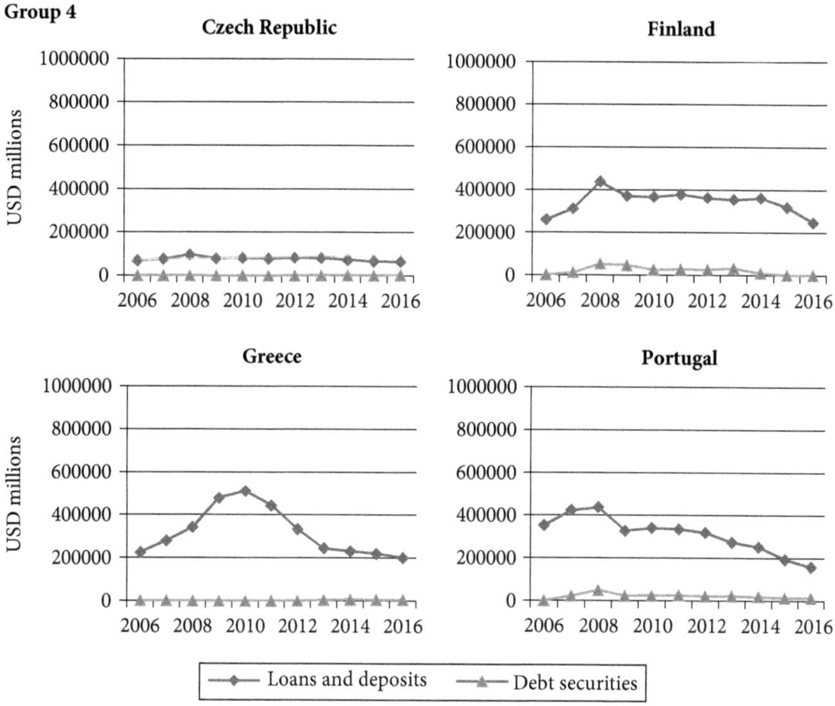

Group 5

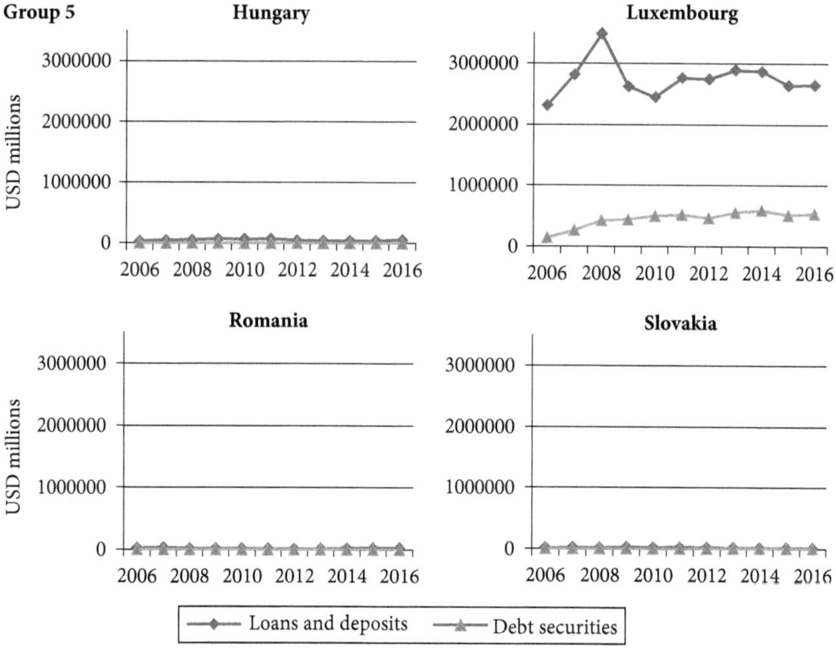

Group 6

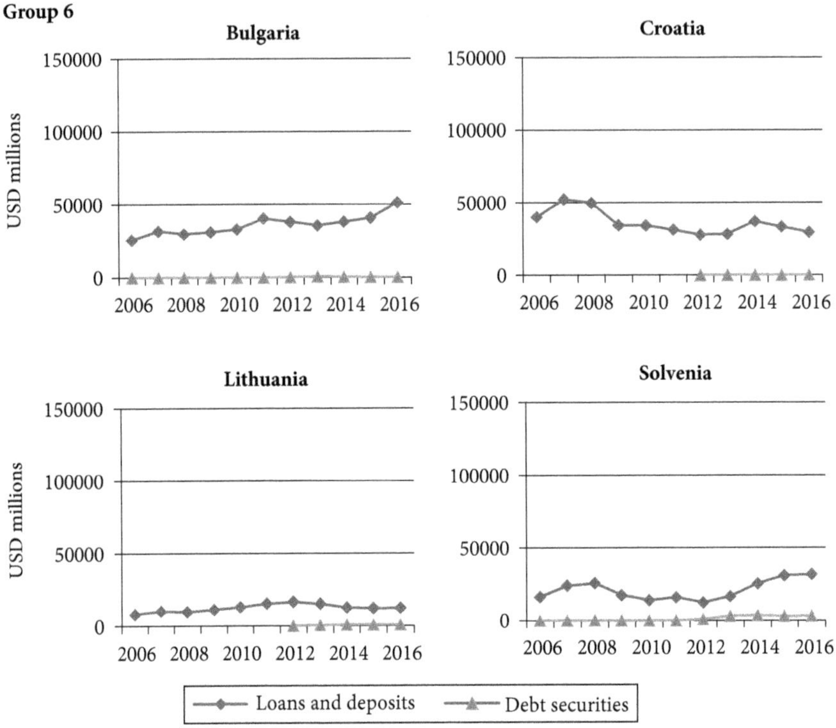

Group 7

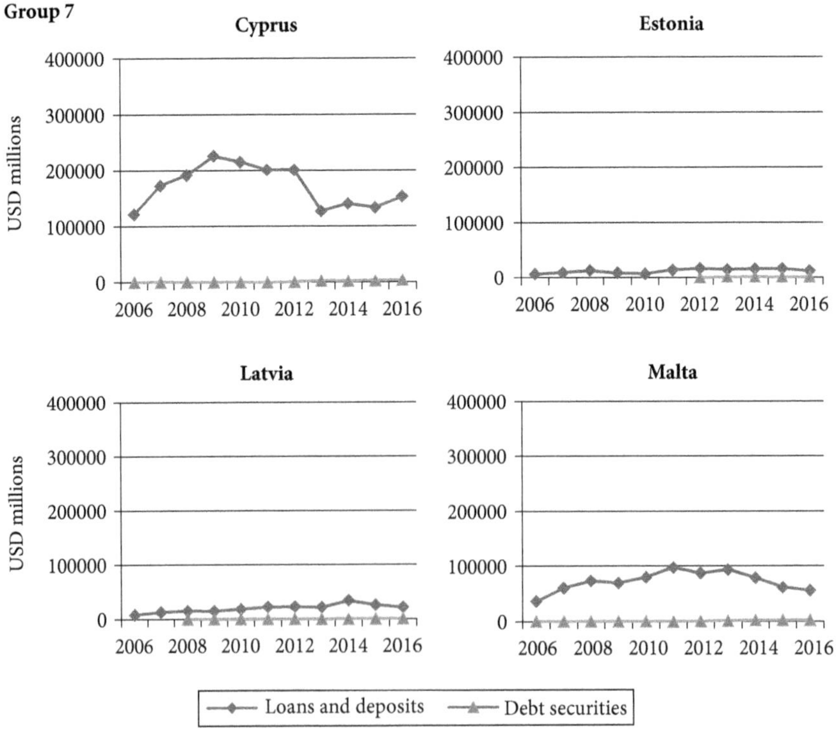

APPENDIX 6

Table Appendix

Table 6.1 ©ECB, Statistical Data Warehouse, except material added by the Author. This information may be obtained free of charge from https://www.ecb.europa.eu/home/html/index.en.html.

Country	Total Number of Credit Institutions in the Member State	EU branches and subsidiaries				Non-EU branches and subsidiaries				Total	
	Total Number of Banks	EU branches	% Branches from EU	EU subsidiaries	% Subsidiaries from EU	Non EU branches	% Branches from non-EU	Non EU subsidiaries	% Subsidiaries from non-EU	Total Foreign Credit Institutions	Percentage of foreign banks
Belgium	87	29	55%	12	63%	24	45%	7	37%	72	82.76%
Bulgaria	26	2	40%	11	85%	3	60%	2	15%	18	69.23%
Czech Republic	56	22	96%	16	94%	1	4%	1	6%	40	71.43%
Denmark	99	21	84%	1	100%	4	16%	0	0%	26	26.26%
Germany	1,599	86	81%	17	50%	20	19%	17	50%	140	8.76%
Estonia	36	6	86%	3	75%	1	14%	1	25%	11	30.56%
Ireland	335	33	94%	6	40%	2	6%	9	60%	50	14.93%
Greece	39	17	81%	2	100%	4	19%	0	0%	23	58.97%
Croatia	28	1	100%	11	85%	0	0%	2	15%	14	50.00%
Spain	204	77	95%	11	58%	4	5%	8	42%	100	49.02%
France	415	65	76%	46	53%	20	24%	40	47%	171	41.20%

(continued)

Table 6.1 Continued

Country	Total Number of Credit Institutions in the Member State	EU branches and subsidiaries				Non-EU branches and subsidiaries				Total	
	Total Number of Banks	EU branches	% Branches from EU	EU subsidiaries	% Subsidiaries from EU	Non EU branches	% Branches from non-EU	Non EU subsidiaries	% Subsidiaries from non-EU	Total Foreign Credit Institutions	Percentage of foreign banks
Italy	517	50	71%	18	90%	20	29%	2	10%	90	17.41%
Cyprus	34	7	32%	3	60%	15	68%	2	40%	27	79.41%
Latvia	52	5	100%	3	100%	0	0%	0	0%	8	15.38%
Lithuania	83	7	100%	4	100%	0	0%	0	0%	11	13.25%
Luxembourg	138	31	72%	49	55%	12	28%	40	45%	132	95.65%
Hungary	60	8	89%	11	85%	1	11%	2	15%	22	36.67%
Malta	25	1	33%	2	50%	2	67%	2	50%	7	28.00%
Netherlands	91	39	93%	2	20%	3	7%	8	80%	52	57.14%
Austria	570	25	96%	16	47%	1	4%	18	53%	60	10.53%
Poland	648	23	100%	17	81%	0	0%	4	19%	44	6.79%
Portugal	141	19	95%	6	75%	1	5%	2	25%	28	19.86%
Romania	37	7	100%	16	94%	0	0%	1	6%	24	64.86%
Slovenia	17	3	100%	6	100%	0	0%	0	0%	9	52.94%
Slovakia	27	15	100%	10	100%	0	0%	0	0%	25	92.59%
Finland	259	26	93%	4	100%	2	7%	0	0%	32	12.36%
Sweden	155	28	85%	4	80%	5	15%	1	20%	38	24.52%
United Kingdom	381	65	41%	14	16%	94	59%	76	84%	249	65.35%

Table 6.2 Author's analysis ©ECB, Statistical Data Warehouse, except material added by the Author. This information may be obtained free of charge from https://www.ecb.europa.eu/home/html/index.en.html.

Eurozone Member State	Total Assets			Assets held by Domestic Banks			Assets held by Foreign Subsidiaries and Branches		
EUR Billions			Percentage Change			Percentage Change			Percentage Change
	2008	2016		2008	2016		2008	2016	
Belgium	1420	1022	–28.0%	1,201	516	–57.0%	219	506	131.1%
Germany	10010	7084	–29.2%	9,005	6,583	–26.9%	1,005	501	–50.1%
Estonia	37	25	–32.4%	0	2	200.0%	37	23	–37.8%
Ireland	1621	439	–72.9%	538	227	–57.8%	1,083	212	–80.4%
Greece	458	233	–49.1%	358	227	–36.6%	100	6	–94.0%
Spain	3637	3591	–1.3%	3,287	3,450	5.0%	350	141	–59.7%
France	7150	7216	0.9%	6,874	6,853	–0.3%	276	363	31.5%
Italy	2758	2700	–2.1%	2522	2469	–2.1%	236	231	–2.1%
Cyprus	126	67	–46.8%	87	53	–39.1%	39	14	–64.1%
Latvia	33	30	–9.1%	11	15	36.4%	22	15	–31.8%
Lithuania	29	26	–10.3%	4	2	–50.0%	25	24	–4.0%
Luxembourg	1008	845	–16.2%	133	103	–22.6%	875	742	–15.2%
Malta	44	47	6.8%	8	19	137.5%	36	28	–22.2%
Netherlands	2995	2533	–15.4%	2874	2358	–18.0%	121	175	44.6%
Austria	1175	947	–19.4%	830	720	–13.3%	345	227	–34.2%
Portugal	477	386	–19.1%	376	299	–20.5%	101	87	–13.9%
Slovenia	53	41	–22.6%	38	22	–42.1%	15	19	26.7%
Slovakia	62	73	17.7%	2	12	500.0%	60	61	1.7%
Finland	386	537	39.1%	116	185	59.5%	270	352	30.4%
Euro area	33318	27910	–16.2%	28247	24183	–14.4%	5,071	3727	–26.5%

Table 6.3 European Bank Presence in Eastern European Member States and Accession Countries

Country	Raiffeisen	UniCredit	Societe Generale	Intesa	OTP	Erste	National Bank of Greece	Alpha Bank	KBC	Commerzbank	Swedbank	Skandinaviska Enskilda Banken (SEB)
Bulgaria	X	X	X		X				X			
Czech Republic	X	X	X			X			X	X		
Estonia											X	X
Croatia	X	X		X	X	X						
Hungary	X	X		X	X	X			X			
Lithuania											X	X
Latvia											X	X
Poland	X		X							X		
Romania	X	X	X		X	X	X	X				
Slovenia		X	X	X								
Slovakia	X	X		X	X				X			
Albania	X		X	X				X				
Bosnia and Herzegovina	X	X		X								
Kosovo	X											
Macedonia			X				X					
Montenegro			X		X	X						
Serbia	X	X	X	X	X	X						
Home Market	Austria	Italy	France	Italy	Hungary	Austria	Greece	Greece	Belgium	Germany	Sweden	Sweden
	11	9	9	7	7	6	2	2	4	2	3	3

Source: Orbis Bank Focus, Bureau van Dijk

Table 6.3a Top 5 Banks in Accession Countries: Domestic and Foreign

	Albania				
	Company name	**Quoted**	**Branch**	**Total assets th USD Last avail. yr**	**Home State of Global Ultimate Owner**
1.	BANKA KOMBETARE TREGTARE SH.A.	No	No	3,940,969	Albania
2.	CREDINS BANK SH.A	No	No	1,817,304	Albania
3	INTESA SANPAOLO BANK ALBANIA SH.A	No	No	1,589,220	Italy
4	BANKA SOCIETE GENERALE ALBANIA SH.A	No	No	732,845	France
5	Union Bank SH.A.	No	No	475,822	Albania
	Bosnia and Herzogovina				
	Company name	**Quoted**	**Branch**	**Total assets th USD Last avail. yr**	**Home State of Global Ultimate Owner**
1	ADDIKO BANK D.D. SARAJEVO	No	No	522,547	USA
2	UNICREDIT BANK DD	Yes	No	3,486,048	Italy
3	RAIFFEISENBANK D.D. BOSNIA and HERZEGOVINA	No	No	2,585,233	Austria
4	UNICREDIT BANK DD	Yes	No	2,613,474	Italy
5	INTESA SANPAOLO BANKA D.D. BOSNA I HERCEGOVINA	Yes	No	1,206,886	Italy
	Macedonia				
	Company name	**Quoted**	**Branch**	**Total assets th USD Last avail. yr**	**Home State of Global Ultimate Owner**
1	STOPANSKA BANKA A.D. SKOPJE	Yes	No	1,684,171	Greece
2	KOMERCIJALNA BANKA A.D. SKOPJE	Yes	No	2,130,685	Macedonia
3	NLB BANKA AD SKOPJE	Yes	No	1,484,296	Slovenia
4	HALK BANKA AD SKOPJE	Yes	No	878,095	Turkey
5	OHRIDSKA BANKA AD SKOPJE	Yes	No	736,817	France

(continued)

Table 6.3a Continued

	Serbia				
	Company name	**Quoted**	**Branch**	**Total assets th USD Last avail. yr**	**Home State of Global Ultimate Owner**
1	BANCA INTESA AD BEOGRAD	No	No	5,523,542	Italy
2	UNICREDIT BANK SERBIA JSC	No	No	4,335,839	Italy
3	KOMERCIJALNA BANKA A.D. BEOGRAD	Yes	No	4,271,109	Serbia
4	OTP BANK SERBIA AD NOVI SAD	No	No	2,097,547	Hungary
5	SOCIETE GENERALE BANKA SRBIJA AD	No	No	3,158,319	France
	Montenegro				
	Company name	**Quoted**	**Branch**	**Total assets th USD Last avail. yr**	**Home State of Global Ultimate Owner**
1	CRNOGORSKO KOMERCIJALNA BANKA AD PODGORICA	Yes	No	744,937	Hungary
2	SOCIETE GENERALE BANKA MONTENEGRO AD	Yes	No	579,711	France
3	NLB BANKA AD PODGORICA	Yes	No	551,422	Slovenia
4	HIPOTEKARNA BANKA AD PODGORICA	Yes	No	580,330	Montenegro
5	ATLAS BANK AD PODGORICA	Yes	No	307,462	Montenegro

Source: Orbis Bank Focus, Bureau van Dijk

APPENDIX 7

Table 7.1 Author's own analysis from Orbis Bank Focus

Country	Listed	Listed %	Non listed	Non listed %	Total banks
Austria	2	33.3%	4	66.7%	6
Belgium	2	28.6%	5	71.4%	7
Cyprus	2	50.0%	2	50.0%	4
Estonia	0	0.0%	3	100.0%	3
Finland	1	33.3%	2	66.7%	3
France	3	25.0%	9	75.0%	12
Germany	4	19.0%	17	81.0%	21
Greece	4	100.0%	0	0.0%	4
Ireland	2	40.0%	3	60.0%	5
Italy	9	75.0%	3	25.0%	12
Latvia	0	0.0%	4	100.0%	4
Lithuania	0	0.0%	3	100.0%	3
Luxembourg	0	0.0%	4	100.0%	4
Malta	2	66.7%	1	33.3%	3
Portugal	1	33.3%	2	66.7%	3
Slovakia	2	66.7%	1	33.3%	3
Slovenia	0	0.0%	3	100.0%	3
Spain	7	58.3%	5	41.7%	12
The Netherlands	2	33.3%	4	66.7%	6
	43	34.9%	75	65.1%	118

Source: Orbis Bank Focus, Bureau van Dijk.

Table 7.2 Author's own analysis from EBA and ECB Data

Member State	Total Number of Credit Institutions	Total Number of Significant Banks	Proportion of Significant Banks	Total Number of O-SIIs	Proportion of Total Banks Classified as O-SIIs
Belgium	87	7	8.05%	8	9.20%
Germany	1,599	21	1.31%	13	0.81%
Estonia	36	2	5.56%	4	11.11%
Ireland	335	5	1.49%	6	1.79%
Greece	39	4	10.26%	4	10.26%
Spain	204	14	6.86%	5	2.45%
France	415	13	3.13%	6	1.45%
Italy	517	14	2.71%	4	0.77%
Cyprus	34	4	11.76%	10	29.41%
Latvia	52	3	5.77%	6	11.54%
Lithuania	83	3	3.61%	4	4.82%
Luxembourg	138	4	2.90%	8	5.80%
Malta	25	3	12.00%	3	12.00%
Netherlands	91	6	6.59%	5	5.49%
Austria	570	8	1.40%	6	1.05%
Portugal	141	4	2.84%	6	4.26%
Slovenia	17	3	17.65%	7	41.18%
Slovakia	27	3	11.11%	5	18.52%
Finland	259	4	1.54%	3	1.16%

Source: EBA and ECB, 2018, <https://eba.europa.eu/risk-analysis-and-data/other-systemically-important-institutions-o-siis-/2018>.

Table 7.3 Author's own analysis from EBA Data

Member State	Total Number of Credit Institutions	Total Number of O-SIIs	Proportion of Total Number of Credit Institutions Classified as O-SIIs
Belgium	87	8	9.20%
Bulgaria	26	11	42.31%
Czech Republic	56	7	12.50%
Denmark	99	7	7.07%
Germany	1,599	13	0.81%
Estonia	36	4	11.11%
Ireland	335	6	1.79%
Greece	39	4	10.26%
Croatia	28	9	32.14%
Spain	204	5	2.45%
France	415	6	1.45%
Italy	517	4	0.77%
Cyprus	34	10	29.41%
Latvia	52	6	11.54%
Lithuania	83	4	4.82%
Luxembourg	138	8	5.80%
Hungary	60	8	13.33%
Malta	25	3	12.00%
Netherlands	91	5	5.49%
Austria	570	6	1.05%
Poland	648	12	1.85%
Portugal	141	6	4.26%
Romania	37	11	29.73%
Slovenia	17	7	41.18%
Slovakia	27	5	18.52%
Finland	259	3	1.16%
Sweden	155	4	2.58%
United Kingdom	381	16	4.20%

Source: EBA, 2018.

APPENDIX 8

The author's own analysis based on data from The World Bank, bank non-performing loans to total gross loans data, <https://data.worldbank.org/indicator/fb.ast.nper.zs>.

Group 1

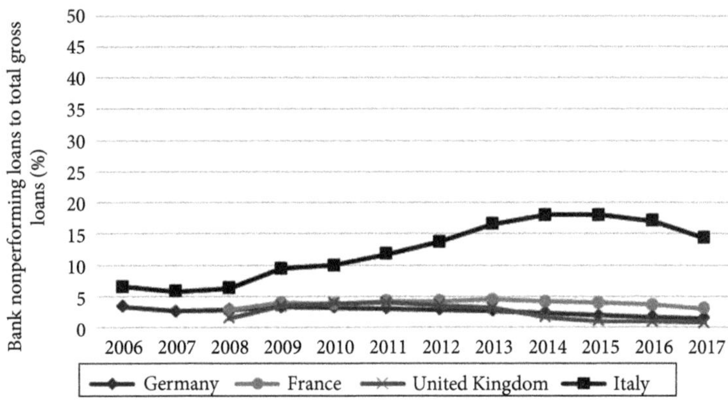

Group 2

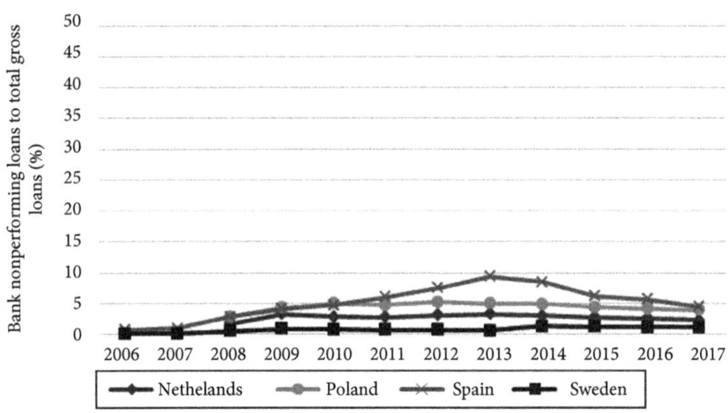

Group 3

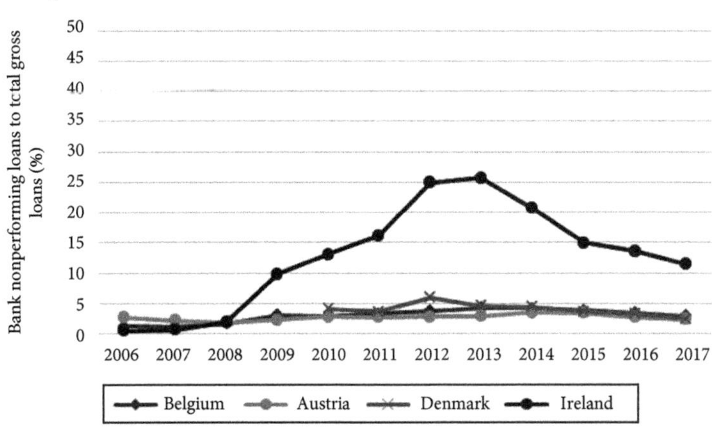

Group 4

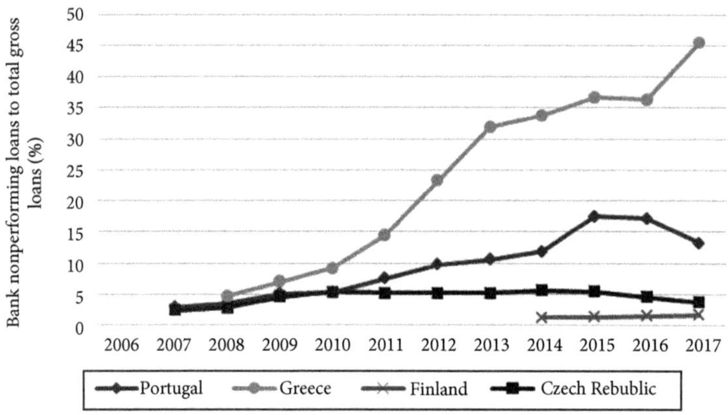

Group 5

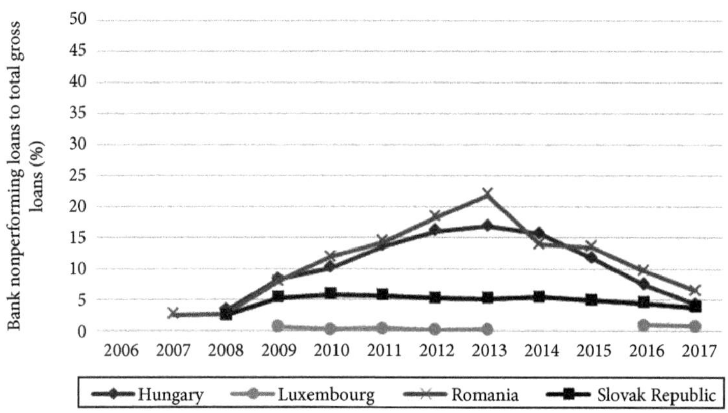

Group 6

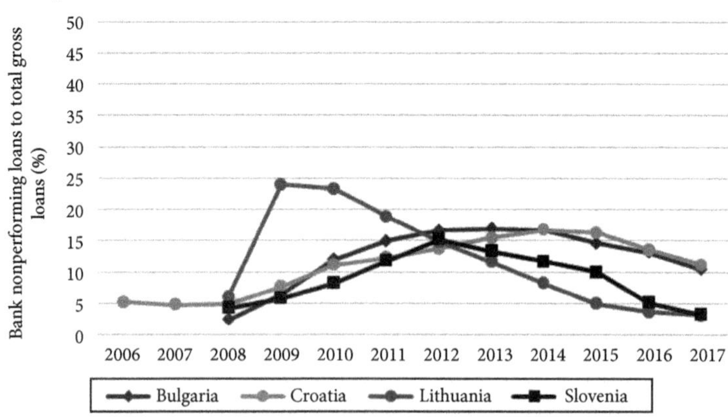

Group 7

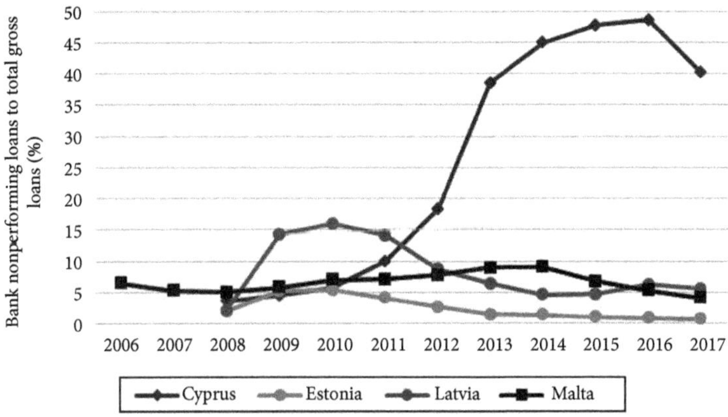

Group 8

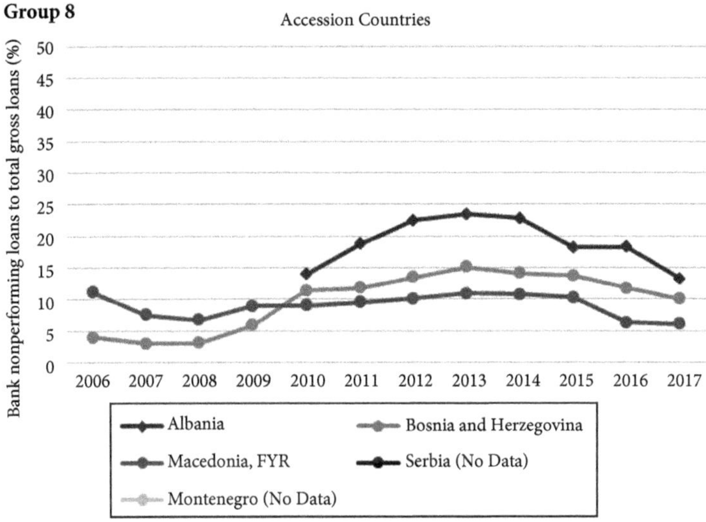

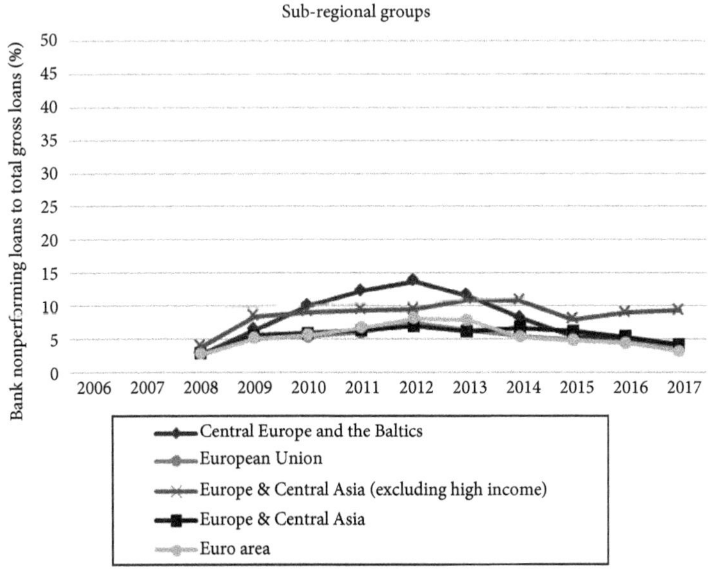

APPENDIX 9

Table 9.1 DGS Covered Deposits and Available Funds 2017

	Covered Deposits	Available Financial Means	Current % Level for DGS	Target level for DGS	Percentage Target Level Shortfall or Surplus +/-
Group 1					
Germany	686,439,260	2,976,440	0.43%	0.80%	–0.37%
France	1,113,415,000	3,649,500	0.33%	0.50%	–0.17%
United Kingdom	1,145,000,000	7,400,000	0.65%	0.80%	–0.15%
Italy	592,081,290	951,640	0.16%	0.80%	–0.64%
Group 2					
Netherlands	485,442,000	915,000	0.19%	0.80%	–0.61%
Poland	721,025,921	12,338,981	1.71%	2.60%	–0.89%
Spain	707,092,900	1,881,000	0.27%	0.80%	–0.53%
Sweden	2,279,500,000	40,084,000	1.76%	0.80%	+0.96%
Group 3					
Belgium	287,278,457	3,356,373	1.17%	0.80%	+0.37%
Austria	67,934,000	156,000	0.23%	0.80%	–0.57%
Denmark	726,341,000	8,816,000	1.21%	0.80%	+0.41%
Ireland	98,968,000	154,000	0.16%	0.80%	–0.64%
Group 4					
Portugal	130,129,398	1,546,021	1.19%	1.19%	–0.00%
Greece	98,831,819	1,430,269	1.45%	1.39%	+0.06%
Finland	51,105,530	1,073,180	2.10%	0.80%	+1.30%
Czech Republic	2,267,438,000	30,284,000	1.34%	0.80%	+0.54%
Group 5					
Hungary	9,256,726,030	32,474,000	0.35%	0.80%	–0.45%
Luxembourg	30,398,100	154,000	0.51%	1.60%	–1.09%
Romania	172,671,682	5,472,517	3.17%	3.43%	–0.26%
Slovak Republic	32,391,897	205,387	0.63%	0.80%	–0.17%
Group 6					
Bulgaria	52,991,480	507,710	0.96%	1.00%	–0.04%
Croatia	185,419,000	4,644,000	2.50%	2.50%	+0.00%
Lithuania	13,036,840	55,070	0.42%	0.80%	–0.38%
Slovenia	17,898,094	32,961	0.18%	0.80%	–0.62%

(continued)

Table 9.1 Continued

	Covered Deposits	Available Financial Means	Current % Level for DGS	Target level for DGS	Percentage Target Level Shortfall or Surplus +/-
Group 7					
Cyprus	16,803,000	65,600	0.39%	0.80%	-0.41%
Estonia	8,457,966	223,120	2.64%	2.50%	+0.14%
Latvia	8,435,000	154,000	1.83%	0.80%	+1.03%
Malta	11,046,313	111,185	1.01%	1.30%	-0.29%

Source: Author's analysis based on EBA Deposit Guarantee Schemes Data, Aggregated DGSD data: <https://eba.europa.eu/regulation-and-policy/recovery-and-resolution/deposit-guarantee-schemes-data>; see also <https://eba.europa.eu/regulation-and-policy/recovery-and-resolution/dgs-data/additional-information-on-dgs-data>.

Table 9.2 Liquidation Cases with DGS Payouts and Other DGS Interventions—Author's analysis based on EBA Notifications EBA Notifications on resolution cases and use of DGS funds, https://eba.europa.eu/regulation-and-policy/recovery-and-resolution/notifications-on-resolution-cases-and-use-of-dgs-funds.

Member State	Name of Institution	Reason for Closure	Administrative authority or court?	Deposits Unavailable	Appointment of Administrator	No. of Depositor Payouts	Size of DGS Payout	Reimbursement Period	Use of a payout agent to reimburse depositors
Croatia	Tesla štedna banka d.d.	Balance Sheet Insolvent	Supervisory Authority	21st February 2018	Appointment of Administrator	7	EUR 1,014	26th February 2018 (3rd Working Day) - 20th February 2021	Yes
	Banka splitsko - dalmatinska d.d.	Withdrawal of the licence Balance Sheet Insolvent	Supervisory Authority	25th May 2016	Appointment of Administrator	8212	EUR 50.74m	June 10th 2016 (10th Working day) -9th June 2019	Yes
Estonia	Versobank AS	Revocation of authorisation[1]	Supervisory Authority	26th March 2018		3606	EUR 93.4m	5 April 2018-20 April 2021	Yes
Lithuania	Taupkasė credit union	Revocation of Authorisation (breach of capital requirements)	Supervisory Authority (initiated bankruptcy proceedings)	13th February 2018	Moratorium Appointment of Administrator	2572	EUR 18.68m	26th February 2018 (8th working day) - 13th February 2023	Yes
	Centro Taupomoji Kasa Credit Union	Revocation of Authorisation (breach of capital requirements and large exposure)	Supervisory Authority (initiated bankruptcy proceedings)	16th January 2018	Moratorium Appointment of Administrator	1000	EUR 10.56m	6th February 2018 (15th Working Day) January 16th 2023	Yes
	Vilniaus Kreditas Credit Union	Insolvent –Balance Sheet Insolvent and breach of capital requirements	Supervisory Authority (initiated bankruptcy proceedings)	10th November 2017	Moratorium Appointment of Administrator	1247	EUR 20.4m	November 28th 2017 (12th Working day) November 10th 2022	Yes

(continued)

[1] National Competent Authority asks the ECB to revoke authorization CRD IV Withdrawal of Authorisation Art. 18(e) and 18(f) Other reasons for withdrawal and those referred to in Art. 67(1) primarily reporting and governance failures.

Table 9.2 Continued

Member State	Name of Institution	Reason for Closure	Administrative authority or court?	Deposits Unavailable	Appointment of Administrator	No. of Depositor Payouts	Size of DGS Payout	Reimbursement Period	Use of a payout agent to reimburse depositors
	Baltija Credit Union	Insolvent – Balance Sheet Insolvency Financial Crime	Supervisory Authority (initiated bankruptcy proceedings)	25th September 2017	Moratorium Appointment of Administrator	967 +58 (additional data)	EUR 8.61m EUR 2.9m	6th October 2017 (9th Working day) 25th September 2022 19th October 2017 (18th Working day)	Yes
	Namų Credit Union	Insolvent – Balance Sheet Insolvency Financial Crime	Supervisory Authority (initiated bankruptcy proceedings)	25th September 2017	Moratorium Appointment of Administrator	319 +10	EUR 1.09m EUR 0.29m	6th October 2017 (9th Working day) 25th September 2022	Yes
	Credit Union "Žemaitijos Iždas"	Insolvent – Balance Sheet Insolvency	Supervisory Authority (initiated bankruptcy proceedings)	7th March 2017	Moratorium Appointment of Administrator	189	EUR 1.63m	20th March 2017 (8th Working day) 7th March 2022	Yes
	Credit Union "Pajūrio"	Insolvent – Balance Sheet Insolvency		17th March 2017	Moratorium Appointment of Administrator	297	EUR 2.15m	28th March 2017 (6th Working day) 17th March 2022	Yes
Luxembourg	ABLV Bank Luxembourg S.A.[2]	Parent Entity placed in to Liquidation Unavailability of deposits	Supervisory Authority and judicial authority	24th February 2018	Moratorium Administrator Appointed	Not provided	EUR 14m	After 7 working days (by bank transfer)	No

[2] ECB supervisor and SRB resolution authority.

Malta	Nemea Bank plc	Withdrawal of Authorisation (Non-compliance with regulatory requirements	Supervisory Authority	30th March 2017	Moratorium Administrator Appointed (limit on withdrawals €250 to €2,500 per depositor per day	Not provided		30th March 2017 (20 working days)	No
Poland	SKOK Wybrzeze credit union	Insolvent Balance Sheet Insolvent	Supervisory Authority and the courts	15th September 2017	Supervisor filed for Bankruptcy	7696	EUR 28.2	25th September 2017- 14th September 2022	Yes
	NIKE Credit Union	Insolvent Balance Sheet Insolvent	Supervisory Authority and the courts	June 2nd 2017	Supervisor filed for Bankruptcy	10439	EUR 27.3	12th June – 11th August 2017- 1st June 2022	Yes
	Twoja Spółdzielcza Kasa Oszczędnościowo-Kredytowa (Twoja Credit Union)	Insolvent Balance sheet insolvent	Supervisory Authority and the courts	12th May 2017	Supervisor filed for Bankruptcy	14019	EUR 39.3m	22nd May – 21 July 2017 – 11th May 2022	Yes
	Wielkopolska Spółdzielcza Kasa Oszczędnościowo-Kredytowa (Wielkopolska Credit Union)	Insolvent Balance sheet insolvent	Supervisory Authority and the courts	17th February 2017	Supervisor filed for Bankruptcy	39575	EUR 66.1m	13th February 2017 (6th Working day) 14th April 2017 – 2nd February 2022	Yes
	Spółdzielczy w Nadarzynie (Cooperative Bank in Nadarzyn)	Insolvent Cash flow insolvent	Supervisory Authority and the courts	24th October 2016	Supervisor filed for Bankruptcy	5595	EUR 33.7m	2nd November 2016 (6th Working day) 30th December 2016 - 23 October 2021	Yes

Index

Administrative Board of Review
  role of, 2.28–3.30
Adverse selection
  non-performing loans, 4.2, 4.4, 4.16, 4.39, 4.41, 4.44
Assets
  asset management corporations, 4.41–4.45
  asset quality reviews, 4.23–4.24
  asset separation tool, 5.65
  foreign and domestic banks, proportion of, 1.41–1.42
  total assets, Appendix 6.2
Available funds, Appendix 9.1

Bail-in tool
  Common Equity Tier 1 capital, 5.71
  generally, 5.66–5.67
  liabilities eligible for bail-in, 5.69–5.70
  minimum threshold, 5.76
  option of 'first resort', 5.74–5.75
  prepositioning, 5.77
  purpose of, 5.68
  registers, amendment of, 5.73
  share listings, amendment of, 5.73
  shareholder treatment, 5.72
Bank insolvency
  branches, 6.10–6.18
  consistency in approach to, 6.3
  creditors' interests see depositor preference
  critical functions, continuity of, 6.1
  cross-border insolvency
    ABLV Bank AS, 6.31–6.39
    Banca Populare di Vicenza, 6.40–6.44
    cross-border proceedings, 6.29
    judicial liquidation procedure, 6.36
    public interest, 6.42–6.44
    suspension of payments, 6.36
    unequal treatment of creditors, 6.39
    Veneto Banca, 6.40–6.44
  deposit guarantee scheme
    cross-border challenges, 6.69–6.76
    funding, 6.55–6.58
    liquidation cases with DSG payouts, 6.59–6.68
    other interventions, 6.59–6.68
    role of, 6.52–6.54, 6.69–6.76
    third country perspective, 6.77–6.78
    total coverage level, 6.55–6.58
  deposit protection issues, 6.79–6.81
  depositor preference
    deposit guarantee scheme, and, 6.48–6.49
    deposit insurance, and, 6.47
    forms of, 6.50
    hierarchy of creditors' claims, 6.45
    IADI Core Principles, 6.50–6.51
    introduction, 6.45
  financial stability, endangering, 6.1, 6.5
  home and host dilemma, 6.9
  insolvency proceedings
    cross-border proceedings, 6.29
    moratoria, 6.26–6.28, 6.30
    negative net worth, 6.24
    rationale of, 6.25
    threshold to trigger, 6.24
  international soft law instruments, 6.79–6.81
  introduction, 6.1–6.9
  moratoria
    large institutions, 6.30
    right to seek, 6.26
    small institutions, 6.30
    suspension of payments and delivery obligations, 6.27
    timeframe, 6.28
  normal insolvency procedure, 6.19–6.23
  principal issues, 6.82–6.83
  public interest, 6.2
  Reorganisation and Winding Up Directive
    branches, 6.12
    burden-sharing measures, 6.14
    contractual rights, 6.18
    forced winding-up, 6.15
    home Member State responsibilities, 6.11–6.12
    introduction of, 6.10
    netting agreements, 6.18
    reorganization measures, 6.13
    rights in rem, 6.18
    scope of, 6.11
    set-off against credit institutions, 6.18
    subsidiaries, 6.17
    third country banks, 6.16
    voluntary winding-up, 6.15
  subsidiaries, 6.10–6.18
  winding-up, meaning of, 6.22
Bank resolution
  asset separation tool, 5.65
  bail-in tool
    Common Equity Tier 1 capital, 5.71
    generally, 5.66–5.67
    liabilities eligible for bail-in, 5.69–5.70
    minimum threshold, 5.76
    option of 'first resort', 5.74–5.75
    prepositioning, 5.77
    purpose of, 5.68
    registers, amendment of, 5.73
    share listings, amendment of, 5.73
    shareholder treatment, 5.72
  branches, 5.7–5.8
  bridge institution tool
    Bayerische Landesbank v Hypo Alpe Adria Bank International AG, 5.63–5.64

Bank resolution (*cont.*)
generally, 5.57–5.58
Goldman Sachs International v Novo Banco SA, 5.59–5.62
capital requirements
compliance with, 5.12
going concern scenario, 5.11
outward facing nature, 5.11
cross-border group resolution, 5.84–5.87
early intervention
assessing whether bank failing or likely to fail, 5.44–5.47
cooperation between supervisor and resolution authority, 5.39
cross-border dimension, 5.51
infringement indicators, 5.40
no-creditor-worse-off, 5.49–5.50
notification of decision for, 5.43
shadow resolutions, 5.42
temporary administrator, 5.41
valuation of assets and liabilities, 5.48
home bias for significant subsidiaries, 5.104–5.107
international cooperation agreements, 5.100–5.103
international soft law instruments, 5.108–5.109
introduction, 5.1–5.4
Member State resolution decisions
Denmark, 5.82
generally, 5.78
Greece, 5.83
Hungary, 5.79
Italy, 5.80
Portugal, 5.81
minimum required eligible liabilities
close cooperation, need for, 5.14
deposit guarantees scheme, 5.17
global systemically important institutions (G-SII), 5.19
gone concern scenario, 5.11
impact of compliance with, 5.11
insolvency, 5.15
introduction of, 5.10
inward facing nature, 5.11
loss absorbing capacity, 5.10–5.13
mandates of supervision and resolution, 5.19
other systemically important institutions (O-SII), 5.19
resolution authority's decision on amount of loss absorbance, 5.15–5.16
resolution fund, 5.17
resolution or insolvency, 5.20
stress testing, 5.18
multiple point of entry approach, 5.21–5.27
principal issues, 5.110
resolution colleges
benefits of, 5.35
cross- border groups, 5.30
group resolution authority, role of, 5.34
information sharing, 5.31
interests of other hosts, 5.37
introduction, 5.28
joint decision-making, 5.36
management of, 5.34
membership, 5.29
rationale, 5.29
resolution coordination, 5.31–5.33
technical standards, 5.38
resolution objectives, conditions and principles, 5.52–5.53
resolvability, assessment of, 5.9–5.10
responsibilities of the home and host resolution authorities
Banking Recovery and Resolution Directive, 5.5
branches and subsidiaries, 5.7–5.8
crisis management, 5.7
information sharing, 5.6
recovery plans, responsibility for, 5.6
sale of business tool, 5.54–5.56
single point of entry approach, 5.21–5.27
subsidiaries, 5.7–5.8
third countries, relations with
branches in third country, 5.95
cross-border resolution regime, lack of, 5.98
implications of lack of coordination, 5.99
introduction, 5.88–5.89
lack of information sharing, 5.94
MPE approach, 5.92
non-binding cooperation agreements, 5.96–5.97
parent companies in third country, 5.90
public interest, acting in, 5.93
third-country cooperation and coordination, 5.91
Banking Union
opting in or out of, 2.4–2.6
overview, I. 1–I.4
third pillar, 7.53–7.54
Branches, foreign
assets held by, Appendix 6.2
bank insolvency, 6.10–6.18
foreign and domestic banks, proportion of, 1.43
home or host country control
asset levels, 3.8
authorisation, 3.3
determination of, 3.5–3.6
general good principle, application of, 3.7
home country control, 3.4
Significant Branch Guidelines, 3.9
non-performing loans, 4.24
number of, Appendix 6.1
resolution
home and host relationship, 5.7–5.8
recovery and resolution plans, 5.6
Bridge institution tool
Bayerische Landesbank v Hypo Alpe Adria Bank International AG, 5.63–5.64
generally, 5.57–5.58
Goldman Sachs International v Novo Banco SA, 5.59–5.62

Capital buffers
international soft law instruments, 3.77
stress testing, and, 3.60

Capital requirements
Basel III requirements, 3.77
breach of, 6.40
determination of, 2.43
early intervention, and, 5.39, 5.42
implications of movement at group level for host authorities, 3.21
joint decisions, improvements on, 3.32
liquidity assistance, 7.34
loss absorbing, and, 5.10–5.15
non performing loans
approach to losses, 4.35
loan loss provisioning, and, 4.3
phase-in period for IFRS 9, 4.37
small banks, 4.50
prudential supervision, meaning of, 3.11
recapitalization, 6.14
'significant subsidiary', 3.66
Centralised decision making
aims of, 2.1
Close cooperation
Bulgaria's application for, 2.47–2.51
introduction, 2.1–2.3
opting in or out of Banking Union, 2.4–2.6
principle issues, 2.52
Single Resolution Mechanism, 2.32–2.38
Single Supervisory Mechanism, 2.7–2.21
Consolidated supervision
capital risk requirements, 3.32
foreign subsidiaries, 3.34–3.35
information sharing, 3.31, 3.35, 3.70, 3.76
introduction, 3.2, 3.30
joint decisions on prudential requirements, 3.36
meaning of home and host Member State, 3.33
purpose of, 3.32
supervisory cooperation, 3.31, 3.33
third country perspective
assessing equivalence, 3.69
consistency of approach, 3.72–3.73
incentivising compliance, 3.71
information sharing, 3.70, 3.76
introduction, 3.2
Memorandum of Cooperation, 3.74–3.75
Consolidated supervisor
capital requirements, determination of, 2.43
close cooperation, advantages of, 2.5
ECB as, 2.13, 2.17–2.18
group recovery plans, 2.44
host supervisor, relationship with, 2.20
joint supervisory teams, relationship with, 2.20
national competent authorities as, 2.17–2.18
Convergence criteria
opting in or out of Banking Union, 2.4
Cooperation and coordination agreements
deposit guarantee scheme, and, 6.69–6.73
supervisory colleges, 3.49
Counter-cyclical buffers
stress testing, and, 3.60
Country exposure
percentage, Appendix 3
USD, Appendix 2
Court of Justice of the European Union
review of ECB decisions, 2.25
Crisis management and containment
ascertaining quality of arrangements, 2.11
asset management corporations, 4.42, 4.45
branches, 5.7, 6.12, 6.78
close cooperation, and, 2.9, 2.11, 2.16
cooperation and coordinate arrangements, 3.44–3.45, 5.3
Crisis Management Group, 3.79
cross-border decision-making, 3.62
European Central Bank, role of, 7.3
European Deposit Insurance Scheme
aims, 7.55
deposit guarantee scheme, importance of, 7.56
high coverage levels, 7.52
introduction, 7.51
raising private finance, system of, 7.57
separating of resolution and insolvency-liquidation, and, 7.58
third pillar of Banking Union, 7.53–7.54
European Stability Mechanism
aims of, 7.60
alignment with national interests, 7.69
assessment of request for assistance, 7.63
assistance available, 7.64
direct recapitalization, 7.66
establishment of, 7.59–7.60
fiscal burden of bank, facilities to address, 7.65
risk-sharing, 7.67
shareholder contribution, 7.61
subscribed capital, 7.62
systemic crisis, likelihood of, 7.68
voting procedure, 7.61
extraordinary financial support, 7.3–7.4
information sharing, 2.16
international cooperation agreements, 5.100, 5.103
international soft law guidance on temporary public funding
cross-border cooperation, 7.73
Financial Stability Board guidelines, 7.71
home and host relationship, 7.74
importance of, 7.70
private funds, use of, 7.72
introduction, 7.1–7.2
legal form, and, 1.36
liquidation aid, 7.28–7.32
liquidity assistance
centralizing, 7.33–7.37
emergency, 7.4, 7.13–7.21
precautionary recapitalization, 7.5–7.12
principal issues, 7.75
resolution colleges, 5.29, 5.33
significant subsidiaries, 3.67
single resolution fund
administration of, 7.40
aims and objectives, 7.41

Crisis management and containment (*cont.*)
appeal against contribution, 7.48
contributions, calculation of, 7.43–7.47
cross-border bank resolution, 7.50
home and host relationship, 7.49
introduction, 7.38
minimizing agency problems, 7.39
underfunding, 7.36
utilization of funds by resolution authority, 7.42
State aid, 7.22–7.27
subsidiaries, 5.7
third country relations, 5.88–5.89, 5.94
Cross-border insolvency
ABLV Bank AS, 6.31–6.39
Banca Populare di Vicenza, 6.40–6.44
cross-border proceedings, 6.29
judicial liquidation procedure, 6.36
public interest, 6.42–6.44
suspension of payments, 6.36
unequal treatment of creditors, 6.39
Veneto Banca, 6.40–6.44

Decision-making
centralised decision making, aims of, 2.1
consolidated supervision, 3.36
European Central Bank
Administrative Board of Review, 2.28–3.30
Court of Justice, review by, 2.25
Governing Council, 2.24–2.27
internal verification, 2.27
Mediation Panel, 2.23, 2.26
non-objection procedure, 2.23
single resolution mechanism, 2.31
Supervisory Board of the SSM, 2.23–2.27
joint decisions
consolidated supervision, 3.36
European Banking Authority, 2.40–2.44
resolution colleges, 5.36
Deposit guarantee schemes
cooperation agreements, 6.69–6.73
covered deposits, Appendix 9.1
depositor preference, and, 6.48–6.49
funding
current funding levels, 6.58, Appendix 9
introduction, 6.55–6.56
target level fund, 6.57–6.58, Appendix 9
lending between schemes, 6.74–6.76
minimum required eligible liabilities, 5.17
payouts
determination date, 6.65
generally, 6.59–6.61
number of depositors paid, 6.62
payment methods, 6.67–6.68
reimbursement period, 6.63–6.65
size of payout, 6.62
statistics, Appendix 9.2
techniques used to execute reimbursement, 6.66–6.67
resolvability, assessment of, 5.11
role of
cross-border challenges, 6.69–6.76
generally, 6.52–6.54
third country perspective, 6.77–6.78
timeframe for payments, 6.63–6.64
Deposit insurance
see also **European Deposit Insurance Scheme**
bank insolvency, and, 6.47
Deposit protection
see also **Deposit guarantee scheme, European Deposit Insurance Scheme**
bank insolvency, 6.79–6.81
Depositor preference
deposit guarantee scheme, and, 6.48–6.49
deposit insurance, and, 6.47
forms of, 6.50
hierarchy of creditors' claims, 6.45
IADI Core Principles, 6.50–6.51
introduction, 6.45
Deposits
DGS covered deposits, Appendix 9.1
international bank loans and deposits 2006-16, Appendix 1

Early intervention
assessing whether bank failing or likely to fail, 5.44–5.47
cooperation between supervisor and resolution authority, 5.39
cross-border dimension, 5.51
infringement indicators, 5.40
no-creditor-worse-off, 5.49–5.50
notification of decision for, 5.43
shadow resolutions, 5.42
temporary administrator, 5.41
valuation of assets and liabilities, 5.48
EDIS *see* **European deposit insurance scheme**
European Banking Authority
non-performing loans, 4.19
recovery planning, review of, 3.56
role of
capital requirements, 2.43
joint decisions, 2.40–2.44
macro-prudential supervision, 2.39
mediation, 2.45–2.46
micro-prudential supervision, 2.39
resolution colleges, 2.40
resolution proceedings, 2.44
Single Rulebook, 2.39–2.41
standardization, 2.39
supervision disputes, 2.42
supervisory colleges, 2.19, 2.40
technical standards, production of, 2.39
stress testing, and, 3.64
European Central Bank
see also **Bank resolution, Single Supervisory Mechanism**
accountability, 2.22–2.31
authority, scope of, 2.7

bias, minimising risk of, 2.22
close cooperation
Bulgaria's application for, 2.47–2.51
centralised decision-making, 2.1–2.3
introduction, 2.1–2.3
opting in or out of Banking Union, 2.4–2.6
principle issues, 2.52
Single Resolution Mechanism, 2.2, 2.32–2.38
Single Supervisory Mechanism, 2.2, 2.7–2.21
consolidated supervisor of significant banks, role as, 2.13, 2.17–2.18
crisis management and containment, 7.3
decision-making process
Administrative Board of Review, 2.28–3.30
Court of Justice, review by, 2.25
Governing Council, 2.24–2.27
internal verification, 2.27
Mediation Panel, 2.23, 2.26
non-objection procedure, 2.23
single resolution mechanism, 2.31
Supervisory Board of the SSM, 2.23–2.27
ESCB Statute, key provisions of, 2.7
Governing Council, 2.24–2.27
independence, 2.22
investigation of significant risks, 2.14
non-performing loans, 4.5
power to make regulations, 2.7
presence of, Appendix 6.3
role of, 2.13–2.14
'shadow' competent authority role, 2.13
European Deposit Insurance Scheme
see also **Deposit guarantee scheme**
aims, 7.55
deposit guarantee scheme, importance of, 7.56
high coverage levels, 7.52
introduction, 7.51
raising private finance, system of, 7.57
separating of resolution and insolvency-liquidation, and, 7.58
third pillar of Banking Union, 7.53–7.54
European Stability Mechanism
aims of, 7.60
alignment with national interests, 7.69
assessment of request for assistance, 7.63
assistance available, 7.64
direct recapitalization, 7.66
establishment of, 7.59–7.60
fiscal burden of bank, facilities to address, 7.65
introduction of, 2.5
risk-sharing, 7.67
shareholder contribution, 7.61
subscribed capital, 7.62
systemic crisis, likelihood of, 7.68
voting procedure, 7.61

Financial Stability Board
guidance on home and host supervisory issues, 3.79
Key Attributes of Effective Resolution Regimes, 5.108
single point and multiple point of entry resolution, 5.21
temporary public funding, 7.71
Foreign branches *see* **Branches, foreign**
Foreign subsidiaries *see* **Subsidiaries, foreign**

Global Systemic Important Banks (G- SIB)
temporary funding, 7.71
Global systemically important institutions (G-SII)
minimum required eligible liabilities, 5.18
risk profile, 7.45
Going concern
conservation of value, 6.25
early intervention, 5.39
information sharing, 3.37
minimum required eligible liabilities, 5.11
supervisory college, role of, 3.44
viability as, 2.11
Gone concern
early intervention, 5.39
minimum required eligible liabilities, 5.11
sale of assets, 6.25
Governing Council
role of, 2.24–2.27
Supervisory Board of the SSM, and, 2.23
Group recovery plans
consolidated supervisor, role in, 2.44
early intervention, and, 5.40
responsibility for, 5.6
Group Resolution Authority
confidence in, 5.36
considerations in restructuring group, 5.56
cross-border coordination, 5.99
determination of resolution options, 2.44
home bias, 5.105
host Member State taking responsibility for, 5.30
information sharing, 3.40, 5.90
multiple point of entry, initiation of, 5.22, 5.26
notification of how MREL will be set, 5.14
resolution colleges, leading, 5.28, 5.34
resolution coordination, 5.32–5.33
role of, 5.33–5.35
single point of entry, initiation of, 5.22, 5.26
Single Resolution Board, role of, 5.24, 5.108
subsidiaries, legal form of, 5.5

Home and host relationship
bank insolvency, and, 6.9
prudential supervision perspective
benefits of close cooperation, 2.6
consolidated supervision, 3.2, 3.30–3.36, 3.69–3.76
consolidated supervisor, 2.20
home bias for significant subsidiaries, 3.65–3.68
information sharing, 3.31, 3.35, 3.37–3.40
international soft law instruments, 3.77–3.80
introduction, 3.1–3.2
legal form of cross-border banking and supervision, 3.3–3.9

Home and host relationship (*cont.*)
macro-prudential classification of banks, 3.20–3.29, Appendix 7
non-performing loans, 4.3–4.4, 4.46
principal issues, 3.81
recovery planning, 3.2, 3.51–3.58
significant banks, 3.2, 3.12–3.19
single regulator, effect of introduction of, 2.20
Single Rulebook, and, 2.41
single supervisory mechanism, 3.10–3.14
stress-testing, 3.60–3.64
supervisory colleges, 2.19, 3.2, 3.41–3.50
resolution perspective
asset separation tool, 5.65
bail-in tool, 5.66–5.77
branches, 5.7–5.8
bridge institution tool, 5.57–5.64
capital requirements, 5.11–5.12
cross-border group resolution, 5.84–5.87
early intervention, 5.39–5.50
home bias for significant subsidiaries, 5.104–5.107
international cooperation agreements, 5.100–5.103
international soft law instruments, 5.108–5.109
introduction, 5.1–5.4
Member State resolution decisions, 5.78–5.83
minimum required eligible liabilities, 5.10–5.20
multiple point of entry approach, 5.21–5.27
principal issues, 5.110
resolution colleges, 5.28–5.38
resolution objectives, conditions and principles, 5.52–5.53
resolvability, assessment of, 5.9–5.10
responsibilities of the home and host resolution authorities, 5.5–5.8
sale of business tool, 5.54–5.56
single point of entry approach, 5.21–5.27
single resolution fund, 7.49
subsidiaries, 5.7–5.8
third countries, relations with, 5.88–5.99

Information-sharing
consolidated supervision
generally, 3.31, 3.35
third country perspective, 3.70, 3.76
importance of, 2.6, 3.37
need for increased requirements, 3.40
requirements for, 3.37–3.39
resolution colleges, 5.31
stress testing, 3.61
third countries, relations with, 5.94
Insolvency
minimum required eligible liabilities, 5.15, 5.20
International claims
country exposures, 1.10, 1.14
interbank financing, 3.24
local positions of total international claims
generally, 1.20–1.24
local resident exposures to foreign bank counterparties, 1.25–1.30
International cooperation agreements
single resolution mechanism, 5.100–5.103
International securities 2006-16, Appendix 1
International soft law instruments
bank insolvency, 6.79–6.81
resolution, 5.108–5.109
supervision
Basel Committee Progress Report 2017, 3.79
Basel Core Principles 2012, 3.78
FSB Guidance, 3.79
introduction, 3.77
lack of reciprocity, 3.80
temporary public funding
cross-border cooperation, 7.73
Financial Stability Board guidelines, 7.71
home and host relationship, 7.74
importance of, 7.70
private funds, use of, 7.72

Joint Supervisory Coordinator
appointment under SSM of, 2.15
Joint Supervisory Teams (JSTs)
benefits of, 2.16
composition, 2.16
consolidated supervisor, relationship with, 2.20
Joint Supervisory Coordinator, 2.15
language issues, 2.15
responsibilities of, 2.15
Single Supervisory Mechanism, and, 2.15–2.21
sub-coordinators, 2.15
supervisory review and evaluation process, 2.15

Liabilities
BIS statistics, Appendix 5
Liquidation aid
crisis management and containment, 7.28–7.32
Liquidity assistance
centralizing, 7.33–7.37
emergency, 7.4, 7.13–7.21
Listed banks, Appendix 7.1
Loan loss provisioning
non-performing loans
adverse selection, 4.39
approach over stages of loan, 4.33
Basel III and IFRS 9 compared, 4.35
cyclical provisioning, 4.27–4.29
expected losses, 4.26
global financial crisis, effect of, 4.30
IFRS 9, 4.31–4.38
moral hazard, 4.39
net loan value, use of, 4.26
Loans
see also **Non-performing loans**
gross loan data, Appendix 8
international bank loans and deposits 2006-16, Appendix 1
non-performing loans, Appendix 8
Local positions
non-performing loans, 4.7
statistics, Appendix 4

Loss absorbing capacity
minimum required eligible liabilities, 5.10–5.13, 5.15–5.16

Macro-prudential supervision
classification of banks
capital requirements buffers, 3.20
classification criteria, 3.23
communication between home and host authorities, 3.27
counter cyclical buffers, 3.21
ECB's role in macro-prudential supervision, 3.20
foreign branches, 3.22
interpretation of EBA guidelines, variations in, 3.28
national designated authorities, approach of, 3.29
O-SIIs, implications of classification as, 3.25
smaller Member States, 3.24
statistics, 3.26, Appendix 7
systematic risk buffers, 3.21
European Banking Authority, 2.39
stress testing, 3.60
Mediation
European Banking Authority, 2.45–2.46
Mediation Panel
composition, 2.26
ECB decision-making process, and, 2.23, 2.26
role of, 2.26
Member States of the European Union
cross-border banking exposure
international loans, deposits and securities, 1.8
introduction, 1.5–1.8
top three exposures per Member State, 1.9–1.19
derogation from ESCB, 2.8
foreign and domestic banks, proportion of
branches, 1.43
generally, 1.31–1.32
intragroup position between banks and affiliates, 1.43
legal form, 1.33–1.40
subsidiaries, 1.43
third country perspective, 1.44–1.47
total assets, 1.41–1.42
local positions of total international claims
generally, 1.20–1.24
local resident exposures to foreign bank counterparties, 1.25–1.30
principal issues, 1.48–1.49
resolution decisions
Denmark, 5.82
generally, 5.78
Greece, 5.83
Hungary, 5.79
Italy, 5.80
Portugal, 5.81
Memorandum of understanding
single resolution mechanism, 2.37
single supervisory mechanism, 2.9
Micro-prudential supervision
European Banking Authority, 2.39
stress testing, 3.60
Minimum required eligible liabilities (MREL)
close cooperation, need for, 5.14
deposit guarantees scheme, 5.17
global systemically important institutions (G-SII), 5.19
gone concern scenario, 5.11
impact of compliance with, 5.11
insolvency, 5.15
introduction of, 5.10
inward facing nature, 5.11
loss absorbing capacity, 5.10–5.13
mandates of supervision and resolution, 5.19
other systemically important institutions (O-SII), 5.19
resolution authority's decision on amount of loss absorbance, 5.15–5.16
resolution fund, 5.17
resolution or insolvency, 5.20
significant banks, 3.19
Single Resolution Board, role in setting, 2.36
stress testing, 5.18
Moral hazard
non-performing loans, 4.2, 4.12, 4.39, 4.41, 4.45
Moratoria
large institutions, 6.30
right to seek, 6.26
small institutions, 6.30
suspension of payments and delivery obligations, 6.27
timeframe, 6.28
Multiple point of entry approach
resolution
generally, 5.21–5.27
third countries, relations with, 5.92
***Mutatis mutandis*, principle of**
close cooperation, and, 2.11, 2.33

National Competent Authority
decision-making powers, 2.25
information sharing, 2.6
observers, role as, 2.17–2.18
Single Resolution Board, relationship with, 2.31
single supervisory mechanism
consolidated supervisor, role as, 2.17–2.18
cooperation with ECB, 2.8–2.10
investigation of significant risks, 2.14
Joint Supervisory Teams, role in, 2.15–2.21
observer, role as, 2.13, 2.17–2.19
role under, 2.13–2.14
sub-coordinator, appointment of, 2.15
supervisory colleges, role in, 2.19
Supervisory Board of the SSM, role in, 2.24
National Designated Authority
administrative discretion, constraint of, 7.12
other systemically important institutions (O-SIIs), 3.28, 5.20
National resolution authorities
single resolution mechanism framework, 2.31
single supervisory mechanism framework, 2.9
Negative net worth
bank insolvency, and, 6.24

Netting agreements
bank insolvency, and, 6.18
No-creditor-worse-off
resolution, 5.49–5.50
Non-listed banks, Appendix 7.1
Non-objection procedure
ECB decision-making process, and, 2.23
Non-performing loans
adverse selection, 4.2, 4.4, 4.16, 4.39, 4.41, 4.44
credit underwriting, and, 4.5
definitional challenges
ambiguity, 4.17
asset quality review process, 4.23–4.24
automatic triggers, 4.21
benefits of consistent definition, 4.20
conflicts of interest, 4.18
criteria for determining performance of exposure, 4.21
criteria for managing NPLs, 4.22, 4.25
EBA standards on supervisory reporting, 4.19
foreign branches, 4.24
foreign subsidiaries, 4.24
quantitative and qualitative evidence, discretion to use, 4.18
European Central Bank jurisdiction, 4.5
home and host dilemma, and, 4.3–4.4
introduction, 4.1–4.6
loan loss provisioning
adverse selection, 4.39
approach over stages of loan, 4.33
Basel III and IFRS 9 compared, 4.35
cyclical provisioning, 4.27–4.29
global financial crisis, effect of, 4.30
IFRS 9, 4.31–4.38
moral hazard, 4.39
net loan value, use of, 4.26
provision for expected losses, 4.26
moral hazard, 4.2, 4.12, 4.39, 4.41, 4.45
principal issues, 4.49–4.51
public and private mechanisms to reduce NPLs
asset management corporations, 4.41–4.45
centralized model, 4.40
decentralized model, 4.40
diversification of NPL credit risk, 4.47
home-host issues, 4.46
introduction of, 4.15
local capacity to undertake task, 4.48
public versus private approaches, 4.42
size of the European problem
local positions, 4.7
mechanisms to address NPL issue, 4.15
NPLs to gross loans, analysis of, 4.8–4.10
quality of bank assets, effect of deterioration of, 4.14
recent decreases in Central and Eastern Europe, 4.16
size of bank, and, 4.13
sovereign debt crisis, link to, 4.11
too-big-to-fail, 4.12
statistics, NPL to gross loan data, 4.8–4.10, Appendix 8

Observers
exclusion from information-sharing, 3.46
supervisory colleges, participation in, 3.46–3.47
Other systemically important institutions (O-SII)
buffer, 3.21
deposit guarantee funds, and, 5.18
financial stability, 3.2
incentives, misalignment of, 5.36
listing discrepancies, 3.66
loss absorption, 5.13
macroprudential classification of banks, 3.22–3.28, Appendix 7
minimum required eligible liabilities, 5.19
number of, Appendix 7
resolution funds, and, 5.18
statistics, Appendix 7.2, 7.3
subsidiaries, classification of, 5.16
systemic risk posed by, 3.40, 5.107

Prudential supervision (home and host relationship)
benefits of close cooperation, 2.6
consolidated supervision
capital risk requirements, 3.32
foreign subsidiaries, 3.34–3.35
information sharing, 3.31, 3.35
introduction, 3.2, 3.30
joint decisions on prudential requirements, 3.36
meaning of home and host Member State, 3.33
purpose of, 3.32
supervisory cooperation, 3.31, 3.33
third country perspective, 3.2, 3.69–3.76
consolidated supervisor, 2.20
home bias for significant subsidiaries, 3.65–3.68
information sharing
consolidated supervision, 3.31, 3.35
importance of, 3.37
need for increased requirements, 3.40
requirements for, 3.37–3.39
international soft law instruments
Basel Committee Progress Report 2017, 3.79
Basel Core Principles 2012, 3.78
FSB Guidance, 3.79
introduction, 3.77
lack of reciprocity, 3.80
introduction, 3.1–3.2
legal form of cross-border banking and supervision
asset levels, 3.8
determination of home or host country control, 3.5–3.6
foreign branches, authorisation of, 3.3
foreign subsidiaries, authorisation of, 3.3
general good principle, application of, 3.7
home country control, 3.4
Significant Branch Guidelines, 3.9
macro-prudential classification of banks
capital requirements buffers, 3.20

classification criteria, 3.23
communication between home and host authorities, 3.27
counter cyclical buffers, 3.21
ECB's role in macro-prudential supervision, 3.20
foreign branches, 3.22
interpretation of EBA guidelines, variations in, 3.28
national designated authorities, approach of, 3.29
O-SIIs, implications of classification as, 3.25
smaller Member States, 3.24
statistics, 3.26, Appendix 7
systematic risk buffers, 3.21
non-performing loans, 4.3–4.4, 4.46
principal issues, 3.81
recovery planning
critical functions, 3.51
EBA review, 3.56
groups, application to, 3.54–3.55
introduction, 3.2
key features, 3.53
'parent perspective', 3.58
requirement for, 3.52
sale of assets or loans, 3.57
sale of subsidiaries, 3.57
significant banks
asset size, 3.13–3.14
classification as, 3.2
classification criteria, 3.12
listed and non-listed, 3.15–3.19
Minimum Requirement for Own Funds and Eligible Liabilities, 3.19
statistics, 3.17–3.18
subsidiaries in two or more Member States, 3.13
single regulator, effect of introduction of, 2.20
Single Rulebook, and, 2.41
single supervisory mechanism
classification by asset size, 3.13
classification of banks as significant, 3.12–3.14
direct prudential supervision of banks, 3.11
division of responsibility based on significance, 3.10
general tasks of supervision, 3.10
specific tasks of supervision, 3.10
stress-testing
cross-border group stress testing, 3.62
customised approach, 3.61
EBA role, 3.64
information sharing, 3.61
macro- and micro-prudential supervision, use in, 3.60
purpose of, 3.59
stumbling blocks, 3.63
supervisory colleges
access to information, 3.46
close cooperation between members, 3.45
generally, 2.19, 3.2, 3.41
levels of engagement, 3.48
membership, 3.43
observers, participation of, 3.46–3.47
potential future issues, 3.50
regulatory requirements, 3.42
tasks of, 3.44
Written Cooperation and Coordination Arrangement protocol, 3.49

Recapitalization
direct recapitalization, 7.66
precautionary recapitalization, 7.5–7.12
Recovery resolution planning
cooperation and coordination, 3.47
critical functions, 3.51
EBA review, 3.56
groups, application to, 3.54–3.55
introduction, 3.2
joint decision-making, 2.44
key features, 3.53
opting in or out of Banking Union, 2.5
'parent perspective', 3.58
requirement for, 3.52
sale of assets or loans, 3.57
sale of subsidiaries, 3.57
Resolution colleges
benefits of, 5.35
cross- border groups, 5.30
European Banking Authority, role of, 2.40
group resolution authority, role of, 5.34
information sharing, 5.31
interests of other hosts, 5.37
introduction, 5.28
joint decision-making, 5.36
management of, 5.34
membership, 5.29
rationale, 5.29
resolution coordination, 5.31–5.33
resolvability of groups, 5.9
technical standards, 5.38
Resolution fund *see* Single Resolution Fund
Resolution proceedings
European Banking Authority, role of, 2.44
Rights *in rem*
bank insolvency, and, 6.18

Sale of business tool
resolution, 5.54–5.56
Securities
BIS statistics, Appendix 1
Set-off
bank insolvency, and, 6.18
Significant banks
classification as, 3.10–3.14
listed and non-listed, 3.15–3.19
Minimum Requirement for Own Funds and Eligible Liabilities, 3.19
statistics, 3.17–3.18, Appendix 7.2
Single point of entry approach
resolution
generally, 5.21–5.27
third countries, relations with, 5.92

Single Resolution Board (SRB)
accountability, 2.35
assessing prospects of entities, 2.38
independence, 2.35
introduction, 2.2
Memorandums of Understanding, publication of, 2.37
national resolution authorities, and, 2.37
role of, 2.33, 2.36–2.38
single resolution fund, administration of, 7.40
Single Resolution Fund (SRF)
administration of, 7.40
aims and objectives, 7.41
appeal against contribution, 7.48
contributions, calculation of, 7.43–7.47
cross-border bank resolution, 7.50
home and host relationship, 7.49
introduction, 7.38
minimizing agency problems, 7.39
minimum required eligible liabilities, 5.17
resolvability, assessment of, 5.11
setting of premiums payable, 2.36
underfunding, 7.36
utilization of funds by resolution authority, 7.42
Single Resolution Mechanism
see also **Bank resolution, Single Resolution Board**
aims, 2.32
introduction of, 2.32
key provisions of SRMR, 2.34
nature of, 2.35
single supervisory mechanism distinguished, 2.31
Single Rulebook
European Banking Authority, role of, 2.39–2.41
Single Supervisory Board
ECB decision-making process, and, 2.23–2.28
supervisory examination plan, 2.15
dialogue between national competent authorities, 2.19
Single Supervisory Mechanism
close cooperation
assessment of requests to enter, 2.12
benefits of, 2.21
framework for, 2.9
information sharing, 2.21
reliance on, 2.10
requests to enter, 2.11–2.12
decision-making process
Administrative Board of Review, 2.28–3.30
Court of Justice, review by, 2.25
Governing Council, 2.24–2.27
internal verification, 2.27
Mediation Panel, 2.23, 2.26
non-objection procedure, 2.23
single resolution mechanism, 2.31
Supervisory Board of the SSM, 2.23–2.27
direct prudential supervision of banks, 3.11
general tasks of supervision, 3.10
governance mechanisms, 2.22
introduction, 2.2
Joint Supervisory Teams, 2.15–2.21
Member States with derogation, 2.8
national competent authorities, relation of ECB with, 2.13–2.14
significance, 2.13, 3.10
significant banks, classification as, 3.12–3.14
single resolution mechanism distinguished, 2.31
specific tasks of supervision, 3.10
SSM Framework Regulation, 2.13–2.14
Supervisory Board of the SSM, role of, 2.23–2.27
tasks to be undertaken by ECB, 2.7, 2.13
Sovereign debt crisis
banks' behaviour, 1.8, 4.6
direct recapitalization to avoid, 7.66
European Stability Mechanism, establishment of, 7.59
impact of, 1.26
non-performing loans, 4.1, 4.8–4.11, 4.15, 4.49
non-performing loans, and, 4.11
Single Resolution Mechanism, and, 2.32
supporting critical functions to avoid, 7.37
State aid
crisis management and containment, 7.22–7.27
Statistics
accession countries
European Bank presence, Appendix 6.3
top 5 banks, Appendix 6.3a
available funds, Appendix 9.1
country exposure
percentage, Appendix 3
USD, Appendix 2
credit institutions, number of, Appendix 6.1
deposit guarantee scheme
covered deposits, Appendix 9.1
liquidation cases with payouts, Appendix 9.2
deposits
DGS covered deposits, Appendix 9.1
international bank loans and deposits 2006-16, Appendix 1
European Bank presence
accession countries, Appendix 6.3
Eastern European Member States, Appendix 6.3
foreign branches
assets held by, Appendix 6.2
number of, Appendix 6.1
foreign subsidiaries
assets held by, Appendix 6.2
number of, Appendix 6.1
international securities 2006-16, Appendix 1
liabilities, Appendix 5
liquidation cases with DGS payouts, Appendix 9.2
listed banks, Appendix 7.1
loans
gross loan data, Appendix 8
international bank loans and deposits 2006-16, Appendix 1
non-performing loans, Appendix 8
local position data, Appendix 4
non listed banks, Appendix 7.1

O-SIIs, Appendix 7.2, 7.3
significant banks, Appendix 7.2
total assets, Appendix 6.2
Stress-testing
cross-border group stress testing, 3.62
customised approach, 3.61
EBA role, 3.64
information sharing, 3.61
macro- and micro-prudential supervision, use in, 3.60
minimum required eligible liabilities, 5.18
purpose of, 3.59
stumbling blocks, 3.63
Subsidiaries, foreign
assets held by, Appendix 6.2
bank insolvency, 6.10–6.18
consolidated supervision, 3.34–3.35
foreign and domestic banks, proportion of, 1.43
home or host country control
asset levels, 3.8
authorisation, 3.3
conversion to branch, 3.8
determination of, 3.5–3.6
general good principle, application of, 3.7
resolution, 5.7–5.8
non-performing loans, 4.24
number of, Appendix 6.1
significant subsidiaries
home bias for, 3.65–3.68, 5.104–5.107
Supervisory Board of the Single Supervisory Mechanism *see* **Single Supervisory Board**
Supervisory colleges
access to information, 3.46
close cooperation between members, 3.45
European Banking Authority, role of, 2.19, 2.40
introduction, 3.2, 3.41
levels of engagement, 3.48
membership, 3.43
observers, participation of, 3.46–3.47
potential future issues, 3.50
regulatory requirements, 3.42
resolvability of groups, 5.9
tasks of, 3.44
Written Cooperation and Coordination Arrangement protocol, 3.49
Supervisory review and evaluation process (SREP)
supervision of significant banks under SSM, 2.15

Technical standards
production of, 2.39
resolution colleges, 5.38
Temporary administrator
early intervention, 5.41
Third countries
consolidated supervision
assessing equivalence, 3.69
consistency of approach, 3.72–3.73
incentivising compliance, 3.71
information sharing, 3.70, 3.76
introduction, 3.2
Memorandum of Cooperation, 3.74–3.75
deposit guarantee scheme, 6.77–6.78
foreign and domestic banks, proportion of, 1.44–1.47
resolution
branches in third country, 5.95
cross-border resolution regime, lack of, 5.98
implications of lack of coordination, 5.99
introduction, 5.88–5.89
lack of information sharing, 5.94
MPE approach, 5.92
non-binding cooperation agreements, 5.96–5.97
parent companies in third country, 5.90
public interest, acting in, 5.93
third-country cooperation and coordination, 5.91
Too-big-to-fail
non-performing loans, 4.12
Total loss-absorbing capacity *see* **Loss absorbing capacity**

Valuation
early intervention, 5.48

Winding-up *see* **Bank insolvency**